Autobiography of an Avadhoota

Author

Avadhoota Nadananda

©Avadhoota Nadananda, 2011

All rights reserved.

No part of this publication may be reproduced, stored in a retrieval system or transmitted by any means, electronic, photocopying, recording or otherwise, without the prior written permission of the author

Original published as THE PYRE OF THE DESTINED by Abhaya Varada 2011

1st completely new edition published by GuruLight 2016

Book and Cover design: Zoran Stefanovski
(Mohana Hanumatananda)

www.gurulight.com

M.R.P: Rs.800/-

Paramaguru Nityananda Bhagavan

Sadhguru Avadhoota Tara Mayee

Avadhoota Nadananda

Endless Love - Avadhoota Nadananda with Mohanji

**Puvapalli Krishnan Namboodri, Gangadevi
Parents of Avadhoota Nadananda**

Avadhoota Nadananda With Brothers and Sisters

Experiencing an Avadhoota

*A*vadhoota Nadananda once told me "When man becomes mad, he becomes a saint. When saint becomes mad, he becomes an *Avadhoota*. When *Avadhoota* becomes mad, he becomes *Bhagavan* (God)." Beings reveling in their non-existence are *Avadhootas*. They are totally occupied inside, so much so that the outside world with its materials and flavours carries no meaning to them. It does not exist for them. Regular human beings for whom the outside world is everything will find it difficult to understand such an existence.

We live in an atomic universe. It is a universe made of particles. They are energy manifested into forms which also means duality or multiplicity. This is the cause of all our delusions. An *Avadhoota* is rooted in the energy beyond the matter within and outside of him. He is never deluded with terrestrial existence.

We float in the river of manifested existence. May the One who is the cause of the atom as well as the inner and outer universe guide us, lead us and protect us. May the One who is beyond all dualities dissolve us too. May our lives be full and complete through the awareness and experience of non-dual perfection. May the power (*Shakthi*) of will, knowledge and action maintain us constant and make our lives complete. May the greatest power (*Maha Shakthi*) awaken in us and melt us into the ocean of abundance and supreme bliss.

The fundamental shift in awareness expresses itself with one question "Who AM I?" and it subsequently flows through further questions such as "What am I" and "Why be I?" This is the story of every seeker. A moment in time forces the naturally extroverted being to look within and ask this question into the seeming darkness of the unknowable. The "I AM" dissolves into "Who Am I?" Ever since time created the thinking man on earth, this question has remained in the canvas of existence of every evolved being. "WHO AM I?" This eventually evolves into the fundamental question "Why Am I?" which leads to dimensional destruction. Dimensional destruction leads to freedom from form, binding identifications and takes one to ultimate liberation.

This question, at some point in time in the life of everyone, naturally evolves and becomes a burning quest. Nothing else in life matters except a convincing answer in the form of a compelling experience to satiate this quest. The realization that nothing that I consider as "I AM" has anything to do with the real "ME" shifts the awareness to a totally different level. This inner momentum also urges man to shed the boundaries of his mind and move from the known to the unknowable which mind cannot perceive. He is forced to seek beyond the mind with the full understanding of the limitation of the substratum called mind. Delusions and misconceptions walk the path as inevitable companions. They serve as tests as well as traps. Many fall prey to it and slip down to where they started from. Domination of mind through fears and doubts are one of the biggest hurdles. Expectations are another. Many also get trapped in powers that inevitably happen when gross melts into subtle spontaneously. It takes a lot of maturity, clarity and steadfast consistency over destination to arrive at the final truth. It may take lifetimes to reach this final destination. What may seem as great accomplishment of an incarnation in one lifetime often contains the invisible consistent efforts to attain truth, running through many past lifetimes. Awareness is the only investment that stays through incarnations without depreciation. Hence awareness is the only investment that is truly worth in a lifetime.

Life evolved through various incarnations that ran through various species on earth. It finally landed a human existence. The thirsty, hungry and most vulnerable existence in the whole jungle of multiple species! The suffering of severe identity crisis of a thinking man versus the speeding time, who like to believe that they are time riders and end up realising that the time has been riding their incarnation beyond any compromises on ownerships. This is the identity crisis of delusional supremacy that leads to the thought process of Man Versus Nature instead of Man in nature! This non-understanding further leads man to his eventual alienation and subsequent search for his real home. We all are searching. We all are usually searching outside. Seldom destiny brings us home into ourselves. Most of the times, we end our search in illusions and corresponding disappointments. Most of us do not know what we are looking for and hence do not know where to look.

Here we have the true story of an *Avadhoota*, a man who went through his physical, emotional, intellectual and spiritual boundaries to climb to the Everest of awareness that only a few could effectively achieve. We have to discard a lot to gain somewhat. It is my deepest privilege and honour to write a foreword to this great work which I am sure that time would nurture in its lap as a guiding light much more than just a book of purpose to the true seekers of truth, often seeking in darkness not knowing what they are seeking and where to seek.

This is the story of you and me. This story will remind us about ourselves. *Avadhoota* Nadananda travelled through the same terrains of happiness, sorrows, accolades and betrayals just like any of us. He did not stop. He did not rest. He did not procrastinate or give up his efforts disheartened by the hardships associated with a pure spiritual journey. But, he travelled beyond his own boundaries. He touched the realms of existence that made him an *Avadhoota* which most of us could never even dream about. Most of us would never have realised that *Gyanganj*, the causal layer of the earth and the world of the *Avadhootas*, exists beyond the human ken, deep in the recesses of Tibet, now within the borders of China, as a location. This is the Shambala of Immortality. This is the Shangri-la minus the imagination of a Utopia. This is the world of existence in non-existence. This is the world of perfection in nullification. Nothing exists except the complete ocean. There are no drops to claim its identity. There are no false and temporary identifications. There is only perfection of completion and an existence to revel this perfection.

Avadhoota Nadananda has the prime possession of the begging bowl that his *Guru*, Maa Tara Mayee gave to him, which she inherited through generations of *Avadhootas*. The same begging bowl that many centuries ago, the great Babaji, who is called Mahatapa in the *Avadhoota* tradition carried in His own hand! The *Guru* instructed her perfect disciple Nadananda, "Do not beg. Do not accept or carry money. Give yourself completely to the will of destiny and grace. If food comes to you, consume, whatever the type of food is, if not, observe spontaneous fasting. Do not go in search of food. Whatever you need will be provided by the tradition through nature or some hands. Do not compromise on your own integrity and the integrity of the tradition. I shall be with you". Nadananda travelled through the tough terrains of Himalayas with no money and not many clothes. This book is a testimonial that such saints exist amongst us, often invisible to the gross eyes. We need extreme subtlety as well as grace to see them and more so to recognise them. They reveal themselves only to guide us.

One who has nothing to do with terrestrial existence is an *Avadhoota*. One who has no emotional value for any events of life is an *Avadhoota*. An *Avadhoota* is totally occupied in bliss supreme. An *Avadhoota* floats through existence like water on lotus leaf, without acquiring any emotional dirt from any happenings of life. They remain clean and pure always. Being born is an illusion for the eternally unborn *Avadhoota*. They live freedom and leave behind the essence of freedom for the people who are bound by emotions of life to witness, experience and merge into. They are spontaneous, unbound and unperturbed about how the society looks at them, evaluates them or "deals" with them. They are not bothered about food, clothing or shelter. They are beyond the insecurities of existence that a human mind carefully nurtures. They are natural and they are real. The looking glass of concepts that an everyday man wears often obscures him to see the wealth of freedom that an *Avadhoota* possesses. Almost everything that a modern man considers important has no value for an *Avadhoota*. Detachment is their garb. Society can only see their seemingly indifferent existence and they mark it as madness or even anti-social.

Avadhoota Nadananda was a sceptical, rational young man like most of us have been in our youth. He asked questions and demanded answers to the regular inequalities of the society and opted to react at various times. The pain of existence soon became the purpose of existence instead of succumbing and surrendering to life's inevitable chores, passively compromising the fire of thirst that glowed in the stomach as inspiration to wreak positive changes in the world around him. The transformation from existentialistic pains to purpose took him to the narrow paths of spirituality only a few even dared to tread. *Avadhoota* Tara Mayee held the reins of his further journey. *Avadhoota* Nadananda was born. As a young man, he asked a wandering monk who visited his house "Can I have your begging bowl?" The saint smiled and replied "This is not yours. Yours is on its way. Be ready to receive it. It is precious." The begging bowl of Mahavatar Babaji, who is known as the eternal Mahatapa in the *Avadhoota* tradition came to him, passing hands through his *Guru Avadhoota* Tara Mayee. The rest is history. *Avadhoota* Nadananda wrote that he met Mahatapa at *Gyanganj* and was ordained as the 48th pontiff of *Gyanganj*. The purpose of leading people to inner awakening continues to fuel the existence of *Avadhoota* Nadananda along with the deep urge to serve the under-privileged despite his compelling physical conditions. He still sings and dances despite the binding ailments of body. He remains unstoppable. Over a conversation about the relevance of physical body, he told me "Mohanji, I will remain in action for 300 years after my physical demise, just as Sai Baba of Shirdi continues to work after 100 years of His physical exit. Sai Baba was the 39th pontiff of *Gyanganj*. I am the 48th. When I told *Gyanganj* that my body is too tired to carry the burden of being a pontiff, I was told "we are carrying the burden, not you", existence will continue. Death cannot stop anything".

Lord Dattatreya is the father figure in the tradition of *Avadhootas*. He is also the father of the *Nath* tradition in its codified form as we perceive it now. Here, you can see the *Kriya*, *Datta*, *Nath* and *Avadhoota* traditions uniting and merging. Lord Dattatreya has had many reincarnations and each one of them has been unique and powerful. The tradition of *Avadhootas* always existed in the terrestrial realms as the highest potential of human awareness where the cosmic consciousness is everything and nothing else ever mattered. The Lord Dattatreya tradition, the *Nath* tradition as well as the *Kriya Yoga* Tradition are all interconnected and mutually complementing. In short, every tradition has its origin and destination at the same source. The seemingly different paths are only aimed at catering to the orientation of the various recipients.

The gateway to locations of higher frequencies is the subtleties of existence. *Gyanganj* is such a world that only those who have eyes of subtlety can witness it, let alone reach it. Grace is the key. *Gyanganj* is the causal layer of the world. The causal layer always remains invisible while effects of the causes become visible manifestations of the existence of the invisible causes. Every tradition of earth has its roots in *Gyanganj*, the realm of masters.

Eligibility for entry into the causal realm is dissolution of personal identities and identifications. Purpose is selfless service to the world. When the operating level is beyond the atoms, the atoms are in our command. Creation is the choice of the creator.

Avadhoota Nadananda says "The words of an *Avadhoota* never go in vain. Words become command to the nature. It can cut across *karma* and bring people back from death". He has literally done that. He has suffered the *karmas* of others and saved people from death. The book takes us through the treacheries of existence. The play of the human mind or its cunningness and betrayals, a naive and innocent *Avadhoota* cannot reciprocate. They operate only in the plane of unconditional love and sincere compassion.

These acts of supreme compassion and kindness are often rewarded back in the form of sheer thanklessness and ingratitude by its recipients, as society standards through generations continue to be ungratefulness to acts of compassion. We are the same society that crucified Jesus, poisoned Socrates and took Sai Baba to court. Generations have come and gone but the psychology remains the same. Contemporaries usually never understood a true master. It usually took them their death and the advent of further generations to birth a reasonable awareness. Yet, unabated, without complaint, the great masters delivered without expectations. This book serves as a mirror to the society of double standards. This could serve as an eye opener to many generations to come. This is one of the major relevance of this book.

My meeting with Nadananda is always cherished as one of the most auspicious moments of my life. When he said, "Mohanji, I shall be always with you. I am with you wherever you are". I knew the depth of these words. He is not a person. He is a tradition. It was a promise from the *Gyanganj*. When the master says "I am with you", the whole tradition is with us. The assurance that the tradition leads us is enough to walk the rest of the journey in this incarnation. Beyond the boundaries of the mind rest the truth. The master represents that truth. While over a casual chat on March 2nd 2016 at Dhar in Madhya Pradesh, Nadananda said to me "You are also an *Avadhoota*. You will know in time". I like to believe that our eternal lineage brought us together. Likewise, it is the lineage of liberation of the soul that united all of us, the readers and the writers.

I refrain from writing further. I shall rather let you read and digest this classic work of modern times. Remember, this is a road map into true spirituality as well as a mirror to the average seeker. Remove your glasses of ego and analysis. Remove your concepts and expectations. Remove yourself and experience this book. This can transform you inside out. Wish you great transformation.

With deepest gratitude and humble surrender to the great masters who guide the beings of universe. And humble prostrations to *Avadhoota* Nadananda who gave me the rights to globally publish and distribute this book. When I agreed to bring this work to the world, my intention was just to bring the pure and unpolluted spiritual tradition of India to the world. True spiritual journey which is essentially a journey to oneself is often obscured in the myriad of ritualistic course oriented modern methods. Enlightenment, like meditation, is essentially a state and not an activity. Likewise, being an *Avadhoota* is also a state which happens when man transcends his identifications and offers himself to total dissolution. My deep gratitude to *Avadhoota* Nadananda for his trust in me to bring his life story into the world and into your hands.

Endless Love to each and every one of you.

Yours

Mohanji

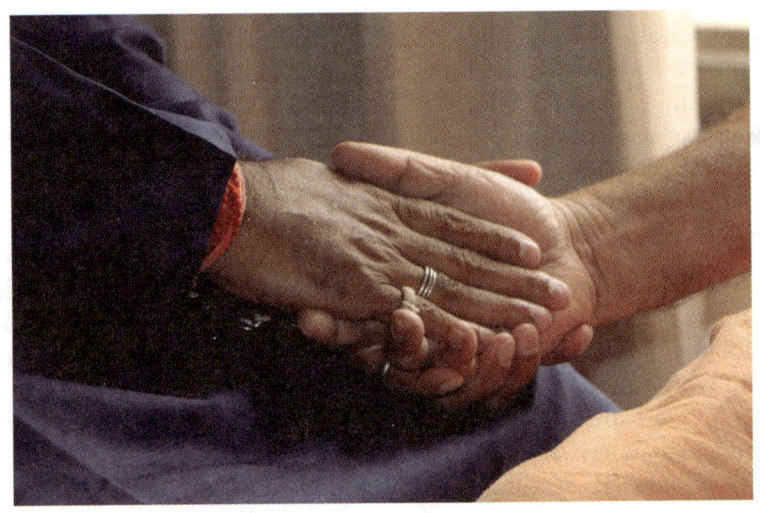

The Tradition Flows Eternally

Important Places in Avadhoota Nadananda's Life

Preface

This is the story of an *Avadhoota*. Who is an *Avadhoota*, one may ask? To paraphrase what Mast Ram Baba of Rishikesh once told me, "*Aakash chath hai, aur bhoomi bichona hai. Aur sirf Guru pe vishwas*". For whom the sky is the roof and the earth is the bed. And one who relies only on the *Guru* (spiritual preceptor) and the Divine for fulfilment of one's needs. What does an *Avadhoota* do? While describing our tradition, my *Guru*, *Avadhoota* Tara Mayee (*Amma*), told me, "A person who lives for himself is an animal and a person who lives for others is a *Bhagavan* (God). Now you have to decide what you want to become - an animal or a *Bhagavan*. If you decide positively, take an oath that you will live for others for the rest of the life, only for others. No matter what the consequences are to yourself." At that moment, I touched her holy feet and took that oath which is the guiding light for every *Avadhoota*. *Seva hi mam dharma*. Selfless service is the religion of an *Avadhoota* and it extends to every being on the planet – humans, animals, birds, plants and all living creatures. An *Avadhoota* sees God in the grass, worms, flowers and all the living and nonliving things on the earth.

When I first thought of writing my autobiography, the first face that appeared in front of me was that of my beloved *Guruji* who is everything to me and is with me, rather in me, at every moment. I was a rough, black and shapeless lump of clay that was moulded into a smooth, beautiful idol in her hands. Due to *Amma*'s skill in transforming that dingy clod of clay, a few kept that idol in the altar of their hearts and worshipped him as their *Guru*. That is me and this is my story.

It is the story of a never ending journey of an *Avadhoota* with all the trials and tribulations of a life enriched with all the tastes - bitter, sour, sweet, hot and spicy. And I feel this is a story that must be told. Not for personal glorification. Far from it. Paramahamsa Yogananda said in *Man's Eternal Quest*, "It is not necessary to go through every kind of human experience in order to attain ultimate wisdom. You should be able to learn by studying the lives of others." Ignoring the unceasing struggles involved in this effort and the naysayings – both from my own self and others, I have bared my soul to reflect the vulnerabilities, the tenacities, the determination, the Grace, the purpose, the miseries and the Masters that illumined my journey. If a single person gets inspiration from these words and changes his attitude towards life, I will consider myself a successful writer.

I have been a lonely traveler since birth, and even now, walk alone in the crowd of my disciples, devotees and well wishers. I have documented the unforgettable experiences of my journey of yesteryears right from childhood through my long life as a *sanyasi, guru, Avadhoota* and a social worker. In this long journey, I have encountered people from all walks of life - a few worth remembering, a few worth forgetting. Some who helped, some who harassed, some who criticized and some who stood by me as a witness to my pain and pleasure. And yet, it is not a story about them or me.

My story is a testament to the power of *sankalpa* – the power of the human will that, when determined to achieve a worthy purpose gets suffused with the Divine Will to circumvent all obstacles in its path. It is a demonstration of the truth in the words of my *Guruji*, "Wherever you are, I will be there". A testimony to the unfailing and complete protection offered by the Divine Mother to one who has completely surrendered to Her. To paraphrase from *The Hound of Heaven*, the Shade of Her hand has outstretched caressingly through each and every step of my life. Even now, my *Amma* is always with me in every moment!

A life lived for one's self is a life not worth living. Animals also exist in that fashion. The value that one brings to others and to the world is the only lasting impact for a human being.

Spirituality is for the welfare of the people. It is not a tool, as used by the contemporary religious institutions, to intimidate the devotees in the name of God and, thereby, control and exploit their ignorance. Throughout my life, I tried to live for the betterment of others. This lovely verse sums up my belief that any selfless service done with dedication and attention is verily the worship of the Lord.

होती आरती, बजते शंख,	*As hymns are sung and conches blow*
पूजा में सब खोए है,	*All deeply engrossed in prayers aglow,*
मंदिर के बाहर तो देखो,	*Outside the temple as you look,*
भूखे बच्चे सोए हैं।	*Hungry children sleep in every nook*
एक निवाला इनको देना,	*Sharing with them a few morsels of thine,*
प्रसाद मुझे चढ़ जायेगा,	*It becomes an offering truly divine*
मेरे दर पर माँगने वाले,	*All what you have come to seek,*
तुझे बिन माँगे सब मिलजायेगा।	*Will be granted even before you speak.*

It is the great thrust of compassion for my fellow human beings that has sprung forth from this tiny heart that has roared forth its voice to dictate this story. It is that roaring from the Ocean of Silence that brings to its shore pearls of wisdom in the form of warnings, admonitions and invaluable illuminations about the real worth and purpose of human birth. This Roaring Silence beckons each human being to get out of the Sisyphean task of seeking out the pebbles of the senses on the shore of life that has engaged him or her for countless lifetimes and strive for the real precious treasure hidden within oneself. That is truly your life's only purpose. If a single person awakens from the deep sleep of his or her ignorance, I would feel successful.

And yet in a sense, I have nothing to convey to you at all. This is an *atma-gatham* – a musing to oneself. In a way, you are just overhearing this conversation. Yet, the sounds are yours, the words are yours, the emotions are yours – only yours. I am just witnessing it and trying to collect the sparks which may take the form of the fire. Some may burn you, some may warm you.

I have tried to pen down my experiences and emotions in its true spirit and value. These words will be merged in the air, in the water, in the sound, in the earth, in the fire and eventually in oblivion. As I too, one day, will merge in the Cosmic Soul. Then, my Roaring will be silenced thereafter. Let time decide the value of the words of this *Avadhoota* to you.

Acknowledgements

A contemplation on my journey evolved a thought in me to put forth my autobiography with the wish that it would enable others to move up the ladder in their spiritual life. This journey which led to who I am today, as well as this autobiography, is only the result of the unceasing and unfailing *kripa* (blessing) of my beloved *Amma* (my *Guru Avadhoota* Tara Mayee Maa). I would like to acknowledge my heartfelt thanks to my disciples, devotees, well-wishers and even some unknown people who have constantly persuaded me to write my autobiography. It is their unfailing enthusiasm that has made me go through considerable effort and turmoil (physical, mental and financial) to write and publish the three volumes of my autobiography – *The Pyre of the Destined, Roaring Silence* and the yet unpublished *Sparks of Oblivion*.

It is my privilege to mention the one person who understands me and has travelled physically, mentally, and emotionally with me for more than thirty years sharing my unconcealed pleasures and pains - my spiritual brother *Swami* Abhayanand Saraswathi. He has the freedom to not only correct my words but also me! His unstinting and crucial literary support for the three volumes of my autobiography deserves the utmost credit. However, I cannot thank him because he is verily a part and parcel of my life. Can one thank one's own mind for a good or positive thought?

I want to thank my loving disciples who served me whole heartedly during my serious illness while pressing me to complete my literary works. I could wholly focus on my writing because they took care of all my daily needs and ensured that I had the privacy required to complete this undertaking. My heartfelt thanks to

Anirudh, Divya, Swapna Akhil, Unni Krishnan, Manikanta and many more that I may have missed. These are my children so I will dispense with the formal thanks. I shower my heartfelt *ashirvaads* (blessings) on them for their co-operation by offering their time, money or skills towards these volumes.

This book is the result of a chance discussion with Mohanji where he remarked that in this world of make- believe and pretensions, spiritual seekers are hankering after feel- good, fake glittering stones rather than real diamonds. Mohanji believes that this could possibly be because the seekers do not have a taste of what genuine spirituality means. To fulfill this need, Mohanji suggested that my autobiography be made available internationally so that its message reaches a larger and diverse global audience of genuine seekers. I consider Mohanji to be a man in the world but not of the world - an *Avadhoota*. I felt the sincerity and clarity of his intentions as well as the purity of purpose and, with great happiness, I gave my wholehearted approval and blessings for this project – to combine my three autobiographical works into this single new book titled *"Autobiography of an Avadhoota"* extended over one or two volumes with the same name. It was Mohanji who suggested that the three different books should indeed be combined so that the readers can easily feel and navigate through it effortlessly. And Mohanji graciously undertook the task of executing his suggestion without any expectations, and with my permission, shouldering the expenses for it himself or through his Foundation. He even offered to give back all the revenue that he may generate from the sale of books after expenses to the charity foundation that I had started. Appreciating the gesture, I suggested sharing the revenue between our organisation and ACT Foundation/Mohanji Foundation that Mohanji founded.

As I have said before, this book is not about me. The message of unconditional love and selfless service it contains is universal. I would like to see this message permeate into the world across age, race, creed, colour, gender, religion, etc. I want all human beings to recognize the innate Divinity within everyone and express that Divinity for the welfare of themselves, and most importantly, others. The only purpose of human existence is to discover the Kingdom of Heaven within our own hearts. Thy Will be done on earth, as it is in Heaven. My life, and consequently, this book is a humble expression of that divine goal and a witness to its universal truth.

I wish to see it available to a global audience and allow them to partake it by all means possible such as translations in different foreign languages as well as the different means offered in this new age such as e-books, audiobooks, and perhaps even video depictions. I express my sincere gratitude and offer my complete support to Mohanji, Mohanji Foundation and its team members and bless them with all my heart to achieve this noble goal. I would like to thank the Team at Manav Seva Samiti, Siddhaganj (Kurnool), Ammucare/ACT Foundation and the entire Publications Team of Mohanji Foundation notably Dr. P. K. Namboodiri, Lata Ganesh, Natesh Ramsell, V. Krishna Murthy, Sumit Partap Gupta, Rajesh Kamath, Sainath Wutukur, Geeta Iyer, Puja Narula, Akila Indurti, Janaky Murli, Vijaya Wutukur, Chandni Dinakaran and Disha Gupta among others.

Avadhoota Nadananda

Table of Contents

Experiencing an Avadhoota   ix
Preface   xix
Acknowledgements   xxiii

1. The Pyre Burns   1
2. Meeting the Same Sadhu in The Himalayas   4
3. The Journey Starts   7
4. My Verandah Life   10
5. Life in the Mookambika Forest   12
6. The Upadesa   16
7. The Path of Renunciation and Service   18
8. Logs in Stream   22
9. Language of Trees and Birds   26
10. The Inevitable Departure   29
11. Endless Journey Begins   35
12. The Journey to the Door of the Almighty   38
13. At Rishikesh   43
14. Towards Vyas Ghat   51
15. At Vyas Ghat   56
16. Days at Vyas Ghat   61
17. Dev Prayag   63
18. Back to Vyas Ghat   68
19. Vyas Ghat Days   73

20.	First Navaratri in The Himalayas	77
21.	Vyas Ghat Life Continues	82
22.	Moving Out From Vyas Ghat	86
23.	Stay at the Ghat	90
24.	Towards Upper Himalayas	94
25.	The Initiation into Bismillah Mantra	107
26.	Life at Uttarkashi	109
27.	The Stay Continues	114
28.	Towards Gangotri	118
29.	Gangotri Life Continues	124
30.	Stay at Ashram Verandah	127
31.	Towards Triyugi—I	130
32.	Towards Triyugi—II	134
33.	Towards Triyugi—III	138
34.	With Ashamayee	141
35.	With Ashamayee— Experience of Pratyangira	145
36.	Towards Tibet	149
37.	The Journey Continues	153
38.	Towards Northern Tibet	156
39.	The Lost Paradise: Where is Gyanganj?	160
40.	Towards Haridwar	165
41.	At Haridwar	168
42.	Haridwar Life Continues	172
43.	Life in the Mandali	175
44.	Navaratri in the Land of Vaishno Devi	178
45.	Mandir and Ashram	181
46.	In Gujarat	184
47.	Life in Karma Yoga	187
48.	Life with Jaunsaris—I	191
49.	Life with Jaunsaris—II	203
50.	Life with Jaunsaris—III	206

51.	Kumbha Mela and Journey to Narmada	209
52.	At Omkareshwar	212
53.	The Journey for Nothingness—I	216
54.	The Journey for Nothingness—II	219
55.	Broken Dreams	222
56.	Running away From Maya	226
57.	Again Haridwar	229
58.	Aimless Journey	233
59.	Journey in South (In Tirumala)	236
60.	Kalahasthi/Pakshi Teerth	239
61.	Srisailam	242
62.	Arunachala Shiva	245
63.	Back to Haridwar	247
64.	Life at Ghat Number 10	250
65.	Life at Ghat Number 10 Continues	253
66.	Towards Kailash Via Jammu	255
67.	Nepal, Pasupathy	258
68.	Manasarovar— Kailash	263
69.	Kailash - End of Sadhana	266
70.	Kailash—The Abode of Self	269
71.	Back to India, Samalkha	273
72.	Again Narmada and Kashi	275
73.	Tantra Sadhana	287
74.	Sadhana at Burial Ground	290
75.	New Horizons	292
76.	Unlimited Bliss	295
77.	Namami Devi Narmade	298
78.	Narmade Har … Har … Har	301
79.	Just a Journey—Neither Pilgrimage Nor Picnic!	304
80.	Life—A Dry Leaf	307
81.	Towards Badri —Via Jammu, Haridwar	310

82.	Badrinath —Chaturmas in a Cave	313
83.	End of Chaturmas	316
84.	Towards Tapovan	319
85.	Tapovan	322
86.	Towards Gyanganj - I	325
87.	Towards Gyanganj—II	328
88.	Towards Gyanganj—III	331
89.	Towards Gyanganj—IV	333
90.	Towards Gyanganj—V	336
91.	Towards Gyan Gunj—VI	339
92.	At Gyanganj	342
93.	Life at Gyanganj	345
94.	Last Days in Gyanganj	348
95.	On the Way to India	351
96.	At Kamakhya	353
Glossary		356

The Pyre Burns

The pyre in me to leave the mundane life started at the age of nine or ten when I was in an elementary school near my parental home. It was my first-ever encounter with a *sadhu* (an ascetic, holy man), who appeared in front of our courtyard one afternoon after my return from school. Usually my elder sister fed me rice, curd with *papad*, the most loving food which I enjoy even today. All of a sudden, a *sadhu* in *kashaya* (orange-coloured robe) appeared from nowhere at our courtyard, begging for alms. My mother invited him with utmost devotion and requested him to sit in the verandah, where he would be served his alms. By that time, I had finished my lunch and with much curiosity was watching the *sadhu* take a black-coloured bowl (which I came to know later, was called '*kappar*', a *pathra* or utensil used by *sadhus* for receiving *bhiksha*[1]), and asked my mother for *bhiksha*. Mother served rice, cooked vegetables, *papad* and pickles, and as I watched in wonder the scene in front of me, he took out another small bowl from his shoulder bag and asked for water to be poured in it. I was astonished with what was going on, as it was my first vision of a *sadhu* taking *bhiksha*. After a few moments, the *sadhu* mixed the food together and gulped it down. While the *sadhu* was putting away his *bhiksha pathra* into his shoulder bag, I asked him with all curiosity and devotion, "*Swami*, will you please give me this bowl?" He looked at me for a few seconds and with a beautiful smile (this vision still remains fresh in my memory) told me, "Oh Son, one day it will come to you ... you will get this *kappar*." Since

---

1 *Bhiksha* is food obtained by asking for alms. It signifies a Hindu, Buddhist and Jain tradition of begging for alms with the purpose of self-effacement or ego-conquering.

his reply was in Hindi which I could not understand, my sister translated his words for me in Malayalam. Before leaving, he put his hand on my head and uttered something in Sanskrit.

After many years when I was initiated to *sanyasi* (asceticism) by my beloved *Guruji Avadhoota* Tara Mayee and was ready to leave for the Himalayas on my onward journey as an '*Avadhoota*'[2] for my *tapas*[3], my *Guruji* gave me a *kappar* in black colour (the same which I had asked for from the old *sadhu*). With a smile on her face, she said a few words which I can translate this way, "This is the *kappar* which you asked for in your childhood. Beware, do not give it to anybody and have your daily *bhiksha* in this. As long as this *kappar* is with you, I will be with you, and once it breaks neither will I be there, nor you."

Even now, I keep the *kappar* with me and take my *bhiksha* in it. After a few years when I had a chance to meet *Avadhoota* Ashamayee (in the Himalayas)—a *Gurubehen* (fellow student of the same spiritual master/lineage, considered as a sister) of my *Guruji*—her first question to me was "Is the *bhiksha pathra* with you?" When I showed it to her, she told me that it was not an ordinary one as it was used by my *Guru Parampara* (lineage of *Gurus* or Masters) for eight generations and now I am the ninth generation person who is using this *kappar*.

Even now, the *kappar* shows its value by helping me whenever I am in need. It is a miracle utensil that always makes me aware of my *Guru*'s presence with me. This *kappar* has performed different miracles for me whenever I am in a fix. I believe that as long as it is with me, I will definitely have the presence of my *Guru Parampara* originating from *Gyanganj*.

---

2 'Avadhoota' is a Sanskrit term referring to a particular type of mystic or saint who is beyond egoic-consciousness, duality and common worldly concerns and acts without consideration for standard social etiquette. He/she is a spiritual guide to many souls and enlightens the path of those on a psychic journey.

3 Connotes certain spiritual practices in India related to asceticism, including meditation, austerities, body mortification and penance.

THE PYRE CONTINUES

Being born and raised in an orthodox *Nambudiri*[4] family (known as '*Kartha*', erstwhile *Samantha* rulers under the Travancore Kingdom), I had lots of restrictions in my day-to-day affairs. *Shuddhi* (purity) and *vrithy* (cleanliness) were foremost practices of a *Brahmin* family, that too very orthodox. However, the pyre started burning the day I met the *sadhu* from whom I had asked for the *kappar* at the age of nine or ten years. Ever since I met this sadhu, I had thoughts of leaving my home and travelling to an unknown distant place. I wanted to be like that *sadhu*. During those days I used to dream or visualize myself being at the foot of a snow-clad hill, at the banks of a ferociously flowing river, at dilapidated temples where a few *sadhus* with big matted hair and long beards covering their bodies or sitting on the banks of the river/at the foot of a hill and chanting something unfamiliar to me. During my stay at Rishikesh and Gangotri, I realized that I was witnessing the scenes I used to dream about.

---

4 The Malayalam-speaking Brahmins of Kerala.

Meeting the Same Sadhu in The Himalayas

During my stay in the Himalayas, somewhere near Gangotri (may be the name of the place is Maneri, on the way from Uttarkashi towards Gangotri), a miraculous experience happened. One morning, during my *pada* (on foot) pilgrimage towards Gangotri, I went for a bath in the *Ganga* (River Ganges in North India, revered as Mother or '*Mata*') at Maneri. I was all alone and was afraid to enter into the stream as the flow of water was frightening. I sat on a rock, thinking as to how to take a bath. Suddenly an old *baba/sadhu* with matted hair and beard appeared, perhaps to take a bath too. He came near me and asked, "Are you afraid to enter into the *Ganga*? *Ganga* is our Mother; enter and bathe; Mother *Ganga* will take care of you." When I looked at him, I remembered the childhood episode and tried to ask with hesitation, "*Swami* have I seen you somewhere?" With a touching smile the *sadhu* said, "'I AM EVERYWHERE,' whether you look at me or not, I am looking at you." I realized that the voice was the same I had heard during my childhood days in my parental home.

The next moment, he entered the *Ganga* River, washed his legs and hands and came towards me where he had kept his shoulder bag. He lifted a *kappar* from his bag which I had seen in my childhood and asked me "Finally you got the *pathra* you had asked for, show it to me." When I opened my bag, to my wonder, the *bhiksha pathra* given to me by my beloved *Guruji* was missing. Again, with the same smile, the *Swami* said "You don't believe me? My boy, do not panic, here is your *pathra* which you got from your *Guru*. You may be wondering how it came to me. Listen, this was actually my *bhiksha pathra* and I am your *Paramaguru*. Devotees call me Nityananda. I have given you a vision to let you know that you are not travelling all alone. *Tara* and I are always with you." He asked me to look upstream. When I looked (behold!), my *Guruji Avadhoota* Tara Mayee was taking a bath there and then she immediately disappeared (my *Guruji* had never left the forest near the Mookambika Temple[5] during her lifetime).

And then the *Swami* again asked me to check my shoulder bag, and to my wonder the *kappar* was there right in my bag. Just moments ago I had seen this *swami* putting my *kappar* into his shoulder bag and now it was there in my bag. There was no time to ask any question or converse, since he had himself told me that he was my *Paramaguru Swami* Nityananda *Bhagavan*. I offered *sashtanga namaskara* (prostration with full body on the ground) before him and to my wonder when I got up he had disappeared and looking into my shoulder bag, wonder of wonders, my *kappar* was there safe.

This entire episode means that a devoted disciple never needs to worry for his food, shelter or anything; the *Guru* will take care of the disciples and their needs too.

I sat there for hours together, lost in thoughts of my *Guruji* and *Paramaguruji*. Then I saw some women dressed in traditional Himalayan village clothing, walking towards me with a small bamboo basket. They came to me and said "*Baba*, take *bhiksha*, we have brought *roti* and *curry* for you." They insisted on my taking *bhiksha* without having a bath and just by washing my hands and legs. I offered the food first to *Ganga Mata* and then ate. It was the most delicious food I had ever had as I was eating for the first time in four days. Before my journey to the Himalayas, I had taken an oath that I would not beg for food and would eat only if somebody offered it to me. I did not know who they were. To my ordinary intellect, they were just villagers. Nevertheless, after some time I realized that they were not ordinary village women.

---

5 The Kollur Mookambika Temple located at Kollur, Udupi district in the state of Karnataka, India, is a Hindu temple dedicated to Goddess Mookambika Devi.

Then with utmost politeness I asked them "Mother, where do you people stay and how did you know that a hungry man was sitting here?" They smiled for a while and said, "We are those mothers whose names you have been chanting since your childhood." Now I understood they were none other than MahaKali, MahaLakshmi and MahaSaraswathi, for whom I used to recite *Devi Mahatmyam* since childhood. My father had initiated me into the *Devi Mahatmyam* prayer when I was in class ten. I feel that when I was afraid to move forward to the Himalayas, my *Guruji, Parama Guruji* and the three Mothers came to me to encourage me and make me understand that I should never look back, just move forward, forward and forward. While having my *bhiksha* I noticed that the three mothers had disappeared.

I will narrate later the same episode, repeated with a slight difference during my journey to Manasarovar and Kailash.

The Journey Starts

It was *Ashada masam* (fourth month according to the Hindu traditional calendar, corresponding to July/August) when I left my home with the blessings of my parents in search of the Self. It had been raining since morning; I told my mother and father that I was leaving my home once and for all in search of the Self. By this time, my father had verified my 'horoscope' (for an astrological reading/prediction) and had told my mother that no force on earth could stop me from leaving home since I was destined to do so.

Everybody is destined to be what he/she will be. So too 'ME'. This is known as '*Poorva Janma Karma Phalam*' (the result of the deeds of one's previous birth).

It was in the morning around 6.00 am that I left my home, my mother, my father, brothers, sisters, and friends in search of 'ME'. On that morning, my friend Sridharan Thomas (who was a unique person, who lived as an *Avadhoota* without knowing his actual identity and who sings songs written by himself), came to me and said, "It is time to leave, I will take you up to the bus stand." I was ready to say goodbye to everybody. I wore my hand-spun cotton *dhoti* (traditional men's garment) and *khaddar* shirt, kept Rs.16 in my pocket and a pocket book edition of the *Bhagavat Gita* with me. When I prostrated before my mother, she with eyes filled with tears asked me just one question, "So far I took care of your food and other needs. Who will feed you from today onwards?" My eyes too started to submerge in a storm of tears, but hiding them from my mother, I said: "Mother, keep one thing in mind, even if a dog walks away hungry in front of your house, I will be hungry on that day. So try to feed somebody before you eat. The food you feed somebody will be served by somebody else to me." I prostrated before my mother and father and left home. (According to the custom, parents are supposed to close the main door of the house with a thundering sound when their child leaves home for *sanyasa*.) I heard the sound of door closing behind me. For a while my feet stopped, the ground shifted from beneath my feet, but my friend Sridharan Thomas insisted that I move on. We travelled to the bus stand on a bicycle. He rode and I sat behind him. I got a bus to Trichur. From there I was supposed to take another bus to Mangalore, to go to Mookambika (the deity, Sri Raja Rajeswari to whom I offered worship during my *Sri Vidya Sadhana* at my residence). At that time, my mind was full of one intention, to reach Mookambika, from where I could start my journey, or where I would be able to find a Guru who could lead me to 'ME'.

The next morning I reached Mookambika. I was left with just Rs.1.50. The previous day I had not taken any food as there was no sufficient money to buy any. I was feeling hungry and went to a shop, took a glass of lemon water worth four *annas* (0.25 paisa). The remaining money, I offered to a person sitting in front of the Mookambika temple.

Now there was no shelter and no food. Except for the sky, there was no roof over my head, and except for earth, no bed. I went to the nearby river (Souparnika) took a bath and with the same unwashed robes (as I did not have another dress to change into), came once again to the Mookambika Temple. It was noon, time for *Arathi* (religious ritual of worship which involves lighting lamp in front of the deity), after removing my shirt and putting it on my shoulder, I went in front of the *Garbhagriha* (inner sanctum) to have *darshan* (ceremonial viewing of a deity) of my mother Mookambika whom I used to worship for a long time as Srividya.

I saw a beautiful woman with long hair, with *kumkum* (vermilion powder usually offered to the goddess in *puja*) on her forehead, wearing a yellow sari and blouse, looking at me constantly. In front was Mother Mookambika, but instead of looking at the idol of the deity, my eyes were being forced to see the beautiful woman with a very wonderful body language. After a moment, she went for *pradakshina* (the ritual of circumambulation in a temple).

The moment she reached the rear of the temple, she stopped and looked back to see whether I was following her or not. Of course, I was following her. She stopped for a while and with a wonderful smile on her face she said, "Go to the verandah of Sri Ramakrishna Yogashram and be there, your *Guru* will meet you there," and then she stepped forward and disappeared into the *Garbhagriha*. It was then that I realized that it was *Amma* (Divine Mother), the Goddess Mookambika herself who had instructed me.

I was hungry and moved here and there, the temple bells were ringing and a tourist told me that the bells announced the time for feeding the poor and directed me to '*oottupura*' a dining hall behind the temple. I was served my first *bhiksha* blessed by Mookambika, at her abode, as the mother takes care of her children who are hungry in the form of Annapurna.[6]

After my first *bhiksha*, I enquired about the route to Sri Ramakrishna Yoga Ashram, which I reached with a bit of difficulty. One aged *Swami* was sitting on an easy chair. I asked him for permission to stay at the ashram's verandah for at least forty-one days, as I wanted to chant *Lalitha Sahasra Namam*, in front of Mookambika daily. Since he was also from Kerala, and may be because I spoke in Malayalam, he agreed and asked me to stay there and take my two meals from the ashram. The swami is known as *Acharya Theertha*, a well-known author, editor, poet and orator, who had been living there for a long time.

---

6 Hindu goddess of nourishment, an avatar (incarnation) of Parvati, the consort of Shiva

My Verandah Life

I started staying on the verandah of the ashram. Every day the bell rang at 11.30 am and 7.30 pm for food. I took my daily food from the ashram along with other inmates, went to the temple every morning and sat at Saraswathi Mandapam and chanted *Lalitha Sahasra Namam.*

Days passed, I failed to meet my *Guru,* and my mind was a bit disturbed with the thoughts of my mother, father and home. One fine day in the afternoon, I was sitting as usual in the verandah— this might have been fifteen days after my arrival there—I saw an old lady in alphy (a long shirt made of cotton), short hair, a stick in one hand and a tin box in the other, walking towards the verandah. She came near me and sat down. The woman was dirty and untidy. All of a sudden my ego awakened and reminded me of my Nambudiri background. I moved swiftly away from the old woman thinking that she was a beggar. But she was immersed in herself talking as a mad woman and I got a little bit afraid looking at her. I moved close to the *Swamiji* who was sitting on his easy chair and asked him who she was. To my wonder, the *Swami* cautioned me and told me not to go near her, because if she got angry I would lose everything, and if she was happy I would be blessed.

Since I had been blessed by the Universal Mother that I shall meet my *Guru* in the verandah, I had the thought in my mind, what did I have to lose now? I had left everything behind and came in search of a *Guru* who could lead me to the ultimate reality of experiencing the Oneness. So I went near her and tried doing *sashtanga namaskar.* All of a sudden she laughed and asked, "You are from a Brahmin family, I'm a beggar as you think, how you can do *namaskar*[7] to a beggar, you will lose your *brahmanatwa*, go away, get lost."

But looking at her face I could read the motherly affection she possessed, which she was showering on me. Immediately I remembered the golden words of the Universal Mother, whom I had met at the rear of the Mookambika temple, that I would meet my *Guru* at the verandah. At that moment without thinking I did a full-body prostration at the feet of that old woman, saying "*Sri Gurudevyei Namah*" (Salutations to the Mother Goddess who is in the form of a *Guru*/Master). She might have heard it, for she laughed loudly for a few minutes and then asked me "Why are you here?" I was unable to find any words, however I managed to say, "In search of a *Guru*, which may be you, *Amma*." Immediately she took her stick and beat me once on the shoulder.

All of a sudden, she left the verandah and started walking towards the Sauparnika River. Without wincing, I followed her like a calf following in its mother's footsteps. She entered the river, crossed and went to the other bank of the river. It was raining, both of us were drenched. She kept on walking deep into the forest. I too followed her.

Thus the journey began...

---

7 A traditional Indian greeting or gesture of respect, made by bringing the palms together before the face or chest and bowing

Life in the Mookambika Forest

This was the first time I was staying in a forest filled with animals, reptiles and birds. It was a dense forest with some parts that were yet to receive rays of the sun.

My *Guruji Avadhoota* Tara Mayee used to stay in this forest under a big tree. She used to stay under this particular tree in rain, hot sun and even cold weather, day and night, except when she went for morning ablutions or to the temple to take *bhiksha*. She used to carry a shoulder bag made of cloth by tying the four corners of a cloth. In it, she carried a *mala* (necklace) made of brass in the shape of a skull (later she gave it to me and finally I handed it over to Mohi at Chowl, Maharashtra, to keep it in the temple), a cloth which she used as a scarf, and a *bhiksha pathra* which she gave to me on my journey to the Himalayas. She wore a *kafni* (a knee-length, loose robe-like garment) made of cotton cloth which looked very dirty as if it had never been washed. *Amma* carried a tin box with a twine handle on it for carrying easily and collected bhiksha in it. These were her possessions. In her *kafni* pocket, she carried lots of half burnt *bidi*s (Indian cigarette) and a few match sticks. She never smoked but, occasionally lit a *bidi* and offered it to me to pull the smoke as much as I could (later I understood that this was a technique used to teach me *pranayama*). She hardly spoke and occasionally uttered a few words.

One morning, when the rain had just stopped and the sun was peeping into the grass, when no bird was making any noise, *Amma* woke me up and showed me a flower at a distance. It was a violet flower, just bloomed with a few bees around it. She said "I want you to be like that, like this flower with bees around it." (At that time I was unable to understand what she meant, but later during my Himalayan life I realized who I was and what my responsibility was and with disciples around me I understood what *Amma* told that day.) By Her grace, now I am like a flower with people around me taking honey (nectar of spirituality) from the child of *Amma*.

I never saw *Amma* sleep or take a bath. She never gave me lectures; I used to sit near her looking at her lotus feet for hours and hours. She allowed me to go to Sauparnika for daily ablutions and to visit the Mookambika Temple in the early hours. *Amma* took *bhiksha* from the Mookambika Temple when the temple bells rang around noon but never allowed me to get *bhiksha*, even from the temple. She brought the *bhiksha* in the tin box to the forest and made a typical whistle putting two fingers in her mouth. Many animals gathered at the whistle and *Amma* fed each of those rabbits, serpents, crows, pigeons, small ants, etc. After feeding each of them fully, *Amma* fed me with a hand full of rice and *sambar* (a lentil-based vegetable stew or chowder based on a broth made with tamarind) or whatever she got as *bhiksha*. Finally, whatever was left (not even half a handful) she ate and then poured some water in that box and drank it. This continued until the end of my stay with her.

I had still not been initiated to any *sadhana*, or order or discipline. I wondered what to ask and was a bit worried as to "what was happening to me". One morning when I woke up, *Amma* was not there. My *Guruji* never left the tree in the morning. I searched for her here and there but could not find her, even in the temple. It was *bhiksha* time and she had not returned. I did not go to the temple for *bhiksha* but came to the old verandah of Sri Ramakrishna Yogashram. When the old *Swamiji* observed my face and asked me what was wrong, I narrated my pain of missing my *Guruji*. The *Swamiji* laughed and said that I was like a calf that missed its mother. He assured me not to worry and insisted that I take food as I had not eaten anything since morning. It was almost evening and I told *Swamiji* that I would not take food and water until and unless I got my *Guruji* back and went back to the verandah with tears in my eyes.

That night in my dream, I had the *darshan* of my *Guruji* saying that I should not be foolish and should have food the next day at the ashram. The next day morning I was sitting with the ashramites to take food when from nowhere my *Guruji* appeared all of a sudden and took away the served food (there the food used to be served on a plantain leaf) and fed a cow standing on the road. *Swamiji* told me that this was a test for me; something good was going to happen to me and asked me not to take any food and consider it as *upavas* (fasting) day. Next day the same thing was repeated; *Amma* took away the served food and fed the cow on the road.

One afternoon, it was very hot and I wanted to take a bath. That old *Swamiji* had already left for bathing in Sauparnika. I asked *Amma* if we could both go for a bath. *Amma* nodded. I went inside the ashram and took soap, *vibhoothi* (sacred ash) and kumkum from somebody. Then I took *Amma*'s hand in mine and walked to the Sauparnika for a bath. I first washed *Amma's kafni* and put it out to dry. I then bathed *Amma* and asked her to wear my towel until the *kafni* dried. Then I washed my clothes, put them for drying and took a bath. After the clothes dried, I put the *kafni* on her body and applied *vibhoothi* and *kumkum* on her forehead. As soon as I put the *tilakam* (marking on forehead, usually with a fragrant paste, such as of sandalwood or vermilion) on her forehead, she placed her hand on my shoulder and said, "Now I look beautiful, will you marry me?" I was very shocked with this question. The old *Swamiji* near us was laughing as if these words had a deep and different meaning. The foolish boy that I was, I didn't understand the words of a great saint like *Amma*. Moreover, I felt bad and thought, "Why is this old lady asking me to marry her?" I got angry and walked back to the verandah with tears in my eyes, thinking, "Is it for this that I left my home, parents, sisters, brothers and friends? Why is this old lady behaving like this?" I sat on the verandah with tears in my eyes, depressed and lost in my thoughts. I had seen the *Swami* followed by *Amma* walking towards the ashram. I sat as if I did not notice them. The Swami went inside the ashram to arrange for *arathi*. I heard a *bhajan* in the background, *Innu sukravara...* (Kannada *bhajan* on Datta *Bhagavan*).

When the *arathi* was over, the *Swami* came to the verandah and sat in his favourite easy chair. *Amma* was sitting near me. It was raining very heavily and may be because of the bath and now the rain, *Amma* was shivering. Though my mind had not settled yet, my heart melted. I found some wooden scraps lying in one corner of the verandah. I asked the *Swamji* for some match sticks, gathered the wooden scraps near my *Guruji,* and started a fire. *Amma* was sitting in the upper verandah and I was sitting on the second step below. I was heating my palms in the fire and passing on the heat by massaging *Amma's* feet. *Swamiji* was quietly watching all that was happening. I heard *Amma* talking to herself saying, "When there is heat inside, where is the requirement of heat from outside." (She repeated these words three to four times as if she was talking to herself.) Foolishly, I continued giving massage to warm *Amma's* feet and hands. Suddenly, she lifted her left leg and gave a kick (blow) on my chest. I fell down on the road unconscious. I heard *Swamiji* say, "The marriage is over, the marriage is over." Because of my foolishness, this time also I was unable to understand what was happening to me. *Amma* came near and uttered the *'Ekakshari'* mantra to me. I was in a trance and had lost control of my body, mind, intellect, consciousness and complexes. I was in a trance for almost sixteen hours and when I came back to my senses, the *Swamiji* gave me a cup of coffee and said that it was my *'Shaktipath deeksha',* initiation from my *Guruji* through a kick on my chest. I had never expected my *Guruji's deeksha* to be like this. After all this, that is sixteen hours of trance and coffee, I followed *Amma* to the forest. It was ten to eleven in the morning. She was silent and I was quiet too. I felt totally blank and there was no awareness of my mind, body, or intellect at that time.

The Upadesa

When we reached the tree under which she normally stayed, she sat as if nothing had happened. I did *pranaams* and sat near her. She started talking of the *Siddha Parampara*[8] and about the *Shaktipath*. She concluded saying, "You have to keep this *Agni* with you forever and make use of it for others. A person who lives for himself is an animal and a person who lives for others is a *Bhagavan* (God). Now you have to decide what you want to become, an animal or a *Bhagavan*. If you decide positively take an oath that for the rest of your life you will live for others, only for others, whatever consequences may befall in the path of your spiritual journey. "Then I took an oath touching her holy feet, "*Amma*, I will live for others, only for others in my life, whatever may happen to me". She said, "Well, my Son, if so, I will be with you always."

No other *sadhana*, no *japa* (chants), no *mantras*, I was just observing what was happening to me within. I always felt a sweet burning sensation within my inner self. Now I understood that the fire within was burning, and the sweetness of my *Guru's* touch created an ecstatic mood whenever I remembered this golden moment of my life.

Days were passing by and my eagerness to go to the Himalayas was raging like a fire within me. But I was afraid to ask, as I believed that without *kashaya vastra* (*sanyasi* initiation), I was not supposed to go to the Himalayas. One day as I was thinking about this, *Amma* told me that a *Swamiji* was coming to Mookambika for *darshan*, and that he would perform the *Sanyasa Sanskara* (rituals

---

8 Traditional lineage of adepts, ascetics who have achieved enlightenment

related to initiation to *sanyasa*). As an *Avadhoota*, my *Guruji* was not supposed to perform any such rituals herself. I was happy that my *Guruji* had read my mind and was now arranging for my *sanyasa* initiation. I was very happy and there were no words to explain this happiness.

I slept that night as a child sleeping near his mother, calm, quiet and dreamless. The expected moment was nearing. I was now getting ready for my *sanyasa*, and these were the thoughts as I woke up in the morning.

The Path of Renunciation and Service

My sanyasa *deeksha*[9] happened on the banks of the Sauparnika River. My *Guruji* was witnessing and instructing the *Swamiji* about the *deeksha*. The rituals were day-long and finally I received my *kashaya vastram* (saffron-coloured garments worn by ascetics of India) and *Presh Mantra*[10] after *Viraja Homam*[11] and a new (spiritual) name was given—Swami Nadananda Tirtha. Now I belonged to *Dasanami Sanyasi Parampara*, a ten-sect order. Adi Sankara had divided *Sanyasa Parampara* into 10 sects, known as Dasanami according to Vedic Philosophy—the details of the sanyasa rituals are a sacred secret between *Guru* and *Shishya* (disciple) hence I am unable to give details. To see everybody in '*samatva bhavana*' (equalism), *sanyasa* is the one path. *Sanyasa* means '*Samyak Nyasa*' (i.e. to renounce worldly and material aspects of living and lead a life of intellectual contemplation), but to me, *sanyasa* means not only leaving everything apart, but also '*nishkaam karma*' (non-attached action without obligation) as my *Guruji* taught me—to live for others.

---

9 Preparation or consecration for a religious ceremony which involves giving of a mantra or an initiation by the guru in Indian religions such as Hinduism, Buddhism, and Jainism

10 Chanting of 'Presha Mantram' signifies the renunciation of the world, worldly relations and material wealth

11 *Viraja Homa* is an oblation to fire for self-purification from ego, performed during the ceremony wherein a Hindu monk takes up the vows of renunciation.

Every moment we live for ourselves is selfishness. To live for others is not easy. But once you have taken the oath, you have to bear and you have to live for others. Shastras say, 'Aatmano Mokshartham Jagat Hitaya Cha', meaning 'For one's own salvation and for the welfare of the world.' It simply means, you live for yourself but it should be for the betterment of others. I tried, am trying and will keep trying to be like that as I have taken an oath touching my beloved *Guruji*'s holy feet.

So now that I had got upgraded to a *sanyasi*, people prostrated before me wherever I went, even on the roads, and in the ashram, they looked at me differently. The value was added. This is the system in Bharat; holy men are given high regard. However I was worried that this should not boost my ego, the ego that will make me fall in the pit. So chanting the *Pranava* or '*Om*' mantra (considered the symbol or representation of the individual soul which *sanyasis* must always chant) and remembering *Guruji* eternally, I remained in the Mookambika forests along with my *Guruji*. One day, she said (for kicking my ego), "Son, now you are a *sanyasi*, you are free, why do you want to be with me always. You should do *tapas* and get your battery charged which will be useful to distribute to the needy." I felt sad. Why was my mother asking me to go? My eagerness to go to the Himalayas was too high, so she surely must have read my mind. After taking up *sanyasa*, one day the old Swamiji invited me for *bhiksha* (as per the Hindu culture, *sanyasis* are invited for *bhiksha* to houses or ashrams); with the permission of my beloved mother I left for *bhiksha*. After all the food items were served on a plantain leaf, I was about to offer it to my *Guruji* as per the tradition of the *shishya*, when all of a sudden *Amma* appeared there in the dining hall of the Ashram with an unusual smile on her face. She told me, "You have offered it to me, let me take it" and she took the plantain leaf filled with rice, lentils, vegetables, *papadam*, etc., and started eating. Finally, as usual, as a mother feeds her child, my beloved mother fed me directly with her hand a handful of food, the moment my lips touched her fingers, tears rolled down my cheeks endlessly. She took me outside the Ashram and told me, "Whenever you are given food with any *sankalpam* (a prayer of offering made with some desire), remember me and offer it to me and then eat it." I did not know the food served to me was with a *sankalpam*. Even now, whenever food is served to me with a *sankalpam*, I just remember this incident and offer it first to my beloved mother and then eat it.

The urge to go to the Himalayas was increasing in me day and night. It looked like it was time for me to depart (physically) from my beloved *Guruji*. But it was not possible for me; therefore, I decided to stay back with my mother for a few more months.

Once a *Shetty* (merchant) came with lots of *idlis* (steamed rice cakes—a south Indian dish) and *chutney* and offered it to *Amma*. After leaving home (more than a year had passed). I had not taken any food other than the *bhiksha* that *Amma* fed me. I looked at the *idlis* with longing and wanted to swallow them at one go. There were two dogs that regularly took food from *Amma's bhiksha*. *Amma* called both the dogs and fed all the *idlis* to them. I felt very bad that not even a single *idli* was given to me and in a fit of anger expressed my disappointment with my *Guruji*. She kept quiet for a few moments and then told me to look around for those two dogs which had eaten the *idlis*. A few yards away from us, to my shock, both the dogs were lying dead under a tree near the Sauparnika River. I asked, "*Amma* why did this happen?" She replied, "Son, Shetty had come with the intention of killing us by feeding us the poisoned food." I again asked her, "But why come all the way to kill you?" She said with a gentle smile, "Shetty is a crooked person and whenever he comes to me he comes with a *sankalpam*, and knowing his nature I never granted him anything that he wanted and because of that he has done this misdeed." I queried her again, "Then you have killed those two dogs." She patted and replied, "Son, the life span of these dogs is over; hence I have liberated them. They will take a human form in their next life and will become your disciples." At that moment, I was not in a position to believe this but since *Amma* said so, I accepted it. After many years, when I was in Haridwar, two Agarwal brothers approached me along with their parents with a request to initiate them. I was uncomfortable thinking how could somebody just walk towards me and request an initiation, but then I heard the thundering sound of *Amma's* voice saying, "Son, do not think again, these are the two dogs that died eating those poisonous *idlis* and as I had told you they have come to you for initiation, do initiate them with the *Devi Pranav Deeksha*." Without hesitation, I initiated them and even today, they are my disciples practicing the *sadhana*. However, I have not told them the details of their previous birth as it may disturb them.

There are a lot of such experiences with my *Guruji*.

Logs in Stream

Life is like logs in the stream. Due to the flow of the river currents, dry logs flowing in the river come together and then separate. All relations are like this. Due to *poorva janma karma*[12] (*karma* related to the previous birth) we come together and then depart.

I knew in the core of my heart that at any time, any day, my *Guruji* will ask me to leave her for my '*tapas*' in the Himalayas. But my mind was in conflict; on the one side I wanted to leave for the Himalayas and on the other I did not want to leave the loving presence of my *Guruji*. I was in a dilemma on this issue and was unable to take a decision. But I am destined to be. Therefore, my destiny would definitely take me to where I should be. During my stay at home, I was unaware that I would come to Mookambika or that I would be initiated into *sanyasa*. It was destined, so it happened. Likewise, I knew that the day was nearing when I would take leave from my *Guruji* and go to the Himalayas in search of me within me.

Once I was sitting with my *Guruji* on the banks of Sauparnika near the tree where she used to normally sit. *Amma* had shown me a small fish which was trying to come onshore, but as soon as it reached the shore, due to suffocation, was jumping back into the river. It repeated this several times. *Amma* said, "You are also like this fish; you want to come to the shore but due to the suffocation on reaching the shore you are again jumping back into the river." She understood my situation where on one side I wanted to go

---

12 The sum of a person's actions in this and previous states of existence, viewed as deciding their fate in future existences.

to the Himalayas and on the other side did not want to leave my beloved *Amma*. With great difficulty, I tried telling her, "I do not want to leave you and go to the Himalayas, but if you promise me that you will be there with me always, then I will not have any issues in going to the Himalayas". *Amma* got angry and scolded, "You still doubt me? Do not worry, I will be with you always, where ever you go I will be there for you." On hearing this from *Amma*, my mind eased a bit.

I had two more *Gurubhais* (males initiated by the same *Guru* are considered brothers). One of them was very much envious of me because I always stayed with *Amma*. He used to come on weekends or holidays as he was working in a college. The other brother was young and energetic, simple, loving, cooperative, and non-demanding. Once I was sitting near *Amma* under a tree during an afternoon, both of them came and after doing the *namaskars*, they sat near *Amma*. The first person, the one who was envious of me, brought some fruits and sweets, and as usual *Amma* offered them to the animals. On *Amma*'s whistle, a fox, a dog and two rabbits appeared from nowhere and fed on the fruits. That was the first time I had seen a dog eating fruit. There were some leftover fruits and sweets, which I thought *Amma* would give all of us as *prasadam* (food that is a religious offering, consumed after worship or religious ceremony); however, *Amma* told the brother who was working in the college to give the leftovers to the animals at his house. We could not understand why she told him that and were surprised. As it was nearing sunset, both my brothers were ready to leave, but *Amma* told them to wait for a while. She asked the brother who was working in a college, "What are you expecting from me?" He asked *Amma*, "*Amma*, you be with me in your last days, I will keep your *Samadhi* at my home." Amma agreed and granted the wish. She immediately asked the younger brother, "What about you?" and he replied politely, "*Amma* with your blessings, I would like to be an *Avadhoota* like you." With a smile, *Amma* granted him his wish. Lastly, she turned towards me with a smile and asked "*Ninte icha entha*?"("What is your wish?")

At that moment I felt as if the earth was moving away from me. I was trembling, shivering, could not even swallow the saliva as my throat had dried up completely, it took a few moments for me to say, "*Amma*, you be with me always, always, till the end of my life." I could not see anything at that moment as my eyes were fully filled with tears flowing down my cheeks like a gushing river. *Amma* opened her arms and embraced me with all affection and love. It was an unforgettable incident in my life; I noticed that there were tears of my *Amma* which had purified my back while she was embracing me. This caring touch of my *Guruji* always stays with me. *Amma* said, "Yes this was the moment I was waiting for; one needs my body which does not have any value, the other needs my capacity and you, my son, only you need me, only me. So I'm with you, I will be with you forever and ever." There was a disturbing silence for a while and my brothers left. I stayed with *Amma* and *Amma* with me.

One day a priest from the Mookambika temple invited *Amma* and me for *bhiksha*. *Amma* never accepted any invitations, but to my wonder, she said, "Yes I will come." We went to the priest's house for *bhiksha* as it was the birthday of his only son, who was ailing from some illness. We entered the house of the priest where we could see a small boy of 3 to 4 years of age lying on a cot at the corner of the house. *Guruji* walked straight to the cot and embraced the boy and told him, "I am not ready to lose you, you are the only son of these people and you have to take care of them, so do not go my son, do not go." While saying this she placed her left hand on the *bhrumadhya* (spot on the forehead between the eyebrows) of the boy and the boy opened his eyes and laughed. I could not understand anything happening there. However, the priest told me that according to the horoscope—astrologically—the boy was just counting his days on this earth. Now it was clear to me that *Amma* had saved the boy from death bed. But *Amma* started vomiting a lot of yellowish fluid, which was worrying. *Amma* told me, "Son, do not worry; get me a handful of coriander leaves powder in a glass full of buttermilk. The priest helped me in serving this to *Amma*; she took it and lo, within a few moments the vomiting stopped and the same old smiling face of *Amma* returned. Instead of sitting and eating there, *Amma* took *bhiksha* in her tin container and we left for the forest.

That was the day *Amma* taught me how to save people (who are in need) even from death bed. Touching and healing process is a part of all religions. The way *Amma* taught me was very different. After her teachings, she cautioned me, "Do not misuse this *vidya* (knowledge) for *kupathras (those not eligible to receive the sacred knowledge)*. Remember that whenever you do this, you will definitely lose a good part of the vital energy. So be very careful in using this." I have done this *vidya* for several people who were ailing and about to leave the world. Of course, it is against the rule of nature. If one man is suffering because of his past 'karma', the *karma phala* (fruit of karma/destiny), he has to undergo that suffering and finish it in the next birth. Now if I am interfering with the rules of nature, the ailing man will be relieved but instead of that ailing person, I have to suffer the pain and agony the person was supposed to suffer.

Several times, I suffered to some extent and am still suffering because of my actions to relieve a suffering person and a dying person. However, there is a plus point to this. Due to the *punya karma* (meritorious karma) which I did by saving a person who is in need for his family or society, my *Guruji/Ishta Devi* (main godhead or deity chosen for worship) gives me back the vital energy, double than what I have spent, and this energy I can use for others.

Language of Trees and Birds

Once I noticed that *Amma* was talking to a bird sitting on the branch of a nearby tree. The bird was making some noise and *Amma* was replying in a language unknown to me. When the conversation got over, I went to *Amma* and asked, "*Amma* what was the bird saying?" She looked at me for a few minutes with her eyes wet and said, "The bird was telling me about your Himalaya pilgrimage." I asked once again, "What language was that?" *Amma* said, "It is the language of nature, I learned this language from nature. If you observe carefully, you will find that the language of nature is already within you because we ourselves are merged with nature. The river sings, wind speaks, trees, birds, animals everything in the *prakruthi* (nature) have a common language. I call it 'LOVE'. If you can be affectionate to nature, she will also reciprocate."

I was astonished; I was unable to understand the mystic language that *Amma* spoke. How can it be possible for me to understand the song of a river, the affection of the wind, or the dialogue of two birds or animals? As I was just contemplating these thoughts, I got a blow with the big stick, which *Amma* used to always carry as her walking stick. I thought why is *Amma* beating me for nothing? *Amma*'s voice was very clear, "Do not have any disbelief or doubts; your disbelief will lead to your downfall." I have never since doubted nor have I looked back. I never regretted choosing the path of renunciation because I know deep within that *Guruji* is always with me. I believe that she has been carrying me on her shoulder and making me eat, drink, think, write and speak, all through.

RUNNING AWAY FROM AMMA

One rainy day—rains in Mookambika are unpredictable—I was sitting close to *Amma* at dawn after completing my usual rituals/prayers. She suddenly removed her stick and gave a big blow on my shoulders. When I received the blow, I felt bad and my ego was hit to the core and I began to think why was this *Amma*, a beggar-like person, beating me a literate person hailing from a very pious family. The very moment such thoughts arose in my mind, another big blow landed on my shoulder. I was furious, and in a fit of anger moved away from *Amma* crying and thinking why had I left my palatial house, my beloved parents, my brothers, sisters, relatives, friends and my village? Why did I end up staying with a beggar woman, begging along with her, living on the steps of a temple, bathing in the river, wearing one piece of cloth, getting drenched in the rain, drying up in the scorching sun, getting dusty in the roads of the village, smelling, wandering in deep forests and mountains—not realizing where I was or where I was headed to, I just walked and walked miles and miles continuously for a couple of hours and finally sat under a Peepal tree. I could not console myself and cried continuously for hours together.

It was almost afternoon when suddenly I could hear the sound of the bells coming from the famous Mookambika temple, which was nothing but the invitation to the *sadhus* and *sanyasis* to have their *bhiksha*. I realized that it was the time for me to take the *bhiksha* from *Amma*, and that she would be waiting for me. I realized that *Amma* would not eat without feeding me *bhiksha*. In spite of that, I decided not to go and continued crying under the tree for hours together repeatedly asking myself, why had *Amma* beaten me? After several hours I got up shivering and moved slowly towards the tree where *Amma* sat. Then I began running towards *Amma*. I was running like a calf running in search of its mother when it could not find her. It did not even occur to me that I was deep in the forest and barefoot; thorns were piercing deep into my feet and blood was gushing out like water. The rough stems of the wild trees were cutting my body and blood was oozing out, but the very thought that *Amma* would be waiting for me to have *bhiksha* and that she would not have had even drop of water without having given me *bhiksha* was making me run wildly towards *Amma*.

In a few moments I was in front of *Amma*. I looked at the *bhiksha pathra*; it was full of food, and *Amma* had neither eaten the food nor given even to the birds and animals according to the regular practice. I saw the wet eyes of my *Guruji* who had been waiting for me for a long time. I went near her and did a *sashtanga namaskar* and told her, "*Amma* please pardon me, I will never ever leave you. Whatever mistakes or blunders I commit please pardon me always and do make me walk through under your grace. As a son I always want to sleep on your warm lap, hence please pardon me for my mistakes." Saying these words, I washed her lotus feet with my tears. There was a deep silence for a moment, and then suddenly there was another big blow from *Amma's* stick on my back. Wincing with much pain from the blow, I got up and with folded hands I told her once again, "Irrespective of what punishment you give me—whether you beat me, kill me or do anything to me—I will not leave you, you are everything to me, my mother, my father, my brother, my sister, my God, my everything. You have all the authority to do anything to me. In the end, whatever you do will be a good thing for me since I am your son and I know it. Hence, please let me sit in your warm lap always and pardon all the mistakes this boy commits."

She stood up, embraced me, and wept. Both of us—the *Guru* and the *Shishya*—wept for some time. And then she sat down as usual as though nothing had happened and whistled for the animals and birds. They came, and we all had *bhiksha*.

Even after so many years, I still did not understand why *Amma* beat me, why I ran away from *Amma* and then why did I return to her. But one thing I had noticed was that whenever she was in a happy mood she would beat me and whenever she was in an angry mood she would embrace me and cry. How can I describe the moods of an *Avadhoota* who has the nature of '*baalavat*' (childish), '*unmadavat*' (madness) and '*pishachavat*' (beastliness)!

The Inevitable Departure

It was summer in Mookambika. I remember the day as if it is happening just now. It was a fine morning, the wind was blowing in the forest and I was sitting next to my *Guruji*'s holy feet. I had noticed a change in my *Guruji*'s face. She was deep in thought; a profound silence was felt between us; I heard the sound of a crying baby bird, then there was silence, again I heard the cry of the small bird.

Amma broke the silence, "My dear son, this is the apt time for you to move to the Himalayas. Since you have lived too long with me now, there is no option. Go, go for the better. "I did not understand her words, but I took the courage of asking, "*Amma* what are you saying, I am unable to understand."

She said, "I know, you are quite anxious to go to the Himalayas. You have been staying with me for quite some time; now it is time for you to start your pilgrimage."

I now thought how could I take leave from my beloved *Guru* and go to an unknown place to lead a lonely life? She read my thoughts and said, "Do not think about anything. You have to leave tomorrow morning itself, go to Rishikesh and over there find a place near River Ganga and do your *sadhana* or meditation."

But how could I go? I had no money to travel, no extra clothes, nothing in hand, except the blessings of my beloved *Guruji*. I never disagreed with *Amma*'s command, whatever she said I accepted as *veda vakya* (great saying or words of wisdom).

But I hesitantly told *Amma*, "I have neither money nor clothes, how can I travel such a long distance." She told me, "You need not worry about all those things, just make up your mind to leave for the Himalayas. "I kept quiet.

After sometime I saw that a known devotee from Mangalore was walking towards us. He came and prostrated in reverence before *Amma*. He was an owner of a hotel in Mangalore. *Amma* started talking to him, "Shiva, my boy is all set to go to the Himalayas tomorrow, take care of him!"

The hotel owner took a bundle of currency notes from his pocket and offered it at the holy feet of my *Guruji*. She never used to accept *dakshina* (donation or payment for the services of a priest, spiritual guide or teacher) or keep money with her. But she always had a four *anna* coin in her pocket. *Amma* told the hotel owner, "Shiva do not show off your wealth to me. I know you are a rich person, if at all you want to do *Guru seva*, take my child with you tomorrow." (In those days there were weekly trains to Delhi from Mangalore. I wondered how *Amma* knew that the there was a train to Delhi the next day!)

Amma continued, "Ah, do not forget to give him a *dhoti* in *kashaya* and a bed spread with a shawl which he can wear day and night. Let it be a woollen cloth. Help him board the train and then come back to me."

The gentleman agreed and left *Amma* after bowing in reverence. He told me to meet him at the Temple (Mookambika) next morning at 6.00 am as there was a bus to Mangalore at 6.30 am. I nodded my head in agreement.

That whole day I sat with *Amma*; neither she nor I spoke to each other for a long time. After the daily routine of eating *bhiksha*, she asked me to sit near her and then she started talking to me. After a long talk, she concluded, "The journey to the Himalayas is not so easy; it is the land of the *Rishis,* my *Gurubehen* Ashamayee stays at Triyuginarayan. Meet her when you feel so. One thing I would like to remind you, this *Amma,* your *Guruji,* has been connected with you for generations. You will be tested by *maya* (name, fame, wealth). Beware of this! If you can keep out *maya,* this *Amma* will be with you always. Do not be a part of an existing ashram. Your way is different. When you need to have an ashram, I will take care of it. Walk barefoot and don't keep any money with you. Accept only *bhiksha;* do not take any *dakshina* or *vastram* from devotees during your *tapas* in the Himalayas. Keep in mind one thing—keep away from '*kamini*' and '*kanchan*' (woman and money). This will help you reach your goal by the grace of the *Guru Parampara.* You have yourself chosen to live in poverty. He who does not possess anything possesses *Bhagavan* himself. Keep up your chosen poverty. As I told you earlier, remember to live for others always. And whenever and wherever you need this *Amma,* I will be there."

I was wondering about the *upadesa* (advice) she gave me. She had never spoken like this before. She concluded saying "Be with me, be as a child who is having the *nishkalankata* (purity and innocence). This is the only quality I expect from you, do not look back, do not be frightened, where you are, I'm there."

Then she told me to go to Mookambika darshan at the evening arathi and take permission of the Universal Mother to go to the Himalayas. She also insisted that I go and tell the old *Swamiji* of Ramakrishna Yoga Ashram that I was proceeding to the Himalayas for my *sadhana.*

In the evening I went to the Mookambika temple. There was heavy rush as it was a Friday, but as the priest was known to me, I went in front of the *garbhagriham* and prayed to Goddess Mookambika to give me the courage to go forward in my *sadhana* in the Himalayas. The priest came and offered some *prasadam* and I was chanting the *mantra* "Amme Narayana, Devi Narayana..." (The famous *mantra* of Chottanikara temple in Cochin, Kerala). There were tears flowing from my eyes. The priest asked me the reason for my sorrow, and I told him that there was no problem at all. Just that I was going to the Himalayas for '*tapas*' the next day, leaving my *Guruji* behind. He asked, "*Enthuku Kaneeru?*" ("Why these tears?") I told him it was not because I was leaving Mookambika, but because I had the *darshan* of *Kula Devi* (family deity—Sri Porkali Maa) on the idol of Mookambika. Once again, he went inside and brought a hand full of *kumkum* that they use for *archana* (prayers offered by temple priests) to Mookambika. I took it. On the way back, I met the old *Swamiji* at his ashram and told him about my program. He was very happy, and offered me a shawl that I did not accept as my *Guruji* had told me not to accept anything other than *bhiksha*.

It was almost dark in the forest; I was walking towards the tree where *Amma* sat. After crossing a few yards, I realized that I had lost my way even though I had walked this path several times. As I walked a few more yards I heard a sound of a cobra hissing. I was afraid; it was not dark yet, so with the dim light from the sky I could see a huge black cobra in front of me. I was shivering with fear, the *kumkum* in my hand had fallen down and full of fear I cried and called "*Amma... Amma...!*" By that time the cobra approached closer and started crawling on my right leg; I was about to faint.

Just then I heard my *Guruji*, "Son, why are you afraid, this is a *samsara*[13] snake. If you chant the names of the *Guru* and the *Ishta Devi*[14], the *samsara* snake would not harm you." When I opened my eyes, the snake was still on my legs, but I saw the face and hand of my *Guruji*. Her hand came close to my leg, and she removed the snake as if she was removing a thread, and she threw it at a distance. Then she laughed and said, "My dear son, while gracing the path of *Advaita* you have to do your work while staying in the *samsara*. I'm with you, you need not worry." Saying these words, she caught hold of my hand and moved quickly to the tree where we used to sit.

Amma slept early. I was unable to sleep as I was departing from my beloved *Guruji*, Mother, Father, Brother, Sister, everything tomorrow. The whole picture of my *poorvashrama* (previous stage of life) came in front of me like a movie reliving all those days that I had lived with my *Guruji*. I could not sleep a wink. It was difficult for me to control my emotions at that time. I do not know how time passed. I heard the *shankhdhwani* (blowing of conch) from the temple as the temple gates opened at dawn. I could hear

---

13 The material world of the cycle of death and rebirth to which earthly life is bound; terrestrial

14 Literally 'cherished divinity' taken from the words iṣhṭa which means desired, liked, cherished or preferred and devi or devatā which godhead, divinity, tutelary deity is a term denoting a worshipper's favourite deity within Hinduism

the temple bells. Time had come to depart from Mookambika, my beloved *Guruji, Guruji's* pets, the birds, the animals, the forest, the Sauparnika and everything. I felt I was losing them all...

By then my *Guruji* woke up and told me to follow her. She took me to Sauparnika River and asked me to strip so that she could give me a bath. Never before had she given me a bath. There were one or two other persons bathing there. In the water, she gave me three dips and asked me to chant the *Presh Mantra*. She took a stone and mercilessly rubbed on my body till blood came out from my back. While I was wondering what was happening she said, "Son, this is only to cleanse the misdeeds you have committed in this life, you have to become *suddhi* (pure). Have you felt any pain? "After bath, she did not allow me to go back to our beloved tree which gave me shelter for such a long time. She asked me to go to the temple and then meet the hotel owner who was waiting for me.

THE MOMENT OF SILENCE

I was unable to talk or think; tears were flowing from my eyes. *Amma* was standing on the banks of Sauparnika River and with gusto she asked me to move. I saw tears in her eyes also. I was unable to move an inch. I just stood still there. I wanted to do a *sashtanga namaskar* to *Amma* but my legs had become stiff, body shivering, and once again, *Amma* gestured me to move on. It seemed that she was also not in a position to say anything.

With much difficulty, I did *sashtanga namaskar* to my beloved *Guruji*. The moment of departure was here and my heartbeat had started rising as if I was participating in an Olympic 100-meter race. I saw the old *Swamiji* reaching Sauparnika for a bath, smiling at me; he asked "Have you not left yet? You were supposed to leave by this time. Why are you becoming so emotional? Come on, go ahead, the bus might leave." Once again I touched the holy lotus feet of my beloved mother; she took me into her arms. I felt I was a small child as she embraced me, gave me a kiss on my forehead— the sweetest kiss I ever had. I heard the bus horn, inviting the passengers to board. I had to move on; there was no other way. I felt it was exactly like death to leave my *Guruji*.

Once again I bowed in prostration to my *Guruji*. Then I took a handful of sand from where my *Guruji* stood, applied the holy '*dhooli*' (dust from beneath the feet of my Guruji) on my forehead, on my head and on my body. Even then I was unable to control my tears. Once again I saw the hands of my *Guruji* coming forward to me for an embrace; once again she embraced me and gave me a good blow on my back with her left hand and said, "*Po da* (go son), it is time for you to leave, you have to leave, *poda, poda.*" She turned her face away. Slowly with shivering legs I went towards the Mookambika temple where the bus was parked and where the hotel owner was waiting for me.

I tried to look back, but in vain. It was as if my neck had frozen, I could not, and I walked towards the bus.

The endless journey begins...

Endless Journey Begins

This was the second time I was travelling such a long distance. A few years earlier, before joining my *Guruji*, I had gone to Rishikesh for a few months to attend the Yoga Vedanta Forest Academy course run by the Sivananda Ashram. So the journey to North India was not a new thing to me, and I had the advantage of talking at least basic Hindi. I had studied Hindi under *Dakshin Bharatha Hindi Prachar Sabha* during my school days. My maternal uncle was a Hindi teacher and I had stayed with him during my high school days.

Before leaving Mangalore, the hotel owner Shiva offered me the rail ticket, clothes and some money as per my *Guruji*'s instruction. I accepted only the rail ticket and clothes and refused the money. At the end of the first day's journey, I was hungry and thirsty and had no money with me to purchase either a hot or a cold drink. I went to the toilet inside the train and took a few handfuls of water from the sink faucet and drank it. It was night and the train was passing through the dense forests in Madhya Pradesh, the central province. Looking at the forest, I was lost in thought of the days that I had spent with my *Guruji* in the Mookambika forests. I slipped into a deep sleep as the cool breeze from the forest touched me, and it felt like the touch of my *Amma* soothing me to sweet sleep.

It was morning when I woke up to the cries of the platform vendors at a station, "Tea ... tea ...*nashta* (breakfast) ...*nashta*, etc." I looked through the window of the train. I was in a third-class sleeper coach and my seat was on the lower side. I noted the name of the railway station as Mathura, the land of Krishna. The train stopped there for at least ten minutes to allow for morning ablutions of travellers, and change of train staff. I hesitated to come out of the train because it was of no use as I did not have money with me to buy any food.

Since I was wearing the *kashaya vastram*, I was sure that had I asked, someone would have surely offered me a cup of tea—but I remembered the words of my *Guruji* as if she were telling me now, "Don't ever beg for anything, I will take care of your needs." I sat quietly on my seat and to my wonder an old lady vendor appeared in front. She said, "*Baba, namaskar,* have some *pooris* and vegetables." I was thrilled, my hair standing on end. With all reverence I asked, "Mother, how do you know that I'm hungry?" The old mother replied, "Since I do not have a license to sell food items, I sit at that corner of the platform where generally travellers from the general compartment come and buy food, and since I'm alone I have to do this to make ends meet." (Her words were in a dialect of Hindi difficult to understand). She concluded by saying, "*Baba* take the *poori*" I was still hesitant to accept the food. Observing my discomfort, the old lady said in a very low voice, "I felt within, someone instructing me to come to the sleeper third-class coach, where a *Baba* would be sitting hungry, and to go and serve him. I thought it none other than my Krishna—now if you do not want it, let me leave." Immediately I recalled my *Amma*'s words, "Wherever you are, I will be there to take care of your needs—food, shelter or anything." The old lady gave me five *pooris* and vegetable curry, and also enquired whether I needed water to drink. On getting an affirmation, she immediately went into the crowd and brought me water in a broken bottle. She said me "*Baba* please bless me so that I should be in a better position financially, since I'm alone." (Now I remember the story of Adi Sankaracharya's first *bhiksha* from a poor Brahmin lady, who had nothing to offer in alms to the *Bala Brahmachari* at her door except for a few gooseberries, seeing which he invoked the Mother Goddess with the *Kanakadhara Stotra* 'Angam hare...',[15] which gave wealth to that Brahmin lady.)

---

15 A hymn called 'Kanakadhara' because when Adi Sankara recited it, the Goddess Lakshmi showered golden fruits to help a poor woman.

I had just started enjoying the delicious *poori* and *curry* offered to me as *bhiksha*, when the train started moving. I could easily see the platform but nowhere could I find the old lady; remembering my *Guru* again and again, I finished eating my meal.

Now it was almost afternoon. The train was fast approaching New Delhi from where I had to take the connecting train to go to Old Delhi. I did not having any money with me as mentioned earlier. Alighting from the train, I started walking towards the Old Delhi railway station by making enquiries from here and there for directions. To my surprise I found out that I had to take a passenger train that was to leave at midnight. I had nowhere to go and rest, and I was tired. The *poori* and *sabji* from that old mother had satisfied my hunger fully. I settled on the platform for a while when I saw a *Sardarji (Sikh* gentleman) come up to me and say something in Punjabi. (I told him that I could not understand his language and hence to please speak in English.) He asked me to join him to have a cup of tea, but I declined. When I asked where he was going, he replied saying he was on a pilgrimage to 'Chaar Dhaam'[16] in the Himalayas and that he was waiting for the train at midnight. At a few yards distance I could see his father, mother, and wife and a boy sitting on the platform on a *dhurrie* (a heavy cotton rug) spread out. He once again invited me to a cup of tea but I declined again. By this time maybe because of the insistence of his mother, the *Sardar* boy came and offered a small packet of biscuits. It may have been the *nishkalankata* in the boy's eyes that drew me, but without any hesitation I accepted the biscuits.

Now we were all waiting for the midnight train.

---

16 Char Dham (literally four abodes/seats) are the names of four pilgrimage sites in Himalayas—Badrinath, Kedarnath, Yamunotri & Gangotri—that are widely revered by Hindus.

The Journey to the Door of the Almighty

After midnight, the passenger train to Haridwar left Old Delhi Railway station. There was not much rush and I sat on the bench by the window. A group of *sadhus* entered the compartment. Among them was a fat *sadhu* in green alfy and turban on his head, who was the *guru* for this group of five to six *sadhus*. The *guru* sat in front of me and the others to the side. They took out a pipe (*chillum*) and started filling *ganja* (cannabis) in it. I saw a name written on their trunk box 'Vasu Dev Baba, Tripura'. I had heard about this Vasu Dev Baba from Tripura as a famous *Tantrik* of that place. I wondered if this was the same man who was also a specialist in '*Surya Vidya*'[17]. The train moved slowly and the man asked me "Where are you going?" I told him that I was on my way to the Himalayas. He said that he was going for the Chaar Dhaam pilgrimage along with his disciples and extended an invitation to me to join them if I was willing. The *chillum* started and the *baba* enjoyed the smoke and offered it to me. During my college days and after leaving the village I used to have *ganja* in *bidi* with my old friend Sridharan Thomas. But I shook my head hesitantly saying that I was not interested. Suddenly I remembered the *Sardar* family who had offered me the biscuits; I got up and started looking for them. Maybe they had entered another compartment, and so I could not find them. I came back to my seat and sat down. By that time the *chillum* was over and the group was discussing something in Bengali. One of the *sadhus* among the group was in a fix and chanting: Oh, Mayeego, Mayeego (O

---

17 The science of solar system, especially the sun

Mother)…" I was feeling hungry and opened the biscuit packet offered by the *Sardar* boy at the railway station. I offered it to Vasu Dev Baba sitting before me. I had been taught by my *Guruji* that before eating anything one should always offer it to people sitting near. He declined my offer and said that they had *rotis* to eat, and that was not the time to eat anything. Anyway since I was hungry, I ate all the biscuits in the packet. Hiccups started and there was no water with me. The Baba asked, "*Kyon, pani nahin hai? Kya baba hai thu? Gaand dhona atha nahi, baba banke ghoom raha hai?*" (What, you don't have water? What kind of *sadhu* are you—can't even wash your dirt and roaming around pretending to be a *sadhu*.) He added, "Didn't your *Guru* teach you that a *sadhu* shouldn't move out without carrying a j*alpathra*." I kept quiet, but he was talking something against my *Guruji*. And I could not take that and got angry and started shouting at him, "Who are you to say something about my *Guru*? Whether I have water or not, I am the one who suffers. Just do not talk about my *Guruji*. Bloody fellow! Do you think you are the only *Guru* in this world—don't try to teach me!" Perhaps that was the first time Vasu Dev Baba was getting a scolding in front of his disciples. There was pin-drop silence in the compartment. I was burning with anger. Then one of the *sadhus* gave me water from his j*alpathra* but I refused it as the hiccups were gone by that time.

Since there were more vacant benches in the compartment, all the *sadhus* except for Vasu Dev Baba, went to sleep. Vasu Dev Baba was still looking outside and thinking. His face was very calm. I stood up and said, "*Baba* please excuse me, maybe I spoke in anger." He very coolly said, "It is ok my son! I was like you too when I was young. I used to get angry very quickly and shout at others, but after some time I used to realize it and say sorry. It's ok, do not worry." Later he said that he would be staying at a Dharmashala in Kankhal for a couple of days before his onward journey to Chaar Dhaam pilgrimage. Once again, he invited me to join him.

In the morning around six, we reached Haridwar railway station. Vasu Dev Baba engaged some cycle-rickshaws and asked me to come along with him. I agreed and went with them. Perhaps they had already informed about their arrival, for as soon as we reached there, the old watchman opened the room for us. The room was stinking and full of filth. The *sadhus* cleaned the room and arranged their *asan* (seats). I too put my *chaadar* (blanket) in one corner of the room and sat down. The place was near *Kankhal smashaan* (cremation ground). Kankhal is famous for the *Daksha yagya* (sacrificial ritual). The holy river Mother *(Mata)* Ganga flows near Dharmashala. I felt sleepy though the room was stinking. The other *sadhus* were preparing another *chillum* and I heard another rough sound from Vasu Dev Baba, "Yeh! Get some tea for the *Madrasi baba* and me." (North Indians refer to southerners as *Madrasi*.) It sounded like an order. He gave me a dirty thermos flask and said, "Get some tea filled in this flask." I had not told him that I had no money to buy tea with, and was wondering what to do. If I did not get the tea, this ferocious *baba* might again say something bad about my *Guruji* which would be intolerable to me. I came on to the street, where there were small shops. I saw a small teashop which was open with two persons drinking tea. I walked towards that shop. I did not know what to do. I just stood there flask in hand. "*Maharaj*! What do you want?" The shopkeeper asked me. (I was wondering about the word '*Maharaj*' as it literally means king, but later I learned that North Indians address *sadhus* as *Maharaj*.) I noticed an old lady who looked like a beggar, rising up from her bed sheet near the tea stall.

Her eyes were beaming. She said to the shopkeeper "*Lala*! Looks like this *baba* does not have money and requires tea, so please take these three rupees and give him a flask full of tea on my behalf." I was shocked; these three rupees might be all her previous day's earnings. I took the tea from the shopkeeper, and was just about to leave, looking thankfully at the old lady. Then I remembered my *Guruji* that very moment and I walked up to the old lady with folded hands, and thanked her for the tea. I had turned back and walked a few steps when I heard the old lady say to the shopkeeper, "He looks new to Kankhal, poor boy. He probably left his parents and came here, that's why I gave him tea. I too had a son around his age." I could not control my tears.

I offered the tea to Vasu Dev Baba. He took his small wooden tumbler and started drinking the tea. Immediately after the second sip, he threw away the tumbler and shouted at me saying, "*Tere maa ki. Itna gandhi chai kaha se lekar aya thu...Yahi tera guru seva hai kya. Fukat me kapda rang kar nikla ghar se ... phoo...phoo...*" (From where did you get this dirty tea... is this the way you serve your *guru*? Dyed your cloth in saffron and moved out of your house pretending to be a *sadhu*.) I also got wild and replied, "You are not my *Guru*, and it is by my *Guru's krupa* (grace) that you got this tea. Who are you to scold me? You may be known as a great *baba*, but you show no control on your anger or on your tongue. I am not traveling with you." My scolding was in English; within a minute I took my belongings and started moving. Vasu Dev Baba was astonished. He got up, came forward, and said, "I didn't know that you were an educated *baba*, you speak so well in English. Now, sorry, let us go together." He was also speaking in English but I would not compromise, and walked out without saying anything.

Thoughts were haunting me. The first experience in Haridwar had been bitter. I went to *Ganga Mata*, had my bath and prayed, "*Maa*, I'm here at your feet, please take care of me." Then I moved to the railway station to enquire how to reach Rishikesh.

The train was ready to leave the platform, but I had no money to purchase the ticket to Rishikesh. I went up to the ticket counter and said to the clerk, "*Sir, mere paas paise nahi hai aur mujhe Rishikesh jaana hai.*" (Sir, I have no money and want to go to Rishikesh.) The ticket counter clerk said, "*Rishikesh ke liye ticket nahi to paidal jao.*" (If you have no money for the ticket, then walk to Rishikesh.) I looked back and saw a Swamiji standing behind me. He said "*Baba, main bhi Rishikesh jaa raha hun, thodi door 24–25 miles, idhar ham baba log ticket lethe nahi, chalo mere saath. Yeh railway wale is gadi ko Babaon-Ki-Gadi kehte hai, koi nahi poochta, chalo mere saath, gaadi chootne wali hai.*" (Come along with me. I'm traveling the same way. It's only 24–25 miles away, and we *sadhus* never buy tickets. Don't worry no one will ask you one.)

My mind was not ready to accept this theory of traveling ticketless on the train. Later I learned that in northern India, wandering monks don't usually buy tickets to travel on trains since they sit in the general compartments, and nobody will ask them for it either. Somehow, I made up my mind in a moment, and followed the *sadhu* who had given the idea to travel ticketless.

A fear-consciousness and guilt feeling was overpowering me. Looking at my face the *sadhu* said, "*Tum ko darne ki koyi jaroorat nahi*." (There is no need to be afraid.)

The train moved. My mind was praying to my *Guruji* to save me from the situations that might occur at any moment. I was praying and praying as the train moved, the thoughts also moved and moved...

At Rishikesh

After alighting at the Rishikesh railway station, I looked around for the *sadhu* who had brought me into the train without a ticket. He was not to be seen anywhere. I came out to the road and asked some people for directions to the Sivananda Ashram, where I had stayed a few years earlier for the Yoga Vedanta course. On the way to the ashram, I saw many *sadhus* walking around. Some of them were bathing at *Maa Ganga*, some walking with foreign devotees. India has been a land of *sadhu-sanyasis* from time immemorial and the land of spiritual wisdom or *Atma Gyana*. I somehow reached the ashram and asked a young man who seemed to be a Keralite at the reception counter. He told me that in order for me to stay at the ashram for more than three days, I had to seek the permission from the ashram secretary. Under his guidance I approached the secretary *swami* and introduced myself, my *Guruji*, my studies, etc. He granted permission to me and instructed the reception counter to allot me a room. As I was about to leave the reception counter, the *Swamiji* added, "It is the rule of the ashram that the inmates are supposed to do service at the ashram for a few hours every day. As you are educated in English, I would like you to be in the printing press to attend to the proofreading and editing of the magazine and books being published from here." Without a second thought, I agreed.

After bathing, I visited the *Samadhi Mandir* of His Highness Swami Sivanandji Maharaj and the temples in the ashram premises.

In the temple, I met a *brahmachari*[18] with matted hair and he spoke to me as if we had known each other for a long time. His name was Shivasankaran and he became my best friend in addition to Brahmachari Jayapalan who was serving in the hospital as a medical assistant and was introduced to me by Shivasankaran. My accommodation was near the room of Swamy Sooryadevananda, who was a good singer, and his *sadhana* was singing and playing the veena. He was also from Kerala and so we had no difficulty in communicating with each other. The next day I went to the press to take up my service in proofreading.

A *Swamiji* known as Vivekananda was in charge of the press. My daily routine in the ashram would begin with proofreading/editing and end with proofreading/editing except for lunch. In those days, the workload at the press was heavy. There was no time left for my *sadhana*. Months passed this way and winter was at our door. This was the first time I was facing the North Indian winter, and I was not aware of the severity of the winter in Rishikesh. The ashram authorities provided me with woollen clothes, monkey caps, gloves, etc. Months passed without any personal *sadhana* other than proofreading and other such tasks, and whenever the secretary *Swamiji* met me, he would enquire about my welfare. In fact, I was fed up with this and thoughts would arise in my mind about whether it was for this that I came all the way leaving my *Guru*. But I could not help it. To be frank, I was worried about my food and shelter. The thoughts about my *Guruji* had vanished and the teachings were no longer in my mind. I used to cry during the nights as I felt I was caged in the premises of an *ashram* with no way out. But again, thoughts of food and shelter overpowered my brain, and I continued to spend my days and nights in a mechanical way.

I could not do away with the situation of ten to twelve hours of work. Of course, I was getting pure South Indian food, a good room to stay, good clothes to wear but I felt out of place as my mind was wandering.

---

18 A student of the Vedas, especially one committed to the vow of celibacy. It represents a virtuous lifestyle that also includes simple living, meditation and training for spiritual living.

One Sunday morning Jayapalan told me that he was going to meet Mast Ram Baba and enquired if I was interested in joining him. I had heard about Mast Ram Baba who was staying under a rock cave on the sands of the *Ganga*, on the other side of the river. I had heard that he was a great *siddha*,[19] wearing a white cloth and living alone, occasionally surrounded by devotees.

Jayapalan and I crossed the *Ganga* over the Jhoola Bridge, which is known as Sivananda Jhoola Pul or Ram Jhoola Pul, and we reached the feet of Mast Ram Baba. He was very old, with a lean body and was sitting in front of his cave overlooking the *Ganga*. As soon as I touched the holy feet, Baba looked at me for a moment and, to my amazement, asked, "How is Tara?" He was referring to my *Guruji*, and I was astonished. How did he know my *Guruji*? In wonder and with a lot of questions in my mind, I was looking at him. Mast Ram Baba told me to sit down. He scolded me in a tough voice, "*Tu isiliye ghar, parivar, Guru sab ko chod kar idhar aaya? Tum Ko Tara ne kaha tha na koyi ashram me nahi rehna, aur Ganga kinare reha kar sadhana karna. Tum ko sharam aani chahiye. Abhi tumko tumhaare Guruji ke upar koyee viswas nahi hai, aisa lagta hai. Sadhu ko aakash chat hai, aur bhoomi bichona hai. Tu yah abhi tak nahi samajh paya. Sansar ko choda aur naye sansar me aakar phas gaya. Chod sab kuch. Ab tum jawan ho; abhi sadhana nahi karega to budhape me karega kya?*"

(Did you leave your home, family and *Guru* and come here all the way, for this? Had not Tara told you not to live in an ashram but to do *sadhana* by the banks of the *Ganga*? You should be ashamed of yourself. It seems like you have no more faith left in your *Guruji*. That a *sadhu* should only have the sky for roof, and the earth for bed, this you have not understood. You left one world and got caught in another. Leave away all this. You are still young, if you don't begin your *sadhana* now, when will you—in old age?)

All this hit me like an arrow from the bow of Lord Rama. I broke into pieces. I told Jayapalan "You go back and tell the ashram people that I'm not coming back. I will stay at the banks of the

---

19 It refers to masters who have achieved a high degree of physical as well as spiritual perfection or enlightenment.

Ganga; I committed a mistake by staying in an *ashram*. Now I don't want to continue there. Mast Ram Baba has opened my eyes. In fact, Jayapalan, these are not his words, but my *Guruji*'s words coming through his mouth. I am not returning to the *ashram*." Jayapalan left me hesitatingly. Mast Ram Baba went inside the cave, brought a glass of milk, and started talking to me about his arrival at Rishikesh a few years back, and his *sadhana* (he was a *Vaishnav sadhu*). He concluded, "*Tumhe idhar bahar Ganga ke ret me rehana. Kal se tum ko apni sadhana shuru karni hai.*" (You shall live here on the sands of the *Ganga* and begin your *sadhana* tomorrow.) I was wondering where to begin and how. The winter was at its peak, and the nights chilly. I did not have any additional clothes as I had left everything at the *ashram*. *Baba* brought me a big piece of gunny sack and said, "This will help you to stop the ferocious cold. And my boy, you have to start your *sadhana* from tomorrow onwards."

I asked him, "*Baba*, what *sadhana* are you talking about, I know nothing." *Baba* narrated the format for the spiritual practice that I was supposed to do from the next day. *Baba* told me, "In the morning after you bathe, all you have to do is to go to the bazaar daily for 21 days and collect the banana peels thrown here and there. You have to move around the market until noon and bring me back the peels. Don't speak to anyone or reply to any comments, since you will be keeping *mauna* (vow of silence) for 21 days. Bring the peels and wash them in the *Ganga*, then stand in the *Ganga* water neck deep, and eat the banana peels which you collected. While in the *Ganga*, chant mentally the '*pranava mantra*' until you finish eating the peels. This is to be repeated for 21 days." I thought that this *Baba* was mad. What type of *sadhana* was this? However, reading my mind he said, "*Bete mei pagal nahi hoon, mujhe maloom hai tum ko kya banna hai, jo tum ko malum nahi.*" (Son, I'm not mad, I know what you are destined to become, but you do not know that.)

I agreed. I was not supposed to take any other food other than the banana peels or *Ganga jal* (water of River *Ganga*) for 21 days. My mind was praying to *Guruji* to help me understand what was going on with me. But there was no reply. The next day onwards, I started collecting banana peels from the market by moving around, without talking to anybody. I brought the collection of peels to Baba and as per his instruction, after washing those in *Ganga jal* I ate them and drank a lot of *Ganga jal*. This was repeated daily. On the third or fourth day, some of the *sadhus* and *brahmacharis* who met me at the market saw me collecting banana peels and asked me what I was doing. I kept quiet. They commented, "Nadananda has become mad." One day while I was collecting the banana peels one of the *swamijis* known to me at the ashram came near and asked whether I would like some *jilebees* (sweet crullers). I was tempted. My legs started moving towards the hotel. I heard a sound "*Khabardar, tu kya kar raha hai me dekhta hun. Bete galat nahi karna.*"(Beware, I am watching what you are doing. Son don't make a mistake). Immediately I withdrew myself from there and reached *Baba's* place. *Baba* scolded me, "*Tuney kya socha hai, mein tumko dektha nahi, jo bola aise karna, nahi to sadhana viphal hogi.*" (What were you thinking—that I was not watching you? Do as I say otherwise your *sadhana* will be unsuccessful.)

That very same day, I had an attack of diarrhoea, and had about 10 to 15 bowel movements which made me very weak. *Baba* was observing my weak body and eyes. This was the 6th day of the *sadhana*, and I had 15 days still left. I felt that I would not be able to go to the market the next day for the collection of banana peels due to weakness. However in the evening *Baba* walked near me and said, "*Tu kyon vrudha chinta kartha hai. Andar ka malinya sab bahar jaana hai. Isiliye tum ko yah dasth aaya acha hai.*" (Why do you worry needlessly—all the toxins within have to go out, it was a good thing you had diarrhoea.) He asked me lie down in *Shavasana* (yogic posture) lifted both my legs by grabbing the big toes and pulled. Lo! From then on, there were no more diarrhoea.

I had become very weak. Days passed by quickly and nobody was there to take care of me other than *Baba*. *Baba* had even instructed his disciples not to come to me or interact with me. I was all alone, doing the same s*adhana* of bringing banana peels, and cleaning and eating them, standing in the *Ganga* for some time, drinking the *Gangajal* and simply lying down on the sands. I felt as if death was swallowing me and the thought of life in the *ashram* was so good, that I was cursing myself as to why I came to see this *Baba*. Reading my mind, *Baba* came to me and said "*Bete*

(Son)... you do not understand what you are doing now. The day when you do understand it, you will not think me mad."

On the last and the 21st day of my *sadhana*, I completed the morning routine and was simply lying down on the sands thinking what was coming next. Mast Ram Baba came to me and said *"Aaj tumara sadhana poori hojaegi. Kal tum ko idhar se jana hai. Idhar se kareeb nav din ki doori mein pagdanti rasta mei jayega to Vyas Ghat aayega. Udhar tumko ek sadhu milega, vah tumko baki sadhana bataayega, kal sooryoday me tum ko jaana hai."* (Your *sadhana* will end today. You have to leave from here tomorrow. After nine days of travel, you will get to Vyas Ghat, where you will meet a *sadhu* who will instruct you on the next *sadhana*. You have to leave at sunrise tomorrow.) After telling me this, *Baba* took a handful of sand from the *Ganga* shore, applied it on my body, and left for his cave.

I was wondering what was happening to me. I was very tired and unable to walk. How could I walk for nine days? With all these thoughts, I slept.

The morning was very cold. I had only the gunny bag cloth which *Baba* had given me. I got up and was feeling very energetic and with all confidence did my morning ablutions. I felt a little thirsty, but not hungry.

While bathing I saw *Baba* approaching me. I greeted him with prostration and asked, *"Mujhe rastha maloom nahi, Vyas Ghat tak kayse pahunchunga, aur Baba yeh bataiye is prakar ki sadhana ka matlab kya hai?"* (I don't know the route to Vyas Ghat, how am I going to reach there and *Baba*, please tell me what is the purpose of this kind of *sadhana*?)

Baba said, *"Tum ko chinta karne ki koyi jaroorat nahi. Yah pagh dandi rasthe se jao. Han, ek baath dhyan rakhna, koyi gaon wale ne bulakar bhiksha di tho khana, nahi tho us din upvas me rahana. Kisi se kuch bhi nahi poochna. Ab chalo, gufa me aakar kuch prasad kha kar jao."* (You don't need to worry, just follow the route of this footpath. Just remember this—only if a villager offers you *bhiksha*, you may eat, otherwise you must fast. Never ask anyone for anything. Now, come to my cave and eat some *prasad*).

I went along with *Baba* to his cave, there were one or two devotees there who were looking at me with great reverence and bowed in prostration before me. *Baba* went inside and brought a glass filled with milk and some *kalkandam* (sugar candy). Baba said, "*Yeh dhood peelo, our yeh misri tumare sath rakho. Jis din bhiksha nahi mili, us din is me se thoda khana, ab Ganga mayya ko pranam kar ke Ganga kinare jao.*" (Drink this milk. Keep this sugar candy with you and the day you are not offered any *bhiksha*, you may eat a little of this. Now offering prayers to Mother *Ganga*, make your way along her banks.) My mind and body were shivering, for what reason I do not know, but they were shivering. With the same frame of mind and body, I drank the milk and offered my salutations to *Baba* and from there started my journey further. I tied the *misri* or kalkandam, which Baba had given me, like a bundle on one side of the *dhoti* I was wearing as I did not have a bag or any extra clothes.

After walking a considerable distance I realized that I was neither tired nor weak, and that my footsteps were firm and steady. I continued my journey towards the next destination. The first day of walking was enjoyable. It was nearing dusk; the night about to cover the hills when I saw an old temple a few yards away, up a hill. The sight of the temple made me think that I should rest there. So I started walking towards the temple and when I entered, the temple priest was performing the evening *arathi* with ceremony. I noticed that this was the temple of the local village goddess. I sat in the small temple corridor. After completion of the *arathi* the temple priest approached me, asking, "Where are you heading towards?" I told him, "Vyas Ghat." He replied, "Vyas Ghat is far away from this place. It will take four to five days to get there from here by walk(villagers walk fast hence my 9 days of walk is equivalent to their 4–5 days of walk). You are requested to grace our house to have your *bhiksha* and take rest there till morning." I replied, "As per my *Guru*'s order, I'm not supposed to stay in any village; hence, if you permit me I shall stay here in the corridor of the temple." The priest agreed to my request and left the temple.

Feeling a bit tired, I was about to lie down in the temple corridor after my salutations to the local deity, when I noticed a small light moving fast in the direction of the temple. There was no need to be afraid—I could see that it was the temple priest along with two of his friends approaching me with a basket covered with a dirty cloth. The moment they reached me, they paid their homage and requested that I eat the *rotis* (flat round bread cooked on a griddle) and *chutney* they had brought for me. When I responded with resistance, they said "You are a guest in our village, and guests are treated as gods in this part of the world, hence please do not say no to our offerings, please have the food we have brought for you." I could not refuse, remembering *Baba*'s word that I could eat food offered by any villager. I was surprised to note the hospitality of the villagers even though they were poor and illiterate. I have found this throughout my journey in the Himalayan ranges.

They served me *roti* and *chutney* made of leaves. I took two *rotis* and returned the remaining to them. The priest took them saying they were now like *prasadam* to them, and that they would distribute them among all the houses in the village. They left after their salutations to me. I could not sleep that night, as it was too cold to sleep in the open corridor of a temple on the shores of the *Ganga*.

Next morning, I woke up and after completing ablutions resumed my journey towards Vyas Ghat.

Towards Vyas Ghat

It was the fifth day of my journey towards Vyas Ghat. I was enjoying the journey and the last four days of the journey I never had to walk without food. Food was offered to me either by some villager, or from any small *mandir* (temple) on the way or from any *sadhus* living in their huts. Sometimes I got *rotis* and sometimes I got rice and *dal* or *curry*. I was enjoying the journey without a second thought. Once I was walking along a narrow footpath. To my right side was the side of a big hill and to the left a deep cliff plunging down 200–250 feet to *Ganga Mata*. I had *darshan* of *Ganga Mata* almost every day, as the trail was along her shore. Certain places it was difficult to go down to fetch water or bathe. On such days I used water from the streams coming down from the hills. I was passing through a difficult narrow path one day, when on the right side of the hills I heard a sound, and saw a buffalo running towards me. It came very close, just a few yards away. There was nowhere for me to escape to or to give way to the wild buffalo. It came so near me that to save my life, I jumped to the left side, or rather my legs slipped and I rolled down towards Mother *Ganga*—200–250 feet down on the hillside. A few ladies were bathing and washing clothes there and must have seen me falling, for I heard the sound of their laughter. I had lost consciousness and did not move for a few minutes and the ladies must have got anxious. I heard the sound of people reaching out to me. Their language sounded different, a strange tongue. Somebody sprinkled water on my face, and one of them helped me sit up straight, leaning against a rock. Slowly I regained consciousness. There was a lot of blood on my body as I was cut and bruised by the rough rocky surface as I was falling down the hill.

I was finally at ease. One of the ladies brought me some *Ganga jal* to drink, another collected some leaves, ground them on a stone, mixed it with *Ganga jal* and made a paste and applied it on my body. I was wearing a *dhoti* only and that was the only set of clothes I had. As I was falling down, somewhere I had lost my companion, the gunny bag cloth given to me by Mast Ram Baba, which used to guard me against the cold weather. Slowly I stood up with the help of those ladies. I thanked them and was about to leave when one of them said, "*Maharaj, aaj ithar ganv mein vishram karo. Tum ko bahut dard lagta hoga. Ganv me ek vaidya hai. Un se davayi lekar jao.*" (Maharaj, today please rest in the village. It must be hurting. There is a physician there who can give you some medicine.) I told them, "*Nahi mata, mere Guruji ki agya hai koyi bhi ganv me raat rukhna nahi, aas pas me koyi mandir hai to bolo, mein udhar rahoonga.*" (No mother, my *Guru*'s orders are not to stay in any village, but if there is a temple nearby, I can rest there.) As I was getting ready to move, one of them said, "*Maharaj, thodi door me ek maharaj rahaten hai. Maloom nahi vah udhar hai ya nahi. Bhagya hai to unko miliega. Do teen din udhar visram kar kea agey badna!*" (Maharaj, at a little distance there is a *sadhu*'s hut. I'm not sure if he is there, but if you are lucky to find him, you must rest there two–three days before continuing.) I thanked them deeply and resumed my journey.

It was difficult for me to climb back up to the footpath in the middle of the hill. With the help of one of those ladies, I could climb the hill and resumed my journey towards Vyas Ghat. My whole body was aching and my legs felt as if they would break into pieces. But I continued walking slowly towards my destination.

After a few hours of journey, I could easily see a *kashaya dhvaja* (saffron flag) on a hut. It seemed as if it were inviting me. When I reached there I found that it was empty. A *dhooni* (fire pit) was burning inside the hut and there was no door to that hut. I just sat outside and, perhaps because of exhaustion, was overcome by deep sleep. Suddenly I heard a sound and woke up to see an old *Maharaj* near me. He sat close and asked, "*Jyada chot to nahi laga.*" (Hope the injuries were not bad.) I wondered how this old man knew that I had fallen down. Some villagers might have told him. In villages news spreads like wildfire. That *Swamiji* told me,

"*Aao, andar aao. Kuch chai peena. Mein kuch roti banatha hun, phir hum log baath karenge.*" (Come on in, and have some tea. I will make some *rotis* and then we shall talk.) He offered me hot tea. Of course it was not the traditional tea; it was perhaps made of some wild leaves. It tasted different. But to my wonder, as soon as I drank the tea offered by the *Swamiji* my tiredness and body pain had vanished. Maybe he read my mind for he said, "*Yeh chai Badari ka tulsi se banaya hai. Sadharan chai patti ke nahi*'. (This tea is not the regular tea, it is made from *badari* and *tulsi* leaves.) After eating *roti* and *dal*, we spoke with each other for some time. At night he offered me a blanket as it was extremely cold. But since the fire was burning, I felt I should not accept the blanket. But he said, "*Tumara sab niyam rahaker Himalaya me jeena mushkil hai. Thandi hai, kambal oadh lo.*" (It is hard to follow rigorous rules and survive in the Himalayas; it is cold, so take the blanket.) I asked him, "*Idhar se kithna door hai Vyas Ghat*?"(How far is Vyas Ghat from here?) *Maharaj* said, "*Subah uthkar tej chalega to shyam tak pahunchega. Lekin muje lagta hai kal tum nahi jayega, acha hai do din bad chalo*."(If you left at dawn and walked fast, you might reach by dusk. But I don't think you will leave tomorrow, better that you leave after a couple of days.) I did not reply. I had drifted into sleep.

I woke up next morning to find the *maharaj* gone. My body was shivering, I felt feverish, yet I tried to get up from the asan which the *maharaj* had spread for me but in vain. I was running a high fever. The *maharaj* then appeared and said to me, "*Uthaaya nahi. Thak gaya soach kar mai bulaya nahi*." (I didn't wake you up because I thought you were tired.)

"*Thodi door me ek jheel hai. Uthar ja kar nitya karm karke aao.*" (There is a stream nearby for your ablutions) Once again I tried to get up but failed. *Maharaj* came near me and touched my body and sensed the fever. He said, "*Bukhar hai. Mei bola tha na, do din visram karke janaa acha hai. Rasthe mein bukhar aaya to kya kartha*?" (You have a fever. Did I not ask you to rest for a couple days? What if you had developed fever on the way?). It is in the nature of the *sadhus* in the Himalayas to help others even if they had almost no possessions themselves. I heard him say, "*Tum let jao Maharaj. Mei kal jaise kuch chai banatha hum. Dhoop aane ke bad uthna.*" (You lie down, *Maharaj*. I shall prepare a special tea for you. Arise only after the sun is up in the sky). I took another cup of tea. The *maharaj* had only a few mud pots and a *thava* (griddle) to make his *roti*. I asked him, "*Maharaj, kitne saal se ithar rahate hain.*" (Maharaj, how long have you lived here?) He said, "*Pahale mere Guruji ithar rahate the. Unki samadhi hone ke baad maine is sthan ko choda nahi. Kareeb 8–10 saal hogaya hoga. Ganv vale kuch kaccha ration lakar dete hai. Us se nirvah hota hai. Mein kabhi yah sthaan chod kar nahi jata hoon kyon ki yah sthaan mere Guruji ka hai, gurusthan ka dekhbhaal karna sishyon ka dharma hai.*" (My Guru used to live here before. After his *samadhi*, I did not leave the place and have been here for 8–10 years now. The villagers bring me rations with which I manage. Taking care of the *guru*'s place or *gurusthaan* is the *dharma* of a disciple.)

From his accent I could make out that he belonged to either Bihar or eastern Uttar Pradesh. He got ready to do some *pooja*; sat near his fire, cleaned it, applied *tilak*, and started chanting some Shiv *stotras* (hymns). Perhaps due to the fever I fell asleep again. A long time passed, and the *Swamiji* woke me up to check on the fever. The morning tea had worked wonders. There was no fever anymore. l went out for ablution and came back to the *maharaj*. He was busy preparing a meal of rice and *dal* and while cooking he was talking to me. "*Din me kuch chaval pakatha hai our raat ko roti. Mein akela hai na, kuch banakar Guruji ko naivedyam lagakar me khata hun.*" (I cook rice for the day and *rotis* for night time. Though I'm alone, I always first offer the food as *naivedyam*[20] (oblation) to my *Guru* before eating.) I was lucky to have the food cooked by that *Swamiji*, as he seemed very pure-hearted. He was always chanting, "Shiva. Shiva. Shiva." We both ate rice and *dal*. The *dal* tasted different from the usual, as the *Swamiji* had put some forest leaves in it. Once again I slept. By the time I could wake up, the sun was about to set. *Swamiji* went for the evening bath. He came back quickly and did evening *arathi*, offering it to the fire and his *Guruji*'s photo. I too did *namaskars* to his *Guruji* and the fire. I told *Swamiji*, "*Raat mein kuch nahi khaoonga. Mujhe bhook nahi lagta.*" (I don't want to eat tonight as I am not hungry.)

---

20 Food offered to a Hindu deity/guru as part of a worship ritual, before eating it.

Swamiji said, "*Aise hai to mein bhi aaj kuch nahi khata hai. Ganv wala kal mujhe to packet biscuit la kar diya. Vah kha kar chai peayoonga.*"(In that case I will not eat either. The villagers dropped off some biscuits yesterday and I will have those with tea.)

At night we had only tea and biscuits. It was quite a cold night. *Swamiji* made fire with more fire. Both of us slept near the fire. It was early morning when *Swamiji* called me and said, "*Thakavat nahi to ab chalne ki tayyaari karo. Ab chalega to shayad raat ke pehele Vyas Ghat pahunchega.*" (If the fatigue is gone, get ready to leave. If you leave now, you may perhaps reach Vyas Ghat before dusk.)

I got up and post *nitya karma* (daily ablutions) was ready to move. *Swamiji* gave me a packet of biscuits and a *kambal* (blanket) and said, "*Vyas Ghat tak rasthe mei koy ganv nahi milega. Bhook lage to yah biscuit kha kar paani pee lena. 'Shiv bhole' aap ki yatra subh kare.*" (There is no village on the way to Vyas Ghat. If you feel hungry, eat these biscuits and drink some water. May Lord Shiva bless you on the journey.) I did *namaskars* to *Swamiji*, to his *Guruji's* photo and to the fire and left. Slowly my legs moved forward to Vyas Ghat.

At Vyas Ghat

I tried to walk fast but could not as I was walking barefoot. My feet were torn by thorns and stones, and both sides of the path were covered with thick forest. The gushing sound of the *Ganga* in the middle of the hills was pleasure to the ears. I was walking down the hills coming on to smaller hills. It was almost noon; however, the sun was not scorching since it was winter time. I was enjoying the journey. Of course there was a little bit of fatigue because of the fever. I reached the shores of the *Ganga* and washed my face and drank handfuls of water, and ate the biscuits which were a boon from the *Swamiji* with whom I stayed last night. As he had said, there was no village within my sight. Both sides of the road were covered with dense forests, and the chirping sounds of the birds and animals welcomed me at every step. I walked as fast as I could, afraid that I might be in the midst of the forest at nightfall. It was evening, and I was really tired due to the continuous journey. My legs started to hurt, and far away I saw a person walking down carrying firewood on his head.

I shouted *"Bhai, ek minute ruko, ek minute ruko."* (Brother, wait a minute). He stopped and looked at me with surprise.

I asked him, *"Bhai, Vyas Ghat kitana door hai?"* (Brother, how far is Vyas Ghat?)

He said, *"Maharaj aap ko kahan jaana hai? Silsu ganv me hai kya?"*(*Maharaj*, where do you need to go? Is it to Silsu village?)

I said to him, *"Nahi bhai, muje Vyas Ghat mein ek maharaj ko milna hai, Vyas Ghat kitna doori mein hai?"* (No brother, I need to go to Vyas Ghat to meet a *Maharaj*. How far is it?)

He looked at me for a moment and said, *"Oh I Wah, ek gufa wala Baba, dekho aage wala mod ke baad aur ek mod aayega, uske baad dahine dekho to ek chotta pahad dikhayi dega, uthar ek gufa hain, shayad tum dhoondnewalla maharaj uthar rehtha hai."*

(After the second turn, if you look to your right, you will see a small hill which has a cave. There is a *maharaj* who lives there and he may be the one you are looking for.)

Again, I asked him, *"Aap ko pakka patha hai vahi Vyas Ghat ke baba hain?"*(Do you know for sure if that is the *baba* of Vyas Ghat?)

He replied *"Dekho maharaj, ham logaon ko maharaj logon ke pas ja kar baithne ke liye samay kahan milta hai. Din raat kaam karna, do roti khana, sona, yahi hamara jeevan hai. Maine ek maharaj ko us gufa me dekha hai. Aur hamare ganv ke janani log unko roti dene ko har din jate hai. Us gufa se door hamara ganv Silsoo hai. Ab rukega to mujhe deri hoga isiliye, me aage jata hun."*(Look here, *maharaj*, we people do not have time to sit near *sadhus*. We work hard all day long, eat simple food and sleep. I have seen a *maharaj* in that cave. The mothers of our village go and offer him *rotis*. But my village Silsoo is far from the cave, and I will be late if I stay here anymore, so I have to go now.)

He started walking fast towards his village with a huge bundle of firewood on his head. I followed him; however I could not match his speed.

After walking for about an hour, I observed that the sun was about to set and I was getting tired, and did not know how far I needed to walk to reach my destination. I tried to walk fast as I did not want to get stuck for the whole night in the middle of the forest. After walking awhile, I noticed a small light from nowhere in the midst of a hill. I initially thought it might be a village, on getting closer I realized that the light was from a cave, and it might be the same cave where the *maharaj* was staying. From the top of the hill I could hear a voice saying, *"Hai maharaj, udhar se sidha oopar chado. Yahee rasthahai."* (Hey *maharaj*, start climbing up right from where you are, that is the way.) As the cave was at the top of the hill, I started climbing up, but it was not as easy as it appeared, since the hill was quite steep and slippery. I was getting tired and started feeling hungry as I had not eaten anything since the morning, and thought that I was losing my stamina. However, I could not figure out what was pulling me up towards the cave. I did not stop climbing. After climbing for an hour or so, I finally reached the front of the cave and could see a small light revealing the inside of the cave.

I could see a *Swamiji* wearing only a loincloth sitting near the light. I stood still at the opening of the cave, waiting to get permission to enter. Minutes passed, but there was no sound from inside. In a low voice, I called "*Swamiji Maharaj.*" Now I heard a sound from inside "*Oh tum aaya, Mast Ram ne bheja hai na?*" (Oh you are here. Mast Ram has sent you, isn't it?) Once again I was completed amazed. How did these Himalayan *swamis* know all about me? He spoke from inside the cave again, "*Kyon bahar khada hai, andar aao.*" (Why do you stand outside, come on in.) I went inside slowly. *Swamiji* was sitting in *siddha* asan. A small earthen lamp filled with some oil was burning there. I looked at *Swamiji* and according to the rules of *sanyasis*, offered my salutations to him by saying "*Om namo narayana, maharaj!*" He asked me to sit down. I sat with difficulty as my legs were swollen because of the long Journey of 7–8 days. I did *namaskars* to the *maharaj*. He was dark-skinned and well built. He looked at me and smiled. "*Tho, tum ho vahi, jo Mast Ram ne bheja hai. Acha hua beta, tum Mast Ram ke saath sadhana kiya. Rastha mai koyi takleef to nahi hui?*" (Ah, you are the one sent by Mast Ram. It's a good thing you did sadhana with Mast Ram, my son. Hope you didn't have any trouble along the way?)

I said, "*Maharaj, aap ki krupa se koyee takleef nahi hui. Mast Ram Baba ne mujhe aap ke paas bheja hai. Kyon mujhe maloom nahi. Shayed aap jante honge.*" (Maharaj, by your grace, I had no trouble. I have no idea why Mast Ram Baba has sent me to you. Perhaps you know why.)

The *maharaj* replied, "*Haan bete, jaroor maloom he. Tumara jeevan ek pratyek kam ke liye hai. Guru kripa se tum yeha tak pahunche. Ab chinta mat kar. Tum thak gaya hoga na. kuch kha kar visram karo. Kal ham bath karenge.*" (Yes son, I know for sure. Your life is for a certain purpose. Due to the grace of your Guru, you have reached here. Do not worry anymore. You must be tired. Eat something and rest. We shall talk tomorrow.)

I looked around. There was nothing other than two or three mud pots. He gave me one mud pot containing water and said, "*Haath mukh dho lo. Kuch khao aur so jao.*" (Wash your hands and face, eat something and go to sleep).

I went out of the cave with the water pot. It was dark, and standing near the cave I washed my hands, feet, and face and came back inside. Once again the *maharaj* went near the mud pots and brought 2–3 *rotis* and some potato *curry* and gave them to me to eat. However, I asked him "*Maharaj aap nahi khaoge?*"(Maharaj, will you not eat as well?)

He replied, "*Bete, main din me ek baar khata hum. Vah bhi ganv vala la kar deta to. Aaj tum ayega muje maalum tha. Isliye do roti bachaakar rakha tha. Tum khao.*" (Son, I eat only once a day and that too only if the villagers bring me food. I knew you would be coming here today so I saved a couple of *rotis* for you to eat.)

There were tears in my eyes while eating the *rotis*, because the *Swamiji* had kept aside food from his *bhiksha* for me, awaiting my arrival. What a divine arrangement! I very well understood this was due to my *guru's kripa* (grace) only. After eating we were ready to sleep. I was very tired and when *Swamiji* just lay down on his bed made of gunny bags, I spread my *kambal* and lay down too. For a few minutes there was a silence.

Then he started talking, "*Tum bachpan se chandi path padtha tha na. Kuch arth samje bina tum paath kiya kartha tha. Ab tum mere paas aneka prayojan yah hai tum chandi paath us ka arth aur rahasya sahit samajhoge.*" (You have been reciting the Chandi Paath since childhood, have you not, but without understanding its meaning? Now that you are with me, you will learn the meaning and sacred secrets behind it.)

I wondered how this old *Swamiji* knew that I used to recite the Chandi Paath since my childhood. He was reading my mind—"*Sab kuch maloom hai, sub kuch. Tum kaun ho, aur tumhara karthavya kya hai vah tum nahi janta hai, par mei janta hum. Tum ko ascharya hone ki koyee jaroorat nahi."* (I know everything, everything about you. You do not know what work you are meant to do, but I do. No need to be incredulous.)

I was thinking about how things were getting linked, how they were happening—first at Mookambika with my *Guruji*, then Mast Ram Baba, now this *Swamiji*, all these people were *antaryamis* (omniscient, knowing the hearts and minds of others).

All these were the thoughts on my mind and as though *Swamiji* was reading my thoughts, said, *"Antaryami hai, vahi, jisne ham ko paida kiya, aur palan kartha hai. Vah jagat janani ham logon ke ooper kuch jimmedariyan deti hai. Us me ek tum ho. Jyada sochne ki kya jaroorat hai. Sab kuch pahele se nirnay ho chuka hai. Ab ham ko kya, vahi nirnaya ko palan karna hai. Tum thak gaye ho, so jao, subhah baath karenge."* (The real *Antaryami* is the One who gave birth to all of us, and is sustaining us. That Universal Mother has thrust some responsibilities on us, and you are one of them. No need for too much analysis, everything is predestined. All we need to do is to go along with that, with the flow. You are tired, you must sleep, let us talk in the morning.)

I was thinking about the reasons. I wanted reasoning for anything and everything; that had been my mentality from childhood. The *maharaj* said, *"Har baath ka kaaran mat dhoondho. Vah tum ko pareshan karega. Jo saamne aathe hai, us ko sweekar karne ko seekho."* There was a little roughness in these words. (Don't keep looking for a reason for everything, it will stress you. Learn to accept whatever situation arises.) *Swamiji* added, *"Subah uth kar Gangaji me jaakar snan kar, aur phir ham baat karega, ab tum so jaao."* (When you wake up in the morning, go and bathe in Mother *Ganga*, we shall talk again, now you must sleep.)

Swamiji was about to sleep and I was lost in my thoughts. After few minutes I heard him snore and I too slowly fell into deep sleep.

Days at Vyas Ghat

My stay at Vyas Ghat was for fifteen days only, but those fifteen days are unforgettable. Everyday *Swamiji* and I used to bathe in the *Ganga* and sit on the shore of the river. *Swamiji* told me details about the *Durga Saptasati (Chandi Paath)*. I used to recite the *shlokas* one by one, and *Swamiji* used to clarify the meanings and the secret meaning of the *shlokas*. In fact, according to *Swamiji* the book is one of the foremost *Advaita* treatises, which common people never tried to understand. The so-called priests only chant the *shlokas* without knowing the meaning. It may not make any difference to them, as they only know the chanting as well as the story part of it. (As there is a book *Guptavati teeka*, I am not giving detailed meanings of the *shlokas*, etc., here)

Swamiji took classes till afternoon and later we would return to the cave where the villagers would bring us food. Sometimes it would be rice and *dal*, and sometimes *roti* and *curry* or *chutney*. I used to walk around the hills and forests as it reminded me of the days with my *Guruji* at Mookambika, and I really enjoyed these fifteen days of my stay at Vyas Ghat.

The days were running fast, and one day *Swamiji* said, "*Kal yeh padhai poori hogi. Main samajhta hoon ki ab tak chandi path ka rahasya pahli pankti samjha hoga. Kal tumko aakar pandrah din ho jayege. Parso tum ko idhar sa jaana hai.*" (Your studies end tomorrow. I guess that by now you have learned the meaning of *Chandi Paath* all through right from the first verse. The day after tomorrow, you have to leave from here.)

In fact, I was not at all interested in leaving the *Swamiji*, the cave and the forests. The day of my leaving *Swamiji* finally arrived. In the morning, *Swamiji* said, "*Agar tum abhi chalega to dopahar tak Devprayag pahunchega. Kuch kha kar chalo, maine ganv valon ko jaldi roti laane ko kaha hai.*" (If you start now, you will reach Devprayag by noon. Eat before you leave. I have asked the villagers to bring *rotis* a little earlier today.)

He was about to complete his words when a lady from the village came with *roti*. I shared the food with *Swamiji*, and bid farewell to him.

I started walking. After half an hour of my journey towards Devprayag, I noticed an old temple of the Mother Goddess down the footpath on the banks of the *Ganga*. I went near the temple and did n*amaskars* and continued on my journey. On the way I witnessed a wonderful scene. A *swamiji* was standing still on the banks of the *Ganga* near his hut, and a *shishya* was taking care of his bathing needs. I sat there for a few minutes and one of villagers I had met along the way also sat down to rest there. The villager told me that he was Khadeswari Baba. For the last ten years he had never sat or lay down. He was always in the standing position, in *Mauna*, keeping his right hand raised up. His disciples took care of his food, water, etc. I had heard about such *sadhanas* in the Himalayas before. This type of *sadhana* is known as '*Asuri sadhana*' or '*Tamoguni sadhana*'. The *sadhak* tortures his body—a difficult penance—in order to attain *siddhis* which will then be used for his pleasures.

I resumed walking towards Devprayag. I was feeling sleepy and tired, which slowed my walk. There were many villagers heading towards Devprayag for purchases; they were talking loudly and whenever they passed in front of me, they paid me respects by prostrating. I would accept them, but never raised my hands to give blessings, as I was myself unaware of my eligibility to bless others. Who was I to bless anybody?

Dev Prayag

Finally I reached Devprayag. It was almost evening. I was delighted to see the beautiful scenery of the *Ganga* flowing through the mountains and the view of the *ghat* (river banks). This is one of the five *prayags* (river confluences) in Uttarakhand. I went to the *ghat* and sat there for a few minutes before bathing. After my bath while I was sitting on the banks, I noticed a lady *sanyasi (sadhvi)* wearing a *kafni* walking towards me. In no time she reached and sat near me and asked *"Tumhari yatra theek to hai na? Meri behen kaise hai?"*(Hope you are having a good journey, and how is my sister?)

I wondered who the lady was asking about. Reading my thoughts she said, *"Tara, tumhare Guruji, vah meri behen hai. Mera naam Asha hai."* (Tara, your *Guruji* is my sister. My name is Asha.) I had heard my *Guruji* mention her name during my stay in Mookambika. I stood up and did *namaskar* to that *Mayee* (Mother). She said, *"Baith jao beta. Tara ne tumko ek bhiksha pathra diya hai na, mujhe dikhao. Maine bahut samay se vah pathra dekha nahi. Vah ham logon ki parampara ka ashirvad hai."* (Sit down, son. Tara gave you a bowl, did she not? Can you show it to me; I have not seen it in a long time. The bowl is the blessing of our tradition or lineage.)

I had been keeping my *bhiksha pathra* very safely and carefully during my journey. It was in my hands, covered with a cloth which my *Guruji* would wear as a scarf occasionally. I opened the cloth cover and showed the *pathra* to Ashamayee. I had never expected that I would meet Ashamayee so soon. She said, "Tara told me that you will be reaching Devprayag today. I have been waiting for you since yesterday. I was supposed to be on my way to Triyuginarayan now. Then I remembered that my son was coming, and I thought since he is on the way, let me wait and see him." The communication system of the Himalayan *yogis/sadhus* is quite wonderful. They have no need for telegram, telephone, or the postal department. Their thought waves with their messages pass from one place to another. During those days I was unaware of this technique. In the course of my stay in the Himalayas, one yogi taught me how to send and receive thought waves.

Ashamayee was telling me again, "*Bete, saptasathi rahasya tum ne vah baba se seekha. Is se poora nahi hua. Tum ko bahut varsh is Himalaya mein rah kar sadhana karni hai, samaysamay se koi na koi aa kar tum ko sab kuch bathayega. Un sab ko guru bhav me dekho. Ye sab log tumhare guru Tara se bhinn nahi. Tatva mein guru sab ek hai. Roop me kuch...Bhinnata jaroor dikhayi degi.*" (Son, you have learned the sacred secrets of the *Saptasati* from the saint, but you are not finished yet. You have many more years of *sadhana* left in the Himalayas. From time to time, people will appear before you to impart instruction. They are not really any other than your *Guru* Tara. Though they may seem different in physical appearance, but the *Guru tattva*, an element or principle is the same in all.)

I understood that all these *yogis/gurus* are interlinked and they easily convey their thoughts to one another. Ashamayee was looking with emotion at the *bhiksha pathra*. She held the *pathra* for a while in her hand and prostrated to it again and again. I saw tears of bliss in her eyes. Ashamayee looked very similar to my *Guruji*, perhaps a bit taller. Her face very closely resembled my *Guruji*'s. At that time I did not know that this Ashamayee was my Guruji's own sister and then *guru-behen* as well. It was almost sunset time when some *sadhus* came to the *ghat* for their *sandhyavandan* (prayers offered three times a day). They saw Ashamayee and paid their respects to her in the traditional way of "*Om Namo Narayana, mata.*" She also reciprocated with "*Om Namo Narayana.*" All of a sudden, Ashamayee stood up and asked me to accompany her. We went to the corner of the *ghat,* and she took a handful of *vibhooti* (sacred ash) from her shoulder bag and dropped it in the *bhiksha pathra*. Then she dipped the *bhiksha pathra* into the *Ganga* and held it inside the waters for a few seconds. She then lifted up the *pathra,* and allowed the *Ganga jal* to slowly come out of the *pathra*. She then handed it to me. To my wonder, the *vibhooti* in the *bhiksha pathra* was not wet even though she had kept it dipped in the water for a few seconds. The *vibhooti* was as dry as before. I looked at Ashamayee with puzzlement. She laughed and said, "*Ascharya ho raha hai na. Yahee is kappar ke visheshata hai. Yah kappar ham logon ki guru parampara ka upyog kiya huva hai. Is se adhik pavitra vasthu is duniya me nahi. Tumhara bhagya hai. Yah tum ko prapt hua. Mujhse Tara ne bola tha is pathra ke yogya tum hee hai. Is ko sada suraskshit rakhana. Jab tum ek Guru banoge, tab iska upyog samaj mei aayega.*" (You are surprised, are you not? This is the speciality of this *kappar*. There is nothing quite as sacred as this *kappar*, which has been in usage in our *Guru Parampara* throughout. It is your good fortune that it has come to you now. Tara had told me that it is only you who has the eligibility to possess this now, so you must safeguard it. When you become a *Guru* one day, you will come to know its usage.)

Once again Ashamayee did *namaskar* to the *bhiksha pathra* and again said, "*Tum idhar baitho. Main raat ke pehele jaa kar kuch khana ko lakar ayee.*" (You wait here. I will go and bring you some food before it gets dark.) She moved away quickly. I was sitting all alone on the banks of the *Ganga* in the corner of the *ghat*, holding the *kappar* in hand. (After few years when I became a *guru* by the grace of my *Guruji*, I understood the value of the *kappar* very clearly and even now I keep it with me always, and have *bhiksha* in it only on selected days.)

Ashamayee returned after half an hour carrying some *pooris* and *curry* with her. She sat near me and put the food into her *bhiksha pathra*. She had brought some water in another *pathra* from *Ganga*, offered the food to Mother *Ganga*. (This is the tradition among Himalayan *sadhus*, that whatever they eat they will offer first to Mother *Ganga* and Shiva before eating it.) Ashamayee did not allow me to eat myself. As a mother feeds her child, Ashamayee fed me with her own hands. There were tears once again in my eyes. I remembered the days with my *Guruji* when she would feed me like this. My mind was full of thoughts of my *Guruji*. In these Himalayas, an unknown place to me, I had met my *Guruji's* sister. And here she was now feeding me filled with motherly affection. I thought how lucky I was to get some *prasadam* from my *Guruji* herself. Ashamayee had vanished before my eyes and I could only see my *Guruji* sitting and feeding her child. I wept.

Ashamayee's voice reached my ears, "*Kyon rota hai re? Tara ki yaad aayi hai kya? Mere aur Tara me kya farak hai? Jo vah hai vahee main hun. Tum ro mat. Poori khao. Mujhe tum se bahut batein karni hai.*" (Why do you weep? Are you remembering Tara? There is no difference between her and me, so don't be upset. Eat the *pooris*. I have so much to tell you.)

In fact, I was unable to swallow the food I was eating; it would not go down my throat. I felt this was enough. I could not eat anymore. I said, "*Amma*, bas, ab tum khao." (Mother, I'm done, now you eat.) Ashamayee was not ready to listen. She made me drink some water and again started feeding me. One *sadhu* came to the *ghat* and looking at us was very amused. He said, "*Asha mata, tum ko apna beta mila hai na? Khilao jee bar kar lekin, ek baat mat bhoolna. Ham sanyasiyon ko itni mamata nahi hona chahiye.*" (Mother Asha, you found your son? Feed him to your heart's content, but don't forget that *sanyasis* should not develop attachments.)

Asha Mata replied to him, "*Sanyasi to jaroor hai, lekin main ek mata hai. Tum log jaise kathor dil ke nahi hai. Meri mamta ka arth hai, ay mere beta, tum log jaise kathor baba nahi banne doongi isko. Isko sada ham matru bhav mei me rakhoongi.*" (I may be a *sanyasi* but I am also a mother and not hard-hearted like you folks. I will always regard him with maternal affection and make sure that he does not become hard-hearted like you.) "*Bahut acha*" (very well), the *baba* said and taking some *Ganga jal* in his *kamandal* (an oblong water pot used by ascetics or yogis to store and carry water), disappeared.

Now Ashamayee finished eating the remaining food and washing her *bhiksha pathra*, came, sat near me and started talking, "*Beta, ek baath dhyan se suno. Mei kal subah Triyuginarayan jaa rahi hum. Tumko kal hee vapas jana padega.*" (Son, listen to me carefully. I leave for Triyuginarayan in the morning, and you need to turn back tomorrow.)

I wondered and asked, "*Kaham vapas jana maa?*" (Where do I have to return to, Mother?)

She said, "*Tum kal vapas Vyas Ghat jaao. Udhar rasthe me tumne ek purana devi mandir dekha hai na? Vah mandir Silsoo ganv valon ka hai. Tum us mandir ke neeche ke gufa mein jaa kar rahana aur sadhana karna. Silsoo vala log tumare roti ki vyavastha karenge. Ab thandi ka mausam hai. Abhi tum baccha hai. Is thandi mei tum Himalaya yatra nahi karna. Agle sal garmi mein tum yatra shuroo karo.*" (Return to Vyas Ghat tomorrow. Remember the temple of the goddess that you visited along the way? That is in the village of Silsoo. You must do *sadhana* in the cave that is below that temple. The villagers will take care of your food. You are but young and the Himalayan winter is harsh, and not a good time to travel. Continue your journey in the summer.)

It was difficult for me to understand but my *Guruji's* words were in my mind, "*Tumhare rasthe me tumhare jaroorat ki vyaystha main karoongi. Chinta mat karo.*" (I will take care of all your needs along your journey, do not worry.)

I asked Ashamayee, "*Amma tum bhi mere saath udhar raho, ham saath rahenge.*" (Mother, you also come with me, we will stay there together.)

Ashamayee declined. "*Nahin beta. Tara kahati hai, jyada mamta aur pyar se tum mere bete ko bigaadna nahi. Main tumere sath nahi rahoongi.*" (No, son. Tara says not to spoil her son with too much love and affection. I will not be able to stay with you.)

Night had fallen and it was very cold as we were sitting on the river bank. Ashamayee told me that as I had travelled the entire day, I should sleep now. Mayee said "*Bahut chala hai na, tum abhi visram karo. Kambal odkar meri godh me sar rahkar so jao. Mei raat sota nahi, jap kar ke baithi hun.*"(You have walked a long way; you must rest, wrap yourself in the blanket and lay your head on my lap and sleep. I don't sleep at night, I will sit and pray.)

I was a bit hesitant to sleep on her lap; so I covered my body with the blanket and lay down on the *Ghat*. But Ashamayee was not in a mood to allow me to sleep separate. She took my head and placing it on her lap began to very gently caress my head. I heard the murmuring sound of her *japa*; it was like *sangeet* with a chorus of the song of the *Ganga*. Slowly, I went into deep sleep.

Back to Vyas Ghat

*I*t was early morning when I woke up to find myself still in the lap of Ashamayee, her hand on my head and still doing her *japa*. I went to complete my morning ablutions right away and when I came back to the place where we had been sitting, to my surprise Ashamayee was not there. I went looking all around the *Ghat* for her, and suddenly in a few minutes she reappeared with tea and bananas. She asked me to take the tea and keep the bananas with me, and start my journey back to Vyas Ghat. She also said, "*Kela tumhare paas rahkho. Vaapas abhi jao. Tumhare pahunchne samay tak mandir ka poojari udhar ayega. Aur unse baat karo, vah tumhara pahala sishya hoga.*" (Keep the bananas with you, and start your journey now. By the time you reach there, the temple's priest will also have arrived there. He will be your first disciple.)

She asked me to get going as she was also in a hurry to leave for Triyuginarayan. I offered my salutations to the mother, and with the thought of departure, tears came to my eyes. She embraced me and said, "*Beta, tum akele nahi, yah chinta chod do, aur jao.*" (Son, you are not alone, cast away your worries and leave.)

I started my return journey to Vyas Ghat with a heavy heart and eyes full of tears. On the way, I saw the odd sight of Khadeswari Baba still standing. As I was nearing Vyas Ghat after a walk of almost 5–6 hours, I noticed an old *Vaishnav baba* sitting in a dilapidated temple surrounded by mango trees. He asked me, "*Maharaj, Seetha Ram! Kaha se aa rahahai?*" (Greetings, where are you coming from?)

I thought, the previous day, on my way to Devprayag, I had not noticed this temple or the *maharaj*. The *maharaj* said, "*Main dekha tha, kal tum idhar se jaate huwe. Lagta the tum kuch jaldi-baaji meinhai, isilyei me bath nahi kiya.*" (I saw you on your way yesterday, but you seemed in a bit of a hurry, so I did not speak with you.)

He requested me to sit and offered some food. As I was hungry, and was carrying the bananas given by Ashamayee, I offered him two bananas and said, "*Maharaj, mere paas kela hai. Is se tript hojavoonga.*" (*Maharaj*, I have bananas and am content with them.)

However, the *maharaj* was not ready to listen to me. He said, "*Dekho, mein abhi naivedyam lagaya. Tum mere sath kuch chaval aur dal khayega to mere man tasalli hoga.*" (Look, I just offered *naivedyam* at the temple. If you share some *dal* and rice with me, I will be happy.) So I had some food with him.

I was very happy to have the food served to me. In the Himalayas I have noticed that there is no *sampraday bheda* (differential treatment pertaining to spiritual tradition) between *babas*, whether he be a *vairagi, sanyasi, naga*, or *udasi*. Everybody is cooperative and offers whatever food they have to wandering monks. This is my *parivrajaka* (wandering monk) life. In *parivrajaka* life, one has to go through different tests. He may be treated like a king, or as a beggar or even a dog. *Maan* or *apmaan* (respect or insult) may be there on the way. He has to accept it. This life is for washing out the ego of the *sadhu*.

I resumed my journey after doing *namaskar* to the *Vaishnav baba*. Walking slowly I reached near the temple. Now I could easily hear sounds of some chanting. I went near the temple and an old priest (*pandit*) was sitting there and chanting. After doing *namaskars* I sat on the small verandah of the *mandir*. By this time the *pandit* had completed his chanting and came near me. He asked, "*Baba. Kahan se aana hua?*"(*Baba*, where have you come from?)

I told him, "*Mere guru agya se main idhar rahane aaya hum. Thandi poora hone ke baad char dham pilgrimage karna hai.*" (I am here on the orders of my *Guru*. When winter ends, I have to continue my pilgrimage.)

The *pandit* said, "*Bahut acha. Aaj tumara khane ka bandobast nahi kar paunga. Kal se jab me pooja ke liye atha hai tumhare liye me khana lekar aaooga. Tum kitane din chahiye idhar thaharo. Ganv me, ek sadhu rahana ganv ki shobha hai. Kuch saal pahele idhar ek Mayee raha karthi thi. Vah Mayee bahut sal tak idhar rahi. Ham ganv vaale unki seva kartha the.*" (Very good. Though I'm unable to make food arrangements for you today, I will bring you food every day when I come to do *pooja* here. You can stay here as long as you wish. A village is graced when a *sadhu* chooses to stay there. Some years ago, a *Mayee*, a woman saint, stayed here a long time and we villagers served her.) It struck me that she perhaps had been my Ashamayee, so I asked, "*Panditji, kya unka nam aadi aap jante hai?*"(Sir, do you remember her name or whereabouts?)

He replied, "*Mujhe naam yaad nahi aa raha hai. Haan, itna kah sakta hun vah aek avadhoot Mayee thi. Kisi se kuch bhi poochthi nahi thi. Ek kappar haath mein tha aur do alphi. Din raat jap karke baithi thi.*" (I can't remember her name. But I can say for sure that she was an *avadhoot*. She never spoke to anyone and was in meditation day and night. She had a *kappar* with her and two *alphies*.)

Now it became crystal clear to me that she was none other than my Ashamayee.

He showed me the cave or *gufa* and helped me clean it. I had only one *kambal* cloth and *kappar* with me. *Panditji* went to the side room of the *mandir* where he would keep *pooja* materials and other things. He brought two–three gunny bags and made a bed for me to sit on, and as well as for sleeping. Then he said, "*Ganga mayya kaafi neeche bah rahi hai. Udhar pass dekho ek jharna hai. Udhar tum naha sakte hai. Peene keliye bhi us jharne ka pani acha hai.*" (The *Ganga* is flowing quite a bit below and over there you can see a waterfall. The water is good for bathing as well as for drinking.) I nodded and observed that *Ganga* water was flowing more than five to six hundred feet down from the cave. It would be difficult for anybody to step down and climb back up every day for water. Again the *pandit* said, "*Ab, maharaj yeh tumhara samrajya hai. Yah chandi maata bahut dayaalu hai. Ganv valo ki icha poori karthi hai. Tum inki saran mein rahio. Tum ko kuch bhi kami nahi hogi.*" (Maharaj, now this is your domain. This Mother *Chandi* is very compassionate and fulfils all the wishes of the villagers. If you too seek her grace, you will not lack for anything.) Pointing to some distance away, he said, "*Udhar dekho ek chotta dookan hai. Hamara ganv vala ka hai. Kabhi khulta hai. Kuch jaroori saman udhar se milega.*" (Over there is a small shop belonging to one of our villagers which is open occasionally where you can get necessities.) I told him that I needed nothing and had no money with me. Then the *pandit* said, "*Koyi baat nahi. Mera beta kal Rajasthan se aaye hai. Vah udhar college me professor hai. Kal subah mein rah jana wala hai. Kal mein ate samay usko sath lata hun aur tumare liya khana bhi.*" (Never mind, yesterday my son came here from Rajasthan, where he is a college professor. I will bring him here when I come tomorrow, along with food for you.) He was ready to leave as it was afternoon. The *pandit* left me and I was all alone there except for the idol of the Goddess.

Once again I went near the temple—it didn't have any doors. I bowed in prostration to the deity and said, "Mother, your son has come here to take refuge in you, do protect me." I looked around, there was complete silence. A few trees covered the area so it was well shaded. The *verandah* in front of the *mandir* was not large enough to accommodate more than 2–3 persons and there was a dilapidated *Dharmasala* (resthouse for pilgrims), which looked ready to collapse anytime, and a small store room behind the *mandir*. Mother *Ganga* was flowing down below the cave, calm and quiet.

From here it was not too far from the place where I had stayed with the *baba* to study the *Saptashati (Chandi Paath)* for 15 days. It would have hardly taken 15 minutes of walking to reach that *baba*. I decided not to go there as Ashamayee had asked me to stay here. It began to rain and some water entered the *gufa* where my bed had been spread. It was extremely cold. During winter in the Himalayas, one can expect rain showers at any time. However, it is often not heavy rain, only drizzles, but it makes the weather much colder. By this time the *pandit* might have reached his village. He had told me it would take at least 3–4 hours for the villagers to reach their village and for a person like me, unfamiliar with the area, it would definitely take more than 7 hours.

I sat in the *gufa* calm, quiet and composed. On the top of the *gufa* was the *moorthy* (idol) of *Amma*. It looked like a very ancient *moorthy* made of clay. But after observing for a few days I discovered that the *moorthy* was really made of marble, and the poor condition of the idol was probably because of neglect. What could this old *pandit* do alone? At least he was coming daily and doing *pooja*. All these thoughts were going through my mind. Suddenly the sun shone and I saw a serpent entering the cave. I was terrified. It was my mistake that I had encroached upon the serpent's territory. It came right in front of me. I was ready to get up and run but nothing happened. It looked at me lovingly and slithered away. I was relieved. But a new thought started overpowering me—what if the serpent comes again at night when I am asleep—the very thought made me shiver. It was almost dusk. There was no lamp or electric light. And I did not even have a matchbox with me. I was helpless. So I left the cave and came to the *verandah* and sat there. Now I could hear the sounds of animals from a distance. I was very much frightened. Sitting there I started doing *japa*. (Usually a person remembers God or *Guru* when he/she is in distress.) Sitting on the *verandah*, I was doing *japa* but was not able to concentrate and kept looking around. It was dark and I could not see anything. I could only hear the sound of the river *Ganga* accompanied by occasional unknown sounds of animals.

Once again it started drizzling. As I was in the temple corridor, I had no choice but to get drenched in rain water as I dare not go inside the cave for fear of the serpent. I was in such a dilemma. The night was growing darker and silence seemed to engulf the temple surroundings except for the gushing sounds of the river. I was overpowered by fear. The silence was disturbing, and hours passed in this mood, and without being aware I had drifted into deep sleep in the sitting posture.

Vyas Ghat Days

By noon the *panditji* and his son arrived. I was sitting in the corridor of the *mandir*. Both came and prostrated in front of me and the *panditji* introduced his son, "*Yeh, Bhagawati Prasad mere bada beta working as a professor in a College at Jaipur.*" (This is Bhagwati Prasad, my older son who works as a college professor in Jaipur.)

Panditji went to clean the *mandir* while chanting some *stotras* of *Maa* while I talked to Prof. Bhagwati Prasad. We both talked in English. He was astonished that a *baba* wearing dirty clothes and having no possessions spoke in English. He was acquainted with *babas* of large ashrams who were well versed in English and Sanskrit. He told me, "The shop you see near is being run by my cousin. I will tell him to supply whatever you need. I know you are a *'virakt sanyasi'*, one who does not keep money with him. So whatever you need, you can take from the shop and I will pay him whenever I visit this village. Be here, please don't go. I will see to it that the *Dharmasala* gets repaired, and then you can shift there. Previously the *Mayee* who stayed here was the avatar of *Maa*. She was very generous to all of us. After few years of stay, she left the place and has gone to the upper Himalayas, maybe Triyuginarayan." I did not tell him that the *Mayee* was known to me, as I feared these people would then start expecting more from me, at least more affection. The professor told me, "I am leaving for Rajasthan now. My father is a great astrologer. People from distant villages come to him for *pooja* and astrological consultations." I asked, "What is your father known as?" The professor said in reply, "He is known as Ghananand Panditji. He is now more than 75 years old. Yet he comes to this *mandir* for *pooja* daily. If at all he has any health problem, my younger brother will come and do *pooja*. Your food will come to you daily from my house. Don't worry about anything and stay here happily and continue your *sadhana*." The *panditji* was doing the *arathi*. After *arathi*, the professor did *namaskar* to me and his father, and left carrying a small bag on his shoulder.

The *panditji* brought me my food of rice and *dal*. I accepted my first *bhiksha* there in my *kappar*. Looking at the *bhiksha pathra*, he said, "A similar one was with the *Mayee* who stayed here for a long time. *Bahut achi Mayee thi. Ek din idhar se chali gayi."*(She was a very kind mother and left this place suddenly.) It seemed like he was unhappy that the *Mayee* left the place. I sat near him after the *bhiksha* and he offered me a *bidi*. Even though I was not smoking those days, I accepted it and smoked. Then I started narrating to him the previous evening's experience of the serpent. *Panditji* told me, "*Us se ghabrana kuch nahi. Vah idhar bahut dinon se rahata hai. Ab tak kisi ko kaatta nahi. Lagtha hai koi acha aatma hai us sarpa yoni mein."* (*You don't need to fear the serpent. It has lived here a long time and never hurt anyone, seems there is a good soul in that serpent.)* Panditji looked at my face thoroughly for a few minutes and asked if he could see my right palm. For a few minutes he was silent and was looking through the lines on my palm. Then he broke the silence and said, "*Maharaj, aap kaun hai? Itna jabardasth bhagya rekha mainekabhi bhi nahi dekha. Aap ka ujwal bhavishya dekh kar mujhe ascharya ho reha hai. Kabhi bhi yah hath kisi ko nahi dikhana."* (Maharaj, who are you? I have never seen such a fantastic line of fortune on anyone's palm before. I'm amazed seeing your brilliant future. Do not ever show your palm to anyone henceforth.) I told him that I was a *fakir* and did not care for the lines on my palms. Again he started saying, "*Aap ko nahi, ham logon ka mahabhagya hai aap jaise mahan purush mila. Ek baath pooche phir bura nahi maan na. Kripaya aap mujhe aap ka sishya bana lijiye."* (It is our great good fortune to come across an extraordinary saint like you. Can I ask a favour? I hope you won't take offense if I request you to take me as your disciple.) I wondered. It was only yesterday that I had met him, and today he was ready to be my *sishya*. I answered in the negative, "*Abhi bhi main shishya hun. Abhi tak guru nahi bana. Mere guru ki agya bina kaise me aap ko sishya banaunga?"* (I am still a disciple myself, and have not attained *guru* stature. Without my *guru*'s approval, how can I even think of taking you on as a disciple?)

"*Fir aap apne guru se anumathi poochiye. Main aap ko guru roop me sweekar kiye. Aaj se aap mere guru hai.*" (Then please ask permission of your *guru*. I have already accepted you as *guru* from today on.)

I felt like laughing. I know nothing even about myself, and how do these people know me? And I don't know how to give *deeksha* either. Anyway I prayed to my *Guruji* to take care of the old *pandit*. *Panditji* asked me, "*Navaratri nazdeek hai. Aap kya karne ka vichar me hai?*" (The *Navaratri* festival is nearing, what are your plans?) I had not yet thought about it. This was my first *Navaratri* in the Himalayas. This was the birthplace of my *Ishta Devi* (The Mother goddess is Himavan's daughter). So I immediately thought that I should do some good *sadhana*. I said "*Hum pratipada se, upvas rakh kar 41 din ka sadhana karna chahate hain. Bhaiya sadhana ke liya sadhan jutana mushkil hai. Isliya me socha ke shodashi mantra ka ek purascharan karoonga.*" (I would like to start fasting from the first day of Navaratri and continue the *sadhana* for 41 days. Since it is difficult to procure materials to do external ritual, I would like to do chanting of the *shodashi mantra*.)

There was a strange glow in the eyes of the pandit. He asked, "*Aap Srividya wala Swamiji hai? Hamara bhagya hai. Aap ke liya ek naya kambal main laya. Yah kambal aap asan keliya sweekar kijiye. Aur sadhana ke baad yah kambal mujhe dijiye. Kam se kam Srividya jap karnewala ek Swamiji baitha hua asan prasad roop mei milega to mere jeevan dhanya hoga.*" (Are you a *swamiji* initiated into *Srividya*? I am so fortunate. I have brought you a new blanket; please accept it for your seat/bed. Please give that blanket to me after completion of your *sadhana*. At least, I will have it as *prasad* and my life will be blessed.)

He added that *Navaratri* was starting next week. Villagers would be visiting the *mandir*. To not have any disturbances, he said he would arrange for a door in front of the cave.

My mind was full of thoughts of *Navaratri* and that also the first time in the Himalayas. I told the *panditji* that I would not take any food made of rice during the 41 days of *sadhana*, and I would only need *Ganga jal*. And not to bring any food or fruit for me. He agreed. He gave the key of the storeroom to me and said, "*Kal jaise barsaat aayi to us kamre me aap so sakte hai. Yah chabhi rakho.*" (If it rains like yesterday, you can sleep in that room and here is its key.) I declined saying, "*Mere Guruji ne bola tha mandir ka neecha wala gufa me rahana. Main udhar hee rahoonga. Mujhe kamra ki chabhi kee jaroorat nahi.*" (My *Guruji* told me to stay in the cave below the temple and stay there I will. I don't need that key.)

Panditji with all reverence said, "*Aap bahut hatthi lagta hain. Gufa mei takleef nahi hona, itana main socha.*" (You seem quite adamant. I only offered the key because I did not want you to suffer discomfort in the cave.) The old man might have been disappointed that I had not accepted the offer of the key. He brought a big clay pot from the store and gave it to me and said, "*Yah ghata ithar rakho. Aur pani bhar lo, bar jharna me jaane ka jaroorat nahi hogi.*" (Here's a jug that you can use to store water in, so you don't have to keep going to the waterfall often.)

I felt that if I did not accept this as well, he would definitely feel bad, and so I took it and kept it in the verandah.

Now *panditji* was ready to go back to the village. By this time another villager came there. He was returning from Devprayag. He talked to *panditji* in their local language (Garhwali). *Panditji* replied, "*Yeh maharaj, kal aaya. Thandi mittne samay tak idhar rukega.*" (This *maharaj* arrived yesterday and will stay till the end of winter.) The villager came to me said, "*Om namo narayana*" and sat near us. He took 2–3 bananas from his gunny bag and gave them to me. I took one and returned the other to him saying, "*Ghar me bachon ko de do.*" (Give them to your children at home.) *Pandit* told the villager, "*Naya khoon hai na. Bhut vairagya hai.*" (He meant to say for a young man I was having too much dispassion.) Both moved towards the village. Once again I was all alone there. The songs of birds were easily heard. And then a deep silence, then the sound of a bird, silence, and the sound of *Ganga* flowing.

I was enjoying every moment there, and sat quietly.

First Navaratri in The Himalayas

This was my first *Navaratri* in the Himalayas. The Himalayas are the abode of the Mother Goddess. On the first day of the *Navaratri* I took an oath for a *purascharan* (repeating a *mantra* for a particular number of time and for a period of time) of *shodashi mantra* (*Srividya*) *japa* to be completed in 41 days and also took a decision of not taking any cooked food. It was not easy for me to obtain uncooked food like fruits or vegetables there, as it was a remote place in the Himalayas. The *panditji* told me, "*Baba*, you are young, you can do it. This is the time for *sadhana* like this. Keep it up." On *Navaratri* days I first recited *Chandi Paath* in the morning. It took nearly three hours to complete. Then I started my *japa* which lasted until noon. All I had in the morning was some *Ganga jal* after my *japa*, and rested for a few hours till about 3 pm or so, when I started my second session of *japa* which lasted till 6 pm or *arathi* time. *Ganga* was flowing there with a smile of affection. *Panditji* told me that he would stay in the *mandir* till the end of *Navaratri*. A few villagers used to visit the *mandir* daily. But they never disturbed me by coming near, or asking anything. *Navaratri* went well with daily recitation of *Chandi paath* as well as *japa*. The *panditji* also did *Chandi paath* after the morning *abhishekam*[21] and *pooja* to mother goddess.

On the 10th day (*dashami*) *panditji* offered rice pudding (*kheer/payasam*) as offering (*naivedyam*) to the Goddess and distributed it among the devotees assembled there. That day more people had arrived from nearby villages. At about 12:30 pm when his *poojas*

---

21 A devotional activity and/or religious rite or ritual involving pouring of a liquid as an offering to

and *naivedyam* had ended, he asked me to take some *prasad* but as I was in *Vrata*, I did not. In the evening, the *panditji* left for his village and once again I was alone there in the *mandir* and my *gufa*.

I was a bit tired because of the ten-day long *Vrata*, of complete fasting with no intake other than *Ganga jal*. My daily routine had been to wake up in the early hours, bathe at the *jharna* and then commence *japa*, continuing till noon. And after taking stomach full of *Gangajal*, to rest till around 3:30pm when I would resume *japa* of the *shodashi mantra* ending at about sunset. Again after a bath I would sit down for *japa* till sleep overcame me. Everything went on well for a few more days. I was becoming weaker. Now it had become difficult for me to even walk to bathe at the nearby waterfall. *Panditji* used to come daily morning as usual and every day he looked at me very sympathetically.

Twenty days had passed; I became very weak because of not eating anything. That day I was unable to move even to the *jharna* and just lay down on the verandah of the mandir. All of a sudden one *Swamiji* with matted hair, dark in complexion, old but moving swiftly appeared in front of me. The *Swamiji* came near and touched my body. I was not sleeping, but was in intoxication of the *japa* and quite tired. *Swamiji* asked, "What you are doing here without eating anything. Are you committing suicide? Fool, this not the way to do s*adhana*. If you cannot keep your body intact, what *sadhana* will you be able to do? This body is the instrument to perform the *sadhana*. You have to maintain it." For a few moments I said nothing. I was adamant in my decision and even if I were to die, it did not matter. I had to continue my *sadhana* without food (*upavas*) and complete the *japa* in 41 days. *Swamiji* may have read my mind for he said, "Okay, if you are very adamant about not taking any cooked food, etc., no problem—but hear me and act accordingly. Observe the leaves which these monkeys are eating. They are of course medicinal leaves, as monkeys are much cleverer than we are. Take those leaves and drink as much water as you can." The *baba* had come to me as if someone had sent him to me for passing on this information.

I asked the *Swamiji*, "Respects to you *maharaj*, tell me where you stay? I have not seen you here since I came." *Swamiji* with a beautiful smile on his face told me that he was staying on the other side of the river, and that he was on his way to Devprayag to purchase some groceries. I could not believe that one could cross that part of the Ganga even by swimming. Once again it seemed like he was reading my mind because with a meaningful glance at me, he added, "See, I need no boat or swimming to cross. I am there and I am here. That is all." He left me.

The next day onwards I was observing the monkeys to see what they were eating. I identified a few trees and bushes from which they had been eating; I went there to collect the leaves as I felt I had to obey the words of that Himalayan *yogi*. It was my very nature that if any *yogi/swami* gave me any instruction, I would take it as an order from my *Guruji* and follow it. I always felt as if my *Guruji* had appeared in their form and asked me to do a certain work. That is why I had agreed to take the leaves which the monkeys ate. I saw a few monkeys on the small trees as well as in bushes. They were staring at me as I was picking up the leaves. They looked at me and smiled very sarcastically. Maybe because they thought I was a fool, that even in a human body I was not more than a monkey, eating like them and living like them without clothes. In those days I used to wear only a loincloth. My hair had started growing and became matted. I nearly looked like a monkey. Just imagine a grown-up man in a loincloth, body covered with dirt and all, and eating leaves and drinking only water from the stream. Of course the monkey's thoughts were correct.

Days passed by in this way. Now I was almost at the end of the 41-day *japa*. But due to eating just leaves, I developed some pain in my stomach. I felt too weak to walk. However, I still managed to walk up to the *jharna* for my daily ablutions, ate monkey food (leaves) and water. *Panditji* used to come every day as usual and after *pooja* would ask me about the *japa*. And it was a wonder that he never once enquired about my health. That day, he said. "*Maharaj*, you are wonderful. When you started the *japa sankalp*, I doubted that you would complete 41 days. But tomorrow is the 41st day. Tomorrow morning after *arathi* you have to complete the *japa* and break your *upavas*. I will bring you some rice and yogurt. In fact, you are also supposed to do '*dasamsh havan*' tomorrow as you would have completed the *japa*. I will arrange for the *homa*.

My son will also come and help us." *Panditji* left for the village. As I was running towards the goal for the last 40 days, I was happy that I would reach it the next morning. I sat on my asan for *japa*. All of a sudden my old friend, the serpent appeared. As I was unable to move from the bed due to exhaustion, I sat still and continued my *japa*. The serpent came inside the cave, moved towards me and looked at me for a few seconds as if doing *namaskar*, or saying thanks, I don't know. It started slithering towards me and made three *parikramas* around me and once again looked at me for a few seconds as if thanking me and moved out—I could not understand why. Even today I can visualize the scene clearly and remember the face of that serpent. To my amazement, the next day I saw the still body of the serpent lying dead in front of the verandah, where I used to sit.

Now the winter was in full swing. It was too cold there. When I noticed the dead serpent, I thought my body too was as good as a dead body, as I had been living without food. I dared not touch the dead body of the serpent on the verandah and I waited for the panditji to come and do the needful.

With great difficulty I bathed and came back to the *mandir*. That day I did not collect any leaves as my *upavas* was ending and *japa* concluding too. I saw our *panditji* and his son appearing at the *mandir*, carrying firewood and some other things.

As soon as the *panditji* saw the dead body of the serpent, he said, "Oh dear, you have left. Good that you were with this *maharaj* for the last few months. The *mantra* which *maharaj* chanted will definitely give *moksha* to you." Then he asked his son to take the serpent and give it a good *Jal Samadhi* (interment in water) in the *Ganga*.

By noon we completed the *homa* and *tarpana*. *Panditji* offered the *naivedyam* of curd rice to the Goddess and some of it he put into the fire. Then offered it to me saying, "*Maharaj*, I am proud of you. You have done it. Done it wonderfully. Even though you were weak, you did not break your vow. I am proud of you." After mentally offering it to my *guru*, I took the curd rice offered to me by the *panditji*. But alas, as soon as I ate the food, I started vomiting. I vomited several times. Every time the *panditji*'s son brought me water and washed my face and mouth. After 5–6 times of vomiting, the *panditji* went to the nearby bushes, and brought a few leaves. He put them in water and made me drink the mixture, and the vomiting stopped immediately. These are the specialities of Himalayan herbs that the villagers have knowledge of, and how and when to use them. Due to exhaustion, I lay down on the verandah of the *mandir*.

Vyas Ghat Life Continues

Slowly days passed and every day the *pandit* would bring me food. It took me at least a month to regain normal health. One day, the *Vaishanav swamiji* came to meet me. He brought disturbing news that the *swamiji* who used to stay on the other hill (from whom I studied *Durga saptashathi* meaning and *rahasya*) had attained *samadhi* the previous night. The *Vaishnav swamiji* was on his way to that *swamiji*'s hut. I also accompanied him. I was filled with grief at seeing the motionless body lying in the hut. Two or three other *sadhus* were there but I didn't know anyone other than the *Vaishnav swamiji*. They were planning to take the body to *Ganga* for *jal samadhi*. This is a custom among Himalayan *sadhus*. Once a *sadhu* attains *samadhi*, he will be given *jala samadhi* in *Ganga*, if he had not desired to keep his body in *bhoo samadhi* (burial at land).

They were awaiting another *sadhu* who had been the disciple of that *swamiji* who attained *samadhi*.

After a while that disciple *sadhu* arrived from Devprayag. He was young, about 30 years of age. His eyes were filled with tears. I was in tears too. Sanyasis are not supposed to shed tears whatever may happen to them. They are supposed to be composed, and keep equanimity. We took the body to the *Ganga* and after bathing it, clothed it in new clothes. The other *sadhus* tied 2–3 big stones to the body of *Swamiji*, and slowly lowered it in the *Ganga*. This was the end of the *Swamiji*. One of *Swamiji*'s disciples came to me and said, "*Maharaj*, are you the *sadhu* staying at Vyas Ghat *mandir*. My *Guruji* had told me about you. I am coming with you now. I would like to talk to you."

The other *sadhus* left as if nothing had happened. They were in their own moods. They had not enquired about us, and I did not talked to them either. The *Vaishnav swamiji* told me that these *sadhus* were staying in separate caves around the hills. *Vaishnav swamiji*, the young disciple of the *Swamiji* and I started walking back to Vyas Ghat. There was deep silence between us for a few minutes.

The *Vaishnav baba* left for his cottage directly. The young *swami* and I came to the *mandir*. We had a bath at the *jharna*. I possessed nothing that I could offer this young *swami*, as I was living on *Akash Vritti* (a life without asking anything from anybody for day-to-day needs, and only accepting the minimum), the life of birds.

After some time the young *sadhu* broke his silence and said, "My *Guruji* told me about you last month. Since then I have been eager to meet you, *Swamiji*. Now my *Guruji* has left and I am all alone." I interrupted him, "*Gurujis* never die, don't worry. Only the body has gone. He is here and now with you. Are you planning to go to Devprayag?" He said, "No, I want to stay with you for a few days and study *Srividya* from you." I was surprised, I had never told the *swamiji* who had attained *samadhi* or even anybody else that I was a *srividya sadhak*. But now this young *swamiji* knew about my *sadhana*!

The young *swamiji* continued, "My *Guruji* told me about you— that you have done the *Srividya* up to *poorna abhishek*, and that you are now in the Himalayas for further *sadhana*, following the order from your *guru*. Will you please teach me the *sadhana*?" It seemed like he had already forgotten about the recent *samadhi* of his *guru*. I had left my *Guruji* recently too and she was still alive but even then I missed her badly. But this young *sadhu*, only moments before we had conducted his *Guruji's samadhi* in the *Ganga* and yet he did not seem sad.

This young *swamiji's* name was Vigyanand Saraswati. He told me that his *Guruji* was born and brought up in Bihar, and stayed there till the day of his entering *sanyas*. His *Guruji* then stayed in that hut for several years. The young *swami* said, "I am from Saharanpur in Uttar Pradesh. I joined him three years ago. He taught me *Chandi Paath* and other *sadhanas*. Six months ago, he initiated me into *sanyas* and asked me to live in Devprayag. Now I feel I am all alone. Please take care of me." I was wondering what I could do for this *swamiji*. My life itself was dependent on others. How could I feed him? Where would he stay? But one thought was powerful—I should not say anything negative as his *Guruji* had taught me *Chandi Paath* and even though his *guru* was a *siksha guru* to me, this young *swamiji* was like my *guru bhai*. I should not say anything negative to him.

He stayed with me for a few days. Whatever the *panditji* brought me as *bhiksha* I shared with him. We both lived on half-full stomach every day. One day I told him, "*Maharaj*, I am not a *guru* to initiate you in *Srividya*. But I will tell you something about the *Srividya sadhana*." But he was adamant that he should get at least the '*Tryakshari*' *mantra* from me. I consulted the *panditji* to astrologically check for a good day for *deeksha*. Now we had another problem. This *panditji* also had accepted me as a *guru* even though I had not given him any *deeksha*. Now I had to initiate both of them. *Panditji* decided on a good day for *deeksha*, reminding me that he was the first person who had requested me for *deeksha*. I had to accept this as there was no way out. It was in the month of January that I initiated both of them in '*Tryakshari Mantra*'.

The night before the *deeksha*, both of them stayed in the *mandir* itself. That night I was thrilled that I was becoming a *guru* at such a young age. I prayed and prayed to my *Guruji* for hours together to give me the strength to give *deeksha* to my first disciples. That night, I had a vision of my *Guruji* in a dream asking me to go ahead and not to worry as she would take care of everything. Next morning all three of us went to the *Ganga* for bathing. Then we sat on the sand and I initiated *panditji* first and then the young *swamiji*. Both were happy and did *namaskaras* to me repeatedly after *deeksha*. Now it was time for accepting *guru dakshina*. *Panditji* brought some money and tried to offer it to me. Pointing to the wild flowers on the banks of the Ganga, I told him, "Don't give me money. Just pick the flowers and offer them as your *guru dakshina*." Both of them picked the wild flowers and offered them as *dakshina* and did *namaskars*. I told them that the real *guru dakshina* is not money or food or clothes but offering me *sadhana*.

That means to do your *sadhana* as has been taught and reach the goal. That is the real *guru dakshina*.

They both nodded and then I said, "*Swamiji*, you are a *maharaj*. Don't stay with me anymore. Go back to Devprayag and do your *sadhana* there as your *Guruji* said. Now you can add this *mantra* also to your *sadhana*. I am depending on this *panditji* for food and shelter. You please don't depend on me. Let me be alone and allow me to do my *sadhana*. As per your desire, I have given the first part of *Srividya mantra* to you. Srividya is a *krama deeksha*. Do this *mantra japa* for nine lakh times and then come back to me. I will give you the 'Panchadasi mantra' then." And I told *panditji*, "This is applicable to you also. *Panditji*, you have served me for several months. Without my permission, you accepted me as your *guru*. Now you do this *japa* for nine lakh times then I will surely initiate you in 'Panchadasi'.

The three of us came back to the *mandir* and bowed in prostration to *Maa*. Now it was time for the young *sanyasi* to leave me. I offered half of the food the *panditji*'s son had brought for me. He was also happy that his father had been initiated into *Srividya mantra* that day. After taking food, the *Swamiji* was ready to leave, and while prostrating he asked, "*Maharaj*, allow me to come and see you occasionally." I agreed, and then he left for Devprayag.

The *panditji* also left for his village. Now as usual I was all alone. But some thoughts came to my mind. Who made me a *Guruji*? First this *panditji* used to call me *Guruji*. Now it was official as I had initiated him into *Srividya* and accepted him as my disciple. I was wondering what was happening to me. I prayed to my *Guruji* to keep me under her care, that I not develop an ego because of attaining *guru* status. I went to the cave and lay down for some time.

Moving Out From Vyas Ghat

Days were passing by very peacefully. *Shivaratri* was near. In the Himalayan hills, *Shivaratri* is as important as *Navaratri*. All the people used to assemble in the courtyard of the village and sing and dance in praise of Shiva and Parvati.

Prof. Bhagawati Prasad came one day to meet me on his way before going to the village. I told him about my plan to move out of Vyas Ghat and to go to the upper Himalayas. My plans were to go to Badrinath/Kedarnath or Gangotri/Yamunotri. The professor told me that the temples would open only on *Akshaya tritiya* (in April). Before the temples opened it would be risky to move on the snow-clad hills. The professor went on to his village. The next day the *pandit* told me that it was risky to go just then. I had to wait for two more months—or up until May. But my mind was not ready to accept this theory. Why should I fear anything, when my *Amma*, my *Guruji*, was with me? That was the thought dominating me. I decided to leave for Gangotri after *Shivaratri*.

A lot of villagers assembled at the mandir on *Shivaratri* day. Day and night there were *bhajans* and *poojas*. Everybody was fasting or in *upavas*. During the night we had four *poojas*. And in the morning the villagers cooked rice, *dal* and vegetables and served everybody after offering to Shiva and *Amma*. We all enjoyed the '*bhandara*' (this is the word often used for common feast in North India).

I remember one day before *Shivaratri*, that young *swamiji* whom I had initiated into *Srividya*, came to meet me from Devprayag. He looked very happy and he said that he had completed the chanting nine lakh times. The *panditji* was also present. *Panditji* had yet to complete the required chanting. I had told both of them that if they completed the nine lakh times chanting before *Shivaratri*, I would initiate both of them into *panchadasi mantra* on *Shivaratri* day. Both had agreed.

Therefore, I initiated both in *panchadasi* on *Shivaratri* day as *panditji* was also able to complete his chanting. I was now ready to move the day after *Shivaratri*. No preparations were necessary as I had no possessions. I told the young *swami* that I would go with him up to Devprayag. From there I would decide where to go. *Panditji* was not happy with my proposal. Prof. Bhagawati Prasad said, "*Maharaj*, in fact we want you to be with us. I don't know what is attracting me towards you. Please don't go. Be here, whatever facilities are needed I will take care of it." However, as I am firm by nature, if I once decide on something, I will not look back or change my decision.

Next day the *Vaishnav Baba* also came to meet me. I was getting ready to move ahead. He also said, "*Maharaj*, winter is still not over. Why can't you wait for a few months?" But I said, "It is my nature that once decided I will not change my programme whatever may happen." This *swabhava* (nature or habit) has been with me from childhood. I paid my homage to mother goddess, remembering my *Guruji* in that form, and then bid farewell to the cave, *panditji* and the few villagers assembled there. *Vaishnav Baba* followed me up to his hut and the young *swamiji* was with me.

On the way I met the same Khadeswari Baba, who was standing still. As it was noon, his disciple was feeding him; I looked at him hesitantly and moved way. A few villagers were moving towards Devprayag. They were bowing in prostration to both of us while we walked fast.

Devprayag was not far from there, we could reach there within a few minutes. The young *swami* said, "Stay with me in my small cottage for a few days and then both of us can go to the Himalayas as you wish." I was not ready to take him with me. I wanted to face all situations by myself, all alone. I told him, "Of course, I have no problem in staying with you for two or three days. But for upper Himalayas, I am sorry; I will not be able to take you with me, because I want to do the journey alone." We reached

Devprayag. The young *swami* was staying in a small cottage made of some leaves and wood. In this cottage he had arrangements for cooking his food—a stove, a few aluminium vessels, and one or two steel plates. He said that before sunset he would bring some groceries and went to the small bazaar opposite the *Ganga*. I also went to the *ghats* where I had met my Ashamayee and stood silent for some time there.

I sat looking at the *Ganga*, and was lost in my thoughts of the days I had with Ashamayee here at this same ghat. One *Swamiji* came to me and asked, "Oh, you are back; you were staying in Vyas Ghat, is it not?" I nodded. "Why have you come to Prayag now? It is too cold now; where will you stay?" I told Swamiji that I would stay with that young *swamiji* for a couple of days and then move to upper Himalayas. In a very rough voice he said, "No, no, this is not the time to move to upper Himalayas. You stay at Devprayag and then move after a few months."

I wondered why these people were dictating terms to me about my movements. I opted to stay at that *ghat* for the night. But the young *swamiji* asked me to stay in his cottage. I declined, as I had decided to stay at the *ghat*. He left and after some time brought me some *rotis* and vegetables. It had become dark with nightfall. I was sitting all alone at the *ghat*. There was the sound of 'hara, hara, hara...' (The sound of Mother *Ganga* flowing).

I think I fell asleep sitting and leaning on the step behind me. The sound of '*beta*' awoke me. To my wonder, I saw my beloved Ashamayee standing near me. But how was it possible? Ashamayee was at Triyuginarayan, very far from here. How could she be here? I said to myself, yes it is a *swapna* (dream) only. But it was not a simple vision.

She sat near me and started talking to me. "Son, you are not willing to listen to anybody's words. What you decide, must happen. Very typical nature you have! But now I am telling you— be here, at Devprayag, and do your *sadhana* till *Akshaya tritiya*. After that day you may leave. Move to Gangotri first." I was not in a position to refuse *Amma* who is very much like my beloved *Guruji*. I accepted her words, but asked, "Mayee, will you please allow me to live in freedom here at this *ghat*? I will go to the nearby village and get my *bhiksha*. But I do not want to be with anybody in cottage or *ashram* or a house. If you permit this, I will stay here at Devprayag as per your orders."

She looked at me once again, "All right, be here, but take care of your health. You don't have any warm clothing other than that blanket. Is that sufficient for you to cope with the cold here?" I told *Amma* not to worry, as both she and my *Guruji* were there to take care of me. Ashamayee disappeared in the darkness. Even today I wonder whether it was a dream or reality. So, obeying *Mayee*'s order I decided to stay on there at the *ghat* for a few more months.

Stay at the Ghat

As I had taken a decision to stay at Devprayag until *Akshaya tritiya*, I did not want to stay there doing nothing. Therefore, I took up a *sankalp* (solemn vow or determination) for the coming 90 days that I would be at the *ghat* and recite the '*shodashi mantra*'—once again another '*purascharan*'. Last time it was a bit difficult for me to complete the *japa* of 16 lakh '*shodashi mantra*' in 41 days. This time I had at least 90 days to do the *japa*. Also I decided not to go for *bhiksha* or accept any money from anybody. If someone called and gave me *bhiksha* I would accept it—that was my decision. Winter was in full swing. Covering my body from head to toe with my blanket, I sat on the banks of the *Ganga*, and did *japa*.

But it was indeed a wonder that during these days even though I did not go to the village or to any other place for *bhiksha*, I was served *bhiksha* daily by someone coming to me. Sometimes food was brought by travellers, at time by villagers or the young *swamiji* whom I had initiated into *Srividya*, or some other *sadhus* staying in Devprayag. I was always remembering the caring touch of my *Guruji* as well Ashamayee. They had seen to it that I should never lack food. As I had opted for the sky as my roof and the earth as my shelter, and possessed nothing else, I felt free and happy like I wanted to be.

As days were passing by, I noticed that my body was again getting emaciated as I had not been taking any nutritious food. Of course there was weakness, since I ate only once a day but I never bothered about that.

One day some young men (college students perhaps) from Delhi came for a trip to Devprayag. I discovered that they were merely educated fools. They came near and sat for some time, trying to tease me with sarcastic words in English. For a while I kept quiet and was sitting as if I was unable to understand the language. But when they crossed limits, I started to speak to them in English and they were surprised that I was educated. I told them, "It seems you are all educated fools. You may have some preconceived notions about a *swami* or a *maharaj*. It need not always be like what you imagine. Look, I will tell you one thing, the life of a *sadhu* is not as you think. You see only his external appearance. You must try to see him with your inner eye. Only then will you understand him. So whenever you go to any *sadhu/maharaj* try to be more polite and enquire about the secrets of life." When I concluded, they were wondering what might happen to them. They apologized to me and offered me some money for my needs. I told them, "I never accept or keep money with me. My *Guruji* takes care of all my needs. I never worry about food or shelter like you people. You have plans to rise up high in your lives in terms of materialism. But I am not like that. Regarding what I need, my *guru* knows it better than I do. So tell me, when your parents were taking care of your needs, were you ever worried?" They understood what I was trying to convey. Once again they said they were sorry for teasing me, and vowed to never do such acts in the future. They were all journalism students in Delhi. One of them asked for permission to come and meet me during his holidays and I agreed. They then left me.

The days were passing smoothly and my *japa* was in progress. Every day the young *swamiji* would come to me and ask if I needed anything. His daily coming and asking was just mechanical. So one day I told him not to come to me daily and that he not need check as I needed nothing. I asked him to concentrate on his *sadhana* instead of moving around me.

One day the old *Vaishnav Baba* from Vyas Ghat came to Devprayag and met me. He was with me for a few hours. He had come to Devprayag for some purchases. He was happy that I had not resumed my journey to the upper Himalayas that winter. He said that in fact he was planning to go the Yamunotri that season.

Sometimes I felt these people were talking only just to while away time. I was not of that type and was trying to be serious in my *sadhana*. If I wasted time I would not be able to complete my *japa* in the fixed time. So I wanted to leave the *ghat*, and find another suitable place for sitting in *japa* where nobody could easily notice me. I found a place just a few yards from the *ghat*, covered with bushes. I was able to sit there for hours together doing *japa*. A few known people who used to bring me food, discovered where I was sitting, but they came only at *bhiksha* time and never disturbed me with small talk.

Almost three months passed with the same routine; my full concentration was on *japa* only. My hair and beard started matting. It was a bit difficult for me to maintain my hair and beard. I was not using any soap or shampoo. So my body stank a bit. There were no additional clothes, so the old clothes started to tear. But my attention was not on all this.

I completed the *japa* in ninety days. Now my mind was again on the pilgrimage to the Himalayas. When the *swamiji* came to meet me I told him that I had completed another *'purascharan'* and was ready to move to somewhere in the upper Himalayas. He was wondering how although I had nobody to call my own, yet everybody and everything were mine, for I had many to bid farewell to, in Devprayag. To the people who gave me *bhiksha* daily, to Mother *Ganga*, to the bushes that had hidden me for months from the eyes of the public, or to the sky that had always sheltered me. I felt they were all within me. And so it follows that it would not be necessary to say any farewell words to anybody, for if I did so, it would be as though I were bidding farewell to myself!

I slept on the *ghat* steps that night. Though it had been a very cold day, the weather was slowly changing. I saw somebody crossing the *Ganga* walking over the water. Slowly the person came into view. It appeared to be an old *swamiji* wearing a white robe, with a white beard and matted hair. I stood up in fear. How could a man have crossed the *Ganga* by walking over water? Even imagining it was impossible. The *swamiji* came close, and I touched his feet. They felt wet as if he had just washed his legs.

Without any preface and as if he had known me for a long time, he said, "You don't' believe it? It is always like that—our own eyes disbelieve what they see. But we believe everything that is in books. I know you have completed your second '*purascharan*' of *Srividya japa* in the Himalayas. Congratulations. But try to continue and keep up this fire within you always." In all foolishness and fear, I asked the *Swamiji*, "May I know *Maharaj* who you are and where you are coming from? Though I have never seen you before, you seem to know everything about me." He replied, "I met Tara Mayee in Mookambika a few days ago. I was on a journey to the South Indian temples. In winter, I travel to the south on pilgrimage. Tara Mayee said that her son was somewhere in Devprayag and asked me to meet him." I wondered about the *leelas* (divine play and wisdom) of my *Guruji*. Sitting in Mookambika, nearly 2,000 km away, she knew where I was, and her loving eyes were looking at me always (in the way a turtle, sitting on one bank of a river, watches over her eggs which are on the other bank). The *swamiji* brought a handful of '*payasam*' which my *Guruji* had given him to pass it to me. It was wrapped in the leaf of a teakwood tree and the payasam had almost dried up, having been sent a few days back. I took it with all reverence and tears in my eyes. Once again I was getting something to eat which had been touched by the hands of my *Guruji*. I was so happy that in my hurry I forgot to offer a part of it to the *Swamiji*. I apologized to him for that act. Then the *Swamiji* said, "While I was returning from Mookambika, Tara Mayee said to take this *payasam* for you. If at all I was unable to meet you at Devprayag, she had asked me to cast this in the *Ganga*."

I wept, and it was difficult for the *Swamiji* to console me. After a few minutes the *Swamiji* left the way he had come, walking on the *Ganga* waters. I sat all alone on the steps of the *ghat*, lost in thoughts of my *Guruji* and the *prasadam* she had sent for me through an unknown person.

Towards Upper Himalayas

The next morning I left Devprayag. The young *swamiji* came with me up to the main road after crossing *Ganga*. He said, "*Swamiji*, if you are going to Gangotri, the route is via Rishikesh, Uttarkashi. If you prefer to walk it is okay, but you can definitely catch a ride on trucks that go in that direction as they will take you to Uttarkashi free of cost." I preferred to walk. Leaving the *swamiji* behind without another word, I moved towards Rishikesh. Rishikesh was not so far from there; I walked and walked and walked.

Near Rishikesh was a famous cave where Swami Purushottamananda Maharaj lived for a long time. I had seen the signboard of the cave and went there. A disciple of Swami Purushottamanandaji was there. He welcomed me wholeheartedly. It was almost sunset time. He asked me to bathe and attend the *arathi*. Before I left for a bath in *Ganga*, he offered me coffee in a steel cup. Since leaving my home, this was the first time I was drinking coffee. Even in Mookambika I never had a chance to have a cup of coffee. I had it, washed the glass and went for a bath. I was tired after walking. After *arathi*, swami offered me some food. As this *swamiji* was from South India, his food was pure South Indian with plenty of masala and chillies. As I had not had such spicy food in a long time, it was not so easy for me to finish the food offered.

Swamiji asked about me, my *Guruji* and my travel plan. Since he had been staying a long time here in this cave, he had not been to Mookambika after leaving Kerala. But of course he said he had definitely heard about the *leelas* of my beloved *Guruji* from the *yatris* (travellers) coming from Kerala. *Swamiji* told me about his experiences during his journeys to Gangotri, and he added that

Uttarkashi was a wonderful place for *sadhana* and that I should stay there for a few months. He also said it was better to go by foot and not depend on anyone for food, as the villagers on both sides of the road were used to wandering monks, and would definitely offer alms. Himalayan villagers consider it their *dharma* to feed wandering monks, even though they may not have sufficient food for themselves. *Swamiji* asked me to move in the early hours before sunrise so as I could cover more miles before sunset. But I was not in a hurry to reach anywhere!

Next day morning before leaving *Swamiji* offered me a cloth and a few hundred rupees. I told him very politely that I needed nothing other than the blessing of a Himalayan saint like him, and added that I was not used to keeping money with me. He pressed me to at least accept the cloth which was *kashaya* coloured. My cloth was almost torn. I accepted the cloth from the *Swamiji* and taking my old cloth to the *Ganga* I threw it in. *Swamiji* was looking at my actions. He said, "Are you a *parama virakt*,[22] you are not willing to keep even one extra cloth with you. I do not understand how you will survive in the cold at Gangotri?" I simply replied, "With the blessings of my *Guruji*," and departed. Now I was moving through the roads in front of Sivananda Ashram. I moved fast as I did not want to be spotted by any *swamis* or *brahmacharis* known to me. After a while I could see the roads climbing up to a new road. This might be the bypass to Uttarkashi.

I saw the tollgate or check post and went there and sat awhile. A forest guard was sitting there and I asked him how many days it would take to reach Uttarkashi. He said it all depends–a minimum of five or six days. I sat for some time there and then started walking.

I was moving constantly. On the way I visited the famous Kunja Devi Mandir and stayed there for a couple of days. The *poojari* was very cooperative. This is one of the famous temples in Uttarakhand, and I noticed that most of the people in the Himalayas were *Shakti* worshippers. The mandir was on top of the hill so it was very cold.

---

22 Person with absolute indifference to worldly pleasures. Renouncer of all material

Along the way down the *mandir,* there were many roadside hotels, since all buses for Uttarkashi halt there for food. A few buses bound for Uttarkashi were there, and *yatris* were taking food. I stood like a fool in front of a hotel, and after a few minutes was ready to move from there towards Uttarkashi. An old man frying *bhoota* (corn) offered me a piece from his basket. That was my lunch and dinner for that day.

It was the third day of my walking and I was as tired as a dog running for hours. In the afternoon, I sat by the roadside, and leaning against a tree, slept for a while. Hearing a sound I woke up. It was about sunset hour. One Muslim lady (maybe a *gujjar,* from a community that keeps buffalos and sheep and moves around collecting grass for them) was standing in front of me. She asked whether I had had food. I said that I had eaten nothing other than just one corn the whole day. She went down the hill to where they kept their animals near a small hut where their family lived. By that time two children emerged from the hut and came towards me. They were staring at me curiously for some time. I called them, but perhaps they were afraid, for they did not come. The Muslim lady came, carrying two big *rotis,* some *chutney* made of leaves and a glassful of milk too. She offered them to me, and with a lot of happiness I accepted the food in my *kappar.* While I was eating, I saw two *Naga sadhus* pass by; they noticed me taking food, and stopped for a while and shouted at me.

They said, "*Saala, sharam nahi aati hai? Muslim ka roti khata hai. Tum koi baba nahi dikta hai. Paakhandi hai.* (Aren't you ashamed? Eating Muslim roti. You are no *baba,* but a hypocrite.) While continuing to eat, I told them, "*Maharaj,* I am not eating Muslim roti, this is wheat roti!" My sarcasm disturbed them and murmuring something they left. I told the Muslim Gujjar lady, "*Maa,* these people seem very orthodox. Don't feel bad about those words." Then I added, "*Mata,* I never take milk. So, please give me some water. She took the milk and went to the other hut to bring some buttermilk and some water. The two rotis made by the Gujjar Muslim lady were very large and with those two *rotis* my stomach was full. I took the buttermilk and sat there for some time. Since the sun was about to set I opted to stay on the roadside for the night. The gujjar woman reappeared. This time her husband was also with her. Both of them sat near me and I didn't mind even though they smelled of sweat, for they were kind. They asked me, "*Maharaj,* can you give us some water from your *kamandal (jal pathra)?* Since the last two days one of our buffalos has been having some swelling, she is not giving milk." I wondered what they would do with my *kamandal* water. Maybe their belief would serve the purpose. I handed them my *kamandal.* They took it over to the buffalo and sprinkled some water from it on her udder and also sprinkled water in their hut and brought me back the *kamandal.* While they were sprinkling the water they were chanting some *mantra.* I asked them what they were chanting. They were quiet for some time. At my insistence they told me it was the '*Bismillah mantra*'. My inner voice guided me to get that *mantra* from them—it might be useful to me too in the future. I asked them, "*Mata,* will you please teach me that mantra? They kept quiet and went to their hut.

Early morning I went to the nearby *jharna,* washed my face and hands and was ready to move. The old woman came with a small glass full of black tea and to my wonder, said, "Because of your *kamandal jal,* my buffalo gave milk and there is no more swelling from where we milk her." She asked me to take the tea and wash my hands and face again.

Avadhoota Nadananda

Avadhoota Nadananda in Younger Days

The First Day of Sanyasa Deeksha

Prasobh Maharaj

Cave of Mast Ram Baba

Shri Mast Ram Baba

Sadhana in Himalayas

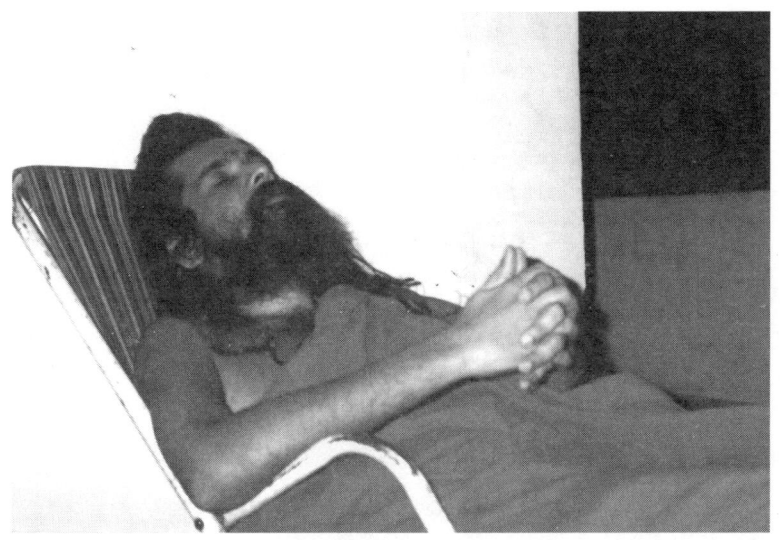

In Bhava Samadhi

Entrance of the Ashram in Jammu

Gaddi at Jammu Ashram

The Initiation into Bismillah Mantra

She sat near me, and said, "Take the *mantra* which we chanted yesterday that you asked for. This will definitely be useful to you in the future." She chanted it in my ears three times. I memorized the *mantra* in no time—another initiation I received from someone other than my *guru*. Then I thought to myself, "Why am I thinking, other than my *guru*." I corrected myself—I must think, my *guru* has appeared to me in another form and given me the *mantra*—yes. Of course, it was certainly like that. She asked me not to leave yet as she would prepare a few *rotis* for the journey. She said Uttarkashi is near and if I start now, I can easily reach there by night.

The Muslim lady brought 2 to 3 rotis with her and the same *chutney*. I told her that being a *sanyasi*, I am not supposed to have '*parigraha*' (accumulate anything for future use), and I would not carry the *rotis* with me, but of course I would eat the *rotis* sitting near her. She was happy. This time the two children came near me again, and when I called out to them they came near, maybe because their mother was also sitting near. I asked the children to share *rotis* with me, and I started feeding them with my own hands. They ate one *roti* and I took one from the remainder. The lady asked me if I would eat anymore, if I waited for a few minutes she could prepare some more for me. I declined and after a few minutes of eating *roti* I was ready to move. The lady had tears in her eyes and asked me to stay there for another day. She said when she saw me she remembered her dead son who had drowned in the *Ganga*. Something was holding me back. I was thinking about the mother who had given birth to me, and my *Guruji* who gave me rebirth. This woman, even though a stranger, had given me the '*Bismillah Mantra*', and had fed me with all love and affection the night before and that morning too. She was like another mother to me. She was remembering her own son who had died in the *Ganga* when she looked at me. I could see tears in her eyes. I decided to stay back that day and then move towards Uttarkashi next morning.

The Muslim lady and her husband both went to collect grass. The children were sitting next to me. Looking at their faces and mud-covered bodies, I could see that they had not bathed for a few days. I told them that I had not had a bath since the day before and that we could all bathe in that stream. While I was bathing the children, the lady returned and was astonished to see the *maharaj* bathing her children. She brought a few clothes from her hut and changed clothes for the children, and I too bathed and went to sit under a tree.

Once again the lady offered a plate of food. This time it was rice and *dal* and the same *chutney*. I noticed that butter had been put in the *dal*. She also brought a few green chillies and salt. I asked her to put everything together into my *bhiksha pathra*. While she was serving me, her husband arrived with lot of grass on his head. Keeping the grass there, he also joined her in serving rice. Even though he had not washed his hands before serving, I accepted the food he served. External cleanliness is much less important than internal cleanliness.

This Muslim couple were very pure in their minds, I thought. When she was serving food, there were tears in her eyes. She was perhaps recalling the days she fed her son who drowned in the *Ganga*. I had a happy time with those people. My mind was attracted to them too, and telling me not to leave them. But I had to go, I must go. Once long ago I had left my mother, my *guru*, and now this mother. I wondered what it was in me that attracted all these people.

Next morning I was ready to resume my journey. The Muslim lady came with tea. I took it considering it *prasadam* from a *guru*, as it was she only who had initiated me into the *Bismillah mantra*. With her permission, I started for Uttarkashi.

Life at Uttarkashi

The days at Uttarkashi were very different. In the evening when I reached Uttarkashi, I spent many hours wandering around in the small town due to unfamiliarity with the place. On the way to the main market I came across a *swamiji* and asked where I might get an accommodation, even though I was not really interested in staying in any ashram. My *Guruji* had given me strict instructions right at the beginning about never ever staying in an *ashram*, and try to remain independent. The *swamiji* informed me that if I travelled one or two miles towards Gangotri road, I would reach a place known as Ujjaily, which was like a colony of *sadhus/sanyasis* where they stayed in different *ashrams*.

I met a *brahmachari* from Rishikesh Ashram who took me to the branch of the Sivananda Ashram at Ujjaily. The *swamiji* there was very generous and said that I could stay there if I wished. But I opted for the *verandah* or the *ghat*. He didn't agree to that and gave me a set of keys to a place across the road known as Sanatkumar cottage. He said I could easily stay there as it was vacant at the time. The owner of that cottage, a Bengali *swamiji*, was in Calcutta and would be back after five or six months. I went there with the *brahmachari* who was also willing to stay with me. The cottage was big, with two/three rooms and a cave in the basement. I opted to stay in the cave.

The system at Uttarkashi was very different. Every *sadhu* had to go someplace in order to receive *bhiksha* except for the aged and sick. In the mornings I would see *sadhus* walking on the road towards the *annakshetras* (almonries, a place where free food is distributed to wandering monks). There were three well-known *annakshetras*. Kala Kambliwala was the oldest, Punjab-Sindh

Annakshetra and Dandi Ashram. At Kala Kambliwala we used to get five *rotis* and vegetables or *dal*; at Punjab-Sindh *roti*, rice, *dal* and vegetable; and at Dandi Ashram rice and *dal*, often vegetables or some sweets. I would usually go to Kala Kambliwala, collect my share of *roti* and then move on to Dandi Ashram for rice. Evenings, all of us *sadhus* would assemble at Kailash Ashram in Ujjaily for *bhiksha*. *Sadhus* at Ujjaily, after collecting their *bhiksha*, took it to their rooms and added some masala or seasoning to the dal, etc. The morning's *bhiksha* would be sufficient for the evening as well. It was only very rarely that we went for evening *bhiksha* at Kailash Ashram.

Once during the *bhiksha* at Kala Kambliwala kshetra, I met *Swami* Mangalananda, who has a well-built cottage at Mangala *ghat* known as Mangala Ashram. That *swamiji* was from Kerala state and had been living in Ujjaily for a long time. He asked me to visit his cottage and so the next day after collecting my *bhiksha* and having it on the banks of the *Ganga*, I went to meet the *swamiji*. He introduced me to other *swamijis* from Kerala who had come from Gangotri. Swami Bhumananda and Swami Samprasadananda were well known for their scholarship in *Vedanta*.[23] They were from Sri Ramakrishna Mission and disciples of Swami Eeswarananda of Kerala.

To my amazement, Ujjaily was full of *swamijis* from Kerala and Bengal. Even now I cannot think of a reason why most of the Bengali and Malayali *swamijis* chose to do their *sadhana* in Ujjaily.

Of course, Ujjaily was a very beautiful location—calm, serene with beautiful scenery. I was staying for more than one week in that Sanat cottage. Feeling guilty that I was staying there in spite of my *Guruji* having cautioned me against depending on *ashrams*, I went one day to the *swamiji* at Sivanand Ashram, and returned the keys back to him. By this time the *brahmachari* who stayed with me had left for Gangotri. Once again I went to Mangala Ashram and asked *swamiji* to give permission to stay at his *ashram ghat*. He refused and said that if at all I wanted to stay, it would be at

---

23 A Hindu philosophy based on the doctrine of the Upanishads, especially in its monistic form.

his *ashram*. The *Ganga ghats* belong to none. They are owned by *Ganga Mata* only. With that impression in my mind, I went back to Ujjaily and started staying at a *ghat* near the Sanat cottage. *Swamis* who used to come to bathe would look at me very suspiciously and cautioned that it is not a good idea to stay there as the *ghat* was frequented by small poisonous snakes. I was in no mood to listen to their words. Days had been passing without any *sadhana*, and I thought I should make proper use of my time and for that reason, I decided to start another *purascharan* of *Srividya* at the *ghat* itself.

The next day I did not go for *bhiksha*; instead started my *japa* in the morning itself, after taking a s*ankalp* of my *Shodashi purashcharan*. Around 11 am Swami Bhumanandji came in search of me and asked why I had not gone for *bhiksha*. He also brought some *rotis* and vegetables for me. The system in Ujjaily is that, if any of the known sadhus is not seen at the *Annakshetras*, then definitely one of the *sadhus* would come to enquire about his welfare and pass on the alms. I told him that as I had mentioned earlier I had started a *purascharan* of *Srividya*, and had not gone for *bhiksha*, and assured him that I would take *bhiksha* from the next day onwards. He also brought good news from Swami Mangalananda that he had accepted my request of staying at his *ghat*. But some ego was driving my mind—now why should I go back to him. I told this to Bhumanandaji, but he laughed that I could not cast off my ego for this small matter. He persuaded me to go the *ghat* of Mangala Ashram. Most of the senior *swamijis* who were well known for their scholarship never used to do much ritual. They just recited the *Shiva Mahimna stotra* in the evening time in their cottages/*ashrams*.

But I was neither a mature *sanyasi* nor a scholar. I had taken the *sankalp* to do *japa* of *shodashi* 16 lakh times, and I was adamant about it. Bhumananda took me back to Mangala Ashram and the *swamiji* who had spoken to me roughly the day before and denied me stay at the *ashram ghats*, now called me and appreciated my courage at staying at the *ghat* and doing *sadhana*. When he heard from Bhumanandji that I had taken *sankalpa* of the *Srividya purashcharan* and this was my third one on the banks of the *Ganga*, Mangalaanand swamiji was very happy to welcome me to his *ashram*. He told me "If you want to stay at the *ghat*, I would not have any problem. Yesterday I was not in a good mood. Or if you want to stay here in this *ashram,* you are most welcome." I told him that though it was comfortable at the Sanat cottage, remembering my *Guruji's* orders, I felt I was doing a mistake by staying in an *ashram,* and that was why I had opted to stay at the *ghats* in freedom. If I lived in an *ashram* I would have to follow the rules and regulations of the *ashram. Swamiji* enquired about my *Guruji.* He was happy to hear her name, and said, "Two years ago, once during my visit to Mookambika, I met that *Amma* at the temple premises. I know she was a well-known *Avadhoota Mayee* there. Oh! You are lucky to be her disciple."

Bhumananda brought some coffee which we all had during our conversation. *Swamiji* asked me about my possessions, offering me space to keep them in the *Ashram.* I told him that all I had was one cloth, one kambal and a *bhiksha pathra* and *jal pathra.* I never kept money. Hearing that, he was wonderstruck, and laughingly said, "These *Malayalis* are all extremists, either this end or that end."

Days were passing smoothly in the calm and quiet atmosphere of Mangala ghat. Every day once or twice, *Swamiji* would come to enquire if I needed anything. I always would tell him that I needed nothing except for his blessings. Every day before and after *bhiksha* I used to do my *japa.* Then after resting for an hour, I continued *japa* until night. I never went for *bhiksha* during the evenings. Sometimes, Bhumanandaji would bring some tea or coffee, and so I was very happy and contented there. One hot summer night, I was sitting and doing *japa* on a rock near the *ghat* by the stream of the *Ganga.* I saw a shadow on the *ghat* steps, and was a bit nervous, wondering who it could be at that late hour? I got up and moved towards the *ghat.* Reaching there, I was in amazement! It was my *Guruji—Avadhoota Tara Mayee—*standing on the *ghat* looking at me. I thought for a moment—I was not sleeping, but sitting and chanting, so I cannot be dreaming. But how can this be true? I pinched my hand to check whether I was dreaming!

Amma held my hands and asked me to sit near her. Now I knew it was not a dream, it was really happening. She opened a small packet she was carrying and gave it to me. It was full of groundnuts fried in ghee with pepper sprinkled on it. She asked me to eat it. I slowly started eating it and wanted to feed *Amma* some nuts too, so I asked her, "*Amma* please have some groundnuts with me." Saying that I extended my hand towards her. She laughed at me and said, "Arre, you forget that I have no teeth?" At that, tears immediately began flowing down my cheeks. I was thinking that even if this were a dream, it should not end. Was it a dream? Or was it real? I don't know. But it had happened, and even after so many years I still remember it as if it just happened now.

The Stay Continues

I was a bit unhappy with the days, as I was unable to do more *japa* due to the flow of visitors coming to me. I tried stopping them but could not do so, and once asked them not to disturb me as I was doing a *purascharan*. I wondered what it was in me that was attracting at least two or three visitors every day, who were talking about Srividya and other subjects for hours together.

One day I told Mangalanand Swamiji that I was being disturbed, and would like to move elsewhere, requesting him to suggest a place where I could be left alone to do *sadhana* without any trouble. He was not inclined to allow me to leave that *ghat,* and said that he would take care of the visitor problem.

Now the visitors were fewer, and occasionally one or two *swamis* or *brahmacharis* did come, and that only when the *swamiji* was sleeping. If he was there on the *verandah* of his cottage none were allowed to come to me.

Winter was over, and the Chaar Dham temples were now open to pilgrims. Almost two months passed like this with the daily routine of *japa* without disturbance. My mind was at Gangotri and I was planning to move there after completing the *japa* the following month. Bhumanandji and Samprasadanandji left for Gangotri, where they stayed in their caves, during the season.

I was surprised to see one of the *swamijis* I had known in Mookambika at Kala Kambliwala Annakshetra one day. I greeted him politely and asked about everything at Mookambika. He narrated that before leaving, he had met my *Guruji* at the Mookambika temple and she told him that I would certainly be at Uttarkashi. My memories went back to my days at Mookambika, and with tears in my eyes enquired about my *Guruji* and about her health.

Swamiji told me that everything was well at Mookambika and that my *Guruji* was doing well. I was happy to hear that. Even though he asked where I was put up in Uttarkashi, I did not reveal the details, because I was afraid of getting disturbed daily by his visits. However, he was moving towards Gangotri next day.

Days passed without any changes to the routine. It was as usual. One great scholar *swamiji* came from somewhere in Gujarat and was teaching classes on *'Panchadasi'* written by Vidyaranya Muni. This book is one of the most revered ones in *Vedanta*. Mangalananda said if I was interested, I could cut short two hours of *japa* and attend his *pravachan* at Kailash Ashram. I was not much interested in hearing about *Vedanta* as my mind was settled on *japa*. I replied in the negative.

My *japa* was about to conclude. For the last few days I had not been going for *bhiksha* in the *kshetras*. I was depending only on *Ganga jal*. If I went for *bhiksha* I would waste two–three hours. I wanted to utilize that time also for *japa*. The hair on my body would stand on end in *romaharsha* (bristling of the hair in delight) during *japa*. I always heard the *mantra* (*shodashi*) around me, whether I be at the *Ganga*, or on the road. Five days passed without food. Slowly I was becoming weak; sometimes I felt I would be unable to walk even to the *Ganga* which was only a few steps away from me.

I was sure that I would be able to complete my *japa* by the following evening. But here, unlike with the *panditji* at Vyas Ghat, there was nothing with me to do *Homa* with. When Mangalanandji came to me, I asked him "*Swamiji*, by tomorrow evening my *japa* will be over. But I wonder how I will do the *Dasamsha havan* and *tarpan*." Then the *Swamiji* replied, "Look, you have done '*Viraja homa*' and now you are a *sanyasi*. You are not supposed to or even required to do any *havan* or *tarpan*. Instead of that you can do '*Dasamsha japa*'." I was happy to hear the solution given by *Swamiji*, but that meant that there would be one more day of *japa*. I agreed to do that one more day of *japa*.

It was the evening hour when the sun had not yet reached the western sky. But as usual in the Himalayan hills, it was getting dark. I was doing *japa*. But I was very hungry. My body was shivering a little bit from weakness. To my wonder I once again saw my *Guruji* in front of me. This time around it was not night nor was I sleeping. I stopped my *japa* and stood up with difficulty. My *Guruji* held my hands and lifted me from the *asan* and embraced me with all warmth and affection. As usual I was crying. She put her hand into the pocket of her '*alphy*' and took a medium-sized packet, wrapped in leaves and gave it to me, and in an aggressive voice she started scolding me, "I have not sent you here for dying. Who told you not to eat anything? You stupid boy, you are disturbing my mind again and again doing such nonsense. Don't repeat such acts in the future. If you want to do *sadhana*, you must eat something. I told you earlier that this body is the instrument for *sadhana*. If you don't keep your room neat, clean and tidy, how can you sit in it? Likewise, your body should be clean and neat, eat properly and do your *sadhana*. I never thought you were so stupid." Scolding, she asked me to sit and she also sat near me. The packet she gave me was in my hands. I was yet to open it. She took the packet back in her hands and opened it. Aha, the aroma of rice and sambar rushed to my nose. I was amazed how *Amma* had come with rice and sambar! It was unbelievable. She opened the rice packet, packed in plantain leaves and mixing with her own hands, she slowly started feeding me.

I wept, and looking at me *Amma* started scolding again, "You are an idiot, no doubt. I am here and now with you, feeding you with my own hands, yet you cry. What for? See I am alive, not dead. Even if I were dead, you know very well that I would be with you. Don't be foolish. Sit quiet and eat properly." There was no end to my tears. She lifted her hand and with her *alphy* she dried my tears once, twice, thrice. But in my mind there was a guilt feeling that because of me *Amma* had been put to trouble. I made her travel all the way from Mookambika to me; since I had not been eating and was weak she had to come. This is the same with all *gurus*. Whenever the disciples are in distress, the *guru* runs towards the disciple to help. *Amma* kept on feeding me. I saw that because of old age her hands were shivering. It was too much for me to bear.

Never had I got such affection from anywhere, even from my own mother who gave birth to me. I was unable to control my tears. By this time I had probably eaten half of the rice and sambar. I signalled to *Amma* with my hand, that I needed no more, but she was not ready to stop feeding me.

Just like a mother taking care of feeding her small child, she was coaxing me to eat a little more, a little more. After a few fistful of morsels I stopped eating, and I said to *Amma*, "You have not taken any food, *Amma*." She laughed and said, "*Tumko maloom hai, main sab ko khilakar khati hai.*" (She would never eat first, and as mentioned earlier, she would feed birds, reptiles, rabbits, dogs, ants, even serpents and then me and only after that would she take a little bit.) I considered my *Amma* as the embodiment of the goddesses Annapoorna, Lakshmi, Kali, Saraswati, Durga, and others. While taking the remaining food from the plantain leaf she again said "I think you can now move to Gangotri. Remember, Gangotri is extremely cold. Stay there in some safe place and don't forget to eat something daily. You should not do *upavasa*. If you do so, it will be trouble for me, and I have to come all the way to feed you. So do not do any such stupidity in future." (After that I stopped doing *upavas* during my stay in Himalayas.)

She took my hand in her hands for a few minutes. I felt as if some current were passing through my whole body. My body shook for some moments. Then removing her hand from mine, she disappeared just the way she had appeared. This was my last meeting with my *Guruji* in this form during my Himalayan days. She never appeared in her own form, thenceforth. But I had many experiences of her presence in other forms.

My *Guruji* was a *Siddha Avadhoota*. She could easily assume any form and be able to appear anywhere at any time. I know that whatever experiences I had during my Himalayan days are only due to her blessings.

I sat for some more time in the quietness at the *ghat*, mentally preparing for the journey to Gangotri next day.

Towards Gangotri

Next morning after conveying *namaskars* to Mangalanand Swamiji I was about to start for Gangotri by walk. *Swamiji* gave me some instructions about life at Gangotri. He added that I could very well stay with Bhumanandji at his cave. By that time a small group of *Swamiji's* devotees from Lucknow arrived there. They had come by car and were on their way to Gangotri. *Swamiji* asked me, "If you are willing to travel by car, join my disciples. They will take care of you." I declined and opted to travel by foot only, as I was very eager to learn about and understand the pros and cons of Himalayan life. Traveling by car, I could have reached there by evening, but it would have been just mechanical. I told them I preferred to walk.

I was walking by the small market in Bhatwadi on the way to Gangotri when I saw the *Naga sadhus* who had scolded me for eating from the hand of a Muslim lady. They offered me a few fruits and asked me to join them in the journey. As I wanted to travel alone, I did not join them.

I reached Harsil the same day and was tired because of the continuous journey. I sat on the roadside by the *Ganga* banks. I noticed a sign indicating the presence of a military camp there. A few military people in uniform were moving here and there. I sat there for more than two hours. After sometime a military *jawan* came near and asked if I was on my way to Gangotri. I nodded. He also asked whether I had taken any food. I shook my head—since morning I had eaten nothing. The previous day, a roadside shopkeeper had given me some boiled potatoes and tea. That had been all the food for the day. The *jawan* then asked me to follow him. When both of us went inside, another *jawan* asked him in

Malayalam, "Ravindran, why have you brought this *maharaj* here?" The first jawan replied that I was hungry and tired, and he was going to feed me from their mess. When I heard them speak in Malayalam, my affection towards my mother tongue rose up, and I spoke with them in Malayalam, and they were happy to hear that I was also from Kerala. Rice and *dal* were served, and while I was eating, Ravindran the first *jawan* went out for some time. The other *jawan* was talking to me and serving vegetables. Ravindran brought me some mango pickles which he brought from his home when he returned from annual leave. After a long time I was eating something made in Kerala. I ate the food very happily. Finally, he served me rice once again and poured some unflavoured yogurt on my plate. (I did not use my *kappar* for the meal since I assumed these *jawans* were used to eating non-vegetarian food. So I did not want to make my *bhiksha pathra apavitrata* [impure]. I took food in their serving plates. I was having yogurt for the first time since leaving Kerala, and it is one of my favourite foods. I remembered my elder sister then, who used to feed me daily with a mix of yogurt and rice after my return from school.

After food they took me to their barracks, where there were some more Malayali *jawans*. They all spoke with me in great reverence and one of them offered me a packet of cigarettes. I took one and started smoking even though I was not used to that. I was ready to move. The *jawans* in this area are very generous and helpful. They believed in *babas/maharajs*, maybe because they live a risky life in those Himalayan hills. I was ready to move. Ravindran offered me a *kambal*. I refused it saying that if I carried that other military people would suspect me of theft.

Then the other *jawan* opened his box and brought out a civilian *chaadar* made of wool. He said he had got it from Harsil and that even at Gangotri one cannot survive without blankets. He requested me to accept the shawl. As this was purchased from the market the military would not suspect me for this shawl, and I accepted it. Now it was nearing sunset, so they told me to resume pilgrimage the next day as it would be dangerous to move at night. They informed me of a small temple in the military campus, where I could rest and took me to that small *mandir*.

One senior officer was at the temple doing *namaskars*, and he looked at me for a few moments. Ravindran told him in Tamil, "Sir, the *swami* is from Kerala, traveling by foot to Gangotri. We would like to accommodate him on the *verandah* of the temple for tonight." The senior officer did not deny the request. It seemed like he wanted to talk to me, but since the juniors were around him, he kept quiet for some time and then signalled with his hand to his juniors to leave that place. Ravindran and his friends left. The senior officer asked me whether I spoke Tamil. I told him I didn't, but that he could certainly talk to me in English. He talked to me at length on life here and there in different parts of the Himalayas, and finally I noticed his face changing and it seemed like he wanted to talk to me about something very serious. I told him not to worry, that he could speak freely. This appeared to embolden him and he said, "I was married to a woman seven years ago. We have no children and doctors say there is no problem with both of us. But I am anxious, and we are eagerly awaiting that good day when a child would be born to us."

I saw a few drops of tears in his eyes. But what could I do? I was thinking about it. All of a sudden a current passed through me. I told him there was nothing to worry, and that *Bhagavan* (God) is very merciful. I asked where his wife was. She was in his parental home in Kerala. Then I told him to go to Mookambika with his wife on his next annual leave. I told him in detail about my *Guruji*, who was capable of doing anything for the welfare of others. I gave him instructions on reaching my *Guruji*, and told him to take with him a few fruits as offering. If my *Guruji* returned a fruit out of the offering, his desire would be fulfilled. He noted down everything in his small pocket dairy. Before he left, I gave him some *kumkum* which I used to keep with me for daily use, and told him to send it to his wife to use for *tilak* every day after her bath. I was tired and ready to sleep. The senior officer wanted to give me some money. I refused it, telling him I that I never ever kept money. (After few years during my visit to Kamakhya in Guwahati, Assam, I met the same senior officer again at the residence of a colonel with whom I was staying. He recognized me and bowed in prostration, and with tears of joy told me of his meeting with my *Guruji* in Mookambika a month after I had met him at Harsil. He had two children now, both studying in Kendriya Vidyalaya at Guwahati. I too was glad to hear the news. The colonel, with whom I stayed, is a disciple from Haryana, and he asked for details of the episode, and the officer narrated everything to him.)

Early morning Ravindran came to me with a mug full of tea and some biscuits. By this time I had bathed near the temple and was ready to move on. We had tea and biscuits together. He did *namaskars* and I resumed my journey towards Gangotri immediately. By evening, I reached Gangotri. It was very cold there and I was shivering. This was my first time in the upper Himalayas. To see the snow-clad mountains around me and the beauty of *deodar* (Indian native variety of cedar) trees everywhere was enchanting. Here the beautiful *Ganga* looked like a big stream. I reached the *Ganga*, and washing my hands and face, went directly to the temple. It was *arathi* time. A few Garhwali villagers and some pilgrims were there and of course few *sadhu sanyasis* as well. It was not difficult for me to find Swami Bhumanandji with whom I had stayed in Uttarkashi. After *arathi* he told me, "Let us go to my cave. If you like the place, stay there with me." He was direct and plain in speech always. We reached his cave on the other side of the *Ganga*. I noticed several huts with tin shed and some caves. Only a few pukka buildings were there.

Samprasadananda was sitting on a rock near his cave. He got up and welcomed me. He was a very nice person and had no ego of scholarship. They were both *guru bhais* and used to live together at Gangotri and Uttarkashi. Since long time they had not stepped down to Uttarkashi. My belongings were one *kambal* and the *chaadar* given to me by the military man. And of course, my *kamandal (jal pathra)* and *kappar (bhiksha pathra)* were also with me. I was wearing a small cloth ending at my knees. Looking at me, Bhumanandji was irritated, "What are you thinking; this is not your Kerala that you can manage with just one piece of cloth. You are stupid. This is Gangotri, covered fully by snow—you cannot survive here without proper clothes, your *Virakti* has no meaning. If it were possible to realize *Bhagavan* by mere nakedness, then dogs and cows would have surely realized *Bhagavan* before you. You don't recognize that your body is an instrument for your *sadhana*." He then handed me a few *kambals* and an *alphy* from his belongings, saying, "If you want to live here at all, dress properly which will protect you from the cold." I did not take the clothes. I was ready to die. I told him, "*Swamiji*, but with my *Guru's krupa* (grace) nothing will happen. I can tolerate the cold here. You don't worry. I will live with my belongings." There was no reply to this.

Samprasadanad came and told Bhumanandji that it was time to go to Dandi Ashram for night *bhiksha*. I felt that I should not accompany them. When I told them that I was not coming for food, Bhumanandji again shouted at me, "I have never seen a fool like you. *Paramatma* (Supreme Soul - God) has made everything for us here. Now you are here, with your stupid things, and you are not taking anything. See if you don't want to eat dinner, okay no problem, but at least have some milk from the Dandi Ashram with us, for god's sake."

I saw affection in his eyes even though he was speaking to me roughly. I went with him. There in Dandi Ashram, I had a glass full of milk and two or three biscuits. I slept in Bhumanandji's cave that night. He also slept nearby. Bhumanandji was a very good person and I knew he loved me, and wanted me to progress even higher in my *sadhana*. That may have been the reason for him speaking roughly to me. I was tired of the continuous journey, and slept very deeply. In the morning I wanted to go bathe in the *Ganga* but Bhumanandji stopped me, advising against it saying it would be dangerous till I had adjusted to the climate. Two or three days passed in that cave. One day I told Bhumanandji that I would like to start *sadhana* of *Shodashi Purascharan* in Gangotri. Also that I would like to stay at Gangotri for at least four months, as I can complete the *japa* in three months and then visit Gomukh, the place from where Mother *Ganga* originates.

He showed me a small cave near his, which had been unused for a long time. The previous year a Bengali *sadhu* was staying there, but this year he had not come to Gangotri and if it was okay for me I could have a good stay there. I started cleaning the cave as it was quite dirty. Bhumanandji also helped me and it took us more than 3 to 4 hours to clean it. Now my abode was ready to be occupied. Bhumanandji gave me a few cartons and gunny bags to use for spreading out on my *asan* to sleep on. I opened the cartons and spread them over the gunny bags. Now the asan was ready. It was time for *bhiksha*, and we went to have it at Dandi Ashram. One thing I noticed was that being a *sadhu* with *kappar* in hand, I was not allowed to sit in the row of *sadhu sanyasis*, but supposed to take *bhiksha* from the *ashram* door, and sit somewhere outside and eat it. There were two or three *sanyasis* who used to take *bhiksha* in *kappar*. A few *rotis*, some *dal* and rice and vegetables were put in the *kappar* by a *brahmachari*. I could easily notice the reverence towards the *sanyasis* who carried *kappars*. I took the *bhiksha* to my cave and sat there for a while. By that time Bhumanandji and Samprasadanad came after finishing their food at the ashram. I was yet to take my *bhiksha*. Bhumanandji came near me and said, "*Maharaj*, I didn't know that you were using the *kappar*. Wait, I will give you some lemon pickle which we made at Mangal Ashram, in Uttarkashi." He brought the pickle and I then had my first *bhiksha* at Gangotri.

I wanted to begin *sadhana* the next day, and conveyed this to Bhumanandji and his *guru bhai*. I told them I would leave the cave only for *bhiksha* since I wanted to spend the maximum time possible in *japa* with a goal of completing it in ninety days. Making the *sankalp* by the *Ganga*, I came back to the cave with a *kamandal* full of water and began my *japa* of *shodashi*. This was the fourth *purascharan* in Himalayas.

I started the *japa* with great joy. There was a deep silence around the cave. Usually nobody came there except for a few *swamijis* who came to visit their *guru bhais* occasionally. I felt at ease there.

Gangotri Life Continues

My *sadhana* at Gangotri was going very well. Every day after *bhiksha* I would walk around the hills/forests with no aim in mind. My mind was in search of something unknown. Months passed without any disturbance. Suddenly one day, the *swamiji* from Bengal who used to stay in the cave which I was using, arrived. He asked me to vacate his cave. I obeyed since he had been occupying the cave for a few years—though of course, none of the *gufas* (caves) are registered in anybody's name! I vacated and came out. About a month was still left for me to complete my *japa purascharan*. Bhumanandji was at a loss for what to do for my accommodation. I told him not to worry, as I considered this a test for me, a test whether I would leave my *sadhana*. I was better without amenities there. I told Bhumanandji that my *Guruji* was always with me and *Amma* would take care of my needs.

I went around in search of a place where I could sit for *japa* without any more disturbances. Finally a few yards downstream by the Ganga, I noticed a flat rock where I saw a *swamiji* getting ready to leave for Haridwar that day. I went to him and told him of my problem. He happily agreed to give me a tent-like thing made of plastic. Now Bhumanandji also arrived there and spoke to that *Swamiji*. *Swamiji* had no problem giving me that place provided I gave him the amount he had spent for plastic and for putting up the tent. I had nothing with me and so was a bit depressed. Bhumanandji said he would pay for the plastic which cost almost 300 rupees! Thus I managed to get a place to continue my *sadhana*. Only the top of the tent was some kind of plastic material—the sides were all open to the merciless wind.

I occupied that place and resumed *japa*. There were no possessions or money or any valuables, and the only valuables were my *kamandal* and *kappar*, so I had nothing to worry about. It was unlikely that anyone would want these things. And if some person did, I did not care about that either. And why did I need to worry since my *Guruji* was always there to take care of everything for me.

The days at that tent were fine. But the nights were terrible. Now a drizzling rain also started. I shivered at nights because of the chilly wind. I just had one *kambal* and one *chadar* (sheet). Late one night I saw Bhumanandji walking up to me with something in his hands. I continued with the *japa*. He came near and gave me two kambals and asked me to layer them and cover my body to save myself from that biting cold. He also told me that on the day of return, I must give back the *kambals* to him. I was thus saved from the biting cold at Gangotri due to the help of Bhumanandji. Every morning this *swamiji* would give milk and biscuit to the *sadhus* staying at Gangotri. For this he used to bring lots of milk powder every year, and daily he would make milk and distribute it. His *sadhu-seva* (service) mentality was wonderful. I too used to go there and get a packet of biscuits and even though he insisted on my taking some milk too, I never did, as I did not like milk.

The next day started with high fever and body ache. This was due to the wind, which had been blowing all night long. By evening, the fever had gone up much higher and I was unable to move my body from the *kambal*. I was shivering. Somehow, Bhumanandji came to know of my condition and reached me with some tablets. He also collected some firewood from here and there, and made a fire near me on the flat rock where I had been staying. That was my first fire. After a few hours the fever vanished, but I was still very weak. Bhumanandji brought some black coffee made from coffee powder and pepper. That helped very much to keep my body warm.

The next day Bhumanandji suggested that it would be better for my health if I left Gangotri as good treatment was definitely available at Uttarkashi. I was not ready to do so as my mind kept saying that nothing would happen to me; moreover at any cost,

I wanted to complete my *purascharan* at Gangotri itself. Soon I recovered and could easily go for *bhiksha*. On the days I had fever and was unable to walk, Bhumanandji would bring me a few *rotis* and vegetables from the *Annakshetra*. His service mentality was wonderful. The 90th day of my *purascharan* was nearing. I was thinking to myself that within 2–3 days I would be able to reach my goal. I met Bhumanandji at *Annakshetra* and said to him, "By the day after tomorrow, my *japa* will be over. I don't feel I will be able to move to Gomukh this time as my health is not good and I am weak. After completion of my *japa* I will return to Uttarkashi and stay there for some more days before resuming my pilgrimage to the next destination." Swamiji agreed and said that within 4–5 days he would also be going to Uttarkashi to purchase milk powder, and that I should join him. I told I preferred to go by walk as I didn't carry money with me. As usual he once again shouted at me, "Your *virakti* has no meaning! Here *bhakts* (devotees) are coming and giving *dakshina* for the use of our people. You are a fool to not accept money, and now when you are in need who will help you? Anyway, it's not a problem; I will take a ticket for you up to Uttarkashi. You can come with me. I will see that you get good treatment for your health at Uttarkashi."

Next day I was supposed to leave Gangotri. I went around the cottages and caves and one or two small *ashrams* in Gangotri and did *namaskaras* to all *sadhus* and *sanyasis* and bid farewell to them. We took the early morning bus to Uttarkashi and reached there around sunset. Both of us went directly to Mangala Ashram, where I stayed before coming to Gangotri.

Stay at Ashram Verandah

With the permission of Swami Mangalananda I started staying on the verandah of the *ashram*. Mangalanandji insisted on me staying in the room, but I was not willing. The next day Bhumanandji took me to a doctor in the government dispensary and after preliminary check-up and a blood test he gave some medicines. I was too weak to go for *bhiksha* at Kali Kambili Annakshetras as it was bit far away from the *ashram*. Bhumanandji left for Gangotri after purchases.

After few days, I recovered from the weakness and fever, and was able to go to the *kshetras* for my daily *bhiksha*. During the days of illness, one *brahmachari* known to Mangalanandji brought me *rotis* and *dal* every day. Those days passed by without any *sadhana*, and I was feeling very bad that I was just sitting and eating. Once, Mangalanandji asked me if I wished to study *Vedanta*. I was not interested in studying, in those days, and was willing to do only *japa sadhana*.

Once again I wanted to start my *shodashi purascharan*, but the *swamiji* said, "You have just recovered from illness. Be here and take rest for a month or two, and then better move to Haridwar and stay somewhere there and do your *sadhana*. I agreed to his suggestion and stayed there. *Swamiji* gave me some Malayalam books on Vedanta and I started reading them regularly. *Swamiji* wanted me to read them loudly for him, so I did that every day and *swamiji* would listen attentively.

After a few days, the thought to move on from Uttarkashi again began to overpower my mind. However, because of the fear of *swamiji*, I kept the idea hidden in my mind only. The book reading was almost complete. Then *swamiji* brought out another famous book—*The Gospel of Sri Ramakrishna*—and asked me to start this one.

This was the second time I was reading that book. During my college days I ran away from home once and reached Sri Ramakrishna Ashram in Thrissur. I told the *swamiji* in-charge of the *ashram* that I wanted to join the Ramakrishna Mission, and after a day's stay there I was sent to the Kancheepuram branch of the mission, to Swami Smaraharananda. That *swamiji* was very old and another young *swamiji* from Ceylon was also staying there. I was entrusted with the work of cleaning the temple utensils (*pooja pathras*, etc.) and mopping the *mandir* hall. Smaraharananda who was also from Kerala gave me the same book in Malayalam, and made me read it daily after lunch. *Swamiji* used to hear about the life and teachings of Sri Ramakrishna. (Just as I ran away from home and reached the Kancheepuram Ashram, the same way I ran away one day from the *ashram* too and went back home. What a foolish boy I was in those days!). Mangalananda and I were enjoying the gospel-like nectar, and he would give me explanations in the middle of the readings, upon the words of Sri Ramakrishna. In fact, this was the book that added fuel to the fire in me, which gave me *vairagya* in my younger days.

Life at Mangala Ashram was going on smoothly. Almost one month had passed when I told *swamiji* one day that I would like to make a move to Haridwar as he suggested. But he said that I should leave only after completing the book. Even though he scolded me sometimes (because of my foolishness) that *swamiji* was a great personality, who loved me very much.

On another day I told the *swamiji* that though I was not going to Haridwar, I would still like to roam around the Himalayas for some more time. He was against my wandering here and there. Whenever I said I wanted to travel, *swamiji* would refuse and make me drop the programme. My mind was with Ashamayee at Triyuginarayan, and after meeting that *Amma* once, I wanted to go to Tibet in search of my roots.

Gyanganj in Tibet is the origin of my *guru parampara*. I had heard this from my *Guruji* several times and once even Ashamayee told me about Gyanganj. I was unaware if I needed a passport and visa to go to Tibet, as it is under Chinese territory. Gyanganj is somewhere in the northern part of Tibet.

Once I talked at length about this to Mangalanandaji but he asked how I would reach there without valid papers. Even though I too understood these practical problems, I was still very adamant about going there as I knew that every wish of mine would be fulfilled by the grace of my *Guruji*. So finally without taking permission of Mangalanandaji, I got ready to move to Triyuginarayan somewhere in the upper Himalayas. *Swamiji* smelt of my plan somehow and came and asked. "You are planning to move. Okay. *Sanyasis* are like wind. They can move anywhere and everywhere, why do they need permission from anybody? Do one thing, whenever you come back to Uttarkashi, come back to this *ashram*. Be with me."

I agreed and left the *ashram* towards Triyuginarayan where Ashamayee resided.

Towards Triyugi—I

Life in the Himalayan hills was like the life of a wild bird—free to fly up in the sky far and wide, rest awhile on a tree when tired, and eat whatever it could find for food. I felt like that bird, so free from the clutches of *maya*, and moving around the beautiful Himalayan hills, in search of what—I don't know. Life was so carefree there in that journey, where I would walk and walk for miles with no destination in mind, and eat whatever was offered by a villager or shopkeeper, and resume my journey towards the ultimate. I was very happy as I was free from the so-called rules and regulations of an *ashram*. When I spotted a *jharna*, I might bathe and sit for a while doing *japa*, then move on. Thoughts of food or shelter never bothered me. And why did I need to bother? *Amma* was always behind me—her loving and caring hands on my head always.

I asked several villagers for directions to Triyugi. Somebody said that I had to go to Guptakashi first and then on to Ukhimatt, and then to Triyuginarayan. I was not worried about not finding the way, and whenever and wherever I felt tired, I would rest by the roadside or in any small *mandir* or near any *jharna*. More than food, water was the important factor. But in the Himalayan hills there is no water scarcity at all, there are big and small streams everywhere.

Once I was sitting near a village at a small tea shop. The tea shop owner served me with some boiled and dried potatoes and then tea. While I was taking the tea, one villager came there and started abusing me and accusing me of having stolen some valuables from his house the previous day. He was fully drunk. He grabbed at my clothes, shouting '*chor, chor*'. The tea shop owner was very annoyed and pushed him away from me. Even then he was not in a mood to leave me and caught hold of my clothes.

I also got very angry and was about to give him a kick, when another villager standing near the teashop came to my rescue and gave the drunkard two or three good blows. He fell down on the road. Since I was an outsider, I wondered what I would do if all the villagers were to band together and attack me as a thief. A few women were near the shop with grass and firewood on their heads. They put their heavy loads down near the shop, and asked what the scene was all about. One of the women loudly admonished the drunkard about insulting a *sadhu* and warned that if a *sadhu* were to curse one of them, the whole village would go to ruin. I was amazed to see the two faces of those villagers at the same time—one side in my favour were praising me, the other side with the drunkard scolding me. Suddenly the shopkeeper came to the drunkard and beat him up and told him that if he suspected me, he could check in my clothes and other belongings. If no valuables were found on me, he cautioned the drunkard that he would haul him to the village *panchayat* for vilifying a *sadhu* on pilgrimage. Everyone agreed. They stripped me, and as I did not have even a single penny or any valuables other than my *pathras* and pair of *kambals*, everyone was ashamed and asked me for pardon. They took the villager to the *panchayat*, asking me to follow them.

In the village courtyard, a few villagers assembled and began questioning me. I told them I was on my way to Triyugi from Uttarkashi and possessed no valuables. And also added that I was passing that way for the first time, and had no knowledge about the villager or his valuables. The Panchayat was distraught that a *sadhu*'s wrath in the form of a curse might ruin the whole village. I told the villagers that I was the last person to curse anybody, as my *Guruji* had taught me that even if others wronged me I should pardon them. One of the village women I had seen near the tea shop then brought some tea without milk and offered it to me with devotion. I sat there calm and composed, and had that tea. By that time the high intoxication of the drunkard had come down. He came near me and touching my feet, wept and begged pardon for his mistake and requested me not to curse the village on his account. I told him not to worry, that I was not angry with him and was ready to move on. It was almost sunset time and the villagers requested me not to travel in the hills at night as it was dangerous. They told me to resume journey the next day. I agreed and went to the village *mandir*, and keeping my *kambal*, etc., on the *verandah*, went to the nearby stream for a wash.

Though no one was near, yet an unknown fear now crept over me. This was the first and most bitter experience I had had in the Himalayan hills. I bathed and returned to the village *mandir* and sat for a while in *japa*. It was almost dark but I could make out that a couple of people were approaching me with a small kerosene lamp in their hand. It was the old drunkard with his wife and another villager, perhaps their relative. They had brought me some rice, *dal* and *chutney*. While eating, the now normal drunkard, asked for pardon again for his mischief. His wife wept and told me that it was his nature to drink a lot and quarrel with her daily. As if nothing had happened, I sat there very calmly and ate the food they brought. The *mukhiya* (chief) of the village then arrived, enquiring about whether I was going to Triyugi. I told him I was on pilgrimage in the Himalayan hills, and that my *Guruji's guru-behen* was staying and doing *tapas* in Triyugi.

During those days my Hindi was not good. In my broken Hindi I told them about my journey and future plans to go Tibet via Triyugi in search of the Almighty. The *syana* (chief) was very impressed and asked if I needed anything. By this time I had finished eating and felt very tired. The drunkard and wife told me they would be very happy if I stayed in their village for a few days. But I told them of my inability to do, and had to be constantly moving till my goal was reached. They requested me to stay at least for two days as they wanted to do *seva* and repent for the sins they have incurred by insulting a wandering *sadhu*. The village '*syana*' also requested me to stay in their village for 2 or 3 days and they would be happy to serve me. Seeing the innocence in their eyes, I told that I would let them know the next morning.

Early morning the drunkard and his wife again came to me with some tea. I told the drunkard that if he promised to stop drinking and beating his wife, I would stay at their village for 2 or 3 days and accept their '*seva*'. He went in front of the temple deity and with folded hands and tears in his eyes, prayed and said something to the deity in the local language. I didn't know the language but the expression on his face showed his remorse. He was asking the deity several times to pardon him for the previous day's misbehaviour. He came back to me and again touching my feet promised that he would never again drink in future, and would take care of his wife and children.

I was very happy to see the face of the villager's wife, and said I would stay in the village for three days. Then that villager said to me, "*Maharaj,* you have pardoned my big mistake of doubting and shouting at you yesterday. I have a request. Triyuginarayan is far from here, at least 4–5 days journey. Please allow me to come with you up to Triyugi as a helper. By this *seva* of accompanying you I am sure I will be purified. Please, *maharaj,* please allow me to accompany you." I felt his request was genuine. I told him that I was staying at the village for 2–3 days and when I was ready to leave, I would let him know my decision. They went back to the village happily, and I sat there peacefully on the *verandah* of the *mandir.*

Towards Triyugi—II

I stayed in that village for two days and the stay there was most memorable. The villagers would assemble at the *mandir* in the evening and chant some *bhajans* sitting in front of me. They were happy that I was there. Both days the drunkard who had scolded me brought me food. The third day morning I was getting ready to leave the place. I had not told the villager whether I was allowing him to come up with me to Triyugi. But in the morning he was ready and came near me with the same request. As was the usual practice, he carried some *rotis* and *chutney* with him.

It was always my preference to travel alone so I could chant my *mantra* at each and every step. If anybody was with me my concentration was disturbed. So I told him to walk at a little distance away as I was chanting my *mantra*. He was walking about fifty steps behind me. He had a shoulder bag and a long stick to help him for a speedy walk.

By afternoon we reached a village. There was a stream coming down from the hills, the water very cold. I sat there for some time for my body to adjust to that temperature, and then slowly began my bath in that ice-cold water. The villager was sitting on the other side of the road. I also invited him to take a bath to freshen up. He did not take a bath. After my bath the villager took some *rotis* and *chutney* from his shoulder bag. He had also brought a few tree leaves on which he served the food. While eating, he told me that his wife was crying because I had left their village.

We rested there for some time after our meal. In the meantime a small truck arrived there and stopped for water. The driver came near and asked me where I was headed. When he learned it was

Triyugi, he invited me to ride in the vehicle so that there would be no need to walk. But I told him that I preferred to walk on these hills to enjoy the beauty and solitude. He looked at me doubtfully and went away. After an hour we resumed our walk. Once or twice I told the villager to go back as if I wanted him to travel back. But his reply was "*Maharaj*, let me come with you at least up to Triyugi. I know I committed a great mistake; now I want to atone for my sins by serving you. By walking with you and serving food, I will definitely be cleared of my sins."

I kept silent and continued the journey. Before evening we reached a village which was very small compared to the previous one. By the roadside, there was a small temple of the village deity. The villager asked me to stay there as the sun was about to set. There was no *verandah* or any additional construction other than a small hut-type mandir. I sat in the courtyard of the temple under a small tree. The villager went to the nearby village telling me that he knew this place very well as his wife belonged to that village. I was wondering what was happening to me. By the grace of my *Guruji* somebody was always there to take care of me, for my food and shelter. I was sleepy due to the continuous journey and had a small nap under the tree. Now the night had covered the hills. I was sitting in darkness and the snow-clad mountains disappeared from my view. Only darkness was there.

I woke up to a voice saying, "*Maharaj*." I saw the villager with two–three persons standing near me, carrying a lantern. The villagers had brought some rice and *dal* and they served it. I told them it was not necessary for me to eat anything now, but since they had brought it, I was taking it.

The villagers moved back to their village and my travel companion brought some firewood and there in the darkness made a fire. Now I could see the temple and the face of the villager sitting near me by the light. I was very quiet. The villager started to sing a Garhwali folk song. Even though the meaning was unknown to me, the *ragam*[24] and *thalam*[25] were very moving and I merged with the *nada* (energy of music) and was in *ananda* (extreme happiness, one of the highest states of being).

Suddenly a drizzle started which grew to heavy rain. The villager said that we should go to the village to avoid getting drenched. But I did not want to, and sat there. I was drenched, the fire was extinguished, and my *kambal* and clothes were now getting soaked. After about half an hour, when the rain stopped, I got up and began wringing out the water from the clothes. I was now only in loincloth, my clothes and *kambal* laid out near the temple to dry. The villager was also drenched, but hesitated to remove his clothes for drying, his theory being that they would easily dry on his body. Wearing a single loincloth I sat under the sky in that biting cold wind, shivering. The villager tried to relight the fire in vain. Sitting and leaning against the tree, I had another nap.

I felt something moving on my body. I cried out to the villager who was still sitting near the temple, and he came running to see what had happened. He came near and lit the match box and to our wonder there was a big rat drenched in water, sitting on my body. I was afraid and the villager took a stick and drove it away. He said it might have come attracted by the smell of food. Even now I was shivering—was it from fear of the rat? Even though I knew there was nothing to be afraid of.

In the morning, the sky was very clear. We were about to resume our journey. My clothes had not dried completely. The *kambal* was very wet, and because of the water, it had become heavier than usual. I noticed that the theory of the villager was correct—his clothes had dried on his body. I was struggling to carry the *kambal* because it was heavier. The villager took it from my hand and put it on his shoulder.

---

24 The six basic musical modes which express different moods in certain characteristic progressions, with more emphasis placed on some notes than others.

25 A traditional rhythmic pattern in classical Indian music

We resumed the walk. After few miles, we reached another village where there was a small tea shop on the road side. The owner had just opened up the place and was getting ready to make the fire to boil water for tea. We both sat near the fire and tried to dry my *kambal*. The shopkeeper continued to make tea. Within a few minutes we were able to dry the clothes and *kambal*, and by that time the shopkeeper brought us some tea in his dirty glassware. We had not asked for tea, yet he had made it and brought it to us.

After tea, my villager companion gave some money to the tea shop owner. At first, he refused to take it, but when the villager kept pressing him, the tea shop owner told him, "Okay, I will take money only from you, not for the *maharaj*. It is my good fortune to be able to serve some tea for this *maharaj* on pilgrimage!" I was wondering about the innocent nature of the poor villagers in that hill. They are very pure in their mind. They were happy with the circumstances. They were good people. After tea and drying the clothes we resumed walking towards Triyugi.

Towards Triyugi—III

We were both walking, the villager behind me. The curvy roads on that terrain were very beautiful, and small terraced fields, cut into steps were visible. We kept on walking. After a while I heard the sounds of a flute playing somewhere from the hills. I stopped and sat on the roadside, looking at the hills trying to find where the sound was originating from. The villager told me it was perhaps some boy who was grazing his sheep. I was listening and wondering at the music from the flute. The air would be full of the melody of the flute and then punctuated by total silence—it was some old Hindi film song. The sound of the flute along with the cool breeze created an enchanting atmosphere. This was the first time I had experienced hearing such a melodious note from a flute.

The music stopped. I felt in my heart that it should continue for some more time. But there was silence. We resumed walking.

I was hungry and there was no village in sight. It was about noon, and though the sun shone overhead, it did not feel hot as the wind from the snow clad hills was making us feel cold.

The afternoon also passed, and we had nothing to eat. We sat on a rock near a *jharna*. I drank a stomach full of water. The villager told me that if we walked fast, we might be able to reach Triyugi before nightfall. Though my legs ached yet I was ready to move. By this time my *kambal* was almost dry. We walked a few more hours. At last at a distance, a village appeared in sight and I asked whether that was Triyugi. He told me that it was not and that we had to walk further for a few more hours to reach there. But for sure we would get something to eat at that village. We reached near the village. My villager companion went to the village in search of food while I sat on a stone on the roadside.

After some time he returned with some food, consisting of plenty of *roti* and vegetables made with corn. As I was quite hungry, I ate more than three *rotis*, and the villager too had his food. Now, with a full stomach, I felt sleepy. But the villager said that if we delayed further, we would reach Triyugi only at night, so it was better to start now. Reluctantly I started with him. The villager informed me that we had one more hill remaining to be climbed and then with one left turn we would be at Triyugi. We tried to walk fast as it was about sunset time.

Finally we reached the Triyuginarayan temple which was located near a village. I sat on the *verandah* of the temple. The *mandir* was closed, as the *pujari* (priest) might have probably left after the evening *arathi*. I told the villager companion to leave me now, as I wanted to meditate on where to move next. I told him that somewhere near here was my *Guruji's gurubehen,* and I wanted to locate her next morning. I would spend the night at that *mandir*.

The villager however was not ready to leave. I told him bluntly not to disturb me anymore. I assured him that with his *seva* to me during the journey, his sins had already vanished. I insisted on him going to the village for the night, and then returning in the morning to his own village since his wife and children were awaiting him.

With much reluctance, he agreed to go to the village, repeating his wish that I accompany him. I explained to him my resolution of never sleeping in a village during my pilgrimage.

He bowed in prostration several times to me, and left unwillingly with tears in his eyes. But I had noticed the happiness on his face when I told him that his sins were washed out. His eyes kept looking to me again and again in gratitude. He then left me.

As usual I was all alone there; it was almost dark around me. But even in spite of the darkness, a small pond-like space near the temple was visible to my eyes. I went there and filled my *kamandal* with water. My birth mother used to tell me that wherever I am at night, I must keep a lamp and some water near me before sleeping. Here though I had no lamp, I did have water. I made a resolution to always keep at least one match box with me.

The night was extremely cold. As I already had some food on the way I was not hungry but felt very tired and also felt an energy pulling towards some unknown place. I was unable to sleep the whole night. My feelings were attached to my *Guruji* and Ashamayee. The pull (attraction) was so intense that I got up and sat on the *mandir verandah* in the early morning.

With the first rays of sunrise, I could see a hill near the temple. The village was below the *mandir*. I looked at the hills and felt the pulling sensation originating from the hills. I looked for few minutes at the hill and then heard the sound of my beloved Ashamayee, "Come this way, climb the hill and reach me."

I was in wonder at all that was happening to me. I washed my face and hands, and with ablutions done, started climbing the hill. Far up on the hill top, I could see a small cave and in front of that I could see Ashamayee standing. My body was thrilled and my eyes filled with tears.

With Ashamayee

I was climbing the hill laboriously, as it was a steep hill which was not so easy to climb. My legs and back ached. Almost half way up the climb, there was a stream coming down the hill. I sat near it for a few minutes and had some water. I saw that my beloved Ashamayee was looking at me. I wondered how Mayee stayed in those hills. Since nobody could easily access the cave, I was thinking about how Mayee got food there. With all these foolish thoughts I once again resumed the climb. Almost three hours had passed but I was still climbing. For a while I thought I would not be able to reach Mayee. I was sweating even in the cold weather. I heard the voice of my Mayee, "Climb son, nothing to worry. You are a young boy and why are you afraid? Climb and climb."

Life is also like this… to reach your goal you have to struggle. I thought it was the symbol of my life. So far I had struggled a lot, even during the beginning of the journey. The struggle was not less even in my *poorvashram* (time of life before taking up *sanyasa*) days. I had struggled for my studies, for my day-to-day food, for my *sadhana*; even now, after reaching the main steps of my life, as a *sanyasi*, the struggle had not left me. As I sat there leaning against a rock, hundreds of thoughts crowded my head. I was thinking about my life, all the way from my childhood down to that point. I felt very tired. I felt I would not be able to reach Ashamayee. My eyes were filled with tears. Then once again I heard the voice of inspiration and encouragement, "Eh! Fool, why do you feel so depressed? Only a few yards more. Climb my son, climb. Look at each step and come forward." The words of Ashamayee were so inspiring. I began climbing again. After an hour-long climb, oh!

Now I was close, the cave was now in clear view. Yes, only a few more yards left to climb, to reach the destination.

At last I reached the feet of beloved Ashamayee. She took my hands in hers, and embraced me for a while as if her long-lost son had returned. The warmth of her body sent an electric current into me. I noticed that she was not wearing any clothes. Mayee's matted hair was covering her old body. In wonder, I drew back to look at her and her eyes shone so bright, it was difficult to meet them; it was like looking at a light bulb. Once again she embraced me and said, *"Bete, mere pass tak pahunchne mein bahut kathinayee hua hai kya, phir bhi tum aaya. Bahut khushi huyee tum ko dekhkar."* (Son, though it was an extremely difficult journey to get to me, still you came. I am so very happy to see you.)

She took me inside the cave. It was rather small. With difficulty perhaps three people could stay there. I observed that she possessed nothing except a few gunny clothes spread there for bed and in a corner there was a tin container and *jala pathra*. I was wondering what Mayee ate. I too was hungry as I had had no food except for some water from the stream. Mayee said, "I know you are hungry. Don't worry. Behind the cave is a *kund* (water pond), go there and wash your feet and hands, you will feel relaxed."

I came out of the cave with great difficulty and went to the water pond. And to my wonder, it was a hot water spring. While washing up, I remembered Nityananda Bhagavan. Wherever he stayed he would create a hot water spring as in Ganeshpuri, in Maharashtra. Ashamayee came near me. It was about sunset hour. There was a small bundle in her hand. She tied it with a stick lying there and immersed it in the hot water. Oh! Endless wonder! Now the bundle had expanded. She opened it and handing it to me, asked me to put it in my *kappar*. It was '*khichadi*'—she had placed rice and *dal* in a piece of cloth, tied it into a bundle and then immersed it in hot water for few minutes and lo, it was now ready to eat. As the water was salty (containing sulphur) adding salt was not necessary. Like she told me, I put the *khichadi* into my *bhiksha pathra*. She then took the *pathra* from me and sat close, and just as a mother feeds her child, she began hand feeding me the *khichadi*. My eyes were full of tears. I felt that one embrace of Ashamayee relieved me from all the tiredness of the day. I felt very energetic.

While feeding me she talked, "I know you have completed three *purascharans*. I am happy with that. I have already informed Tara about you coming to me here today." (I was wondering how these two mothers communicated with each other without any telegram or telephone or post offices, and not even any human being near—another foolishness of this poor boy, who was unable to understand the systems of *yogis*. After a few years a Himalayan yogi taught me how to receive and send thought vibrations.)

It took more than half an hour to complete the food. Just as a difficult child protests about eating, I too was telling *Amma* again and again that my stomach was full, and that I needed no more. But this was Ashamayee—she never cared about the protests. With all her love, she coaxed me again and again and made me eat the whole food.

It was almost dark and a cold wind blew. I thought I was living on the very roof of the world. She asked me to follow her to the cave. After cleaning my *bhiksha pathra* (that also Mayee did not allow me to do, she did it herself) we both went to the cave.

As mentioned earlier, there were a few gunny sacks spread out as asan on which Mayee used to sit or sleep. She said, "I know you are tired from the last few days' journey to Triyugi, and also because of today's climbing. That is why I do not go down from here. I am happy to be here alone. A few villagers bring me some rice and dal occasionally. And you know here on the top of this hill, one will not have much hunger or thirst."

Once again a stupid thought came to my mind. If *Amma* was not ever moving out of these hills, how had I seen her at Devaprayag and how had she fed me there? And before I had even finished thinking that thought, as if she had read my mind, she said, "Arre, buddhu, you have to walk a long way to understand all this. Himalayan *yogis* have the capacity to reach anywhere and everywhere instantly. If you doubt me, you have to doubt your Tara Mayee too. Hasn't she appeared to you at Uttarkashi and fed you with *sambar* and rice? Beta, the Himalayas are full of wonders.

Do not doubt. Accept what you experience. After a few years of *sadhana*, you with be able to realize all this." (Again my mind was in doubt about how Ashamayee could know that my *Guruji* came to Uttarkashi and fed me *sambar* and rice with her own hands.) And she continued, "Just now I told you not to doubt. But you still do. Tara Mayee and I always know where and how we are moving. We convey our feelings through thought waves which are easier than your telegraph and we don't need instruments for this either. Now you are still young—when the time comes you will understand all this. See, you are tired due to the journey. It is night and it is very cold outside. Now you sleep." She insisted that I sleep and she was also ready to lie down. She asked me to lie down near her. As a child sleeping near his mother, I slept near her and *Amma's* hand on my body felt like a gentle soothing massage. The warmth of *Amma's* body was enough to lull me to sleep, and on this cold night in the highest mountain range in the world, I slept without any *kambal* or *chadar*.

With Ashamayee—
Experience of Pratyangira

I woke up late. Ashamayee was nowhere to be seen. I went near the hot water spring and had a nice bath and came back to the cave. Ashamayee was now sitting there, thinking about something. She spoke to me at length on her life with Nityananda Bhagavan and also about Gyanganj. She said, "Gyanganj is the origin of our *guru parampara*. We belong to the *siddha yoga parampara*. The place is not easily accessible. Only if the *maha guru 'Maha Tapa'* wishes, will we be able to enter there. The area is covered with dense fog." I informed her about my wish to go to Gyanganj. She said it was all right but I had to be careful traveling on the snow-clad peaks of the Tibetan Himalayas. I said I did not have any requisite documents such as passport or visa. *Amma* told me not to worry about it as none of the military and police would ever stop any Himalayan *yogi* there.

Then she began talking about my *sadhana*. I told her that my *sadhana* in *Srividya* was at a standstill since I did not have knowledge of the *'prayoga vidhi'* of the three aspects of *'Pratyangira sadhana'*. I only had the *mantra* with me. *Amma* said, "What do you know about the three aspects of *srishti, stithi,* and *samhar.*" Immediately her face changed. She stood and asked me loudly, "You want see what *'Pratyangira'* is? Look here!" She beat on her breast three times and shouted in a wild voice. Lo and behold! The form of Ashamayee was no more visible. I saw the first form of *'Pratyangira'* and was shivering with fear as she beat her breast and the second form of *'Pratyangira'* appeared in her body, and then the third. Every time she was shouting like a wild beast. I was stunned and shocked. She fell down in the cave and I fearfully went near her and called out, "*Maa*, wake up." It took more than half an hour for Ashamayee to come back to normal. She then went outside to wash her face and soon returned to her old self.

She sat near me and told me that if I got permission to enter Gyanganj, I must ask the ruling *acharyas* about the *Pratyangira sadhana*. Putting her hand into the tin container, she took out and handed me something. It was a '*saligram*'-like object. *Mayee* said, 'This is the '*Beejam*' of your life in spirituality. Keep this with you till the *Srividya sadhana* ends." (After returning from Gyanganj, I passed on that *saligram* to one my best friends—the *baba* of Anandamayee Peeth and it is now in his pooja room in Indore, Madhya Pradesh.)

Just as she had done the previous day, she packed some rice and *dal* in a cloth bundle and went outside. I was very curious to see the cooking system *Mayee* had. She put it in the water after tying it with a stick and cooked it by dipping it in the water for a few minutes. She put part of the boiled rice and *dal* in my *kappar*. While I ate, she also had the food.

It was in the afternoon when I sat in front of the cave and looking around, taking in the beauty of the snow-clad Himalaya hills. *Amma* came near me and sat and told me again about 'Gyanganj'. To find the place I had to go to north of Tibet. "On the way," she said, "you can get the help of a few *lamas* who will take you near the destination." But I was afraid of crossing the border and anyway how was it even possible without any valid papers. *Amma* told me not to worry about the journey. Nobody could disturb me on the way, since I would be having the '*saligram*' with me. She instructed me that I must visit Manasarovar and Kailash also. (But it did not happen that time as I had to return to India after my visit to Gyanganj. A few years later I had a chance to go to Kailash with a group of *sanyasis*.)

I was sitting near Ashamayee, calm and composed for hours together. There was deep silence. It was close to sunset hour. Mayee went inside the cave and called me to come inside, as there was a wild wind starting to blow. I went inside and sat with several thoughts on the journey to Tibet. *Amma* said, "You must start tomorrow morning. Move upwards from here towards the north. After a few days' walk, you will reach the border. Just cross it. Nobody will see you. Better you set out early tomorrow morning. Do not worry about your food in that unknown terrain. Their language is different. Tara will take care of you." When asked whether *Amma* had visited Gyanganj, she got angry with me. "Why do you ask such silly questions? Whether I went there or not, what difference does it make to you? Mind your business—you need not ask questions about my life!" I felt sorry about having questioned this loving Mayee and kept quiet. In a few minutes *Amma*'s anger vanished and she sat near me, and placing and moving her hand on my head, told me, "You have a long journey from tomorrow onwards. Now you better sleep." I was not interested in sleeping as I wanted to talk further with Mayee.

When I told her that after my journey to Tibet, I wanted to come back to her, she told me, "No, not at all. This is our last physical meeting. Do not come back. Go on from there back to Haridwar and stay there a while. During that time, try to study *Vedanta* and continue your *sadhana*. No, do not return to me." (After a few years, during my stay in the Anandamayee Ashram in Indore, I experienced a strong pull to move to the Himalayas, and with the financial help of my friend *baba*, I started for Uttarkashi. But at Uttarkashi, I learned about the *Samadhi* of my beloved Ashamayee and returned to Indore.)

Again and again, she insisted that I sleep. I lay down near Mayee just like the previous day. Her hands were caressing my head affectionately. I slept with dreams of Tibet.

Early morning, before the first rays of sun hit, Mayee woke me up and asked me to do my ablutions. After about an hour when the sun's rays had touched the hills, she asked to move on to the north, leaving her behind.

There were tears in my eyes. I was unable to control my feelings and emotions. I touched Mayee's feet with all sincerity and devotion as if they were my *Guruji*'s feet. She lifted me up and embracing me said, "Beta, we will not meet again. I pray for success in your life of *sadhana*. Carry on and never look back. Keep moving towards the goal." Once again she embraced me, and coming out of the cave, gestured in the direction that I had to travel. My legs would not move. I remembered having experienced the same feeling in Mookambika, when I had left my *Guruji* to leave for the Himalayas.

Mayee repeated, "It is no use wasting time here. It is time to depart from me. Go son, move on towards the north. One day or the other you will definitely reach your goal with the blessings of our *Guru Mandal*."

I looked at her face for a few seconds and with tears rolling down my cheeks, started moving with shaking legs. With a mind full of thoughts and an unknown fear, I slowly started climbing a hill towards the north.

Towards Tibet

I was climbing the hill. All around, everything was covered with snow. I did not know which way was east and which west. Still, I continued walking towards the direction that Ashamayee had indicated. Now it was almost noon. There was no village in sight. I was wondering where I was headed, what was next.

I thanked God, when after traveling a few more hours I spotted a small village. I climbed down to the village, which appeared a small one of just 10–12 houses. An old man sitting on a small wooden bench welcomed me, "*Aayiye maharaj. Is rastha me kahan se aana hua.*" (Welcome *maharaj*, where are you coming from?) I told him that I was on the way to Tibet. He stood up and bowed in prostration to me, touching my feet and saying it was very rare that they got a chance to see any *sadhu* or *sanyasi*. He invited me to his home but as usual I was reluctant to enter any house. I saw colourful flags resembling those in Buddhist *viharas* (Buddhist monasteries), and the old man confirmed that it was indeed a Buddhist *vihara*. I was willing to take rest there for some time if they would allow me to. The old man accompanied me to the *vihara* and called out to them in the Bhotia language. One *lama* came out and asked me about my particulars.

I told him of my plans to go to Tibet. In addition, if they permitted me, I would take rest there for some time. He happily agreed. By this time the old man had vanished and while I was sitting on the verandah of the Buddha *vihara* (I never used to enter inside any *ashram* or temple for my stay, as I had decided to stay only outside), he reappeared with a few *rotis* and potato curry for me. I was happy to receive the *bhiksha*, as I was hungry. I had nothing to eat or drink since the morning, not even water. This is the special quality of the Himalayan hills—one will not get hungry or thirsty even if one hasn't had any food for a day or two. The pure atmosphere and unpolluted oxygen of that area itself is enough for a man to survive.

After my *bhiksha*, I decided to stay there for that night. It was still afternoon. Again the *lama* came out and invited me inside, as it was very cold outside. I told him I was happy where I was, on that *verandah*. He sat near me, and asked about my details. He told me this was the last village before Tibet. When I told I was moving towards north Tibet in search of Gyanganj, he said there would be no roads and that I must depend only on the small footpath on the hills. I was happy to hear from him that a few *lamas* of this *vihara* would be going towards Tibet in a day or two. I decided to meet them and informed the *lama* about my wish. He told me they would meet me after the evening prayers and then we could all sit and sort out the journey programme.

In the evening I met the four *lamas* who were supposed to leave for Tibet after two days. They told me that they would accompany me up to one point, from where they would move off towards the Arunachal side while I would have to separate from them to go north. I agreed. I told them I was not carrying any valid documents for the journey except my *Guruji's ashirvaad* (blessings). They said not to worry, only a minimal check would be done on the border, and they never asked questions of *lamas* and *yogis*. (The *sanyasis* in that area are known as *yogis*.) So I decided to stay on the *verandah* of the *vihara* till the *lamas* were ready to leave.

I slept on the *verandah*, the *kamba*l wrapped tightly wrapped all around my body; it was extremely cold as the area was in a high altitude. I dreamt that Ashamayee appeared in front of me and praised my decision to travel with the *lamas*. She said that I must go with them, and to eat whatever they offered me.

Next morning I walked around the village for some time. The Bhotia tribals were staying there and they were looking at me devoutly. One of them invited me to sit in front of his house. His wife brought out some black tea (without milk) and offered it to me and asked whether I would like to take some dry rotis. As I had an offer from the *vihara* to take food with them I declined. Some villagers assembled near me. Their language was very different from Hindi, and in my broken Hindi I conversed with them for some time. They all felt happy and one villager came forward and after doing *namaskars*, offered me a one rupee coin as *dakshina*. I never took any *dakshina* or kept money with me. When I told him that, he looked disappointed and kept the money back in his own pocket.

In the afternoon, at the Buddha *vihara verandah*, I had some rice and *dal*. The rice had a *payasam* texture (like liquid), cooked with some leaves. This was the system of cooking rice in Tibet. Even though it was a paste-like thing, I ate the whole thing happily, which they had served me in my *kappar*. They were looking with curiosity at my *kappar*. Usually Buddha *bhikshus* (monks) carried a different type of *bhiksha pathra*. They asked me to show them my *pathra* after my meal. When I told them I had got it from the *guru parampara*, and that I was the ninth one who was using this *pathra*, they calculated that this *pathra* would then be more than 600 years old. I too agreed. I narrated to them about my journey and said, "I am on the way to my roots. In search of the roots I have to reach Gyanganj. From there my *guru parampara* originates." They had never heard of Gyanganj but they were aware of a place called 'Shangri-la'. They said that 'Shangri-la' was a mystic place hidden in the Himalayas covered with snow and mist. I told them that the place I was in search of was also like that. Since we were supposed to head out the next day, they went inside the *vihara* to make arrangements.

One of the *lamas* came back to me to ask about my belongings. I told them I had the clothes I was wearing, one *kambal*, the *bhiksha pathra* and a *jal pathra*. He wondered how I would survive in that biting cold, since I didn't even have shoes. I told them not to concern themselves and that I had the stamina to face any circumstance because of my *Guruji's ashirvaad*.

In the morning, five of us (four *lamas* and I) were ready to move. They were fully equipped to move in the snow-covered hills. They had *pitthu* (big bags on the back) and good shoes and their bodies were covered with fur pullovers. One old *lama* came out from the *vihara* and offered me a fur pullover, saying it would be useful for my journey, and requested me to wear it. He said that it had been given to him by a *lama* when he had once gone on a journey to Manasarovar, and these days he was not using it. I tried several times to convey that I did not need it as I was happy with what I had. But the other *lamas* also joined the old *lama* in telling me to use it for the Himalayan journey. Finally I had to accept it. Even though it smelled bad, I used it to cover my body to satisfy the *lamas*. The pullover went down to my knees. After all buttons were secured, not even a bit of air could penetrate.

Now we were ready to move. The *lamas* did some chanting in their language. Perhaps they were praying for a safe and successful journey. I also prayed to my *Guruji* to take care of me and the *lamas* in such a long and arduous journey.

We started moving towards the north. I mostly stayed quiet, not knowing the language of the *lamas*. One of them knew a little Hindi. Slowly and steadily we started moving. It felt as if the Himalayan hills were inviting me to climb over them. I felt happy and was chanting the '*devi pranava*' in my mind as I walked.

The Journey Continues

This was the second day of our journey to Tibet. The previous night we had stayed inside a small cave covered with snow all around. The *lamas* had brought *rotis* and fried vegetables with them. They served it with a butter-like thing. The night was unbearably cold. However, the pullover given to me by that old *lama* helped me very much to escape the cold.

There was no water in sight. The *lamas* had already done their ablutions. I was wondering how to attend to the call of nature without water. One *lama* taught me how to do it without water. I had to take a piece of snow and make it into a ball, and rub after nature's call. This was the first time I had ever done such a thing. My mind was conditioned to washing up the body properly after completing nature's call.

Somehow, with a lot of hesitation I completed my morning *karmas*. The *lamas* were ready to move. They told me that they carried a small stove with kerosene and we would have some black tea later that morning. We again began the climbing of the hills up and down. Everywhere it appeared frozen, and no water within visibility. I had an idea to keep some snow in my *kamandal*—it might melt after sometime and then I could use it for drinking as well as for using after answering nature's call. I tried and it was successful. But it was difficult to also carry water during journey. However, there was no way out.

After walking for a few hours, we reached near the border. They told me the border was visible but even then, it would still take more than a day to reach there. We all sat on a terrain where there was no snow. One of the *lamas* started preparing tea. During tea they were talking a lot in their own language, we continued walking after taking tea. There was no food or water for us during the day-long walk. Even by sunset we had not reached the border, so we decided to stay somewhere for the night but could not find a place or a cave or a *vihara* there. After walking a while we saw an open place without snow cover where a small stream was flowing. If one sat for half an hour, he might collect a litre of water, as the stream was very small. It was coming from snow-melt on top of the hill.

We had no tent or anything to accommodate ourselves in. As there was no other alternative, we had to prepare ourselves to stay in that open place in the biting cold. Those *lamas* were habituated to such situations but I was new and was suffering due to cold and unable to open my eyes. The darkness descended slowly. The *lamas* were ready to sleep. They had sleeping bags made of leather. Poor me, I was looking at them and thinking about the facilities they had brought. I thought the *rotis* that the *lamas* had brought might be finished. I felt little hungry also, but I was feeling bad to ask them for the *rotis*.

They slept in their sleeping bags. I was sitting near them looking into the darkness and wondering what else we would have to face. On such a beautiful hill, with the natural wind and song of silence, I felt as though in hell, as I was finding it difficult to save myself from the biting cold. It started drizzling. It was not rain, but light snowfall. The *lamas* slept happily in their bags. I was sitting near, wearing the fur pullover. I covered my head with the *kambal* to protect myself from the snow. The snowfall started getting heavier. I was afraid I might be buried under the snow that day, but thank god, to my relief the snowfall stopped. Snow and rain are unpredictable in those hills. Sitting there, I was looking below and, to my wonder I saw a small lamp on the other hills. I told myself that it might be the border check post.

Now that the snowfall had stopped, I too tried to lie down there. There was nothing to spread. The *kambal* was very wet so I removed it and kept it aside, and tried to sleep.

We woke up in the morning to the welcoming sun rays. We got ready immediately and started moving ahead. By noon we had reached the border check-post. We crossed easily, and the duty staff never bothered to ask us where we were going. We moved with speed towards the north. Since the previous day, there had been no food. We were moving continuously. By afternoon, we spotted a lot of flags flying and Tibet became visible. Now we were in Tibet. In history class, I had studied that this land was part of India until 1962. After the war we had lost it. We all reached under the flags. The *lamas* entered into a tin shed-like house. It was a small Buddha *vihara*.

There were four *lamas* there. They welcomed us and spoke in their own language. One of the *lamas* knew their language, as he used to travel a lot in those hills. When he told them that we were heading towards north, the *lamas* were happy. We all sat in a small room inside the hut made of tin. One of them offered us tea, and asked us to rest for some time. By that time the prayers would be over, and they would prepare and serve us some food. I was glad to hear about food as I had been hungry since the previous night.

We all had some paste-like rice and *dal* prepared with a lot of chillies. I quite enjoyed the food and maybe it was because of the hot chillies, I forgot about the cold. The *lamas* of that *vihara* told us not to leave now as the sun was about to set, and we were all tired. While they all sat and discussed something, I slipped into a deep sleep.

I woke up in the night, wanting to urinate. When I went I discovered there had been heavy snowfall. The *lamas* had been right in telling us not to leave at that time. When I came back to the room, the four *lamas* were still sleeping. I also lay down, but could not fall back asleep, full of thoughts about what was in store for me next!

Towards Northern Tibet

I had never thought the journey to Tibet would be this painful. Every moment I was struggling to save myself from the ferocious cold wind, and we walked continuously for seven days. Evenings we would reach some village or *gompa*[26] or Buddha *vihara*. Due to the help of the *lamas*, I was allowed to stay there and some food was also served by the villagers or *vihara lamas*. Even though it was a struggle, I was happy to be present in the land of *Gurus*.

It was the seventh day of our journey. My feet were swollen and torn, because of snow bite and with great difficulty I was walking with the *lamas*. They walked at speed, as they were accustomed to the Himalayas. Moreover they were wearing shoes which also helped them walk faster. After noon we came to a junction of footpaths at the top of a hill. They told me that from then onwards, I had to walk alone, since they were traveling towards Arunachal. After a few minutes they left me and moved on. But before going they showed me the way towards the north and assured me that I would definitely reach my goal soon—within a day or two.

I started walking. There was some anxiety since I did not know the language of the land. If somebody spoke to me, how would I reply! I tried to walk a little faster, thinking that I should reach some village or Buddha *vihara* before sunset.

It was almost dark when I reached a village. It was a very small one, of 8 or 10 houses. I saw an old lady sitting and sewing some

---

26 A set of small Tibetan temple buildings and other places of worship or religious learning

cloth, with a needle and thread. I went near her but perhaps seeing a stranger, she went inside the house. All the houses there were very small in size. One young man came out of his house and asked me something. As I did not know the language I tried to show with gestures that I wanted to go to north.

He pointed me to a small *gompa* near the village and asked me to go there. Maybe he took me to be a pilgrim. I moved towards the *gompa*, which was also small in size. I saw a middle-aged *lama* sitting there turning his *japa chakra* (prayer wheel) and went near him. Looking at me, he also said something in the local language. I told him in English that I was coming from Hindustan in search of Gyanganj. He went inside the *vihara* without saying anything. Another young *lama* appeared in front of me. Thank God, he knew a little bit of English. While talking to him, I told him of my plan to go to the north in search of my roots in Gyanganj. He had also never heard of Gyanganj, though of course he had heard about Shangri-la. He happily welcomed me into the *vihara* and asked whether I would like to take some tea. I accepted gladly since I had not taken any tea or had anything to eat since morning. After some time he brought tea and started talking to me in his broken English about his journey to Gaya, Varanasi and other places in India. He was very helpful and asked me to rest there for a few days before resuming my journey. When he saw my frostbitten and torn legs, he brought some hot water with salt and started washing my legs with all love and affection. I saw '*karuna bhava*' (compassion) in his eyes. Even though I tried telling him that I could wash my legs myself, he did not allow me to do so. The other *lama* also joined us, and the young *lama* told him about my journey to north. It was almost night time. The prayers were over. There was one more *lama* staying in that *vihara*. He was unable to move as it seemed his legs were paralysed. He was lying on a wooden cot and moving his *japa chakra*. After prayers, we three sat for our food. The young *lama* first fed the paralysed *lama* for few minutes. Even though I was hungry, I was unable to eat the rice as it was cooked in a different way. The rice was cooked with some leaves and was salty. There was no *dal* or anything to accompany the rice yet they were eating it as if it were a delicious food. One could describe it as a different form of north Indian '*khichadi*'. Only instead of *dal* the *lamas* had put some leaves and salt in it.

I was not supposed to throw away the food served in my *bhiksha pathra*. Therefore, with difficulty, drinking water again and again, I finished the food. It was a rare experience for me.

The three of us slept in one room. I could easily hear the sound of the wind outside. Due to exhaustion I fell asleep soon. I woke up a little late. By that time, the morning session of their prayer was over. The young *lama* brought some black tea and told me that after tea I could do my ablutions. Just near the *vihara*, there was a small hot spring. It was a wonder of nature that in this snow-clad region, on the top of the hill, there was a hot water spring!

The water was very hot and I dipped the *kamandal* in the hot spring. After leaving Triyugi, this was the first time I had a good bath, but of course without soap. I repeatedly poured hot water on my body. The young *lama* came there and wondered that this bath would make me catch a cold and get fever. I was enjoying the hot water bath. I rubbed my body with the chadar, bathing to my heart's content, and then put the chadar and cloth in the sun to dry. Now as I was having no other cloth to wear, I was wearing my *kambal*. By this time the young *lama* who had seen my situation of wearing the *kambal*, brought a piece of maroon cloth for my use. I did not accept it saying my cloth would soon be dry and I would use the same.

I told him I wanted to move to north that day itself. But he insisted that I must rest for a couple of days before leaving. With the affectionate words of the *lama* I agreed to stay there one more day. How strange! This *lama* was no one to me. But he was behaving as if he had known me for many years. This I attribute to the *kripa* of my *guru*, that wherever I went, I would get a warm welcome and the people I met loved me for no reason!

I went to the *vihara* and sat for a few minutes, lost in thought. The *lamas* thought I was meditating. No, I was thinking about the future journey. I was all alone and didn't know how many more days I had to wander this way. The young *lama* came to me and asked me to join them for food. The previous day's experience of food was still fresh in my mind, and the hot water bath had invigorated me. And I felt a little hungry also. I was unable to refuse as he kept calling me again and again that it was time for food. We all sat down to eat. They have some ritual similar to our *naivedyam* before they commenced eating. I prayed to my *Guruji* with folded hands and thanked her for giving me timely food. In this meal, it was not the same rice. It tasted like '*bajra roti*' but I wasn't sure, it may have been corn too. There was some *chutney* made of garlic and chillies. I enjoyed the food immensely and thanked them several times for accommodating and feeding me.

It was almost noon and I retired to the room for a nap. The hot water bath, the food and the environment had made me sleepy. I went to collect my dried cloth and *chadar* which I had spread on the back of the *vihara*. But alas! My cloth was missing. I searched for it everywhere. The young *lama* came again and saw what was happening. He told me that the strong wind may have blown away the cloth to the neighbouring hills. Was this a curse of *Vayu Bhagavan* (wind god)? He had taken away the only piece of cloth I owned. The *lama* was laughing at me. He was telling me "I had offered you a cloth to change into. You did not accept it. Perhaps due to anger at this, the wind has taken away your cloth." I apologized to him for disturbing his sentiments, and accepted the maroon cloth (Buddhist monks wear this colour). He was happy that I had accepted the cloth. I returned to the room. There were dark clouds looming and it was about to rain it seemed.

I returned to the room and spread my *kambal* on the floor and lay down with the *chadar* on my body (it was yet to dry) and slept.

The Lost Paradise: Where is Gyanganj?

I stayed for one more day at the *vihara* and then resumed my journey towards north. I was walking alone without knowing how to reach the destination. I walked till afternoon and there was not even a single village or *vihara* in sight. All of a sudden, it started to rain. Since there was snow all around, and raining, I slipped and fell down when I tried to walk. I thought these would be my last moments. But it was not to be. The rain soon stopped and I saw some hills ahead covered in mist. Even though my legs were aching, I kept walking. Soon I could see a village and nearby, a big Buddha *vihara*. Slowly I reached there.

The sun was about to set and the distant hills were slowly enveloped in darkness. One of the *lamas* at the *vihara* was fluent in Hindi. I spoke with him about the journey towards Gyanganj. He told me that the Himalayan hills were full of mysteries. He also told me about the mist-covered hills which were not accessible to anybody.

I rested at the *vihara*. They were very generous and fed me with some *rotis* and vegetables. I was on the *verandah* of the *vihara*, the wild wind making me shiver. It was so cold, that my leg and back pain increased manifold. The *lama* who had spoken in Hindi asked what the problem was and when I informed him that I had slipped down from the hills and that my whole body was aching, he brought some balm to apply on my legs. He would not allow me to apply it myself and he himself applied it wherever I had pain.

Perhaps because of the exhaustion or the affectionate massage of the *lama*, I could sleep for some time. When I woke up it was still dark. All the *lamas* were sleeping and there was no light in that *vihara*. Seeing the darkness, I lay down again.

The next day when I was ready to move towards the mist covered hill, the *lama* cautioned me that I was playing with my life. It was dangerous to climb those hills. I told him even death was okay—I had to search for my roots and find my *Gurusthan* (place of the *Guru*). I started walking and the *lama* was staring spellbound.

I reached the valley of the hills by noon. There was no food or water with me. I sat there for a few minutes and tried to climb again. However, something was stopping me from climbing the hills. A cold wind was blowing and I shivered. I tried walking forward several times but could not take even a single step as if some invisible power was stopping me. I sat on a rock and prayed to my *Guruji* and Ashamayee to show me the path. My calls remained unanswered. I felt angry with myself. After such a long and tedious journey towards this place, now at the last moment, why was I afraid to climb? I do not even know that there was a place called Gyanganj. The mists grew thicker. I sat there and wept.

Who was stopping me and why? I had no answer to this question. After a while the density of the mist reduced, and I could easily spot the top of the hill. Once again I tried to walk ahead, but my legs would not cooperate, as if they had been chained. I could not move an inch. There was nothing to do but to cry in frustration. I cried for nothing—nobody was there to hear me in those lonely hills. But lo, after a few minutes I saw somebody from afar walking towards me. I sat quietly.

He was an Indian *sanyasi*. He was wearing *kashaya* clothes and had a long stick in his hands. He came near and spoke something in the local language. I told him in Hindi that I was in search of Gyanganj and I did not know how to reach there.

The *swami* also talked to me in Hindi—"What are you talking about? There is no place called Gyanganj. It is just a myth, even a philosophical term. I have been living here for long, and I never heard of it." When I asked him about the mist covered hills, he replied hesitatingly, "*Maharaj*, don't think about going to that place. It is not accessible to anybody. Don't go there." I asked, "What is up there on that hill?" He was silent and then got ready to leave saying, "Don't try to be here for long. Move out. Go back. Go back."

I was wondering what was happening there! After such an arduous journey for more than ten days, when I was about to reach my destination, this *Swamiji* was saying that it was dangerous to be in that area. What was the last danger for me? Finally I would die here, that is all. I was ready to, if only once I could see and experience Gyanganj. That *Swamiji* then sat there. The night was about to fall. Leaning on a rock I simply sat there. I could not sleep. Even though I was tired I simply sat on the ground covering my body with the *kambal*.

The next morning I again tried to climb the mist-covered hills. And just as the previous day, that day too I was unable to move. I was getting mad, and cursing myself, sat down. I did not know where to go and how. The topography of that area was unknown to me. Another thought also came upon me—why should I go anywhere, I shall be here and die with no food or water. But I was also sure that one day or the other I would be able to climb the hills covered with mist!

But nothing happened. Three days passed without food or sleep. I was tired and slept on the ground. In a dream I saw Ashamayee telling me to leave that area and return to Haridwar. I woke up to see nothing except darkness. I simply lay there with the thought that I would not go anywhere.

In the morning I was exhausted. I was depressed and started walking here and there aimlessly—sometimes towards one direction and sometimes towards another. I was almost mad. The paradise was lost for me. Was Gyanganj a myth? Or did I lack the *pathrata* (eligibility) to enter there? I had once heard from Ashamayee that entry into Gyanganj was only possible if the *Mahatapa guru* wished so. How could I make him wish that I be allowed entry there?

I felt as the whole journey and life itself had become useless. I was moving here and there aimlessly. Far from the hills I saw a village and a big Buddhist *gompa*.

After a few hours of walking I reached the village. Near the *gompa*, as if he was waiting for my arrival, an old *lama* came near, welcoming me and asking about my whereabouts. I told him of my pathetic condition and of searching for Gyanganj. The *lama* offered me some black tea and told me in broken English. "Gyanganj is there. It surely exists. One lady called Alexandra David Neel has written about it. Gyanganj is like a university. All spiritual practices under the sun are taught there. The problem is not with Gyanganj—it is with us, even a small impurity will not allow us to enter there."

He was happy that I had at least seen the mist-covered hills. Nobody in that area was aware where Gyanganj was exactly. The only thing visible was the mist covering the hills all around. But he told me not to give up my intention to visit Gyanganj, but before the next attempt, I should make myself purer. He also added, "It is better to obey your *Guruji's* orders to go back to Haridwar." This *lama* had travelled extensively all over India. Every year he used to go to Varanasi and Gaya. He was planning to go again the following week. As he was having some stomach pain he had postponed his journey. He said he used to travel alone on these hills as well as in India.

I did not know what to do. I sat in the courtyard of the *gompa* while the *lamas* were preparing food. The *lama* came and offered me some food in the courtyard itself. They did not allow me to sit with them for food. It may have been because of my dirty appearance, my clothes and depressed expression. The *lamas* may have thought that I was mad.

My mind was wavering. One the one hand I wanted to go back to the hills. But on the other were the orders of Ashamayee. I know I had failed to reach my destination after such a gruelling journey.

The *lama* came near me again and told me to stay back there until next week, and if I wished I could join him on the journey up to Varanasi. I was thinking about what to do. I didn't know how to come out of these snow-clad hills, and I was tired and depressed.

I said nothing to him, and leaving everything to my *Guruji*'s hand, I stayed there.

Towards Haridwar

I was in a great dilemma. I was unaware of my mind-set, as it was wavering constantly. I woke up next morning ready to take a decision. In any case the *lama* would be leaving after one week. Better to stay there and in the meantime, ask other *lamas* about Gyanganj, or perhaps even some old villager might give me some information. So I decided to stay at the *vihara*. In the morning after my ablutions, I wanted to take a bath. The *lama* informed me that if I walked some distance down the hills, there would be a small hot water spring where the villagers bathed.

After a nice bath, like the other day at the Buddha *vihara*, I was very cautious about my clothes. I placed a stone on the cloth so this time the wind could not blow it away. As usual I wore my *kambal* till the cloth dried. The *lama* came up to me and informed me that it was mealtime. I went with him and had my food in my *kappar*. This time to my surprise, the *lamas* allowed me to sit with them and eat. I was given a room beside the kitchen. I went back to collect my clothes and then back to the room. I wondered what I would do till the *lama* was ready to leave for Kashi. I just went around the village to see and understand the life of Tibetans in that village.

I observed that the villagers were very poor. Their clothes were torn and they looked as if they had not had food in a long time. I went near a villager who was sitting on the *verandah* of a house and asked him something in Hindi. This man did not know Hindi, but his son who came out, did, and spoke to me in broken Hindi for some time.

He had visited India once or twice and worked in a Buddha *vihara* in Varanasi as a servant. That was why he was able to understand, though it was broken Hindi. I asked him to enquire about 'Gyanganj' from his father (what a fool I was!). The young man asked his father something and the answer was negative.

The temptation to go back to the mist-covered hills (assuming that was where Gyanganj was) arose again in my mind. I brought this up with the *lama*, but he was unwilling to accept my proposal and said that I wouldn't have to wait for too many days, as he would start on his journey to Hindustan as soon as he recovered from the stomach ache.

I stayed at the *vihara* for three more days. While there, I attended the prayer sessions. This was when I first learned the meaning of the Buddhist *mantra* 'om mani padame hum'. This *mantra* has some *tantric* significance. It is related to *yoga* as well. The *lama* explained the meaning and use of chanting the *mantra*.

After five days of stay there, I felt that I was now fine to travel. The body pain and fatigue had vanished and we planned on leaving the next day. The *lama* told me it would take a minimum of five to six days to reach the Indian border, and from there we would catch the bus to reach Varanasi. I told him that I had no money with me and had no idea how I would reach Haridwar. He told me not to worry, as he had some Indian currency which he brought over from his last journey.

We started the journey towards India. I felt miserable though, like a student who had failed an examination, in spite of having studied and written it well.

For a few days, we walked incessantly, staying at *gompas*, *viharas* or any villages along the way when necessary. Since my companion, the *lama*, was very helpful, I found no difficulty during the day-to-day travel, and moreover the confidence in my *Guruji's ashirvaad* (blessings) gave me courage to move ahead fast.

On the fifth day we crossed the Indian border at Arunachal. The *lama* took me in a bus going from Arunachal to Guwahati, and we travelled from there to Varanasi by train. He paid for all the expenses, including railway and bus tickets and for food purchased in the wayside hotels or in the train. I was desirous of visiting Kamakhya while we were in Guwahati. (My *poorvashram* brothers were working at Maligon Railway Headquarters. Both brothers were employed in good positions in the railways.)

As I felt reluctant to meet them in Maligon, I did not venture out to go there, even though it wasn't too far from where we were staying in Guwahati. The *lama* told me that since it was night already and that we had to start for Varanasi by train next morning, it was not possible for us to go to Kamakhya this time. When we started next day from Guwahati for Varanasi, my mind was full of negativity about my life as my mission had failed. We both sat in the general compartment which was crowded. Though we got seats to sit down, the situation in the general compartment was like hell.

We reached Varanasi at night the next day. I thanked and bid farewell to the *lama*, as he was busy preparing to go to Sarnath which is a famous Buddha *vihara*. This was my first time at Varanasi and I did not know anybody there. I went to the *ghats* of the *Ganga* and sat there the whole night. I was hungry. In the morning after bathing in the *Ganga*, I went for *darshan* to the Vishwanath temple. I prostrated at the Annapoorna *mandir* and received a ticket from the *poojari* for my *bhiksha* there. I accepted it happily and waited for food for some time. In that *Annakshetra* I did not use my *kappar* as it was not allowed there. After food, I went to the railway station in search of the train to Haridwar.

At Haridwar

There was a passenger train to Haridwar from Varanasi that night. For hours together, I waited on the platform. When the train was ready, I boarded it; this was the second time I was traveling without a ticket. Since there weren't many travellers, I got a bench to sleep on. In the morning when the train halted at Lashkar railway station, a ticket collector entered the compartment. I was afraid. Before he could come to me I went up to him and speaking in English, said, "Sir, I do not have a ticket, and am coming from Varanasi. I have to go to Haridwar." This probably impressed the ticket collector for he told me to go back to the bench to sit, then came near and asked me about my details. When I told him I was returning from a Tibet pilgrimage and that too without money, he was amazed. The train started to move and a tea vendor appeared. The ticket collector asked him to serve me with a cup of tea. This was another surprise to me.

I was thinking to myself about how my *Guruji* was present in every form. Now here she was, in the form of the ticket collector. Through the entire journey from Mookambika to Haridwar, she had taken care of me in various forms. This was my first '*Advaita Bodham*'.[27]

I had visited Rishikesh previously but this was my first trip to Haridwar. I recalled Vasudev Baba with whom I had a fight before I had gone to Rishikesh. I went towards the *Ganga ghats*. Since I did not know the way, I asked people along the way for directions. I reached 'Har-ki-pauri' and had a bath and waited there on the

---

27 Understanding of non-dual reality or experiencing omnipresence of the Divine

ghat till my cloth dried. I noticed that a *baba* had been staring at me for a long time. He came near and enquired, "*Haridwar me pahali bar aaya hai kya?*" (Are you visiting Haridwar for the first time?). I affirmed and then he added, "Where are you planning to stay? If you go to the Sapta Sarovar, there are a lot of *ashrams* there. You will definitely find a spot in any of the *ashrams*." I didn't know about the 'Sapta Sarovar' and how to get there. The *baba* said, "You sit here, and I will be back soon after purchasing some medicines. I am also going to Sapta Sarovar. I will take you there."

After walking a few miles, we reached 'Sapta Sarovar'. This is the place where the *Saptarishis* had done *tapas*. The *Ganga* splits into seven *dharas* (distributaries) here. The history of the place was narrated to me by the *baba*. He said, "You go to Rishi ashram. There you can meet one Swami Shivananda, who is very helpful. He is also a *dakshini*, and since you are a *dakshini* yourself, he will definitely help you." He pointed to the gate of Rishi *ashram*. I saw a *sadhu* drying clothes in front of his room. Rishi *ashram* was one the bigger *ashrams* there and with its three-storied building and a small dispensary, it had an elegant look. I wondered how I could stay in an *ashram* even after my *Guruji* had told me not to depend on any *ashrams*. But this was not a conventional *ashram*. Datta Mallji and his sons from Delhi were running this *ashram* only for the purpose of *sadhu seva*. I saw a *sadhu* drying clothes in front of his room and asked the *swamiji* where I could meet Swami Shivananda. He showed me a room and I went up to the door and said, "*Om Namo Naràyana*." Even though Shivanandaji was busy doing *japa*, he came out immediately. I spoke with him in Malayalam about my journey and requested him to help me to get some accommodation.

He told me that the *ashram* was for *virakt sanyasis*, and if I was not accepting any *dakshina* or any other type of *parigrahams* (possessions) he would talk to Datta Mallji about allotting me a room at that *Ashram*. Then I told *Swamiji* about my *Guruji*'s orders on not depending on any *ashram*, and that I was fine with staying at the *Ganga ghats*. He disagreed, and said, "This *ashram* is not a conventional one. It is meant exclusively for *sadhu seva*. The Punjabi family owning it is doing *seva* only for *seva's* sake. They do not have any *sankalpas* in their *seva*." He then took me to meet Datta Mallji, and told him about me wanting to stay here and sought his permission. Dutta Mallji was glad to grant it, and asked his son Tara Singh to open up a room for me on the first floor.

This room was near Shivanandaji's room. I entered the room and kept my belongings there. When Shivanandaji saw that I had no extra clothes and just one *kambal*, *kappar* and *kamandal*, he was pleased and remarked, "You definitely look like a *virakta*. In this attire, you did pilgrimage to Tibet? That is a wonder, unbelievable!" Shivanandaji went to his room and brought me a new set of *kashaya vastra* and told me, "Your cloth looks like that of a Buddhist. Use these clothes. This is new. Have a bath in the *Ganga*, and throw away the Buddhist cloth." My loincloth was torn too. I think Shivanandaji noticed it while I was removing my cloth.

He returned to his room and brought another piece of cloth and tore it in four pieces, which I could now use as two sets of loincloths. I wondered at his way of doing things and his affection towards me.

I returned from the *Ganga* after a bath and changed clothes. Even though I wanted to keep the Buddhist cloth as a memory of my Tibet pilgrimage, I don't know why but hearing the words of Swami Shivanandaji, I threw away that cloth into the Ganga. When I returned to the room, I was surprised to find Shivanandaji waiting for me with a few *rotis* and *vegetable*. He sat near me and asked about my *Guruji* and the *sampradaya name* (traditional religious title) of my *sanyasa*. While I ate, he told me that the next day onwards I could join him in going for the *bhiksha* in *virakta mandala*.

In Sapta Sarovar there were more than 18 *annakshetras*. Daily the *mandali* (group of *sanyasis*) went together to take *bhiksha*. Whether we ate or not, we had to attend all the *kshetras*. Different food was being served in different *annakshetras*. One would give out *roti*, the other *dal*, the other vegetable, the other rice, etc. The *virakta mandali* had its own rules and regulations. We had to stand and eat what we accepted as *bhiksha*. Then wash our hands and go to the next *kshetra*. This is known as '*swan bhiksha*' (meaning just as a dog wanders here and there and eats whatever he gets at the doorstep). This system of *bhiksha* is inevitable to wipe out the ego of the *sadhus*.

I felt very happy to be with Shivanandaji and he introduced me to some other *sadhus* staying in the nearby rooms. In the evening I did not go for *bhiksha* as I had taken food late in the afternoon. Every evening the *virakta mandali sadhus* would assemble at Virakta cottage near Rishi *ashram* for evening meals at 5 pm and afterwards most of them would walk on the *Ganga bund* till sunset.

This was a new lease of life for me; I had never stayed with such a big group of *sanyasis* before. Since I was using a *kappar*, everybody viewed me differently. I used to wear only one cloth and hold the *kappar* in my hand while walking with the mandali.

Shivanandaji was very pure and generous but often got angry, speaking roughly some times. He never compromised in the matter of *shastras* (scriptures) and used to be very tough. Even though not highly educated, he was famous among the *sadhus* for his *virakti* and *tapas*. He did *japa* always, sleeping very little at night.

So, in a happy mood and praying to my *Guruji* again and again, I began my stay at Rishi ashram.

Haridwar Life Continues

Life at Haridwar was so monotonous. I felt bored, every day was the same—bathing and then going for *bhiksha* together, then back to room, sleeping, the same again at night, then repeating the same next day. The repetition of the same routine was very boring. One day I decided to start a '*purashcharan*' of *Srividya japa* and informed Shivanandaji about this. He was very happy to hear this. Mornings I would go for *bhiksha*, and the rest of the time I would do my *japa*.

The next morning I went to the *Ganga* and scooping water in my cupped hands, took a *sankalpa* (vow) to start and complete *japa purascharan* in 90 days. This would be my fifth *purascharan* of *Srividya*. I was satisfied at having engaged myself in the *japa* and stopping the interaction with others and walking about here and there. In the mornings I would go with the *mandali* for *bhiksha* and after returning resume my *japa*.

In the meantime, Shivanandaji introduced me to a famous scholar who was staying at that *ashram*. His name was Gopal Muni of *Udasi Sampradaya*. Gopal Muni told me that as I now had more free time after the daily *japa*, I must concentrate on the studies of *Vedanta* and that he would be happy to teach me the *Prashtana Trayee* (i.e., *Gita, Upanishads* and *Brahma Sutra*). I agreed and the classes on each of the *Upanishad*s started, and even though I was not much interested in studies, I tried my best. So the days went by smooth and peaceful.

But somehow I was unhappy with the stay at Rishi *Ashram*. Almost three months had now passed by. I was keen on moving elsewhere. The *japa* was about to conclude. One day I told

Shivanandaji that my *japa* would be over within a week and that I would like to leave Rishi Ashram, as I did not like the crowd at the *ashram* as well as the surroundings. Shivanandaji first differed on the matter but finally agreed to do something about it.

The day after the completion of my *japa*, Shivanandaji asked me if I was willing to move with the Gangadev mandali. This *mandali* had originated in the state of Punjab, and been founded by Swami Gangadev and Gyan Dev Maharaj. Shivanandaji said he had been part of that *mandali* for a few years and after the sad demise of Gangadev Maharaj, he had left it to stay at the Rishi Ashram.

The *mandali* had split into two after the demise of Gangadevji. He said that if I were willing to join the *mandali*, he would too, and then we could travel with the *mandali* together. In those days the *mandali* was staying near Dehradun. After two days, one or two *sadhus* came to Rishi Ashram from the *mandali*. Shivanandaji discussed the plans of the *mandali* with them and asked them where their next destination was going to be.

Shivanandaji and I joined the *sadhus* and travelled towards Dehradun. Since both Shivanandaji and I never carried money with us, one of the *sadhus* who had come bought us the bus ticket to Dehradun.

Shivanandaji was known to all the *mandali* members. He told them about my Tibet pilgrimage and the stay at Rishi Ashram. The head of the *mandali* was from Kashmir. He spoke to me kindly, describing the rules and regulations of stay at the *Virakt mandali*. As *viraktas*, none of us were supposed to accept any *dakshina*. Only just the basic clothes, bed and *bhiksha* were to be accepted. The *mandali* stayed at Dehradun for a few days.

In those days I only had a set cloth for my body and a *kambal* for my bed as well as for sleeping, other than my *kappar* and *kamandal*. The stay at the *mandali* was good. All the *sadhus*, numbering around twenty, were very co-operative and generous. After a few days' stay at Dehradun the *mandali* left for Vikasnagar on the banks of the Yamuna River near Dehradun.

One old *sadhu* used to stare at me for a long time every day. One day I asked him what the matter was. He said that he was from the Jammu region and had a cottage near the village. He was retired from the military and had been living in that cottage since long and of course was not a *sanyasi*, but a *vanaprasthi* (forest-dwelling ascetic). He said that if I wished to go to Vaishno Devi for *darshan*, he could easily take me there on his next visit to his village.

We came to Vikasnagar by foot.

One of the devotees of the *mandali*'s chief, arranged for our stay at his mango garden. The place was full of greenery, on the bank of the Yamuna River. The devotee had constructed a few huts of grass and paddy leftovers, and they accommodated us there. The food was cooked there itself by the group of devotees and served to us both times. Every evening we would all chant the *Shiva Mahimna stotram* after the *arathi* in front of the portable *mandir* which the *mandali* carried wherever it went. A very beautiful *Shivalingam* was in that *mandir*. I felt free to do my *sadhana* in the small hut made of grass and paddy leftovers. We stayed at Vikasnagar for more than three months.

Life in the Mandali

Life in the *mandali* was very smooth. We used to bathe daily in the Yamuna River, and the routine *sadhana* was going well. But I was not satisfied with the *sadhana* as I used to still be left with a lot of free time. I thought it was time to begin my sixth *purascharan* in *Srividya*. But first I needed to know for how many more days the *mandali* would stay there. I was informed it would be for more than four months and they would move only after the end of 'chaturmas'. It was good and encouraging information for me. Shivanandaji told me that two days later was *Ashtami* day and that I could start my *purascharan*.

Early on *ashtami* morning I went to the Yamuna River and after bathing there, I took the *sankalpa* for *Srividya shodashi purascharan* for 90 days. On these *purascharan* days I used to consume only milk and fruit. Even though I was never in the habit of taking milk regularly (as I had never liked milk since childhood), during *purascharans* I would take a glass of milk in the morning and evening each day and few of whatever fruits were available that day.

There was a devotee there, one Attar Chand, a very pious person. He was a wholesale merchant dealing in wheat, rice and *dal*. He would come to all of us usually asking whether we needed anything. And to my wonder he would cook for the *sadhus*, leaving his brother to take care of his business.

The *japa purascharan* days went very well. I was very happy to get a chance to do my *japa sadhana* on the banks of the Yamuna.

One day the *Swamiji* from Jammu came to me to say that he would be going to his village after *chaturmas*. He added, "Please come with me. You will like my village. You can stay in my cottage and let us go for the Vaishno Devi *darshan* once. As you are a *bhakta* of *Mata* you must visit Vaishno devi."

I had also heard about the Vaishno Devi *Mandir* earlier and wanted to go there for *darshan*. When I said that I would accompany him after completion of my *japa sadhana*, my words made that old *Swamiji* very happy.

I completed my *purascharan* in time, in 90 days. After concluding the *japa*, Attar Chand arranged for a *homa* and a special feeding for the *sadhus*. (Being a *sanyasi* I was not supposed to perform *homa* but with the help of two *brahmacharis* at the *mandali*, I did the *homa* on the banks of the Yamuna.)

Somehow my mind was reluctant to go to Jammu to the village of that old *Swamiji*. But he kept insisting again and again that I must accompany him, and one day with the permission of Shivanandaji and the head of the *mandali*, I started for his village along with him.

In those days there used to be a daily train between Dehradun and Jammu. The old *Swamiji* paid for the ticket and both of us sat in the train bound for Jammu. He said that we had to alight at Pathankot and then catch a bus to his village. We tried to get some sleep in the train, though of course we had to do it sitting. We had brought with us some *rotis* and fried vegetable from the mandali which we ate late at night.

In the morning we reached Pathankot, and went to the bus stand to catch a bus to his village called Keerian Gandyal. All the villagers had come there in 1947–1948 during partition. More than 200 Kashmiri *Brahmin* families had settled there. Even after the second generation, the village was yet to have *pucca* (permanent, concrete) buildings—there were only a few *pukka* buildings there. This village was on the banks of Ravi (River 'Iravati' of *Puranas*) river. We reached the village around 11 am. The old *Swamiji* opened up his cottage and cleaned it. By that time his son, who was working with the electricity department in Jammu, came there with some tea. After tea, I bathed in a small stream nearby and sat near the fire, maintained by that *Swamiji*.

To my wonder, a middle-aged lady arrived there carrying two big food containers and entered the cottage. *Swamiji* was getting ready to make his food—the small kerosene stove was already lit and water kept on it. The lady entered and told him not to cook food now as she had brought food for both of us.

I asked her in wonder, 'Who told you that we were here?' She replied, after doing *namaskar* to me and *Swamiji*, that an hour earlier while she was busy cooking food, she heard a voice telling her that her *Guruji* has come to the village and to carry food for him.

I thought first that she was referring to the *Swamiji*. But *Swamiji* introduced her to me as Kaushalya, his daughter-in-law. She was the wife of his second son, working in the military. I told her that I had never before visited that village or initiated her. So how did she feel that I was her *guru*? The reply was very logical and simple. She told me that she used to pray at the Mata Vaishno Devi shrine to be granted a *guru*. The voice she had heard while cooking food was definitely that of Vaishno Mata. I was wonderstruck!

I had my *bhiksha* along with the *Swamiji*. She was coaxing us to eat more and more. We finished the food and the lady left for her house. I felt I should sleep for a while as we could not sleep comfortably on the train.

Navaratri in the Land of Vaishno Devi

Every day more and more villagers began coming to me for *darshan*. One evening when few villagers, women and men, were sitting near me, I told them, "*Navaratri* is very near. I know all of you are devotees of Mata Vaishno Devi. If you all feel so, on *Navaratri* days, I will perform a *satsang* (gathering of people for a spiritual discourse) for you. Mornings I will *recite Chandi Paath (Durga saptasathi)* and evenings around 4 pm or so, I shall tell you stories of *Mata*, based on the *Devi Bhagavatam*." All were very happy to hear that.

MY FIRST GADDI

The next day a few women from the village came there, and collecting stones and soil, they made a 3'×3' size *gaddi* (cushion) for me to sit on, in front of the cottage. They also cleaned the ground in front of the cottage. Since the gaddi was made of clay and stones, it took about four or five days to dry.

There was no drinking water facility (no hand pump, tap, etc.) near the cottage. The elder son of *Swamiji*, after discussing with other villagers, installed a hand pump there. While the digging was going on, I saw a *Shivalingam*-shaped stone among other stones. I asked them to just stop the digging and bring that *lingam*-shaped stone to me.

They tried to lift it, but even though it didn't appear to be a very big stone, they failed. I called *Swamiji* and told him that his Shiva had appeared there (he was a Shiva *Bhakta* [devotee]) and asked him to lift it. I gave a good bath to the *linga* and next day being Monday (the day of Shiva) I installed the *lingam* near *Swamiji's* fire, and everybody was happy.

Swamiji's daughter-in-law used to bring my *bhiksha* daily and *Swamiji* cooked for himself. His ego was a bit high as he was a pensioner. He did not accept anything from the villagers, not even from his children.

Navaratri was to start in a day or two and the *gaddi* made of clay was now dry. Before *Navaratri* I informed the villagers that I would be in *Upavasa* for nine days, taking only water (as was the usual practice) and on the tenth day all the villagers were to come there for *prasadam*. I also told them that we would do *Srividya Homam* every night. I asked them to also prepare three or five boys for '*Yagnopavita sanskar*'[28] before *Navaratri* so that they could participate in the *Homam*.

So, with all such arrangements the *Navaratri* started. Every morning I would do *Chandi Paath* sitting near the fire. In the evenings there would be a good-sized gathering in front of me for *satsang*. In the beginning of course there were fifty or sixty villagers but by the end of *Navaratri*, the crowd had grown to more than three hundred. The daily *satsangs* and *homams* at night went very well.

On Navami day, the villagers started bringing rice, jaggery, ghee, etc., to the cottage. I understood that this was for preparing the '*prasadam*' meant for all. The *Chandi Paath, Satsang,* and *Srividya Homa* were all completed by *Navami* itself.

During the early hours next day (i.e., *Vijaya Dashami*) some villagers came with big utensils from their house and started the cooking of the sweet rice (similar to the payasam of south India).

---

28 A traditional rite of passage that marks the acceptance of a student by a guru. The sacred thread (yajnopavita) is received by the boy during this ceremony, that he continues wearing across his chest forever thereafter.

As early as 6am, people began pouring in. *Bhajans* and *Keerthans* (singing of devotional songs) started. Around 10 am, the *naivedyam* was ready. I was told that they had cooked nearly 6 *mann* (around 240 kilogram) rice for the common feeding of *prasadam*. I asked *Swamiji* and other elders to first offer the *naivedyam* to Mata Vaishno Devi and then start serving. *Bhajans* on *Vaishno Devi* were in full swing and immediately thereafter, the *naivedyam prasad* distribution started. It was about 12 noon when I noticed the appearance of an old man in torn clothes but in good physical condition. There was something special about his eyes. I thought he might be a great *yogi* and invited him inside the cottage to take some *prasadam*. But he sat under a tree and we served him sweet rice and bananas there. After taking the *prasadam* he gave *Swamiji* and me a banana each and told me, "*Maharaj*, this is your 'Karma Bhoomi. Do it and be blessed!" He walked towards the village road and disappeared. I asked some boys to search for him but it was in vain. None of the villagers had ever seen him before. I was wondering who it could be?

People from five neighbouring villages had also come there to have the *prasadam*. Everybody ate to full stomach and carried some to their homes as well.

By evening 6 pm everything had ended. Some village elders were sitting near me. One Madanlal and Paramanand were prominent among them. They asked me if I could stay permanently in that village—they would make arrangements for a cottage. They said that since the village did not have a Mata Mandir, they had been making a plan earlier for constructing one, and with my help and presence, they wanted to build a *Mandir* along with the proposed cottage for me. I kept quiet. *Swamiji* said that I would definitely accept their proposal as I used to do Mata pooja daily.

The villagers left at night and *Swamiji* went to do *japa* in his cottage. I was sitting near the small stream and thinking what to do about the proposal of the elders of the village.

Mandir and Ashram

THE MAYA OF EXISTENCE

Once long ago I had a chance to attend a conclave at Varanasi. This was a workshop on *Vedanta*. I had never done a conventional study of *Vedanta*, but I had read books on the *Upanishad*s and *Gita* by Dr. S.Radhakrishnan during my college days. It was mere chance that I was at the conclave since I was with one of my friends, and a *swamiji* was attending it. There were more than eighteen great scholars and the public included *swamis*, professors of Banaras Hindu University and a few other students of *Vedanta*. There were some hot discussions and I too participated in them. One of the great scholars of Kashi (name withheld) used some abusive and sarcastic language when I tried to prove '*Advaita siddhi*' in perspective of *Shakti sadhana*. Basically I am a *Shakta* (worshipper of *Shakti*) from Kerala. I felt very bad as the scholar *swamiji* ridiculed my viewpoints. In those days I had neither manpower nor money power. I tried to explain my view based on my *Shakti sadhana* experiences. His words hurt me badly. I came out to Manikarnika ghat, where cupping *Ganga jal* in my palms, I prayed to *Ganga mata* with a *sankalp* to one day give me the strength to prove that I was correct.

Perhaps the universal mother had blessed me then, for now in this unknown village some villagers were offering me land, and seeking my help in constructing a *mandir* and *ashram*.

The next day when the villagers came, I accepted their proposal. Then I told them, "We will construct a *mandir* and *ashram* and of course it shall be a *Srividya peetham*, where research work on *Shakti sadhana* especially *Srividya* will be done." All agreed and took me to a spot where there was a small hut-type *mandir* with photos of Vaishno Devi. It was surrounded by at least two acres of barren land with no owner. They told me that the River Ravi had been flowing there years before but now the course of the river had changed. The villagers wanted to construct the *mandir* and *ashram* there.

A day was fixed for *bhumi pooja* (foundation-laying prayers) and the villagers started collecting some money among themselves to initiate it. *Swamiji*'s elder son took the responsibility of getting the idol of *Mata* from Jaipur at his own expense. Paramanand, a senior villager, who had retired from the military, was chosen as treasurer. Madanlal, who worked as an accounts officer with the Jammu & Kashmir government, took over all responsibility of the construction work.

I was not inclined to sit quiet. Even though I had no money with me for construction, I started my *Srividya purascharan* once again. This would be my seventh one.

A very old villager who was known as the 'president' there (he was president of the village committee for rehabilitation in 1947 when they had migrated) came to me with his son and said, "Maharaj, when we came and settled here in 1948, we had a plan to construct a small *mandir* of *Mata*, but somehow it did not materialize. A partially built *mandir* still stands near my house. If you wish so, please make use of those bricks for the construction work." He added that since he himself had made the *sankalpa* of constructing a *mandir*, though it was half done and stopped for lack of funds, he had not dismantled it. He said that I could take those bricks after doing a pooja to Vaishno Mata. After a few days I went there with a few youngsters and performed a small pooja with water and flowers and then removed the bricks. With these we constructed a small cottage of size about 8'×10' near the proposed site of the *mandir*.

I was still staying at the same old cottage belonging to the *Swamiji*. The construction work was going on slowly. Almost three months had passed. But I don't know why my mind was not settled with that *Swamiji*. Sometimes he behaved in an arrogant and egocentric way, even though he liked me a lot. Kaushalya and her children used to visit me daily with my *bhiksha*.

Once after discussions with the villagers, I told her that it was not good that only she had the opportunity to bring me *bhiksha* every day. We selected seven families to provide for my *bhiksha* every week. Even now after so many years with a full-fledged ashram with kitchen and other facilities, the practice of bringing *bhiksha* for me at 12 noon still continues, even though I am not present there. They bring it and offer it as *naivedyam* and leave.

One evening, the old *swamiji*'s son arrived from Jaipur bringing the idol of Mata with him. It was about 3 feet in height and made of white marble and looked very fine. All the villagers came to view it at Madanlal's residence and we placed it in *dhan adhivasa* (paddy fields) till the completion of the construction work.

My mind was very disturbed and I wanted to go to Haridwar or elsewhere for a change. I told the villagers to continue the work and one fine day left for Haridwar. Many villagers offered me money for the journey and it totalled to more than three thousand rupees. Keeping aside a thousand rupees for the journey I handed over the balance to Paramanand to be used for construction.

Winter was now near and I was still having the same old *kambal* and a pair of clothes and of course, my *kamandal* and *kappar*. While on the train, I was thinking about where to go. At Haridwar, I did not go to Sapta Sarovar or any *ashram*. After having a bath, I simply sat at Ganga ghat, thought-free. I decided upon travelling to Gujarat for a pilgrimage to Dwaraka, Somnath, etc. and went towards the railway station to find out whether I would be able to catch a train.

I purchased a ticket to Ahmedabad and sat in a Delhi passenger train, as there was no direct train to Gujarat.

In Gujarat

After reaching Ahmedabad, I was wondering where to go. Shivanandaji of Rishi Ashram had told me once that his *gurusthan* was near Rajkot, in a village known as Thoriyali. His *Guruji* was from the same *'parampara'* that I belonged to. His *Paramaguru* (*Guruji's Guruji*) was the direct disciple of Sri Shivanand Paramahamsa of Vatakara in Kerala (which was why his *Guruji* had given the same name to Shivananda). This Shivananda Paramahamsa of Vatakara is the elder *gurubhai* of Bhagavan Nityananda, all of who belong to the *Siddha Yoga Parampara* of Gyanganj.

I thought that I must visit that place once, and made my way by bus to Rajkot. At that time there was no bus to Thoriyali so I got a ride on a milk van going there. I got on this vehicle at Padthiri, a small *kasba* (walled township) from where nearby villagers made purchases.

I reached Thoriyali, and with the help of a villager reached the *ashram*. Swami Shantanand Giri was the head of the ashram at the time. Two or three of his *gurubhais* were also staying there in that *Ashram*. They welcomed me happily and arranged for my stay in a cottage. I had met these *swamijis* earlier during my stay at Haridwar, and Shivanandaji had introduced me to them.

The *ashram* was very big. There were several single-roomed cottages, the *samadhi mandir* of the *Guruji*, *goshalas* (cowsheds) and a lot of farmland around. I had *darshan* at the *Samadhi mandir* and attended evening *arathi*. In the evening after meals, when we were all discussing sundry matters, I told them that I was on my way to Dwaraka for *darshan*. *Swamiji* told me not to be in such a hurry to leave and asked that I stay there for a few days with them.

The next day, a *brahmachari* also came there who was known to me for a long time. He was the direct disciple of Samprasadananda of Gangotri and later this *brahmachari* took *sanyasa deeksha* from the Swamiji of Omkareswar on the banks of Narmada, in the name of Abhayananda Saraswati. He was a good friend of mine and while in that *ashram* he stayed near me in a separate cottage.

My mind was becoming very disturbed for no reason. I was caught in negative thoughts most of the time, about leaving my *Guruji*, the fruitless journey to Tibet, the trip to Jammu involving the construction, and leaving it behind for no reason—all such thoughts perturbed me. The main problem was that I had no vision of my *Guruji* in a long time. In fact, I was very depressed with the situation and felt like running away from life itself. Suicidal symptoms developed in me. I saw no meaning in a life like that. Food intake came down drastically, and there was no sleep. A type of uneasiness was always within me. Loneliness led to a kind of fear with increase in depression.

I tried to do some *japa* to come back to my normal mood but it was in vain. One day I went to meet a doctor in Rajkot. After hearing about my problem the doctor directed me to his friend, who was a psychiatrist. After long counselling and studying my case, the doctor suggested some medicines for thought control and proper sleep. One was Mellaril and other was Dizepam and I started the medication. But nothing worked. I was slowly becoming violent in my thoughts. There was only one thought in my mind, to leave the body by any means. I was thinking of committing suicide. The thought multiplied so much that one night I consumed more than 10 sleeping tablets together, with the intention to die.

Now I knew that I was dying. It was night, and nobody was near me. My throat felt dry and I wanted some water to drink. I tried to lift my *kamandal* but it fell down and I felt as if I was sinking into oblivion.

When I opened my eyes, Abhayanand was sitting near me. It was the second day since my attempt to die. I was unable to lift my body and Abhayanand lifted me and made me sit leaning against the wall and had me drink a lot of milk. It took more than a week to come back to normalcy. I slept for almost a week, unable to walk or bathe. Even though Abhayanand understood what had happened, he never asked what and for why all this had happened.

Due to all that had occurred, I had grown very weak. Due to the dedicated care and attention of my friend, I began eating again. I wrote a letter to Sri Bhaskar Rao Kalambi of Vanvasi Kalyan Ashram about my mental state and the folly that I had committed. He was known to me since my childhood days, as a *sangh pracharak* (volunteer of a civil organization) in the area where I was born and brought up. I wrote to him saying I wanted to join the Vanavasi Kalyan Ashram which was a pioneer of seva programmes like schools and dispensaries in tribal areas all over India. (Bhaskar Raoji was very close to my *poorvashram* family and I had a special affection for him. I used to go to the *shakha* (branch) with him whenever he visited our village.)

Abhayanand left for Haridwar while I continued staying there to recover my health. Within a week I received a letter in the mail from Bhaskar Raoji enclosing two hundred rupee notes therein. He wrote that I should go to Bombay, as he would be available there at the Kalyan Ashram office in Wadala (Dadar) the week onwards. I sent a reply to him confirming that I would meet him the next week.

I dropped my programme of travelling to Dwaraka and told the head of the *ashram* that I was leaving for Bombay to join a social service organization pioneering tribal development activities.

My mind-set had changed from *japa yoga* to KARMA YOGA! I did not know what the force behind me was or who had changed my mind's inclinations.

Praying to my *Guruji*, I sat inside the train leaving for Bombay from Rajkot.

Life in Karma Yoga

During my college days though I had read the books on *Karma Yoga* by Swami Vivekananda, Maharishi Aurobindo and Mahatma Gandhi, they were very difficult for me to digest. But I had some ideas in my mind regarding '*nishkama karma*' (selfless work) that it would definitely lead one to '*Antakarana suddhi*' (internal purification). But all these were theories to me. Now I was going to enter into '*karma yoga*' in a practical way.

It was not very difficult for me to reach the Vanavasi Kalyan Ashram office in Bombay. I was very happy to meet Bhaskar Raoji again after a long time. He knew that I had left home and been initiated into *sanyasa* but was unaware of my whereabouts during the past few years. After my bath and food, he spoke to me about the activities the organization was doing. He briefed me regarding the main details of what I was supposed to do in the field and what not. Finally he told me that I should go to Dehradun and then to Jaunsarbavar, which is situated in Chakrata tehsil of Dehradun district. He arranged for my ticket for the journey next day by Doon Express from Dadar to Dehradun and gave me a letter to show the manager of the project. Another letter was given to Dr. Nityananda who was the Pranta Karyavah of the Sangh at Dehradun. This was for him to take care of my needs at Chakrata where the Vanvasi Kalyan Ashram had a project of a school and dispensary.

As the train was late, I reached Dehradun after two days in the early hours. I stayed on the railway platform itself till sunrise, and then went to meet the person who was in charge of the project. He was a doctor and well-known social activist of that area. He directed me to go to the Moti Bazaar at the Sangha Karyalaya to meet Dr. Nityananda as he was taking care of things. I did my ablutions and had food at the Karyalaya and met Dr. Nityananda, who was a retired professor looking after the tribal development project at Makhti Pokhri (at Chakrata) and briefed me about the *seva* programmes that were being done there.

The plan was to develop the village so that it can represent a model village. Dr. Nityananda said, "We are not going there to teach them anything, but are there to study them and learn a lot from the poor Himalayan tribals in Jaunsarbavar—keep this always in mind and only then will we be able to do real *seva* for them. Nobody needs our sympathy there. Don't go there with that attitude. Be there, study the situation, and do the needful for the upliftment of the tribal people. We have a dispensary there, which Dr. Dinesh takes care of. And a small school with a couple of teachers. I want you to be there as an overall coordinator of the project."

I assured him that there would be no negative steps from my side in the project. This being the first time that I was getting a chance to work with a big organization like Vanavasi Kalyan Ashram, I should understand what I was supposed to do there. I told Dr. Nityananda that I needed some time to study the situation there.

I was not going to start any work as soon as I reached there. I needed to be there for at least one month and then start the work, with his permission and instructions. Before starting work, I would definitely go to him and describe my observations to finalize the mode of work I was supposed to do. He agreed to this.

I stayed at the *karyalaya* for a couple of days to study about the tribals with whom I was going to stay in the near future. Dr. Nityananda gave me some books about the Jaunsari tribals and I also spoke with the *sangh* workers who used to visit occasionally. Vijayji, the *zilla pracharka* (district in-charge) of the *sangh* told me a lot about the life of Jaunsaris.

During the stay at the Dehradun *Karyalaya* I had a good opportunity to learn about the Jaunsaris. Two young boys studying in the 12th grade were staying at the *karyalaya,* both from the same village where the project was and where I was supposed to go. They were Khajan Singh Rana and Ramesh and were under the guidance of Dr. Nityananda. They were the first group of students who had left the village for the city to study, staying at the *karyalaya*. Dr. Nityanand told Khajan Singh Rana to accompany me to Makhti Pokhri village the next day.

There was a bus going to Nagthat via Makhti in the morning, and we left for the village on the third day. After an hour's journey when we reached Vikas Nagar, I told him about my stay there with the *mandali* and about my *sadhana*. Kalsi was the next stop from where the Jaunsarbavar hills start. From Kalsi to Chakrata the road was one-way. Only after the buses or other vehicles going up reached Sahiya, could the buses coming down start. We left for Sahiya and after reaching there we had to wait for some time for the road to clear. This road and the vehicular traffic were controlled by the military. By evening we reached Chakrata, the *tehsil* headquarters from where we had to travel further for 16 km in order to reach the villages.

The onward journey was on *kaccha* (unpaved) road. By sunset we reached Makhti Pokhri village. The bus continued to Nagthat, which was further away by a few more kilometres.

I handed over the letter meant for Dr. Dinesh written by Dr. Nityananda regarding my arrival and stay there. He had clearly mentioned therein that from that day onwards I would be the manager of the project. Dr. Dinesh had been staying there for a few years with his wife and son. It was a building with three rooms. One was used for the doctor's stay and the other for the dispensary. The third one was vacant. Khajan Singh and I cleaned the third room and put my belongings there. Khajan Singh then left for Makhti village which was a furlong down the hills.

Dr. Dinesh and wife were very cooperative. They fed me at night with rotis and *dal*. He described to me his experiences during the stay there. He told me in detail of life with the tribals and about his attending to more than 60 patients every day. We were talking till late in the night when his wife called him to sleep. I too went to my new room with very positive hopes in mind.

Time is very cruel. I had been doing *japa yoga* previously, leading the life of an ascetic. Now time had brought me in to another shore. I recalled my college days when I was one among some young boys who had formed a small group in the village to do some *seva* activities. Whenever there was help needed in the village, whether it was during weddings, death ceremonies or illness, these villagers used to call us for assistance. Our group of young men would extend the maximum help possible to the needy for which we were always looked upon with special affection and hope. That was the only previous experience in *samaj seva* for me.

Now time had shown its real face and I was content with the thought that it was definitely my *Guruji's* plan to bring me back to normalcy in my spiritual life. I was happy, and I fell asleep thinking such thoughts.

Life with Jaunsaris—I

The Jaunsaris were very different in their beliefs, way of life, etc. They practice polyandry and polygamy as well. Most of them are non-vegetarians. These tribals wear colourful attire and on festive occasions eat, drink and dance day and night as other tribals of India do. They believe that they are the descendants of the *Pandavas*. As such, only the older brothers marry and the other brothers are also the husband of that lady. Surrounded by Himalayan hills, Jaunsarbavar is situated at an altitude of about 10–15 thousand feet. Snowfall during winter is heavy. Mussorie is about 70 km from the place where our project was situated.

The next day I visited Makhti village with Dr. Dinesh and met the villagers. One Param Singh was the village *syana* (head of the village). All of us sat together and discussed about their life there. I did not mention anything about what I was expected to do for them, as I myself was not clear about it. The winter was now coming to an end and *Shivaratri* was near. There was a dilapidated *mandir* of *Kayalu devata* (Kala Bhairav), the presiding deity of the village. It was in a bad shape due to ill-maintenance and I felt that I should start my work from there. I thought if the villagers permitted I should try to renovate the temple and make it the centre of my work.

The room where I was staying was very cramped with no facility for water. For answering calls of nature, we had to go to the forest carrying water in a container. Water was also not available nearby. Dr. Dinesh assigned a lady for carrying water for all of us. Now that *Shivaratri* was approaching, Dr. Dinesh wanted to go to his village somewhere near Etawah (in Uttar Pradesh). I was all alone there after his moving out of the project. I had no other way than depending on someone else to prepare my food.

For a few days, I had rice and *dal* from a small tea shop once a day. This continued till *Shivaratri*. Rajendra Singh Chauhan (son of the village head) and his friend one Chattar Singh were very cooperative. They suggested that instead of depending on the tea shop for my food, it was better that I cooked food myself, and they would also help me to do so. Dr. Dinesh's stove and utensils were in the small kitchen on the *verandah*. I began using them for cooking. I was not a good cook. Somehow I managed to prepare rice, *dal* and vegetables once a day and heated the leftovers for dinner. The self-cooking practice went on well. I was using most of my time to move around the villages nearby (a belt of 25 villages known as '*sell khat*') and sometimes I would take food in the villages if it was offered to me by the villagers. I used to interact with them regarding their life and what they were expecting from my organization. Our school was very small with just a few students but I wanted to enrol more. So whenever I visited a village I would talk to them about the importance of education and ask them to send their children to the school. Slowly the number of students increased and the number of teachers as well. The school was run under the Saraswati Sishu Mandir, a network of schools all over India.

One of the relatives of Rajendra Singh Chauhan was very poor as the head of the family was a drunkard. It was a family of husband, wife, and five children. I had noticed that their elder boy who was a student in the 5th grade was irregular in attendance. I told Rajendra Singh to ask whether that boy was willing to stay with me for his studies. After discussing with his parents, the boy agreed to stay with me.

Chaitra Navaratri was near. I had previously observed both *Navaratris* with fasting and reading *Chandi Paath*. This time I was in a dilemma. Now that I was in the field of '*karma yoga*' should I mix this with '*bhakti yoga*'? With this question in mind, I wrote a postcard to Dr. Nityanand about my intention to celebrate *Chaitra Navaratri* in that village, so that I could be in close touch with the villagers as well during my nine days of stay there. He sent his reply of consent with the bus driver.

After discussing with the village head and some other elders I decided to camp at the village for nine days during *Navaratri* and to do the *Chandi Paath*. A *Brahmin* named Milky Ram from the nearby village came forward to assist me in the programme. Everyday we recited the *Chandi Paath* in the morning and in the evenings the villagers sang some *bhajans* and songs. I was fasting for the nine days. This gave me plenty of time to observe and study the life of the villagers very closely. As mentioned earlier, most of the villagers were non-vegetarian and they drank country-made liquor which was prepared at every home and stocked. I said nothing against it as the geographical conditions were such that they are habituated to eat and drink as they did. Before concluding the *Chaitra Navaratri*, we all sat together to discuss the Kayalu Devata Mandir renovation. All were happy to hear that we could accomplish it with '*Sramadan*' (donation of time and effort, but not money, for a good cause) and that I would arrange to get an idol of *Kayalu Devata* sculpted in marble from Jaipur. There was a small idol of 6 inches height made of copper in that dilapidated *mandir* and Khajan Singh made a sketch of the idol for sending to Jaipur.

Navaratri went well and on the last day of *Vijaya Dasami*, people from nearby villages also attended. We had a community-feeding programme of rice and *dal* as *prasadam*. Param Singh and Amar Singh Rana took the responsibility for this. I went to Dehradun to meet Dr. Nityananda, to speak about my proposal for the development after my interaction with the villagers. He agreed with me. Dr. Dinesh was not returning now and Dr. Nityananda arranged for a new doctor from Dehradun. He had just completed medical studies and was ready to join the project. It would have been difficult for the villagers if there was no doctor in the project, as they would then have to go 16 km to Chakrata to get medicines. Dr. Mukesh was supposed to join within a couple of days. I waited and stayed in Karyala so that I could accompany the doctor on my return.

Cooking for Common Feeding in Jammu Ashram

Gomata Pooja at Jammu Ashram

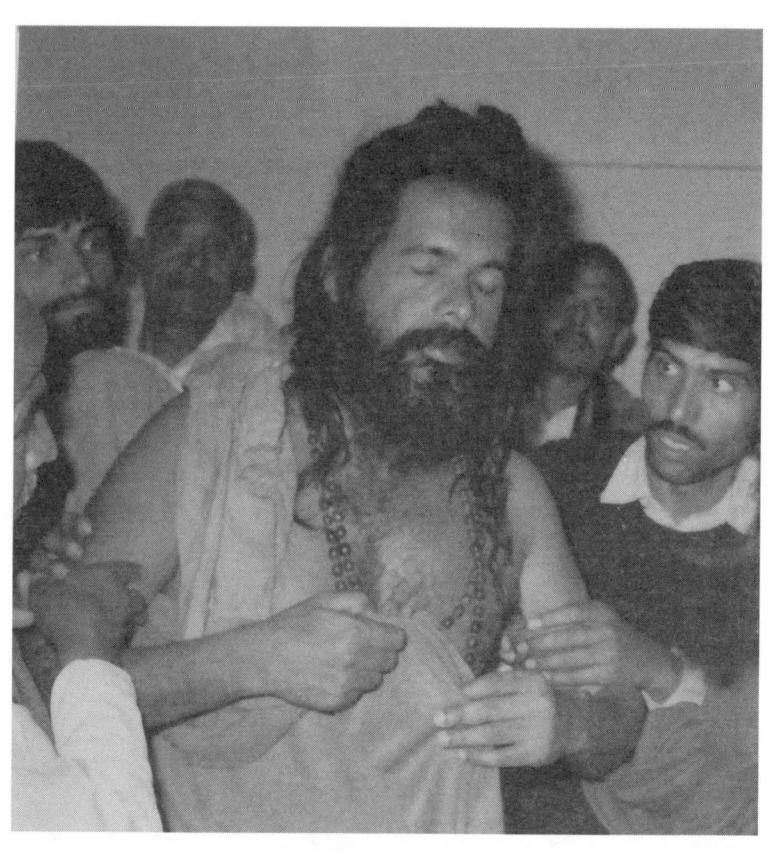

Bhava Samadhi

Deeksha of Mohi – Disciple of Avadhoota Nadananda

Doing Puja

Avadhoota Nadananda at Girnar

Mt. Kailash

Manasarovar

Bhagavan Nityananda

On the Return From Gyangunj

Life with Jaunsaris—II

After returning from Dehradun I concentrated on temple renovation work. All the villagers volunteered to join the work. It took more than four months to complete the renovation. A young lad named Vikram joined me during these days, an innocent and naive boy, who was studying in the fifth grade. He was attending the nearby elementary school, run by the government. I noticed that he was not aware of how to take a bath or wash his clothes. So I started to give him a bath daily in the afternoon when he returned from school, as well as washing his clothes and cooking for both of us. Slowly he picked up everything, bathing, washing and helping me cook food for both of us. When the renovation was almost complete, I brought the Kayalu Devata idol from Jaipur with the help of Rajendra Singh Chauhan.

Dr. Nityananda and others decided to make it a grand programme of installing the idol in the renovated temple. They invited the Dehradun Member of the Legislative Assembly (MLA), who was the Minister for *Gram Vikas* (Rural Development) and a few other dignitaries to the function. This enabled the construction of a road leading to the village, by the department with the help of the government. Mr. Harbans Kapoor, the minister who came to inaugurate the *Mandir*, made arrangements for the road. The local MLA Munna Singh Chauhan and other dignitaries were also present on the occasion. The villagers arranged for a community feeding programme on that day. Villagers from Sally Khat (from 25 nearby villages) came and there were drum beats, dances and songs. I took care of the *Moorti Sthapana* (installation of the idol with rites and rituals) with the help of a village friend and priest called Mali.

For the villagers, Mali's words were final. He was an oracle, who would throw some rice in to the sky and then catching a few grains in his hands, give predictions on the health and other day-to-day matters of the villagers. And before idol installation too, they took permission from Mali to do so.

But before the idol installation I called the elders of the village to discuss ending the slaughtering of goats and other animals at the *Mandir*. I told them that they could still offer an animal by tying it at the pillar of the *Mandir* as a symbol while breaking a coconut instead of slaughtering the innocent animal.

Since the custom of offering *bali* or sacrifice on an auspicious occasion had come down from time immemorial, the elders were at first uncomfortable about accepting my proposal. But I took Mali in confidence and convinced him to tell the villagers to accept the proposal. The villagers were afraid that if the sacrificial animal was not offered, the gods would get angry and it would be harmful for the village. Finally Mali convinced them to do as I said. Param Singh, the village head, also reassured them that the gods would not be angry by just symbolically offering the animal at the temple on the idol installation day and not actually sacrificing it. And in future there would be no animal slaughter at that mandir.

The second step that I took was the prohibition of liquor making and drinking in the village. They also accepted this proposal, except on festival days when they would offer liquor to deities and drink. Thus, the age old system of slaughtering and drinking in the village ended. They took an oath in front of the village deity as well. The newsletter/publication *Rajasthan Patrika* and *Panchajanyam* wrote in detail about me and my work in this direction.

But some villagers were not happy as they used to make country liquor and sell it to the other villages. They got angry with me and that was why one night, a few days after the function, one of the villagers attacked me with an iron rod. I was hurt on my head and was bleeding. This incident created a sympathy wave among the villagers as they thought I was doing something good for them yet a villager had attacked me. They called an assembly of the village *panchayat* and insisted that I tell them who had done the deed, but even though the culprit was sitting right in front of me, I told the *panchayat* that I had not seen his face and that I could not identify him. This action of mine created a change of mind in the person and he came to me and apologized the next day. To my wonder, he stopped making and drinking liquor from that day onwards.

Life with Jaunsaris—III

I was in charge of the project for more than five years and the experience was wonderful. The school grew to eight grades. Two other children besides Vikram began to stay with me. I used to go around the 25 villages often but work was totally concentrated only on Makhti village. After few months of stay with Dr. Mukesh I observed that he was selling medicines which he brought over from Dehradun for our dispensary. The medicines were supposed to be distributed free of cost. I had a talk with him, brought the matter to the notice of Dr. Nityanand, and Dr. Mukesh was removed from the project. For two months the project had no physician and then one Dr. Shyam Bihari, also fresh out of medical school, replaced him.

He had studied at Gurukul Kangadi Medical College and had a BAMS Degree. He was a very generous person who helped me in all my work and also tutored Vikram and the other two boys.

Winter was once again at our doorsteps. I had the same old *kambal* with me which I had been using previously, but now the *kambal* had to be shared with two more children. As I was only taking 500 rupees from the project for my personal expenses, I was not left with much money to spend on their warm clothes. Sri Tilak Raj Kapoor of Vanvasi Kalyan Ashram used to send DD or check to meet the expenses of the project—Rs. 2,000 to pay the doctor, Rs.5000 for medicines, and Rs. 500 for my expenses and some sundry expenses like rent, etc. One night I heard the sound of villagers in the courtyard of the building. They were around twenty people who had brought in a woman in labour pain. Dr. Shyam Bihari attended to her and then came to my room. As there were no other women in the group of villagers, the doctor wanted me to assist him in delivery. I was afraid. A patient was usually brought by villagers only in the case of emergencies. It was a practice with the Jaunsaris tribes to cooperate with any patient or a person in the village facing any problem, to help each other—one member from every household would accompany a patient in emergency, at night. When Dr. Shyam Bihari asked me to assist him in the delivery, I was full of doubt. There was a dilemma in my mind but the words of my *Guruji* suddenly came to mind—'Live for others'. I changed into a *lungi* borrowed from the doctor and went with him to the room where the expectant mother was lying and crying. The doctor gave her an injection and handing over a lot of cotton to me asked me to clean the blood, saying he would take care of other things. This incident will always be etched in my memory. I was neither a nurse nor a doctor. I was a *sanyasi*, and moreover a *brahmachari*. But praying to my *guru*, I helped the doctor in the delivery by cleaning blood and consoling the woman. It was a shock for me and an eye-opener. By the grace of Almighty it took about three-quarters of an hour to complete the delivery process. The baby and mother were fine and I too felt relieved.

The next day I wrote to Dr. Nityananda about the episode and requested him to also arrange for a midwife for the dispensary, and thank God, within a short time a retired midwife also joined our project.

My mind was growing restless and disturbed and I lost interest in my work. I had occasional chest pain and Dr. Shyam Bihari gave me medication.

Winter started in all ferocity. The two children and I used to share the single *kambal* which I possessed. They both slept on either side of me, and like a hen with her chicks under her wings, we were together. One of the boys had been suffering from some stomach disorder for a long time, and he used to emit a lot of gas (with a very bad smell) frequently. I tolerated this bad situation too, as we had no choice but to sleep together to share the single *kambal*. In addition due to insufficient rest with disturbed sleep, my chest pain also had increased. So Dr. Shyam Bihari asked me to go to Dehradun for a check-up with a heart specialist. Due to the snowfall there were no bus services and so with the help of

Rajendra Singh Chauhan, and some other villagers, I went up to Sahiya by walking through the hills. We had to stop along the way in one or two villages, and it took two days to reach Sahiya from where we caught a bus to Dehradun. I had become very weak by then and unable to walk even a few steps due to the chest pain. At Dehradun the heart specialist scolded me for coming so late in my illness, and that too by walk. I had symptoms of cardiac arrest and was admitted in the hospital for a few days.

After discharge from the hospital, I came to the *karyalaya* at Moti Bazaar to meet Dr. Nityananda. He asked me to rest there for a few days. I rested there for a week and returned to the project, up to Sahiya by bus and then by walk. The winter was still in full swing and so I took rest in my room for a few more days. Due to continuing ill health, I left the project.

Kumbha Mela and Journey to Narmada

The Kumbha Mela[29] at Allahabad was about to commence. I was with the *mandali* at Ludhiana. The chief of the *mandali* asked me to take all the food items to Allahabad, in a truck going from Ludhiana to Allahabad. I agreed. The devotees filled the truck with gunny bags of wheat, rice, *dal* and other such things for daily use of the *mandali* members. This was my first time traveling in a truck. I reached Allahabad on the third day. We reached Jhusi village where the *mandali* used to stay during Kumbha melas. Jhusi village is on the other side of the Ganga Sangam. A few Sikh devotees were there already to make arrangements for the stay of the *mandali*. The *sadhus* of the *mandali* were on the way to Allahabad by walk. They would reach in a day or two and I had to make arrangements for their stay and food before their arrival. With the help of the Sikh devotees, it was easy for me to do the work. When the Kumbha mela began, I took care of the *pooja/satsang*. A lot of *sadhu/sanyasis* stayed at our Virakta mandali. Swamy Shivananda was also with me. One day, a friend *brahmachari* of Shivanandaji was discussing his plans to go for '*Narmada parikrama*' (circumambulation of the Narmada River—from Omkareswar back to Omkareswar, about 1,800 miles, which usually takes 3 years, 3 months and 13 days to complete). He had done it once in 18 months. As I had never visited the Narmada, I had a strong urge to go there. The *brahmachari* was planning to go after the '*Kalpavas*' (41 days stay at Kumbha Mela) to Omkareswar,

---

29 One of the largest human congregations of a faith, involving pilgrimage to one of four holy towns of Hindus and bathing in a sacred river

and from there he would start his 'Narmada Parikrama'. With the consent of Swami Shivanandaji, I too planned to go. But as usual, I had no money for bus fare to Omkareshwar. Shivanandaji spoke to one of his friends known as '*Mauni*' (who had kept *maun* or vow of silence for a few years during his stay with the *mandali*) to help me out with some money to go to Omkareshwar. As I was not even handling money in those days, I asked '*Mauni*' to hand over the bus fare into the *brahmachari*'s hands.

Kumbha Mela was in full swing. Lakhs of *sadhus/sanyasis* reached *Prayag* (the *sangam* or confluence of the Rivers Ganga, Yamuna and Saraswati) for the holy bath and stay for 41 days. Once I heard from Shivanandaji about 'Mahavatar Babaji', who is the first *guru* of Gyanganj. (Mahavatar Baba is well known—he appears to devotees as a young man, aged fifteen or so.) I was very eager to search for and find him. Somewhere in Paramahamsa Yogananda's book I had read that *Babaji* attended the *Kumbha Mela* and that one could meet him—if one was lucky enough—among common beggar folk, sitting and controlling the devotees of Gyanganj. I was proud to be one of the *sanyasis* of Gyanganj. After my failure to reach Gyanganj I was deeply disappointed and the information about Mahavatar Babaji gave me new energy to search for him.

During the Kumbha Mela, every day after my ablutions and *bhiksha* I used to wander here and there, in search of *Babaji*. Days passed but my daily movements were not producing any results. One day during my search, it was almost sunset time when I reached near a group of people sitting in a row near the *sangam*. Now, I could easily make out the face of *Babaji* (which I had previously seen in a picture in Paramahamsa Yogananda's book). I tried to reach closer to him, but found that I could not move. It was as if my legs were chained. Again and again I tried to move, but in vain. I could see the face of *Babaji* from a distance. Now as I inched forward, I saw *Babaji* gesturing me, asking me to go. I prostrated standing there itself and once again tried to move towards him. Alas, he was not there and had disappeared from the vicinity. I felt sad and sat near the *sangam* for a while. I was in a trance for a long time. Mere vision had given me such intoxication! I felt a hand on my shoulder. Turning back, I saw a *swamiji* standing behind me in white robes, white matted hair and beard. He told me, "Look, *swamiji*, to have *darshan* or *sparsan* (touch) of great saints, we need to have a separate *pathrata* (eligibility)—purity of body, mind and intellect is very important. You failed to reach Gyanganj or *Babaji*. Why? You know, even now you have some impurity in your mind. *Sakamata*—the desire to gain something materialistic—is your problem." I was wondering to myself how this stranger, a swami unknown to me, knew that I had tried and failed to reach Gyanganj and *Babaji*. He then added, "I know what you are thinking now. You doubt me! You need not tell me anything as I know everything. I know all about you—that you have done good *sadhana* on *Srividya*, and that you are planning to travel to Narmada. But just be aware of one thing—a small impurity in mind or body or intellect, or any materialistic thought will hinder you in reaching your goal." Saying this, he merged back into the crowd.

It was almost night-time. Thousands of fluorescent lamps were burning all over the Kumbha Mela grounds. I felt bad about myself, my mind full of stress. Slowly and with much difficulty I tried to get up and moved towards the *mandali*. The forty-one day stay at the Kumbha Mela had been full of experiences. Meeting some great saints and *siddhas* gave me much courage. I made a resolution never to look back to materialism even though that *maya* was trying to eat me away and my life.

It was time to leave the Kumbh Mela. With instructions from Shivanandaji, I went to the bus stand with the *brahmachari*, and took a seat on a bus going to Indore. Thus began the journey to Narmada.

At Omkareshwar

We reached Indore the next day around noon and changed to another bus from there and reached Omkareshwar by evening. The *brahmachari* took me to the Markandeya Sanyas Ashram on the banks of Narmada. Swamy Ramanand Saraswati, a well-known scholar of *Vedanta*, was the head of the *ashram*. The *brahmachari* and I stayed there. There were about 20–30 *sanyasis* staying there and studying Vedanta. Swami Ramanandji took classes in the morning every day. Even though I was not a student of *Vedanta*, I also attended the classes.

I was introduced to *Swamiji* by the *brahmachari*. I told him about my journey to the Himalayas and my desire to do the Narmada parikrama. Swamiji had done it in his younger days, and told me about the difficulties of the journey. The *brahmachari* and two of his friends (all the people in the *ashram* were *brahmacharis*) and one Swami Budha Das were also ready to travel.

The Narmada flows right by that *ashram* and on the opposite bank was the famous Jyotir Lingam of Omkareshwar. On the bank along the *ashram* was Amaleshwar. I visited these *mandirs* with a few other *sanyasis*. The Omkareshwar Jyotir Lingam is on top of a hill. Down the hill, just near the Narmada was a cave that had once been occupied by Bhagavan Govinda Pada (the guru of Adi Shankaracharya). This was the place where Adi Shankaracharya had studied and practiced *Vedanta* under his guru's guidance. The cave was restored and is now maintained by the Kanchi Sankara Mutt. Swami Ramanandji asked me about my *sadhana* in the Himalayas. When he heard that I had completed seven *purascharans* on *Srividya shodashi mantra*, there was no end to his wonder. He asked me to study *Vedanta*, but for some reason I was very reluctant. *Swamiji* asked me to stay for a few more days at the *ashram*. I used to sit on the banks of the Narmada for hours together in the evenings. One day, the *brahmachari* and the others told me that they were ready to start on the journey. We then took a letter of introduction from the *ashram* and embarked on the journey next day.

The path on the banks of the Narmada was full of stones and thorns. We were supposed to walk barefoot. The beginning itself was very tedious. After two hours' walk we reached Khedi Ghat (Moretaka) where we decided to stay for the night. Swami Budha Das knew somebody there as he had stayed at Khedi Ghat previously. Some villagers brought us food and we rested there.

I was enjoying the journey. On reaching a village, our group of five travellers would split and go for collecting *bhiksha* separately. Though the villagers were not very rich, yet they had made arrangements at every *mandir* on the banks of Narmada, for 'Sadavrat' (giving alms to one on *parikrama*). They used to give wheat flour, salt, oil, rice and cooking utensils and *sanyasis* were also allowed to take cooked food from any house in the village. On the fifth day we reached Raj Ghat. From there on, the dense forest region known as 'Sool Paneeswarea Jhadi' starts. If the traveling devotees on a pilgrimage had any valuables, they could keep them at the village chiefs' residence and when they reached the other side of the Narmada during *parikrama*, they could send a message with any boatman fishing there, and their valuables would be returned!

We continued on our journey and by evening had reached the big bend in the Narmada. We spotted a small cottage and all of us reached there. An *Avadhootswami* in his loincloth was sitting there alone. He had nothing in the cottage except for a small fire. After we had done prostration, he asked us to go and bathe and return there to rest. When we were ready to leave for bathing he asked, "What would you like to eat at night?" I wondered about that since there was nothing in that cottage, yet he was asking us for our requests for dinner. Swamy Budha Das was a very egocentric person. Without a second thought he said, "*Dal, baati, churma.*" (This was one of the famous foods of Madhya Pradesh, which wealthy people serve their guests.) I felt embarrassed at the way Budha Das behaved.

But, lo! When we returned after bathing, to my wonder I saw a few clay pots full of *dal, baati* and *churma*! I was a bit reluctant to eat, as it made me nervous. Of course it was the miracle of the *Avadhoot Baba*. Others had their food and I came out and sat under a tree, where a small Narmadeswar Shivaling was installed. My mind was full of fear and anxiety. By this time, the others were ready to sleep. They spread out their bed inside the cottage and slept.

The *Avadhoot Swami* came out and sat near me. He asked me why I had not eaten even though I was hungry. I told him the truth, that I was afraid to see the pots full of food, presuming it to be a miracle. Then I asked him in all my innocence and fear, "*Maharaj*, when we came inside your cottage there was not even a single pot. But after returning from our baths, there were many pots full of *dal, baati* and *churma*. How was it possible?" Pointing to a small stick in his hand, he said, "Shiva is sitting here. I will show my stick to him if anyone tests me."

There was silence for a few minutes. Then the *Avadhoot Maharaj* said, "Even now you have not recognized me. You are my grandson. Tara told me you would be on Narmada pilgrimage. I would like to caution you on one matter. Do not travel with this group. Just like you have travelled in Tibet, be alone. The company of this group will disturb your pilgrimage." I was wondering; it had been more than three or four years since the *samadhi* of my Paramaguru Nityananda Bhagavan in Ganeshpuri. But how was he here now, taking the same form? There were no limit to my foolish thoughts. Reading my mind, he said, "You are still a child. Everything is possible. One should have belief in the Almighty, everything is possible. Everything!" He stood up and went into his cottage. I was sitting all alone and praying to my *Guruji* to give me a clear idea of what was going on.

Following the *Avadhoot Maharaj's* instruction, I decided not to continue to travel with the group. The next morning I told them that due to a stomach problem, I was unable to travel with them that day. They left in the early morning itself. After ablutions I came to the cottage. There was nobody there! I sat near the fire which was almost extinguished. I waited for my *Paramaguru, Avadhoot Baba*, for a long time but in vain. After some time, a villager came inside the cottage and deposited his clothes and some packed food (maybe his lunch) there. He was ready to go fishing. I asked him about the *Avadhoot Maharaj*. He laughed at me and said, "*Maharaj*, I was born and brought up in the nearby village and am now about 40 years old. I have never seen any *Maharaj* staying here in my life. This *tapara* (cottage) was made by the village fishermen. You were tired at night and probably had a dream about that *maharaj*." There was no end to my wonder. Was it a dream? If so, how could I still see the empty pots and Shivalingam there? This cottage, extinguished fire? Thinking about all this, I fell asleep in that cottage. By afternoon, the fisherman villager returned to the cottage. There were three or four *rotis* made of *bajra* (millet) in his packed lunch. Before eating he asked me to take one or two *rotis* and some fried vegetables. In another packet, he had some fish curry too. He washed his hands again and again, and sprinkled some water on to it and offered me two *rotis* and vegetables. I ate it happily and decided to take rest there for the night.

The Journey for Nothingness—I

Next day early in the morning, I resumed my journey. I was moving through a dense forest on the Narmada banks. There was no village in the vicinity. I could hear the sounds of animals very well. After a while two women and some men appeared in front of me out of nowhere. They were tribals of the forest and to my wonder, they wore only loin cloths. There were no upper and lower garments on their bodies. Coming near, they uttered, "*Muk, Muk*" (stop, stop). I had been warned at Omkareshwar about the tribals, that they would come and loot the *yatris*. Of course I had nothing valuable other than my kappar and *kamandal*. They stripped my clothes one by one and took them all, and even the two small pieces of cloth and the *kambal*. Thank God, they spared my *kappar* and *kamandal*. They turned me into an *Avadhoota* without clothes and any possessions! The tribals disappeared and once again I resumed my journey. Now I was wearing only a loincloth, with a *kamandal* and *kappar* in hand.

By afternoon I had reached a tribal village. As I was very hungry, I went to the village (a small village of less than ten huts) in search of food. I observed that most of them didn't have proper clothes except for small pieces of cloth that only covered their private parts. One of the women offered me some *atta* (wheat flour) and I came back to the Narmada. As I had no utensils or fire to cook with, I put the Atta into my bhiksha pathra, and poured in some Narmada water and drank the mixture. I started walking again and was feeling a little shy as I was not clothed.

On the banks of the Narmada I saw a small cremation ground. I thought that since it was evening, it was better to stay at this cremation ground for the night. I sat there calm and composed.

There was a piece of burlap lying near a pyre (funeral fire). It seemed like a body had been cremated a few hours ago and it was still burning. The villagers might have brought the dead body wrapped in the burlap. I picked it up as it was comfortable for me to wear. I washed it in the Narmada and laid it out to dry. Now it was almost sunset hour. I was afraid how I would spend the night here without any light. I only had the funeral fire for support.

Around me there was only darkness and the sounds of wild animals. The wheat flour mixture which I had had was creating a problem in my stomach. But I was very hungry too. I saw two shadows appearing—it was that of two villagers who had come there to fish. They came there and asked me about my journey. The tribals on the banks of Narmada are called '*Mama*' (uncle) as they consider themselves brothers of '*Maa*' (Mother) Narmada. Narmada is called as '*Maa*' so mother's brother is '*Mama*' (uncle). The villagers told me it would be risky to stay there alone at night, since the animals from the forest came there for drinking water, and they might attack me as they become wild when they see some person. I told them that my *Guruji* would take care and I opted to stay there itself, near the fire. The tribals adjusted the firewood to build up the fire. They told me that they had not come there for fishing—they had come just to adjust the fire wood. They once again cautioned that sometimes crocodiles also came to the shore and it would be more dangerous. They asked me whether I had taken any food and I told them about the *atta* mixing-in-water that I drank at noon. When they were ready to go back to the village, they asked me to accompany them. But I refused to go. After an hour or so I saw both the villagers return to me. I was sitting near the pyre. They came and offered me two *rotis* (large in size) made of *bajra* and a few green chillies and salt. I took it happily and the villagers said they would also stay there, as I was staying there alone that night. I told them several times that I was not afraid, but they slept near me on the sands of the Narmada.

In this remote village, and unknown tribal area, nobody was near me—but who arranged for those strangers to look after me, not just provide food but my security as well. I knew that behind all this was the hand of my *Guruji*. It was my *Guruji* alone who was arranging for my safety and food.

These are the ways of *sadgurus* (true gurus). They will take care of their children wherever they are. Otherwise, these unknown tribals were strangers to me. Not my friends, relatives or disciples!

But they had come due to the impulse of some unknown person and had taken care of my food and security. I was amazed at my *Guruji's* love towards me!

The Journey for Nothingness—II

I woke up a little late in the morning. By that time the tribals had left. I saw that the burlap cloth was almost dry and that the funeral pyre had also become cold. I bathed but having no cloth to dry my body, I sat on a rock for some time to dry out the water. As I had laid out my loincloth to dry, I was now just like a new-born baby, fully naked. As it was a forest, and there was no villager nearby, I did not mind it, but was feeling a bit shy thinking perhaps the *vandevatas* (forest angels) were looking at me. I left that burial ground after a while, wearing the loincloth and the burlap cloth.

I had a thought. What was wrong in being naked? It is the nakedness of mind and body that led one to God. I had read this somewhere but that was a just a thought only. I was not prepared to keep my body naked—though my mind was always naked. I kept nothing in my mind.

As I started walking, my stomach was upset from the previous day's wheat flour mixture. I started having diarrhoea. I had almost six or seven bowel movements within a few hours. And I had not eaten any food. My throat was dry and I felt very weak. Before sunset I reached some unknown area which was less forested and as I was tired I rested there on the banks of the river Narmada. I drank a lot of water from Narmada and lay down on the sand.

As the diarrhoea continued through the night, it became very difficult for me to even sit up in the morning. I was praying to my *Guruji* to reverse this very bad situation. With great difficulty I got up and somehow started walking again, but the diarrhoea continued to trouble me.

By noon I had reached the edge of the forest. A village, known as Hapeswar, was visible. I sat on the banks of Mother Narmada. I saw an old woman from the village coming towards me. She was carrying some firewood on her head and came and sat near me and enquired about my *parikrama*. I told her about my diarrhoea problem and asked if there was any doctor available at a nearby village. With a beautiful smile (resembling my *Guruji*'s smile) she said, "What can a doctor do? Just wait—I will get some medicine for you!" She disappeared into the nearby bushes and brought a few leaves and washed them in the Narmada. She then put the leaves on a stone and crushed them to a paste and mixing it with Narmada water, poured it into my *kappar* and asked me to drink it. I took that herbal medicine prepared by the tribal woman without any hesitation. She sat by me, loudly singing a tribal song as if she was giving some solace to my body and mind.

On the other bank of the Narmada, there was a Shiv *mandir*. With the help of a boat man, the *mandir*'s priest brought me rice, *dal* and vegetables and then returned to the *mandir*. After leaving Omkareshwar this was the first time I was getting to eat rice. (As a south Indian, I always prefer to eat rice.) That old lady was about to leave but I asked her to be with me for some more time and to share some food with me. At first she was reluctant, but when I invited her again to eat with me, she agreed. She washed her hands and shared the food with me from my *kappar*. This was the first time that I was allowing somebody to eat directly from my *kappar*. After eating the food she left. I was thinking that this woman could not be just an ordinary village woman. She must be either Maa Narmada or my *Guruji* in that form. As I had eaten a stomach full of rice, I felt sleepy. After an hour or so of resting there, I was ready to start moving again. Now my stomach felt much better.

But a while later, my stomach started bothering me again. It was full of gas and a severe pain had also developed. The diarrhoea began again and by evening I had had more than ten bowel movements. It was around sunset. I was exhausted from the diarrhoea and stomach pain. I could see that some construction work was happening nearby and some tin sheds. A hydroelectric dam was being constructed on the Narmada there (in the future this dam would be known as the Sardar Sarovar). I came up to the *verandah* of a tin shed and lay down there.

A few labourers came up to me and asked me what the problem was. When I told them of my physical condition, they brought the construction engineer and the site physician. I spoke to them in English. The doctor gave me two-three tablets, asking me to take one now and the rest the next day. They also informed me that outsiders were not permitted to stay there, and if I walked fast I could reach the Soolpaneeshwar Mandir in an hour where I could rest at night. I walked for some time and reached the *mandir* at dark. The *arathi* had just ended and the priest and two *sadhus* also in *parikrama* were just about to start dinner. They asked me to join them but as I was not well I told them that I would not take any food. I just lay down on the floor of the *mandir*. The stomach pain increased and I again had four-five bowel movements after reaching there. The priest and *sadhus* were worried and were discussing among themselves if I should be taken to Kevadia colony where I could get good treatment. They asked me to go along with them. And they were ready to carry me on their shoulders.

They were talking about one Narpat Bhai who had a hut near the bridge to Kevadia. Narpat Bhai and his wife had been doing *seva* to *parikrama vasis* for the last few years by offering them food, medicine and shelter. He was famous among the people doing *parikrama*. With the help of those two *sadhus* and priest, and resting my weight on their bodies, I started moving with them. On the way there also the diarrhoea continued. It took more than two hours to walk to the house of Narpat Bhai. Somehow, we managed to reach Narpat Bhai's residence.

I just lay down at his residence. It was a big thatched hut. Narpat Bhai went to Kevadia on his scooter and brought a doctor, and medications were started with an injection and saline drip.

Broken Dreams

The next day they took me to a hospital in Kevadia colony. This colony had been made for the staff and workers employed in the dam project. Even though it was not a big colony, all facilities were available there. I was admitted into a private hospital. I was not fully conscious, yet I remember the feeling of deep sadness at having broken the *sankalpa* of *parikrama* by crossing the Narmada and thus my long-standing dream of completing Narmada *parikrama* was now unrealized. After three days' stay at the hospital, I was discharged. During these three days, Narpat Bhai or his wife were always by my side. It was a wonder and an evergreen memory for me that in Gujarat, in an unknown remote area, there was someone to take care of me. These people were total strangers to me. I was only a wayside traveller and yet the way they had served me was indeed a matter of wonder! But one thing was certain, without *Guru krupa* all such things would never have happened. I recalled the words of my *Guruji*, "Wherever you are, I will be there." In each and every step of my life, I had felt the presence of my *Guruji*, and even now, in every moment 'Amma' is with me!

It took more than a month to return to normal health. I slowly started eating a little rice and yogurt. Now I could walk up to the Narmada for my morning ablutions, etc. On the other side of Narmada, after walking a few furlongs upstream, there was a school by the name of Sri Rama Krishna School, run by a *swamiji* from Bengal. He had come there a few years ago and had constructed a small Shiva *mandir* and a school. Moolshankar was the priest there. Once or twice I visited the *swamiji*, and whenever I met him, he would ask me to join him to stay there to look after the school. I was still staying with Narpat Bhai and his wife. They told me that they were performing the *seva* to people doing *parikrama*, under the orders of Narmada Mayee! And they were blessed with two children due to the *ashirvaad* of Narmada. Narpat Bhai and wife had done parikrama for three years. He had sold all the land he owned in his parental village, and was spending it here for *seva*. He was also working as a driver in the state transportation department. His wife was doing *seva* for me when I was unable to get up or walk. I was extremely weak and she used to give me bath and feed me, and hold my hand when I tried to walk. The priest Moolshankar used to visit their house. Somehow he could not reconcile to the fact that a young woman was serving a young *swami*. He made distasteful comments that if such *seva* continued the *swami* would run away with the woman. When I heard this it gave me deep pain; at a time when my health was not yet back to normal. The next time when Moolshankar came over, I asked him about his comments. He told me that being a *sanyasi* I should not accept *seva* from young women. I was enraged at his comments and thrashed him again and again till Narpat Bhai came there and restrained me. The *swamiji* also heard the news about Moolshankar's comments and sacked him from his job as the *mandir* priest. The next day Moolshankar again came to me and asked forgiveness for his mistakes. He told that he had lost his job, and that it would be difficult for him to look after his family now. I went to the *swamiji* with him and due to my requests, the *swamiji* reappointed him as priest. After a month's stay with Narpat Bhai and family I went to the *swamiji*. He gladly invited me to stay there. He was quite old and was running the school, which had a good number of students and seven teachers. The school had classes up to eighth grade and was recognized by the government. The medium of instruction was English. Swamiji provided me a room for stay in the school building itself. A *vaishya* family (who ran a grocery shop in the nearby village) provided residence for *swamiji* and they were his disciples. I began taking my food with *swamiji* at their house as well. After a few days' stay *swamiji* asked me to take charge of the school as administrator. He gave me a few *kashaya* clothes too. But still something was keeping me away from getting attached to that school and to my post as administrator.

But due to the affection shown to me and also in their way of dealing, I decided to take charge of the school. Only during school times did I wear the *kashaya vastram* given by *swamiji*. In the mornings and evenings I would go to the Narmada bank to sit for one or two hours of *japa*. A lot of work had been pending in that school and I had to set everything in order. For more than one month, I worked hard to set up the school records properly.

There arose a thought in my mind to do some *sadhana* on the banks of the Narmada. This place was very peaceful and quiet. So one day I told the *swamiji* that since I was free before 10 am and after 4 pm (10 to 4 was the school time) and as I didn't want to sit idle, I would like to start another *purascharan* of *Srividya japa* (this would be my 8th *purascharan*); *swamiji* was very happy to hear about my will to do a *japa purascharan*, since he was himself a devotee of Mother and used to do daily *Chandi Paath*. That was his only *sadhana*.

Even though not very wealthy, the *vaishyas* (with whom *swamiji* and I were staying) were very generous and good people. They had a scooter and the family head's sister-in-law, Meena who was a college student in Kevadia colony began teaching me to drive a motor scooter on the school grounds in the evenings. She used to sit behind me and instructed me in riding in ten days and then *swamiji* helped me get a driving license. This was helpful to me in going to the market or Rajpipla (a nearby small town) for some work.

One *Panchami* day after doing a small *pooja* to the Goddesses Lalitha and Narmada, I took the *sankalpa* of doing *purascharan*. Every day before sunrise I would go to the Narmada and sitting there on a flat rock, do *japa* till 10 am and in the evenings after school hours, I would go again to the Narmada for *japa* at 5 pm. The evening *japa* session sometimes went on till midnight.

I was very happy there. Almost a month had passed by when the *swamiji* received a letter from his *gurubhai*, and went to Bengal to meet his ailing *Guruji*. He gave me a power of attorney to sign the cheques and other documents. I was thinking about how even though I was trying to run away from *maya*, yet it was retaining its ferocious grip on me! Even though I was in charge of the school, I did not allow my work to disturb my daily *japa*.

Running away From Maya

I was doing my *japa purascharan* daily on schedule. I was also attending to the school work every day. The teachers were all very cooperative. Recently a girl had joined our school as an art teacher. She was very good-looking and used to help me in office work too. But I did not realize that it was another form of *maya* trying to get its clutches on me. She was slowly moving close to me. On some days she used to bring *dhokhla* (a type of steamed dumpling made of chickpea flour—a Gujarathi dish) for me. Even though I had lunch and dinner at the *vaishya* family's house, she used to make me eat during leisure time, and one day she said, "It is my bad luck that you are a *sanyasi*. If not, I would have preferred to marry you! "In the preceding days I had sensed that she was in love with me, her actions and work were such. I was shocked to hear her words. Here I was, a '*Sarva Sanga Parityaga Sanyasi*', and this teacher here was in love with me. (One sided, of course! I had sealed off my mind to '*kamini* and *kanchana*'.) I felt very bad for her and told her that if she behaved that way I would have to fire her from her job.

I told the principal of the school about the girl's words. The principal (a woman who was an ex-employee of the government) also scolded her. The next the girl again told me,—"Oh I do not know if you feel bad or good about it but I am opening my heart out to you. I love you. If you can give up *sanyasa*, I would definitely like to marry you!" I got angry and asked the school clerk to type up a termination letter to give the art teacher. I was about to sign the termination letter when the principal told me about her pathetic life. Neither her father nor her mother were alive and she was the only earning member of her family which consisted of her grandmother and her two younger brothers (who were going to school in Rajpipla) and she had to look after them. I called the art teacher and showed her the termination letter. Then I tore it into pieces and threw it in the garbage. Then I told the teacher, "See, you can love me. But not as a person to satisfy your sexual desire. Become a disciple of mine. I too will love you as my daughter. So, be prepared for a *deeksha*. Don't look upon me as a lover. Look to me as your *Guru*." I asked her to follow me to the banks of the Narmada, where I initiated her with the Bala Mantra and returned. The principal was happy to hear about the ending to the episode.

Two more months passed without much problem and my *purascharan* was in progress. This time it seemed that it would take more than four months, since I was not having much time available to do *japa*, as I did in the Himalayas.

One day I received a letter from *swamiji* that his *Guruji* had attained *samadhi* after prolonged illness. And that the *swamiji* would be back by the month end. I had already made up my mind to go to Haridwar as soon as *swamiji* returned. *Maya*'s hands were very fierce and I had to somehow get rid of them. By the end of the month *swamiji* returned from Bengal. I had done calculations and found that if I continued *japa* this way, the *purascharan* would be complete within 20–25 days. I returned the power of attorney and other documents to *swamiji* and told him about what had happened during his absence. He was happy that I was almost finishing my *japa*. When the *japa* was over, *swamiji* arranged for a community feeding for the school children and villagers. I told *swamiji* about my plans to go to Haridwar. But he was not ready to accept my proposal. Within a week after *purascharan* my health again turned for the worse. This time it was the same old chest pain which I had had during my stay in Makhti (Jaunsar bavar). *Swamiji* took me in our school bus (a 15-seat Swaraj Mazda) to Surat for a check-up. Once again there were the symptoms of a heart attack! The doctor asked me to get admitted in his hospital. But I was not willing, and came back with the prescribed medication. I came back to school, where I took rest for some days. Now I could not attend school regularly. The art teacher (who I had initiated) helped me with daily needs during the rest of the fifteen days. I noticed now, a tremendous change in her attitude. The way she looked upon me had changed. Now she was helping me as her *Guruji*, not as a lover. I was happy for her—she had changed, and I assured her she would be married one day to a good person and would lead a good family life.

The rest of fifteen days was over. I felt I was all right since as of now, there was no chest pain or restlessness. Only the body was weak. I was ready to leave for Haridwar. Finally after a lot of pressure, the *swamiji* agreed to me leaving him. There were tears in his eyes, when he permitted me to go.

One of the committee members took me to Baroda by bus and purchased a railway ticket for me. I had left my *kashaya* clothes in the school and came away with just my gunny cloth. Yes, I was still carrying my *kamandal* and *kappar* with me, a part and parcel of my life as a *sanyasi*. The man who accompanied me tried giving me some money. As I didn't have the habit of keeping money I refused it.

Now the train started moving. I was on my way back to Haridwar.

Again Haridwar

By the afternoon next day, I reached Haridwar and went directly to Sapta Sarovar. I could not get a room at the Rishi Ashram where I had lived earlier, since I was wearing a gunny cloth. One was supposed to wear *kashaya* to be able to stay there. I came to a nearby ashram called Ram kutir and got a room there. Krishna Malhotra (fondly called as Krishna Mataji) was very generous to offer me a room to stay there. After her *Guruji's samadhi*, she was looking after the *ashram*. *Mataji* hailed from Ludhiana in Punjab. Even though I was wearing a gunny cloth, they gave me accommodation at that *ashram*. (Usually *swamis* in *Avadhoota* attire will never stay in *ashrams*.) During my stay at Ram kutir I did not go for *bhiksha* with the *mandali*. In the mornings I took *bhiksha* at Ram kutir and in the evenings at Virakta kutia.

I met swami Shivanandaji daily. We used to go for walks along the banks of the *Ganga*. Once, Gopal Muni (who had earlier taught me *Vedanta*) asked me to continue my lessons. I was happy to join him for classes on the *Brahma sutra*.

Days were passing in good mood and health. One day I told Krishna Mataji that I had completed eight *purascharans* on *Srividya shodashi mantra* and would like to do it a ninth time if she permitted to do so at the *ashram*. Mataji happily agreed. But Shivanandaji said that it would be better to do the *japa* on the Ganga banks. I too felt that was right. During those days I used to take injections of Fortwin daily to treat my chest pain. In the beginning it was one or two injections. But then I got addicted to it and was taking four or five injections daily. As I had no money to purchase the medication for the injections, the manager of Ram kutir ashram, Harish, used to get them for me.

By this time Dr. Shyam Bihari had left the dispensary at Makhti (Chakrata) and joined the dispensary run by Ram kutir ashram. He also helped in supplying the Fortwin injections from his dispensary. He used to write in his records that the injections were supplied to his patients, but instead he supplied it to me. I felt that this was malpractice and asked him not to do so, and that he should give them to me only if he was willing to supply injections by purchasing them. He did so accordingly.

During my stay in Kohima (Nagaland) at a project run by Vivekananda Kendra (this project at Kohima is known as Rama Krishna Society, started by *Poojya* [respected] Swami Ranganathanand of Ramakrishna Mission and there was a full-fledged hospital, school and other social activities) I had initiated two *brahmacharis*, Godan and Mohan, both from Kerala. (Later Godan passed away due to peptic ulcer in a few years at a young age.) I left the Kohima project after a few years of staying there, and the whereabouts of Mohan were unknown to me. One day a *swamiji* of my acquaintance brought a *brahmachari* to meet me. I was astonished to see that it was the same old Mohan, in yellow clothes. Now, he was known as Narayan Chaitanya (he was given this name and yellow robe by one *swami* in Palghat in Kerala). Narayan Chaitanya recognized me and said, "*Swamiji*, somebody told me that you had died due to heart problems during your Narmada *parikrama*, and there has been no contact between us since you left Nagaland. I have taken *brahmachari deeksha* and left Vivekananda Kendra and am now staying at Kerala ashram in Rishikesh." He was happy to see me again and came to meet me at Ram kutir occasionally.

Once during his visits, I told him, "Now *Guru Poornima* is near. I am going to initiate you into *sanyasa* on that day. Be ready, we shall do the *sanyas sanskara* on the banks of the *Ganga*." It seemed like he was happy. I asked him not to worry as I would make arrangements for *Viraja homam*, etc. I added, "One *brahmachari* Narayan from the *Virakta mandali* (who is also from Kerala) is here in Haridwar. By his request, I will be initiating him into *sanyasa* as well on that day." I asked him to go to the forest to get a '*palash* stick' for *sanyasa sanskar*. *Mataji* of Ramkutir arranged for a *bhandara*[30] on that day for the invitees (*sadhus/sanyasis*). One day before the *sanyas sanskara*, Madanlal from Jammu (where the construction work of the *ashram* was going on) also came to meet me. One of my friends, Udasi Swami, was staying in a small *kutia* (hut) on the banks of the Ganga. He had an *akhanda dhuni* ('eternal flame', or incessantly burning fire) and with this Udasi swamiji's permission we performed *viraja homam* at his dhuni and in the early hours of *Guru Poornima* day at the Ganga ghat of Sapta Sarovar, I initiated both *brahmacharis* into *sanyasa*.

These two were my first *sanyasi* disciples. One was given the name of Swami Omkaranand Tirth and the other Swami Pranavanand Tirth (this Pranavanand left me the day after *sanyasa* initiation towards the *mandali* and till today his whereabouts are not known). Omkarananda stayed with me. After few days we decided we needed a small *parnasala* (hut made of leaves) on the banks of the *Ganga*. Udasi Swamiji showed me an old *parnasala* near his *kutia*, and we repaired it with leaves, and Omkarananda and I started staying there. For *bhiksha* Omkarananda would go to the *mandali* while I had it at Ram kutir.

My injection habit was still continuing. Omkarananda felt uncomfortable about this habit. But I did not know how to come out of it.

I used to teach Omkarananda the *Upanishads* every day. In the early morning I had a habit of taking tea. I didn't have money to buy it from a tea stall and even if I did it would not look good to take tea from a stall. As the *sanyasis* there were very orthodox, they would not regard us well. Even then Omkarananda used to bring tea for me from the tea shop every morning in his *kamandal* (made of steel).

I was enjoying the stay on the *Ganga* banks and days passed thus uneventfully.

I was planning to return to the old *mandali* of *sadhus*. Madan Lal informed me that the construction work was progressing and

---

30 Devotees prepare food on large scale as a religious offering to god and eat it later in a community setting.

asked me to go with him. But I was reluctant to go to the village where the *ashram* was being constructed. Leaving Omkarananda at Sapta Sarovar, one day I left for the *mandali* (which was in Punjab then) with Shivanandaji.

Aimless Journey

My frame of mind changed on reaching Ludhiana, and I told Shivanandaji that I was not interested in going to the *mandali,* as I wished to go elsewhere. Shivanandaji had always been very cooperative, and understood my feelings. He left for the *mandali* at Phagwara, towards Ludhiana, while I too left for the bus stand. I had no particular place in mind to go to. At the bus stand I spotted a Rajasthan State Road Transport Corporation (S.R.T.C.) bus getting ready to leave for Jaipur. I felt like I should go to Jaipur and from there on to Pushkar. As usual I didn't have money on me. I approached the bus conductor and told him that I had no money and wanted to go to Pushkar. He was a very helpful soul. Taking some amount from his pocket he bought me a ticket to Jaipur. And the aimless journey had now begun. He also offered me food on the way, when the bus stopped for lunch at a *dhaba* (roadside eatery) in Haryana. The journey was quite long, with the bus passing through Delhi towards Jaipur. We reached Jaipur late at night. The bus conductor guided me to another bus going to Pushkar via Ajmer. He spoke to the conductor of the bus, who also agreed to take me to Pushkar even though I was unable to pay.

The next morning I reached Pushkar. I went to a nearby *ashram* (Dasnam Sanyas Ashram) to seek accommodation. To my surprise, Swami Maneeshanand (who was previously at Chinmaya Mission) was in-charge of the *ashram.* We were known to each other from earlier days. He gladly offered me accommodation there. I went around Pushkar, and visited Brahmaji Mandir and other places.

I stayed there for a few days. Swami Maneeshanand had long been a good friend. His *guru bhai* was also staying there who was a very calm and composed *swamiji.* One day after dinner, all of us along with a few *brahmacharis*, sat down for a discussion on our experiences along the spiritual path. During the conversation one of the *brahmacharis* spoke unkindly to the *guru bhai* of Swami Maneeshanand. The *brahmachari* in his rage was about to hit that *swami*. I felt hurt and angry as well. Picking up a shoe lying on the *verandah*, I hit him several times till Maneeshanand saved him from my anger. My mood was very disturbed. I got ready to leave Pushkar, and the two other *swamijis* (one known as Mithaiwala Baba and one as Meghananda Puri also joined me.

As there was a train from Ajmer to Omkareshwar we opted to go there. One of the *swamjis* paid for the rail fares and we started from there on a meter gauge train. By next day afternoon we had reached Markandeya Sanyas Ashram (of Swami Ramanand Saraswati) where I had stayed before my first failed Narmada parikrama. I narrated to *Swamiji* about how I had failed in my journey of *parikrama*. With *Swamiji*'s permission I stayed there for one day and told him about my intention to restart the *parikrama* once again. Since it was the rainy season, *swamiji* didn't agree to this proposal. Some of the other inmates were planning on a south India pilgrimage. That idea also attracted me. They were going to go by train to Andhra Pradesh and Tamil Nadu, to visit famous temples there. Even though I didn't have money with me, I too wanted to accompany them.

Swami Arghyananda (who was a renunciate from Sri Ramakrishna Mission) was the *Kothari* (in charge of the store and money) of that *ashram*. We used to sit daily on the banks of the Narmada and sing ghazals or bhajans and had become good friends. One day I told him of my will to travel to the South on pilgrimage. Hearing this, he gave me Rs. 2,000 and now my mind was made up on traveling with the two *swamijis*, starting with the destination of Tirupathi. One day we purchased our railway tickets and commenced the journey to the South.

Somehow my mind was not adjusting to these two *swamijis*. We travelled together up to Hyderabad and then I told them that I wanted to part ways and would like to continue on my journey alone. They went to visit Hyderabad while I sat at the railway station waiting for a train to Tirupathi scheduled to leave at night.

I reached Tirupathi in the morning. I was left with nearly Rs. 1,500 after paying the rail fare. I was visiting Tirupathi for the first time, and somehow after wandering for a few hours, I found a place to stay in one of the Vaishnav mutts (name was probably Hathi Ram mutt). I rested there well for two days.

Journey in South (In Tirumala)

This was the first time I was visiting Tirumala. Being a *shakta*, there was in my mind some aversion to visit *Vaishnav* temples. But since I was on an unplanned and impromptu pilgrimage to the South, I thought to myself that now that I was here, I must first visit the famous Venkateshwara Mandir too. In those days my *Advaita* experiences had not yet matured fully, and though I had read about the theory of 'Oneness', I had not quite digested it. I had known and experienced only the *Shakti Tatva* during my *sadhana*. To be frank, I was reluctant to go to Tirupathi or Guruvayur, as I used to visit only *Shiva-Shakti mandirs*. Anyway starting from Tirupathi, I began climbing the hills. Slowly and steadily, while resting along the way, I climbed the hills. I considered it like a picnic, not a pilgrimage. People passing me were chanting "*Govinda, Govinda*."

By sunset I had reached Tirumala. There was heavy rush of crowds in and around the famous hill shrine. I went to get in line and it took more than three hours to reach in front of the *garbha griham* (sanctum sanctorum). Without any feeling of devotion I just did *pranams* and came out in a hurry. The hue and cry of devotees had irritated me very much. I decided to walk down to Tirupathi. Since I was hungry I went to have some food at the *Annadanam* place. Some of the priests gave me a ticket for food. I felt tired after taking the heavy meal, and went in search of a place to rest. Near the temple I saw the signboard of the Hathi Ram mutt, and I got accommodation there. I was given a room, and it seemed like it had not been cleaned for years. I managed to clean up the room a bit and slept there. At night, some *Vaishnav swamis* came up and asked me to join them for dinner. As the lunch had been heavy, I declined the offer. I sat on the *verandah*, looking at the temple. An old lady was lying down on the verandah near me. After some time she sat up and said something in what sounded like the *Telugu* language. When I told her I could not understand what she was saying, she spoke to me in *Hindi* with an accent. The old lady said, "Tirumala is *Bhooloka Vaikuntam*.[31] Be happy and proud that you are here." I said, "I don't have any feeling other than aversion to *Vaishnavas*, as I am a pure *Shakta* of Kerala." She laughed and said, "You look like a *sanyasi* of the *Adi Shankara* order! You are supposed to be an *Advaiti*.[32] You should not have any type of discrimination between *Shakti–Shiva* and *Vishnu*. *Dvaita bhava* (duality in beliefs) will not give you salvation." She was then silent for a moment. I was amazed to hear these words from a lady looking like a beggar. She smiled as if she had read my mind, and then spoke again, "Son, cast away this duality of mind. Shiva is Vishnu and Vishnu is Shiva. And moreover your Mother (*Lalitha Tripura Sundari*[33]) is none other than the sister of Venkateswara." (Venkateswara is Vishnu, and one of Mother's one thousand names in the *Lalitha Sahasranamam* is 'Padmanabha Sahodari' or 'sister of Vishnu'.) She concluded by saying, "In the morning, you must once again visit the Lord. You will realize this truth." Then walked away into the crowd near the temple. I was a little confused—who was this lady, was she my *Guruji*? Or was she *Padmavathi* (consort of Venkateshwara)? I felt ashamed of myself and the egoic feeling of being a *Shakta* that I had always had in my mind. I could hardly sleep that night—I sat all night long on the verandah and thinking about what had happened!

The temple bells rang in the early hours, and after bathing, I went for my second visit to see Lord Venkateshwara. Now it was not so crowded. The line of devotees moved slowly and in an hour or so, I reached in front of the idol of Venkateswara in sanctum

---

31 'Heaven on Earth', where the deity reveals Himself to His devotees.

32 Follower of Hindu philosophy of non-dual nature of reality.

33 Lalitha Tripura Sundari is the highest manifestation of Goddess Adi Shakti. Parvati is believed to be the complete incarnation of Lalitha Tripura Sundari is considered the primary goddess associated with the Shiva–Shakti tradition.

sanctorum. One of the priests asked me to stand by the corner and have the darshan. And lo and behold! When I looked at the idol, it was not the idol of Venkateshwara—but I saw my *'Ishta Devi'* (Maha Tripura Sundari's idol) there. My body was shivering. One of the priests gave me some *chandan* (sandalwood powder) and *tulsi* (holy basil) leaves. My eyes were full of tears and my mind humbled at my duality-based thoughts and my aversion to Vaishnavism. My ears were hearing too, as if coming from a distance, chants of the *Lalithasahasranam*. I saw the faces of *Bhu Devi* and *Sri Devi*, looking and smiling at me. Was this all a dream? I was in wonderment, sweating and my tears flowing. The priest showed me the way out. In an altered mood, I came out of the temple and sat near the verandah where the *prasadam* was being distributed. Somebody brought me a *laddu* which I ate with all devotion. Now the aversion was wiped out. My mind had become very light. I came out and walked towards Hathi Ram mutt.

I had walked but a few steps when I heard a woman's voice behind me, "Is the darshan over?" I turned around to see the woman who had spoken to me the previous night. I stepped back, touched her feet, and did pranams. She said, "Son, of course all this was not a dream as you imagine. All are one. We call it by different names and worship in different forms. In principle, everyone is one—the one energy which you call 'Shakti'. Keep this in your consciousness, wherever you are, and the energy can be experienced always." Once again I did pranams to her. Now I was certain that the woman was none other than my *Guruji Avadhoot Tara Mayee*, in that form.

Kalahasthi/Pakshi Teerth

I had set out towards an aimless journey in south India. But I was also experiencing a strong urge to go to the Mookambika temple to visit my Guruji. I was in a dilemma. Leaving Tirupathi I reached Kalahasthi by evening and directly went to the temple there and had darshan of Lord Shiva and mother goddess (*Gyana Prasoonamba*) and then tried to look for a place to stay. There was an *ashram* near the temple, but they were reluctant to give me a room or food. I then returned to the *gopuram*[34] and sat there when a devotee appeared in front of me and offered a packet of *Pulyodhara prasadam* (spiced tamarind rice offering to deity). And of course, I was hungry too. My pocket was also gradually getting emptier through paying train and bus fares or eating at small hotels.

I stayed near the gopuram. Another swami was sleeping there too. He started talking to me in Telugu and when I told him that I was not a local, he spoke in Hindi and gave me information about Pakshi Teertham and Srisailam.

Down below the hills of Pakshi Teertham, there was a very small village-type *kasba*. I reached there between meal times, so I sat in a small tea shop and had some tea and *vada*. There was a photo of *Swamy Ayyappa* behind the hotel owner's table, and a small lamp was lit. Upon seeing this I was quite certain that this owner was from Kerala. I asked him to confirm. Oh, he was indeed from Kerala and was very happy that a swami from Kerala was in his shop. He offered me a stay at his shop

---

34 A pyramidical tower, usually ornate, at the entrance of any temple, especially in southern India.

that night. In the night, after he had closed the shop, both of us sat to have dinner. His wife was a local, who had picked up a few Malayalam words. Keshavan Nair, the owner of the tea stall, had left Palghat, Kerala, a few years back in search of a job and destiny had brought him here. He had set up a small tea shop which had grown to a small hotel after a few years of laborious work. He had married a local woman, who was a widow. He told me, "We are both alone and with no children. I never returned to Kerala. Recently my sister's son has joined me to help run this hotel."

Keshavan Nair told me about Pakshi Teertham. Every day after naivedyam, the temple priest would keep a ball of rice as an offering to '*Garuda*' and at exactly at the same time every day the bird would reach there and eat it. I didn't think this was unusual, since if you are ready to feed any animal/bird every day at a particular time, it will come every day at that time. I had observed this during my stay with my Guruji in Mookambika. I did not think this had any spiritual or religious importance or significance.

My analytical mind refused to believe the story and when I conveyed my theory to Keshavan Nair he may have felt bad.

Next day, after ablutions and breakfast of some *idlis*, Keshavan Nair came up with me to the hills to witness the bird's arrival and eating the offering. I saw a few devotees climbing the broken steps on the hills. At about 11 or so, we reached there and sat waiting under a small tree. Nair told me not to go near the place where the priest offered *naivedyam*, since if the Garuda saw me, I might be cursed or attacked. Around noon the priest brought two big rice balls and placed them on a rock on top of the hill. A few devotees were sitting around to witness the arrival of Garuda. After a few minutes, we saw a huge vulture (from the Garuda family) appear like an airplane and landing near the rice ball, the bird ate it. I felt no wonder about this at all.

I asked Keshavan Nair about the route to Srisailam. I was told that there was a bus from Kalahasthi to Srisailam in the evening and that I could reach there by the next day morning. Now I had to return to Kalahasthi to take the bus. We climbed down and had some coffee from Nair's shop and I got ready to go the Kalahasthi by a local bus. Keshavan Nair gave me Rs. 500 for my journey and as I was running out of money I accepted it and went to Kalahasthi to board the bus to Srisailam.

Srisailam

I reached Srisailam in the morning around 8 am. The journey in the night had been through forests. I felt tired and went around looking for accommodation in an ashram or *dharmasala*. I was surprised to see name boards of dharmasalas, in the name of communities. I saw that the communities of *Brahmins, Reddys, Vaishyas, Yadavas* and so many other others as well were running their own dharmasalas. Not anywhere during my journeys in the last few years had I ever noticed dharmasalas meant exclusively for their own communities. I could not find a single dharmasala where I could accommodate myself—since I never considered myself as belonging to any particular community or sect, be it Brahmin, Kshatriya or Vysya community. I belong to the *manava* (human) community. There were no dharmasalas for 'manava' in Srisailam! On seeing the signboard of *Sringeri Shankar* mutt, I went there to seek accommodation, but the manager of that mutt started questioning me about my *'poorvashram'* and *'sanyas ashram'* details. I felt that it was like the father of a marriageable girl asking for 'horoscope details' from the prospective groom's father before marriage. I was angry with him, and asked, "Do you not recognize me as a sanyasi of Adi Shankara order, by my dress and name? Why then do you ask for my horoscope details? If you have some place for me here, then go ahead and give me accommodation. Else just say no!" He said they accommodated only 'Dandi Swamis'[35] and asked me where my *dand* (a long staff) was.

---

35 A subdivision of the Shaiva tradition where the followers carry a long staff (dand/dandi) to signify their belonging to the sect.

I was enraged at his way of deciding and differentiating between swamis. Whether he be a *'Dandi'* or a *'Paramahamsa'*, a *sanyasi* is a sanyasi. I came out of the mutt without another word and went to the mandir gate. Near the gopuram I saw old dharmasala-type rooms made of stones on both sides of the road leading to the mandir.

I kept my belongings there. Some devotees were staying in some of the open rooms of that dharmasala. Of course some of the rooms where also permanently occupied by beggars.

I noticed another *parivrajaka sanyasi* (a wandering monk) sitting in front of the open room. I went near him. He was from North India and on a pilgrimage to the south. He had already visited most of the South Indian temples since he had covered Kerala, Tamil Nadu, Karnataka and Andhra! And now he was going to return to the north with a bad opinion about the temple priests and ashram authorities of south, since he was denied food or shelter in most of the pilgrim places. It was my experience as well.

In South India, parivrajaka swamis will not get food or shelter in most of the mandirs and the annakshetras are also divided by caste or creed. Sanyasis belong to no caste or creed. So they do not get food or accommodation in *satrams*[36] or ashrams.

I kept my belongings (except for the *kappar, kamandal*, a pair of clothes and a *kambal*, I had nothing else) near the North Indian swami and had a lovely bath with the public water supply faucet by the road side. Then we both went for darshan, and as it was not crowded, it was easy to get darshan in a few minutes. At the *'jyotirlinga darshanam'* I had no reactions, but when I had darshan before the idol of *Devi Bhramaramba* (an incarnation of Mother Goddess), I failed to control my emotions. It felt like I was in standing in front of Mookambika. I feel this type of emotion whenever, and wherever I visit a temple of the Mother Goddess. Whether she be *Mookambika, Chottanikara Bhagavati, Kodungalur Bhagavati, Vaishno Devi*, or *Nayana Devi*—my emotions are always

---

36 A resting place for pilgrims where rooms and food are provided by a charitable institution for nominal rates or free.

the same! I see everywhere the living deity, not an idol made of stone. And of course, I know this feeling was due to the kripa or grace of my guru, the living embodiment of *karuna* (compassion), love and everything to me. I came out of the mandir and sat on the verandah and the North Indian swami was also near me. He was relating his visit to Tiruvannamalai near Madras, and insisted that I must visit the *Agni Lingam* and Ramana Maharshi Ashram and the Arunachal hill too. Those days, there used to be a bus at night to Madras from Srisailam and I decided to take that bus.

Arunachala Shiva

It was not a very difficult journey to Tiruvannamalai. This place is very well known all over the world because of Ramana Maharshi. I reached Tiruvannamalai around noon via Madras by bus. I went around the mandir and had darshan of the *Arunachaleswara lingam* and then went out in search of a place to stay for a couple of days. I failed to get an accommodation at Ramana Ashram and finally I met a swami whom I had known from my Gangotri days and he was ready to accommodate me in his hut at Mulappal Tirtham. Swami Madhurananda was a good person, who not only accommodated me, but took me around Tiruvannamalai. The next day I did a '*Giri Pradakshina*' of Arunachala hill, which is known as '*Dakshina Kailash*' (Kailash of the South).

In the evening I went alone to climb the hill to visit the caves where Ramana Maharshi had stayed. It was almost dark when I reached the top of the hill. I could hardly move because of the darkness. I sat on a flat rock, and decided to stay there for the night. There was total silence in and around me. In the full darkness, and all alone, chanting my *Guru Mantra* I sat on the rock.

It seemed that sitting there I must have dozed off, for a sound woke me up. I could easily see an old man in white robes, standing near me. He spoke to me in Tamil (I could understand Tamil as it is not much different from my mother tongue Malayalam). The old man told me that it was not at all advisable to stay there at night all alone, and that it was better to go down the hills and stay at some Gopuram. He was ready to show me the way down.

But my mind was questioning me. I was never afraid of being alone in the Himalayas, so why would I be afraid here? I told the old man that I was prepared to do my *japa* the whole night all alone there and was not afraid as my Guruji was always there to take care of me. I rejected his proposal to go down to some gopuram for staying the night. Around the Giri Pradakshina *Veedhi* there are many Gopurams or sheds made of big stones, where wandering monks used to stay at night. The old man seemed unhappy that I had not appreciated his proposal, and he disappeared into the darkness. I sat on the rock and continued my japa till sunrise.

Then I went to Madhurananda Swami who was worried about me as he didn't know where I had gone at night. I stayed in Tiruvannamalai for three days and everyday took bhiksha standing in a line with beggars, swamis and pilgrims. On all those three days I did the Giri Pradakshina. Now I had about 800 rupees with me. I had plans in mind to go to Thanjavoor, Kumbhakonam, Swamimalai, Kanchi, Madurai, etc. but as the pocket was getting empty I decided to go back to the north after visiting Dharmasthala. Swami Madhurananda also agreed to this.

So, on the fourth day I left for Madras for my onward journey to Dharmasthala. But at the Madras bus stand, I changed my mind and went to railway station instead to find out about the trains going to the north. The Dharmasthala yatra got postponed and I purchased a ticket to Delhi and boarded a train.

Back to Haridwar

On the evening of the second day, I reached Haridwar and went to Sapta Sarovar. I had decided while I was on the train that this time I would not depend on any ashram for my stay. In the past few years of staying in ashrams or temples I had got accustomed to little comforts. I had forgotten the words of my Guruji to not depend on existing ashrams for stay or food as she would take care of my needs. I went directly to the Sapta Sarovar, to reach the hut in which Omkarananda and I had stayed previously. Now it was occupied by some other *sadhus* so I went to '*ghat* number 10' (this ghat number 10 is very important for sanyasis as here the dead bodies of sadhus are given jal Samadhi). Under a big tree there, I kept my *asan* and decided to stay. I was left with a balance of Rs. 450, which I didn't want to keep with me. So I went to my old friend Udasi Swami, who was staying in the hut where I had done *viraja homa* to initiate Omkarananda, and handed over the amount to him. I told that Udasi swami (who was known as 'Muni') that I would be staying under the tree at 'ghat number 10'. He was glad to see me. I slept under the tree on the banks of Ganga. To my wonder, the next morning, Krishna *Mataji* of Ram *kutir* came to meet me and insisted that I stay at the Ram kutir with her. But I was reluctant to go to any ashram for stay. I agreed though to take *bhiksha* daily from Ram kutir ashram, and Mataji was happy.

I was disappointed that I had wasted time on an aimless journey to the South and decided to start my next '*purascharan*' (this would be the tenth time) of *Srividya shodashi mantra*. I told Krishna Mataji that I would take some milk and fruits from her ashram as bhiksha, as I was beginning my japa purascharan the next day.

It was almost the onset of winter. Mataji gave me a kambal and a plastic sheet to spread out for my asan, which I could use for sleeping as well. The next day, some swamijis of acquaintance came over to invite me to stay at Ram kutir or Virakta kutia, for the winters at Haridwar are very harsh. However, I humbly requested them to not disturb me as I was going to start my japa sadhana the next day. This time around, I wanted to complete my '*japa sankhya*' in three months. Navaratri was now over (October) and by Makara Sankranti[37] (January) I should have completed my japa. In January it might be difficult to survive the cold wind in Haridwar in an open place.

The next morning I made my '*sankalp*' and started the japa. Every day around noon, I would go to Ram kutir for my bhiksha of milk and fruit. The rest of the time, I did japa sitting under the tree, looking at the flow of Ganga. I used to do japa for more than 15 hours daily. I tried to avoid the visits of sadhu friends. Daily after bhiksha at noon, I would sleep for some time (about an hour or so) and then bathe and do japa till late night. This japa *anushtan* (firm conviction to do japa and mantra recitation a prescribed number of times) was one of the best ones that I ever did. I had different experiences at that ghat during my stay.

One of the sadhus I knew told me it would be dangerous to stay at that ghat number 10 at night, as this place was said to be haunted by ghosts. A sanyasi who did not attain *moksha* (salvation) may appear there as a ghost and disturb me. I did not mind his words for I was not afraid of ghosts since I was doing Srividya japa. Moreover, my Guruji's presence was with me always; that was my firm belief!

Late one night while doing japa I noticed an old sadhu appear near me. He was in *kashaya* robe, with a white beard and not much hair on his head. Usually no sadhus would come at that time

---

[37] A Hindu harvest festival that marks the transition of the sun into the zodiacal sign of Makara (Capricorn) on its celestial path. The day is also believed to mark the arrival of spring in India.

of night. I was gripped with fear. He came near and after doing pranams, asked my permission to sit near me! I thought to myself, "Okay, what was wrong in that?" I permitted him to do so and he sat to my left, gazing at me. He asked me to chant my mantras loudly so as he could hear me. When I asked him why, he said "*Baba*, if you chant the Srividya Mantra loudly, I will definitely get salvation from this *preta yoni* (ghost state after death). Now I was terrified. One *preta aatma* (a spirit that has unfinished business in this world) was sitting near me! And it needed my mantra sounds for its salvation?

My friend sadhus had warned me already. But because of my mistake in not heeding to them I now had to face this dangerous situation. And now there was no other way other than to obey the order of the 'ghost swami'!

I chanted my japa loudly and sometime later, to my amazement, the ghost swami did pranams to me and jumped into the Ganga.

I was sweating in fear, even in that cold winter.

Life at Ghat Number 10

The japa purascharan was going on very well. It was only rarely that some of the known sadhus were visiting me. Due to lack of proper food my body was once again becoming weak. During those days I was having only milk and fruit once a day.

One day just as I was lying down to take rest under the tree in the afternoon after my morning session of japa, I heard the sound of someone calling out to me. Opening my eyes, I saw a sadhu in kashaya, with a long stick in one hand and a kamandal in the other, standing near me. He had long matted hair and a white beard. I looked at the stranger who started talking, "Son, though you may not know me, I have known you very well from the first day of your spiritual journey. I know how much you are depressed at not being able to reach Gyanganj. I am Bhruguram Paramahamsa. I am coming from Gyanganj with a message from Mahatapa Guruji. You need not be depressed at this never-ending journey of yours. After completing your purascharan return to your ashram in Jammu. In a short period you will get a chance to go to the Himalayas again. Go and have the darshan of Kailash Manasarovar." I was amazed! This was not a dream. I had once heard my Guruji talk about Bhruguram Paramahamsa, who was a senior guru. This swami could be my '*Paratpara Guru*' (i.e., my Guruji's Guruji).

Swami added with a smile, "You have to scale to higher heights in your spiritual path, don't look back and proceed without thinking about what happened in the past. Remember one thing: never, never reveal yourself till you reach the destination. Hide your identity till you reach the stage of an *Avadhoota*! Remember the message of our great Mahatapa Guruji. Go back to your ashram after completing your anushtan and then wait for the time to go to Kailash. One day of course, you will get a chance to go to Gyanganj too."

Swamiji turned back and walked away quickly. I wanted to ask about my sadhana, but he had disappeared into the distance.

Of course it was not a dream. This was in the daytime, around 2 pm. I was not sleeping. I remembered my Guruji's words, "Every moment the *Guru mandala* is watching you. Don't worry about your progress in spiritual life. They will take care of it. Understand and obey their instructions. You will reach your goal."

Yes, these are the ways of great gurus. They are always watching their children. I am a young boy in front of the great gurus. There are likelihoods of slipping on this path of spirituality. According to the *shastras*, the path of spirituality is like walking on the edge of a sword. I know it and have experienced it. Several times have I come out of occasions that were making me fall into the clutches of *maya*, and every time the *Guru Mandala* has saved me and shown me the right path. All these incidents were in my destiny. Only the destined happens. If the 'pyre' within a sadhu burns properly, (the 'pyre' to reach the ultimate reality), our *Guru Mandala* will definitely take care of it.

I was filled with a new energy in my body/mind/intellect, with the mere vision of a great guru of my *parampara*.

Winter started in all ferocity. I had only two kambals, one for spreading and one for covering my body. And I was content with what I had. Some of the swamis who I knew told me to go to a room to stay during winter. But as usual, my mind was very reluctant to do so. If I continued my japa at that speed, I could finish in a month or so. I had no calendar or *panchang*[38] to track dates. But using pebbles for counting days, I knew that it was now the middle of December. I was ready to face anything adverse during the japa as I was sure nothing would happen since my Guruji was taking

---

38 A Hindu calendar and almanac which follows traditional units of Hindu timekeeping, and presents important dates and their calculations in a tabulated form.

care of me. My mind was filled with an inexplicable happiness. Some times during japa I used to lose my body consciousness. Then the *japa mala* (a string of prayer beads) in my hand would fall down, and I would be in trance for hours together.

One day during the stage of trance, I had a rare experience of a big fish coming out of water and reaching for me. It was of golden colour and with beautiful eyes. Staring at me, the fish spoke, "*Maharaj*, you have no idea who you are! But I know. Hurdles will come. Don't be afraid!" The fish jumped into the Ganga and reappeared, looked at me for few seconds from the shore, and jumped again into the Ganga. I was wondering what was happening all around me. Who was this fish and what was the meaning behind the words? I tried to contemplate on this. I was drifting into trance more often and found it difficult to walk to Ram kutir for milk or fruits. Due to the trances, I decided to stay put there, and subsist only by drinking only *Gangajal* for a few days

Life at Ghat Number 10 Continues

As I had grown too weak to walk up to Ram kutir (about one or two furlongs' distance), I stopped going there for my daily *bhiksha* of milk and fruits. Now I was depending only on *Gangajal*. I remembered the vision of my Guruji who had appeared before me and told me strictly not to do any *sadhana* without food. Even though I had not taken any *sankalp* of fasting, I was forced to do so as I was too weak to walk. On the first evening itself, Krishna Mataji came to the ghat to enquire what had happened to me as I had not gone to take the *bhiksha* of milk and fruit that day. When she realized I was unable to walk due to weakness, she arranged to send me milk and fruits daily through Mishra, a watchman at the *ashram*.

She pressured me to go to Ram kutir and continue *japa*, but I refused the offer due to my stubbornness of not wanting to change a decision once made. Mishra brought my *bhiksha* daily. Krishna Mataji used to mix some honey (to give me more energy) with milk and she increased the quantity of milk too. The winter was very harsh and the cold wind from the Ganga made me shiver. The cold in the Upper Himalayas is of a different intensity, and here on the banks of Ganga, with nothing proper to cover my body except a woollen blanket, it felt like the rough wind was penetrating my body and touching my very bones. But I decided that no matter what happened I must complete my japa anushtan sitting only over there.

I learned from a visiting *sadhu* that there was a discussion going on in the *mandala* about my tapas in winter on the banks of Ganga. That *swami* was familiar to me from my days of stay in the *mandali*. He hailed from Punjab, and was a good person and service-oriented. He returned to me again in the evening, bringing along two other *swamis* from Virakta kutia. They brought a lot of firewood in large pieces, and made a fire near my asan. Another *dhuni* for me. It was very helpful to me to escape the biting cold.

Sitting in front of the *dhuni*, I recalled the day I had made a fire for my *Guruji* on the steps of Ramakrishna Yogashram in Mookambika. Now my *Guruji* had arranged fire for me through some unknown *swamis*. This is the way of *gurus*. They will definitely repay the *sevas* accepted from a disciple or devotee. In that burning fire, I could see the loving smile of my *Guruji* and with that vision again I went into a trance. I was in trance the whole night sitting by the fire. But to my wonder, even though I never rearranged the firewood in the night, the fire had continued burning throughout night. In the morning when I was out of trance and back to normalcy, I could see that some new firewood had been put in the fire which no one could have done, since there was nobody near me. I was all alone at night. Now it was crystal clear to me that if one does *sadhana* with a staunch *sankalpa* and firm belief, the *Guru* will take care of every moment.

In the last few days I had stopped bathing due to weakness. Now that I had a fire near, I felt better and wanted to take a bath that day. When Mishra came with *bhiksha*, I asked him to help me take a bath. He arranged the firewood well to make a roaring fire. I had a bath with his help and went back to my asana. The *japa sadhana* was near conclusion. Krishna Mataji came one day and informed me that it would be Makar Sankranti after three days and by that time my 90 days would also be over. She was arranging for a *bhandara* (common feeding of sadhus) as my japa would conclude and my fruit and milk diet would also end on that day.

On Makara Sankranti morning I concluded my japa. But I was reluctant to go to the ashram, as some emotions were prevailing in my mind as I was leaving the *asan* and banks of Ganga, which had accommodated me for three months. With the help of Mishra I walked slowly towards Ram kutir after doing *pranams* to Ganga Mata, and to my *Guru Mandala*.

Towards Kailash Via Jammu

I stayed at Ram kutir for a few more days. Due to having stayed in an open place and not eaten proper food in three months, my body had grown weak. Krishna Mataji looked after me like a loving mother, and would feed me with almonds and milk which helped me regain my health. One day Madanlal, from the village where the ashram work was in progress, came to meet me. He insisted that I accompany him to the village as the *kutia* work was almost at completion and I could now stay there without any disturbance. I remembered the words of Swamy Bhruguram Paramahamsa instructing me to go to the ashram and await the day of journey to Manasarovar, Kailash. I agreed to go with Madanlal and the next day we started by bus towards Pathankot.

The *kutia* was constructed well. Of course, it was only suitable for a sanyasi. Flooring work needed to be completed and temporarily the floor was finished with cow dung paste as was normal in rural areas. I started staying there. Even though the construction work of the temple hall was still in progress, as the villagers had already installed the idol, I preferred to stay in the hall in front of *Maa*, overlooking an open courtyard. Now, this was January and winter here was worse than that at Haridwar. Kaushalya used to bring my daily *bhiksha* and then one day we rearranged the system by allocating the days to seven different houses. Whatever they brought was first offered as *naivedyam* to the deity before I accepted it as *bhiksha* in my *kappar*. One Brahmin from the village, Maya Rama, used to come in the early hours to do *pooja* daily and he also did *sandhya arathi* in the evenings. Villagers used to call him '*Poojariji*'. I was considering forming a committee of the villagers to look after the temple and the proposed ashram. A panchayat was called and a committee of seven people constituted with Madanlal as head of the committee. Every day I would have a lot of villagers visiting me and they would simply sit and chitchat on various matters, and I wanted to make use of that time for *satsang*. But I had another plan in mind as well. I told the villagers that I was prepared to go to different houses for *Chandi Paath* and whatever offerings were made in front of the Chandi Paath *vedi* (altar), were to be used for the construction work. A list was made and this new venture started from the next day onwards.

Paramanand and a few other villagers used to accompany me to the houses when the *Chandi Paath* was arranged. I carried a *Sri Yantra* and a photo of *Vaishno Devi* to each house and arranged a simple *vedi* decorated with a few flowers, lit the lamp and started *Chandi Paath*. The family members of the house and a few of their relatives as well as some neighbours used to be there to witness the *Chandi Paath*. There were two advantages to this—first that I could study the life of each family, and second that whatever offerings were collected could be used for *ashram* construction. On some days the offerings were 50 or 60 rupees and some days 200 to 500. I was not very particular about the money. Paramanand handled this, as he was the treasurer of the managing committee of the ashram.

One day a poor old woman came to where I was doing *Chandi Paath*. She was a widow and a non-Brahmin. She requested me to do Chandi Paath at her house too. Being a non-Brahmin, she was afraid to ask. Some of the villagers objected to my going to her house for the Paath. I told her that the following Tuesday I would go to her house, and not only do the Chandi Paath, but take *bhiksha* from her as well. Her happiness knew no limits. On Tuesday there were only three villagers with me when I went to her residence. There was Paramanand, his sister Kaushalya and another Brahmin boy named Ashok, in addition to me. I felt unhappy about the narrow-mindedness of the villagers. The poor old lady offered 11 rupees after the Paath. She had already prepared some rice, dal and chilly chutney for my *bhiksha*, and all of us including Paramanand, Kaushalya and Ashok took food from that old non-Brahmin lady. She had tears in her eyes while she was serving me food.

In the evening, a few village elders (all Brahmins) came to me very angrily and said that they had decided to boycott me and that in the future they would not be cooperating with me in any way. I did not try to convince them, but said, "Look, *Maa Vaishno Devi* dwells in everybody, not just only in the bodies of Brahmins. Being a *sanyasi*, I know that what I am doing is correct. If you are not cooperating with me, it is your will and pleasure. But I dislike your mentality of discrimination. If any devotee of *Maa* calls me, even a Muslim, I will definitely go and do *Chandi Paath*. I care the least about your age-old superstitions."

They left me without any comment, but after few days I learned that a group opposing me was being formed. Omkarananda was with the mandali in Nepal those days. One day I received a letter from him that the mandali was planning to go to Kailash Manasarovar yatra from Nepal. The head of the mandali, Swami Viswatmanand, wanted me to join them. I remembered again the words of Bhruguram Paramahamsa. I discussed with the committee members of my plan to go to Nepal and then to Kailash with the mandali and they all seemed to be happy. I told them that I would be leaving them within a day or two.

Most of them contributed funds towards my journey which totalled more than Rs. 6,000. I kept only Rs. 1,000 with me and gave the balance to Paramananda for use towards construction work. I left the village next day for Haridwar—enroute to Nepal.

Nepal, Pasupathy

I stayed in Haridwar for a day to enquire about the route to Nepal. The next day I took a train to Lucknow and from there a bus to Sonali. Sonali is on the Nepal border. I reached there on the evening of the second day and caught a bus to Kathmandu (the capital of Nepal). Even at that point I was not well equipped with warm clothes. I carried a woollen blanket on my shoulder and a small shoulder bag with a pair of clothes and my permanent companions, my kamandal and kappar! Sonali is a small border village with a few shops and I accommodated myself on the verandah of a small tea shop. The shop was closed, but I noticed a fire still burning on the cooking range in the shop. Through the whole night I sat near the cooking range, covering my body with the blanket.

The next day by noon I had reached Kathmandu. I saw a few sadhus sitting near a dhuni in a tin shed near the *Pasupatinath* Temple. They directed me to the building where the *mandali* was staying. Viswatmanandji and other *sadhus* were happy that I was going to be with them. Viswatmanandji told me that it would take ten more days more to start as we had to wait for preparing some papers for the yatra.

I was meeting Omkarananda after a long time. He was not inclined to go to Kailash, but willing to go to Haridwar and stay there. I did not object as it was his will whether to go to Kailash or not. After two days Omkarananda left for Haridwar with another *sadhu*.

A few of the *swamis* of the *mandali* known to me from my previous time in the mandali—Narayanananda, Srinivasananda, Sandranananda, Prasad, Satyananda and Ramu—were there now.

PASUPATINATH

The next day I visited Pasupatinath and Guhyeshwari temples. Both the temples were old, but not kept clean. At Guhyeshwari, *bali* (slaughtering for sacrifice) of animals was being practiced. The worship rituals at that temple were of the old *Vamachar Tantra*[39] tradition. I could stay for only a few minutes at the temple. The *bhiksha* in Kathmandu was sponsored by one of the Seth (Marwari)[40] families who had come two generations ago and settled there. They had arranged a grand *bhiksha* for us and offered us clothes too. During the stay in Kathmandu I wandered and visited a few more temples in and around the city.

By this time our journey papers were ready, and we all went to Nepalgunj by a chartered flight. Most of the sadhus enjoyed the flight journey, as they were flying for the first time. From Nepalgunj, Viswatmanand, a guide we had engaged and I went to Bhajang on a 16-seater helicopter. The other *sadhus* went to Darchula by walk. We also had to reach Darchula early, which is why we took the shortest route via Bhajang and then by walk to Darchula. A few *yatra* papers needed to be collected from Darchula for the journey.

Walking through hills at Nepal was very much invigorating. On the way to Darchula from Bhajang we engaged three or four *coolies* from a village to travel with us to Kailash. After two days' walk we reached Darchula. By this time other the *sadhus* of the *mandali* had also reached there. Darchula is a small village on the banks of the Kali River. Across the river on the other side is the

---

39 Branch of Tantra, a particular mode of worship that uses the kind of elements of deity worship which are not used in the orthodox religion. This known as panchamakara (five 'M's) five species of pleasure, namely: meat (mamsa), cereal (mudra), fish (matsya or machli), wine (madya or madira) and ritual sexual intercourse (maythuna).

40 A native or inhabitant of Rajasthan in India.

Hindustan side of Darchula. We stayed in that village for three days before final preparations of the journey.

As I had been walking barefoot for a long time on the hills, the soles of both my feet had tears everywhere and were bleeding too from the thorns and pebbles that had pierced them. I was walking, but was in too much pain. Viswatmananda got me a pair of canvas shoes for the journey and it was easy for me to walk now.

We all began our journey on the banks of the Kali River, through the Nepal Himalayan hills. There were about 35 people including some workers, guides, etc. I was told it would take a month or so to reach Kailash if we travelled continuously. But we were not bound by time. From early morning till afternoon we walked climbing up and down the hills and in the afternoons we stayed either in some school building or in open places, where our group cooked ourselves—*rice, dal or khichadi*. After food, we rested for the day and early in the morning again resumed journey. This was the practice during the whole journey.

After a few days of travel, I felt tired, my legs swollen. Now we were almost near the Tibetan border. We stayed at the Tibet–Nepal border for a couple of days for clearance from the border check post. On the third day the journey resumed.

During the journey I noticed one thing. If we were walking as a group there would be talks about this and that, petty matters. In fact my plan was to do *Devi Pranava japa* and walk. So I decided to walk a little behind the group and with every step I chanted the mantra. We were now in the land of mysterious *yogis* and *mahatmas*—Tibet. Everywhere around us, we could see the snow-clad hills. My second visit to Tibet was filled with hopes, and I thought I might get a chance to go to *Gyanganj* this time.

More than fifteen days had passed by, and we were still walking. Due to swelling and pain, it was very difficult for me to walk the way the others were walking. I had already thrown away my shoes and was walking slowly.

One day I had fallen far behind the others in the group. My legs were now swollen up to the knees and my movements become very slow. I could easily see that the group was moving on to the next hill. In the Himalayas, though it may seem like the hills that are visible are nearby, it is only when you start walking towards them that you realize how far they really are! It was afternoon and the group had already disappeared from visibility. I was extremely tired and felt as if I would not be able to move even a step. I sat under a tree. Seeing a small stream nearby, I went there, and washed my face, hands and legs and came back to the tree and sat under it. I thought that perhaps now the *mandali* (group) might have reached some place suitable to set up cooking. A breeze coming from the snow-clad hills embraced me, and it was like the energizing embrace of mother to her child. I was lost and did not know what to do. At any time it could be sunset, or rain or snowfall. I was all alone there. The documents of journey were with the head of the mandali. If a military man or any villager spotted me, what would I do? I was worried. As I was tired, I was unable to move. I sat there on the same spot, continuing my japa. It was almost sunset time. I was not sleeping but had closed my eyes and was thinking about the three aspect of the Mother Goddess. Why three? What for? Saptasati says, "I am only one but appear in different forms and names." Some question regarding the '*tritva bhava*' (*Maha Kali, Maha Lakshmi, Maha Saraswati*) was bothering my mind. I heard a sound nearby and opened my eyes. I was stunned when I saw a very tall and beautiful woman in front of me, well decorated with ornaments and flower garland, and wearing a shining *sari*. I tried to look once again at the form that had appeared in front of me. I was certainly not dreaming since I was not asleep. The beautiful lady touched me and I felt now like a small child of six months or so. She raised me in her arms and started nursing me, feeding me milk from her breast. (I feel the taste of that milk is even now on my tongue.) A few minutes passed thus and I felt like I was diving into very shining light.

Hearing the sound of horse hooves, I woke up. I saw a person (looking like a cowboy) near me on his horse. He said something which I could not understand. By gesturing he indicated that the group was on the neighbouring hills, and if I wished, he could take me to them on his horse. I declined, and he went off. It was morning and I got up. I felt more energetic. And there was no more swelling or pain in my legs. Now I was able to realize what had happened and all my doubts vanished. I knew of course, that it was the Mother who had appeared and fed me milk. My mind became very pure and strong. I walked fast and climbed the hills at good speed and reached the mandali. They had been worried about me. The mandali was ready to move and I joined them and continued my journey carrying my unexplainable experience of the previous night.

Manasarovar— Kailash

We continued the journey, and reached Takalkot, where we were supposed to have our papers endorsed by the Chinese authorities. We stayed for two days in Takalkot, which was the place where we could purchase everything needed for the onward journey. We collected the things needed: I kept a bottle of chutney made of garlic and chillies for good digestion as well keeping body heat intact. On the third day we resumed journey and were walking through snowbound hills. My mind was exhilarated at seeing and walking once again through Tibet. As I had experienced Himalayan life earlier, the cold wind or high hills were not a surprise to me. In some places, we experienced oxygen deficiency and some of the sadhus used oxygen kits brought for that purpose. To reach a goal is not so easy—and be it materialism or spirituality, one has to struggle to reach the goal.

My mind was questioning the idea of Shiva actually residing in Kailash. To me, Shiva is not a form but pure consciousness. 'Kailash' literally means *Sahasrara*.[41] I wondered of my mind that was eager to search for Shiva externally; but is not Shiva in the form of pure consciousness already dwelling in everyone's body in their Sahasrara? Instead of this external journey towards Bhukailas or earthly Kailash, I felt that I should instead have traveled to the Kailash within me. To reach Shiva means to attain the pure consciousness level, which will give the realization of 'what I am'

---

41 Sahasrara or crown chakra is generally considered the seventh primary chakra, according to most tantric yoga traditions and is the one which integrates all the chakras with their respective qualities. It is the last milestone of the evolution of human awareness.

or the 'theory of existence'. I had read in books that this state was known as '*Turiya*'. But according to *Shakteya*[42] theory, the journey does not end there. One has to travel one more step to reach *Shakti* or '*Turiyateeta*' or 'being'. This is known as awareness, when you experience the practical existence. In scientific terms, Shakti is energy. The oneness of these two: theory and practical, Shiva and Shakti, knowing and being, is termed *Ardha-Nareeshwara*, which is *Advaita Siddhi*.[43]

All these thoughts were overpowering me during the journey. It started raining and there was not even a small tree under which to take cover. It was almost 25 days since our journey had begun. At sunset we reached a large lake, and some of the sadhus said this was Manasarovar! There were a few huts made of mud and stones nearby and we stayed in them for that night's halt.

To me 'Manasarovar' means 'the heart filled with love and affection'—a mind filled with love like an ocean! A *sadhu's* mind should be like that—on the one hand full of devotion towards the Almighty or the *Guru* (both are the same, if you look deeply enough), and on the other, full of love towards all beings, without any differentiation. The shastras say that 'equanimity is yoga'—to feel for others as you feel for yourself. So my mind was saying that the journey to 'Manasarovar' implies the journey to one's pure heart that loves every being equally. The external Manasarovar will give good scenery to the eyes, but diving into the internal Manasarovar will lead one to ecstasy! It is the everlasting experience of Bliss. That is why Christ said, "Love your neighbour as yourself."

These thoughts were all rising and subsiding in my mind, so I was unable to sleep the whole night. In the morning I sat on the shore of Manasarovar. The water was crystal clear, like the pure mind of a small child. One of the sadhus told me that the mandali

---

42 A sub-sect of Hinduism in which the followers worship Mother Goddess in Her various avatars and incarnations.

43 Advaita Siddhi means 'attainment of non-duality, or 'realizing the Self': that there is only one real unchanging entity in this world called 'consciousness' and every name and form visible in this world, be it living or non-living, is a different face for it.

would stay here for a few days. And if we were lucky we might chance to see a 'hamsa' (swan)[44] too.

I fell into contemplation on this word 'hamsa', that means *Soham* ('I am He/That' in Sanskrit; in Vedic philosophy it means identifying oneself with the universe or ultimate reality—is the meaning of this Mahavakya) and 'hamsa soham' is also one of the last mantras of *Srividya*! *Hamsa* implies 'prana' or vital energy. When *prana* through *soham dhyana* is taken up to the sahasrara to reach *Shiva* (or Pure Consciousness), it takes the sadhak to *Shakti* (or Awareness). Now the theory was crystal clear to me. To bathe in the Manasarovar meant to ascend in the '*pranashakti*' through *hamsa soham* (or the technique of pranayama) and reach *Sahasrara*. In other words to join the '*pranashakti*' to *Shiva* (or Pure Consciousness) and *Shakti* (or Awareness) will lead the sadhak or practitioner to reach *Advaita Siddhi* (ultimate reality)—that is, *Moksha* (salvation). I understood that merely washing the physical body in the lake Manasarovar upon reaching the hill known as Kailash will not grant moksha—but through the path of yoga and tantra one can definitely attain moksha.

I never before had contemplated on thoughts such as these. Perhaps, as this was the land of yogis and mahatmas, perhaps their vibrations had reached my thoughts. I sat there on the shore of Manasarovar till noon, and though I was not meditating yet, the meditation was still happening within me!

---

44 In Indian mythological literature, 'hamsa' is a mythical bird with knowledge and represents the individual soul or spirit.

Kailash - End of Sadhana

I had not been taking food for two or three days since I had neither felt hunger nor thirst. I was as if intoxicated after the experience of Manasarovar, and in the stage of 'Being'. I had felt my body grow very light, with tears of ecstasy in my eyes. It was the evening of the third day and I did not know for how long I had been sitting thus on the shore of the 'Sarovar'. It may have looked like I was simply gazing at the crystal clear water, but of course the '*Hamsa Soham*' mantra was echoing in my brain.

I saw a light emerging from the '*Sarovar Taal*'. In a few seconds it became clear that it was not light but my revered *Guruji* (*Avadhoota Tara Mayee*) appearing before me. My whole body shivered due to *romaharasha* (goose bumps). Tears overflowed my eyes! Yes, it was not a dream. I pinched myself to confirm I was awake. I got up and with shivering legs tried to move towards my Guruji. I was wonderstruck at how my Guruji had again appeared there.

Amma placed her hands on my shoulders and embraced me. She said, "Son, what is all this childishness? I told you to eat properly every day during sadhana. It is your foolishness that you don't understand my words. Look, this *yatra* (journey) of yours to Kailash and Manasarovar is only because of the *niyogam* (plan of destiny) of our great Guru Mahatapa of Gyanganj. Be happy always!" I was crying. As a mother wipes away the tears of her child, Amma lifted her hand and wiped my tears. But it was difficult for me to control my emotions.

Amma said, "Come, come with me. I have something for you." I walked a few steps with Guruji. Now I could see a *yogi* sitting on the shore of the lake and we both went closer to him. *Amma* told me, "Do *pranams* to him. The yogi is Keenaram Paramahamsa—my *Paramaguru* from *Gyanganj*. He has something for you." The *yogi* was clad in white clothes, with a long beard and white hair, and a well-built body. With his eyes closed, the *yogi* was lost in his seventh sense. I did *sashtanga* pranams to him. He opened his eyes and gestured me to sit near him. *Amma* was standing behind me. Keenaram Paramahamsa, my *parmeshti guru (Guru's Guru)*, was in front of me. I was thinking that the most unexpected things were happening. But reading my mind, the *yogi* said, "No, these are not unexpected. These are destined. You are destined to burn yourself in this pyre. You had the experience of '*Soham*'. Yes, this was destined! Now I have something for you. Through Tara, I am destined to pass my yogic powers on to you." The *yogi* closed his eyes again and told my *Guruji* to touch my *Bhrumadhya*.[45] Amma just touched me. There was a sound of '*Soham*' in and around me. I felt like my body was on fire. For a minute my body shivered as if I were running a high fever. My eyes closed on their own. I heard the voice of the *yogi* again, "Son, these are the *siddhis* which you are supposed to keep with you. Now onwards, you are a Siddha Yogi, who has the *siddhis* of '*Doora Sravan*',[46] '*Doora Darshan*',[47] healing powers and '*Sankalpa Siddhi*'.[48] Do not misuse these. You have taken an oath to live for others. To keep that oath you need these powers. Keep it and live for others."

At first I was unable to digest all this. I had the experiences of '*Advaita Siddhi*' two days before and now this! Keenaram Paramahamsa disappeared in thin air. I looked back to see my *Guruji* (*Amma*) still standing there, with her usual smile. I tried to get up, but *Amma* sat near me instead and didn't allow me to get up. She said, "Son, this is the last part of your Shaktipaath Deeksha.

---

45 The point in the centre of the forehead, commonly referred to as the third eye.

46 A siddhi or extrasensory ability to hear conversations far away, without the use of any instruments or equipment.

47 A siddhi or extrasensory ability to see things not in range of eyesight, without the use of instruments or equipment.

48 A power to fulfill your desires or wishes effortlessly.

Now you are a perfect adept. But remember, do not reveal your identity now. I will tell you when the time comes. As I prepare you for '*Loka Sangraha*' (living for the entire humanity), you prepare any one of your disciples to carry out this work in the future." I wanted to ask Amma something, but was fearful.

Amma stepped into the Manasarovar and brought some water in her tin container and had me drink it. She kissed me on my forehead and moved away in a hurry. I wanted to get up and follow her but was unable to get up or walk.

The sun was setting now. Though I was sitting at quite a long distance from the mandali, I could see *sadhus* moving here and there. I was neither in *dhyana* or *samadhi* but in a different stage. The pyre in me was still burning and my head felt heavy.

I saw Narayanananda walking towards me. Speaking to me in Malayalam, he said, "You have been sitting here since a long time. Have you bathed yet? It is time for *arathi* and *Shiva Mahimna* chanting!" He was on his way to answer the call of nature and for a bath. I did not feel like bathing. Even in that cold wind, my body was sweating and my mind trying to recollect what had happened a few minutes before. The face of my Gûruji was still visible in front of my eyes.

Slowly I moved towards the mandali.

Kailash—The Abode of Self

The next day the mandali started moving towards Kailash. It was a day long journey and the mandali reached base camp by evening. Everybody assembled in a small room made of stones and mud. Here and there some tents had been erected for travellers. A cold wind was blowing all around. All of us were tired. Now we had reached Kailash—of course, the external Kailash. This abode of 'self'—the Shiva. This is *'sat-chit-ananda'* (truth, consciousness, bliss). That is 'I'.

The next day, everybody started for the Kailash *parikrama*. I walked with them for some distance and came back. Two or three other *sadhus* also didn't go for the *pradakshina*. I felt like taking a bath in the water coming down from upper Kailash. Sitting near the stream on a rock, I was thinking about my destiny—where I was born and brought up in the southernmost corner of India, and where was I now, in the uppermost Himalayas! Sitting there, I had a vision of the *kundalini*[49] of *Bharat Mata*.

---

49 The dormant yogic life force that is held to lie coiled at the base of the spine until it is awakened and sent to the head to trigger enlightenment.

KUNDALINI OF AKHAND BHARAT

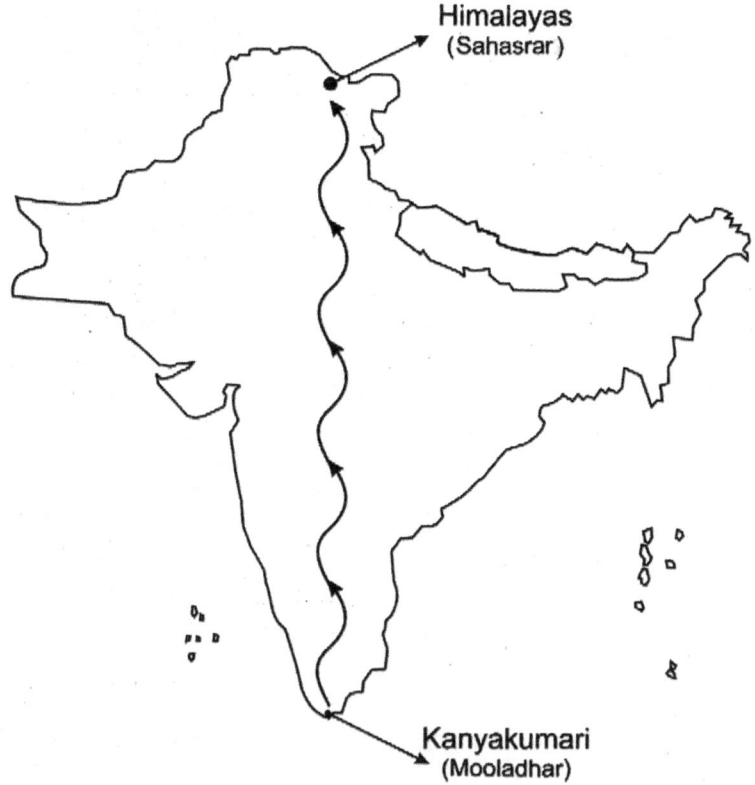

Kailash—The Abode of Self | 271

The melted-ice water was very cold and I was trying to bathe in it. I had been told by some experienced sadhus that to bathe in such cold waters we have to make our body heat become equal to the temperature of water. For that one needs to slowly apply cold water on the body and after a few minutes if you pour on ice water, you will not shiver! I had a good bath. The sun was shining but even then it was very cold. I lay down under the sun and slept. By sunset the mandali had returned after finishing *parikrama*. Everyone assembled in the room again and had something to eat (I remember it was *khichadi*) and slept. But I was unable to sleep.

In my childhood I had heard my mother sing *bhajans* on Shiva and Parvati and Kailash. Until my arrival at this place, the picture of Kailash I had in my mind was based on the bhajans—Shiva with matted hair and *trishul* (trident) in one hand and *damru* (a small, hourglass-shaped hand-held drum) representing the cosmic sound in the other, dancing with Parvati! Here the snow-clad Kailash is the symbol of *Nirakara* (formless) Shiva. Kailash is, of course, in the form of a shiva linga. If we look and imagine, we can visualize three eyes on Kailash as well. But it is imagination. The visualization and imagination is different from real experience. My *Guruji* had granted me the experience of '*Soham*' at Manasarovar. To me, that was the real 'Kailash' that I had reached!

The next day the mandali was planning to move down, retracing the same route. Everybody seemed tired. But there was no other way and we had to walk. Everything was packed up and we all started moving down to Manasarovar.

On the return journey too, we stayed one day at Manasarovar. Everybody collected water from the Sarovar in bottles, except for me! Somehow, these rituals of collecting *teertham* (holy water associated with a temple or deity), etc., were not digestible to me. The return journey was a bit easy. I was easily walking with the other *sadhus*. They were wondering how my behaviour had changed. Not much talking, or if there was talking it was too much.

We reached Darchula and stayed there for a couple of days. There was heaving rain on the way to Nepalgunj. Several streams were flowing down from the hills above. Once I was almost washed away. Swami Sandrananda extended his walking stick and pulled me up and saved me. Without much difficulty we reached Nepalgunj. The head of the mandali had arranged a bus to Kathmandu, and we reached there by evening. Everybody seemed happy and was telling stories of the *yatra*.

Back to India, Samalkha

After returning from the Kailash *yatra* I stayed with the *mandali* for a few more days. The *mandali* was moving around Nepal. We stayed at Narayan ghat for a few days and went to Hathoda. I left the mandali at Hathoda and travelled to India via Sonali. From Sonali I went to Ayodhya and stayed there for a couple of days. I was not in a mood to go to Jammu where the ashram work was in progress. I remembered that one of my sanyasi friends, Swami Lalithanand, was staying near Panipat (Samalkha village) where he was constructing a *mandir*. I decided to go and meet him. From Ayodhya, via Delhi, I reached Samalkha in the morning. I had previously visited that place a few years ago. There was a businessman there named Jagdish Bansal who I knew and I went to his residence, and with his help, I met Swami Lalithananda. They arranged for my stay at an old Shiva *mandir* in Samalkha village. Except for a *poojari* and his family (from Mathura) nobody else was staying there.

My *bhiksha* and other needs were arranged at the house of Iswar Pandit. His wife Uma and her sister Brijalata used to take care of my food, etc. Everybody was enquiring about my journey to Kailash, as Lalithanand had told them about it. For a few days I rested there in the mandir; but I was beginning to feel bad about myself for simply sitting around and eating and sleeping! I told them that I was planning to start a daily *satsang*, at the mandir, based on the *Adhyatma Ramayana*.[50] This was the first time I was holding a satsang on the *Ramayana*. As *satsang* was held during evening time, a sizable number of villagers used to attend the gathering. Lalithanand also started staying with me. An old lady was engaged for cooking food. Jagdish met the expenses for my stay there as he was one of the owners of the Shiv Mandir.

The satsang went on for 21 days. One Surendra Sharma and his wife Latha along with Birjalatha were looking after the requirements of the *bhajan* and *satsang* sessions. By this time the number of villagers had increased and they asked for *deeksha* (initiation by a *guru*) as most of them considered me their *Guru*. A day was fixed and more than 150 persons took *Guru mantra deeksha* on that day. Those days I was not in the habit of taking *dakshina*. But the villagers used to bring some money or fruits for me. I asked Lalithanand to take the offerings and make use of them.

The villagers used to invite me to their homes for bhiksha. I gladly accepted the invitations and would go for bhiksha along with Surendra Sharma and Umakant Kaushik who accompanied me every day. Now I had a good number of disciples at Samalkha and I was getting invitations for bhiksha every day. They stopped cooking for me at the *mandir*. After concluding the satsang of 21 days, I stayed there for three more days. Instead of going to Jammu, I decided to go to Omkareshwar once again. A ticket was booked to Indore, and from Delhi I started my journey towards Omkareshwar again.

---

50 A medieval Sanskrit text extolling the spiritualism in the story of Ramayana. It is embedded in the latter portion of Brahmānda Purana. The text philosophically attempts to reconcile Bhakti in god Rama and Shaktism with Advaita Vedanta, over 65 chapters and 4,500 verses.

Again Narmada and Kashi

Once again I had reached Omkareshwar. I stayed there for a few days. Most of the sadhus I knew were asking me about my journey to Kailash with the mandali. Withholding certain personal experiences, I described my journey to them. Every day, I would sit on the banks of the *Narmada* (river). Swami Arghyanand had already left the ashram and was constructing a small kutia somewhere near Khal ghat on the Narmada banks.

During one of the discussions with Swami Ramanandji I expressed my desire to go to Kashi in order to practice *Tantra sadhana* of the Das Mahavidya. I had completed *Srividya* (*Shodashi*) sadhana. Swamiji was not inclined to accept my proposal, and said, "During your Kailash *yatra*, you have experienced *Advaita Siddhi*. Now why do you want to enter into a fierce *Tantra sadhana*? I see no justification of your desire to do *Tantra Sadhana*. Better that you stay here and study *Vedanta*." This logic did not appeal to me. In Sri Ramakrishna Paramahamsa's biography, which I read during my college days, Sri Ramakrishna tried all types of *sadhana*, even Muslim and Christian ways of *sadhanas*. He had been my model saint in life from childhood after I read his *Gospel of Sri Rama Krishna*.

I did not argue with Swamiji to prove that my desire was genuine. After a few days' stay at the Markandeya Sanyas Ashram, I was ready to move to Kashi to test whether I would succeed in my *iccha* (desire) I had Rs. 500 with me, a pair of clothes and one blanket. And of course my permanent companions, my *kamandal* and *kappar* too! I went to Bhopal by bus and from there to Varanasi the next day. After two days' journey I reached Varanasi. This was the second time I was going to Kashi. The first time had been on my return from Tibet after failing my attempt to reach *Gyanganj*. I knew nobody there. But I knew that there was an *ashram* of Swamy Ramanandji (Abhya Sanyas Ashram) at Manikarnika Ghat. After a few hours of searching and walking here and there, I reached Abhaya Sanyas Ashram. I failed to get an accommodation as I was not known to anybody there. Moreover, with my matted hair, long beard and unkempt clothes I had a very awkward look! I went to Manikarnika Ghat and sat on the steps. It was getting dark and night was near. As I had a little amount of money left with me, I went to a nearby hotel on the *ghat* itself and had some *roti*, etc. I had a balance of about hundred rupees with me. I felt that I should not keep it. I had seen a beggar-type old man on the *verandah* of the next building. I went to him and gave the money to him, walked away quickly to the *ghat* steps again. I decided that no matter what happened to me, I would stay only at that *ghat*, and that one day I would definitely get a guru to teach me *Tantra Sadhana*. Like me, there were a few people who had already occupied the steps of the *ghat* for night shelter. I saw a few pyres burning here and there at Manikarnika Ghat. I simply sat on the steps, looking at the flow of Ganga.

I slept on those very steps that night. The awful smell of burning dead bodies was entering my nostrils. I felt very bad for some time, but after an hour or two, I was at ease. In the morning I answered the calls of nature in the nearby bushes. After bathing I was back at the steps. I made a firm resolution in my mind—if *Annapoorna* was indeed in Kashi, she would take care of my food. I would not ask anybody for my food and nor would I knock the doors of any ashram for my stay. I recited a *sloka*—"Mata Cha Parvati Devi, Pita Devo Maheshvara." So, if both my father and mother were in Kashi, why would they not take care of me? These were the thoughts in my mind. I sat there chanting the *Shodashi mantra* for some time. Occasionally I would slip and started chanting "*Nama Shivaya.*" People (pilgrims and *sadhus*) came to the ghat and bathed, but went away carelessly. Nobody looked at me. It was almost noon. I was hungry. Looking to Mother Ganga I said, "*Maa* Ganga, it seems that *Maa* Anapoorna is not in Kashi. If not, why would her son, a poor sanyasi, be sitting here hungry?" Time was passing quickly and seemed like it was almost 3 pm already. I was a little tired due to hunger and being a little angry with Annapoorna I did not drink even *Gangajal*. Pyres were burning around me and a sound of 'tap-tap' (of burning wood logs and bones) arising from them. In that hot sun, I slept on the ghat for a while. When I woke up after an hour or two I saw a beggar woman sitting near me. She was opening her *pottli* (a small cloth bag), in which she collected food and bringing out three rotis and some vegetables to me, she asked me to eat. I was wondering and looked at her face for a few seconds. There was a maternal affection on her face. At first I hesitated to eat from a beggar's hand. But she kept insisting. I asked her, "*Maa*, where is your food? You begged the whole day and got some *roti*. If you feed all that to me, what about you?" She showed me a few more *rotis* in her *pottli* and asked me to eat. Taking the *rotis* from her hand and putting them in my *kappar*, I began eating. The beggar woman also started eating from her aluminium plate which looked very dirty. While eating I heard the voice of the '*Dom*' (the man responsible for burning corpses), "*Arre Nakuli, tere ko apna beta mila kya? Yeh tum kisko roti khila raha hai?*" (Hey Nakuli, have you found your son or what? Who are you feeding *rotis* to?)

I now knew that the old woman's name was Nakuli. The Dom came down the steps and told me, "Maharaj, I have been watching all night that you have been sitting here. Any problem? Do not believe this mad old Nakuli. Why are you not going to some *ashram* for your stay?" I told him my story and my decision to stay there till I met a guru who would teach me Tantra Sadhana. Nakuli had finished eating by that time, and washing her hands and her *patra* in the Ganga, she came near me and said with a smile on her face, "*Idhar hi thero! Kahin nahin jaana.*" (Stay right here, don't go anywhere.) She slowly ambled away. The Dom also left, climbing up the steps. It was evening. I sat there quietly.

Disciples Welcoming Guruji After his Visit to Gyangunj at Panipat

Dhuni Sthapana In Chowl (Maharashtra)

Srividya Kulagraja Award to Avadhoota Nadananda in 2000

Avadhoota Nadananda

Avadhoota Nadananda with his Gurubhai Prasobh Maharaj

Avadhoota Nadananda

Chandi Parayan at Siddhaganj

Guru Mandala Pooja at Siddhaganj

Aksharabhyasam at a Tribal School at Kurnool

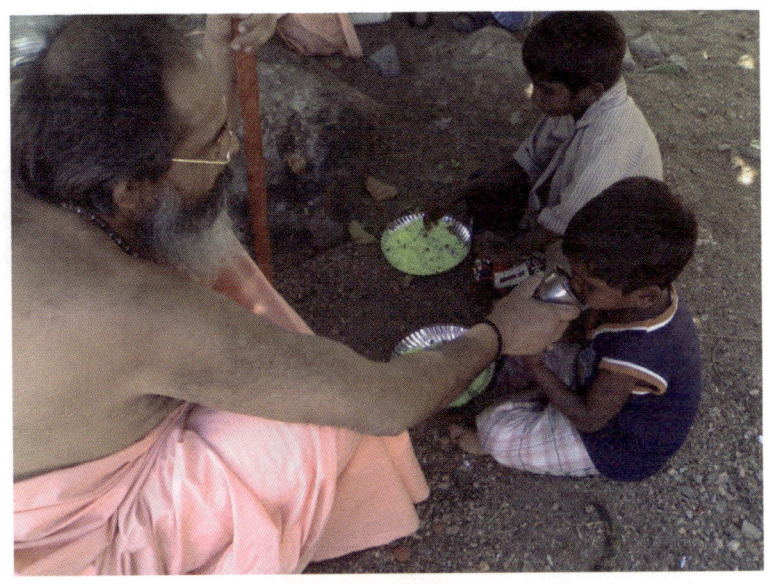

Feeding Children

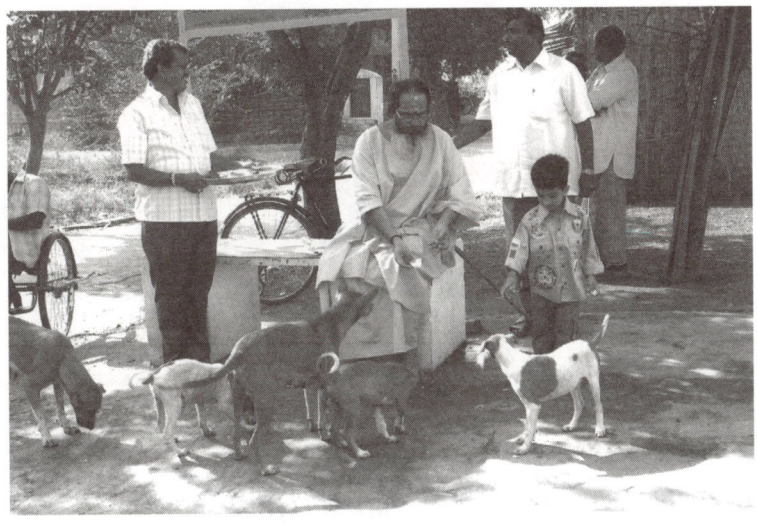

Feeding the Hungry

Guru Pada Pooja at Hyderabad

Tantra Sadhana

I was staying at Manikarnika Ghat. A few days passed this way. Every day in the afternoon Nakuli would bring some rotis which she had collected during her begging. Sometimes I felt very embarrassed at my behaviour of accepting and eating food given by a poor woman who had begged to get it. But in reality who is not a beggar? Even the richest person is a beggar as he begs the Almighty for more wealth. I was a beggar of beggars! But I knew there was definitely some reason behind my eating from her begging.

One day the *Dom* (who used to talk to me daily) introduced me to a Bengali *Baba*, a well-known *Tantrik* of that time. His looked very fierce, a middle-aged man with a well-built body, matted hair and beard, in red clothes and wearing *rakta chandan* (red sandalwood) and *kumkum tilak* (marking on forehead with vermillion). I spoke to him about my intention to practice *Tantra Sadhana*. I replied to his questions about my life so far. Even though he looked fierce, his manner and way of talking were very mild and positive. He agreed to teach me *Tantra Sadhana* and said, "You have to stay only at this *smashan* (cremation grounds). After initiation I have to go to Tarapeetham in Bengal, and will be back in two or three months. Nakuli and Dom will help you meet your needs." But he also placed another condition for initiation. If I wanted to study *Tantra Vidya*, I must first initiate him in Srividya of the Kerala Aacharam. I agreed to it. He opened his shoulder bag and took out a *panchangam* (Indian almanac), did some calculations and decided upon a date (which was after three days) for the initiation.

Two days went by just in anticipation of the arrival of the date of the initiation. After sunset the Bengali Tantrik came to the ghat along with the dom. Nakuli was sitting on the steps near me. We both bathed in the Ganga and after *tilakam* and other rituals he took me to a nearby pyre and sat near it. Opening a bottle of 'local liquor' he poured some into the fire of the pyre as an offering, and uttered some mantra. He took some ashes from the pyre and applied them as tilakam on my forehead, and asked me to initiate him into *Srividya*. I was mesmerized. Praying to my Guruji, I initiated him with the *shodashi mantra, mudras*, etc. Now it was my turn to receive initiation from him. He instructed me about certain rules regarding entering in a *smashan, digh bandham*', how to sit near a 'pyre', and how to start japa of certain mantras of Tara (one of the Dasha Maha Vidyas). Every day, 1 *yama*[51] after sunset, I was supposed to sit near a pyre and after applying '*chita bhasmam*' (ashes from pyre) I had to continue my japa till midnight. He told me that a lot of *pralobhans* (temptations) would come to me during my japa sadhana of Tara but to ignore them. He told me to take the bhiksha which Nakuli would give me and complete the japa within 45 days, and he would try to return by that time. Even if he was late in returning, I should continue the japa sadhana till he returned. He said, "This is the first step of your *Tantra Sadhana*. After completion of the japa you have to then do *homa* in the pyre. If you are successful, I will teach you '*Shava Sadhana*' as well. Leaving me alone, he got ready to go someplace.

The darkness around me was frightening. This was the first time that I was sitting near a pyre for such a long time. Nobody was near me. *Dom* had also left earlier. Nakuli was not visible at the ghat. There was only the light of the burning pyre. At a distance near another pyre I saw two or three *sadhaks* sitting and doing homa in the pyre. Like the Bengali Baba had told me, I was looking at the pyre and concentrating on my japa. It was almost morning when I completed my first day's japa. The fire at the pyre was about to die. Pilgrims and *sadhus* were coming to the *ghat* to bathe. I got up too. My body was covered with ash from the burning corpses nearby. Feeling a little tired I went to the ghat for my morning ablutions.

I felt happy that I could begin the *sadhana* that I had wished for. All day long I would sit or sleep at the *ghat* and in the nights I

---

51 A Hindu unit of time; one-fourth of a day + night is a yama.

would be doing *japa* sitting near one of the burning pyres. Nakuli brought some *rotis* daily for me to eat. Days were passing by without any troubles.

Sadhana at Burial Ground

I was continuing my *Tantra Sadhana* very happily. Dom used to bring local liquor for the offering every day, and Nakuli would feed me a few *rotis* from her *bhiksha*. At about midnight once when I was doing *japa* near the pyre, I saw a very fierce form appear in front of me and asked me to stop my *japa*. I was afraid to look at that form of a woman, naked and wearing a skull *mala* around her neck. She said, "What do you want? Money, fame, good house, a beautiful maid? You can choose all—I am granting them all to you now. But stop this *japa*." The *Baba* who had initiated me had cautioned me about that: "*Pralobhans* will come. Beware of them." I asked the form of that ferocious woman, "Who are you? Why do you want to disturb my *sadhana*? I need nothing from whatever you offered to me. Let me do *japa*. Go away!" She laughed loudly, which was frightening. She said once again, "Your *japa* is disturbing me. Ask for whatever materialistic thing you desire and take it from me. I am pleased with your *japa*. But you must stop the *japa* and take whatever you want." I got angry, and said, "Get lost now. I need none of your materialistic things. I want you to be with me. Can you do that, if so, I am ready to stop this *japa*." Then she smiled in a very calm and beautiful way, and said, "Son, I was testing you to find whether you are doing it for materialistic needs. Okay, I understand you now. Continue the *japa*. I will be yours from the day of your completion of *japa*." Now I understood that this lady was none other than Tara, whose *mantra japa* I was chanting. I was happy that one day Tara would be mine. Of course I had to complete the *japa*.

Almost one month of japa was over. I had been hungry for the previous two days as Nakuli did not show up with my bhiksha. I asked Dom about Nakuli, but he also didn't know where she had gone. On the fourth night, Nakuli came back to me. She looked very tired. I asked her, "*Maa*! What happened to you, I didn't see you the last few days? I was hungry and was waiting for you." She took out two biscuit packs from her pottli and giving them to me said, "I was in the Ganga, doing my *sadhana*. So I was unable to come to you. I know you are hungry. But I have to do my *sadhana* on *Trayodashi*, *Chathurdasi* and *Amavasya*. Son, don't feel hurt because of this old woman. I am your mother. Eat, eat the biscuits! Tomorrow I will bring you some rotis."

Now I realized that Nakuli was not an ordinary beggar. To hide her identity, she had chosen to dress like a beggar. I was sure she must be either a *yogini* (a woman who is proficient in yoga; a female yogi) or a *Bhairavi* (devotee of Mother Goddess). I thought how lucky I was. A Yogini/Bhairavi was doing seva for me by bringing my *bhiksha* daily and was feeding me with motherly affection. I stood up and did pranams to her by touching her feet. She said, "*Arre Baba tum kya karte ho. Main ek bhikkari, tum to maharaj hai, mere pair kyon choote ho?*" (What are you doing? I am just a beggar woman and you a *sanyasi*. Why do you touch my feet?) I had tears in my eyes thinking about my *Guruji*'s *kripa* on me! I told her, "*Maa*, I don't know whether you are a *bhikharin* or my *Guruji*. You feed me every day with motherly affection so, of course, you are a mother to me. Let me do pranams to you again and again." Saying this, I once again touched her feet with my head. I was washing her old feet with my tears. She held both my hands and lifted me up. With her shivering hands, she wiped my tears and started feeding me biscuits.

I went into a trance and was in that state for a long time. The biscuits lay in front of me, but I could not eat them even though Nakuli kept trying again and again to make me eat. Tears flowed from my eyes. Of course, this was all only my Guruji's *kripa*. In this unknown place, an unknown beggar type woman was feeding me! And she was not a beggar at all but a great *sadhika* in *Tantra*. A *Yogini* or a *Bhairavi*! How lucky I was, who was it that wrote my destiny to be like this. It must be my *Guruji*, *Paramaguruji* or whoever. It might be that all this was happening, only because of my destiny. I was in a trance, tears coming out of my eyes, and I was laughing and crying like a madman.

New Horizons

I was thinking often about my *Guruji's* affection towards me these days. That she was always supporting my *sadhana* in various forms. In some way or the other, she had always helped me during my *sadhana*. Even though she lived far from me physically at Mookambika, she was always near me, taking care of my needs every moment. I know that my Guruji is a unique '*avatar*' of love. Even if I write thousands of pages of her love towards me, they would not be enough to express it. Without her support, it would be impossible for me to complete even a day of *sadhana*.

On the evening of the 45th day of my *japa sadhana* on *Tara Mantra*, while I was sitting on the Manikarnika *ghat* steps, thinking of what next, the Bengali Baba returned there to meet me.

He asked me about the days of my *sadhana*. I had not known that he was a *Mahakaula*. (Mahakaula is the most advanced Sadhak Guru in Tantra.) He had different *siddhis* with him. Even though he looked fierce and dangerous, he was very gentle in his behaviour. He said, "I know that you had the vision of Tara during your *japa sadhana*. It is good that you have come out of the temptations offered by Tara. Now I shall teach you '*Shava Sadhana*', which is one of the important steps of your *Tantra Sadhana*. Dom will arrange for a corpse for you to use as an *asan* (seat) and you have to sit on it after decorating it with *chandan* and *kumkum*. He described in detail about the preparations for that *sadhana*. I had to wait until *Amavasya* (new moon night) for it. Till then I decided to continue my japa of Tara Mantra.

It was *Amavasya* and early in the morning, the Bengali Baba arrived. I did not know where he stayed or ate and never asked him either. Dom was also with him and he said he would arrange for a corpse, if any dead body was brought that day for cremation, for my *sadhana*. He brought a full bottle of local liquor and gave it to me. He also brought a few coconut shells, flowers, *chandan* paste, *kumkum*, etc.

It was my good fortune to get a corpse on that *Amavasya* day. It was that of a middle-aged woman. The relatives brought the body and handing it over to Dom, left in the evening. (This is the system in Kashi.) One yama after sunset, at night, both Dom and Baba took the body to a distance from the pyre. There was deep darkness. Dom left after arranging the *pooja samagri* (worship materials). Baba gave me instructions on how to wash the body, how to apply chandan and kumkum and other procedures.

After giving detailed instructions of *Shava Suddhi* (purification of the corpse), *Lepanam* (application of sandalwood paste and vermillion), *Disha Bodham* (cognition of the exact direction), '*Digh bandham*', etc., Baba left me saying that he would return in the early hours next morning. He cautioned me, "Do not be afraid. If you are frightened, you cannot do the sadhana, you will definitely fail. Be careful. I am around here."

From the beginning I had a fear in me. I was all alone near the dead body. I prayed to my *Guruji* to give me courage to do this fierce *sadhana*. As instructed by the Baba I undressed the dead body. I undressed too. After washing the corpse, I applied *chandan* paste and *kumkum* to it. Now my '*Shava Asan*' was ready and as *Baba* had told me, I lit earthen lamps to the left, right and above the head of the corpse. My hand was shivering. To my right I kept a coconut shell full of local liquor near the head of the corpse.

I sat on the dead body with a shaking mind and body. This was my first ever experience of touching a naked female body. Of course, I had attended several funerals, but this way of washing a naked woman's body, applying *chandan*, *kumkum* paste, or sitting for *sadhana*, I had never expected it to happen in my life. I started doing *japa* looking into the opened eyes (I had opened them as Baba instructed) of the body. After a few minutes the dead body started shaking and shivering, and all of a sudden the dead body opened its mouth and made a ferocious sound. I was a bit afraid, and as Baba had said, I poured the country liquor in its mouth and put in a burning wick. It closed its mouth, making a strange sound. Now the dead body stopped shaking. I continued the *japa*. My whole body was sweating. I saw a shadow appearing near me.

While I was wondering what it could be, the form of a naked woman with skull *mala* (the same as I had seen before, during my *japa* near the pyre) appeared near me. She was standing still, and staring at me. My speed of *japa* increased as I was full of fear. She said, "Are you after *siddhis*? What do you want? *Ashta Siddhis*? I know you have the greatest *siddhis*, which you gained during your stay in Manasarovar. What do you want now?" I kept silent and continued *japa*. (That had been the instruction of Baba, to do nothing other than *japa* till the early hours, or until he came.) After a few minutes the lady vanished in thin air. I could hear the barking of dogs from a distance. It was the darkest, most dangerous and frightful night I had ever faced. But with my *Guru's kripa* I could complete the *japa*.

Early in the morning Dom came with Bengali Baba. It may have been about 4.00 am or so, when Baba came near me and asked me to stop japa. He instructed me on how to do 'Japa *Samarpan*' (offering of my chants). Following him, I forcibly opened the mouth of the corpse and poured some country liquor in it. Baba then asked me to drink a little liquor as *prasadam* and give the remaining to Dom. After a few rituals, I was asked to get up. As I had been sitting more than 6–7 hours on the cold dead body my legs had become stiff. Dom helped me stand up. Baba asked me to follow him to the Ganga for a bath. He said that Dom would take care of the body.

I had a bath at Manikarnika Ghat. It was dawn, and pilgrims and sadhus were just starting to arrive at the Ghat for bathing. Bengali Baba told me that he would meet me in the evening and left. Nakuli was waiting for me at the steps. She brought me a glass of tea from a shop nearby. I was tired and felt sleepy too. I lay down on the step and slept till Nakuli brought a few *rotis* for me.

Unlimited Bliss

The Bengali Baba came back in the evening. At that time, I was sitting peacefully on the steps after eating the rotis brought by Nakuli, who also sat by me. She was telling me in me in detail about Yogini Sadhana. I had learnt the '*Swayamvara Parvati*' (a *Yogini*) *mantra*, taught to me by my father. She said that a single *mantra*, if practiced properly was sufficient, as it had the capacity to give all *siddhis*. This *mantra* can be done for the betterment of others too. Nakuli told me about her *Tantra Sadhana* done at Kamakhya, during her stay with her *Guruji*. Her husband had passed away a few years ago, and her only son left her after her husband's death, as he did not want to be labelled a *Tantric* woman's son. She then came to Varanasi for her sadhana and had been here since then. I asked her what it was that made her want to feed me every day, after begging for food. She said, "On the day I first saw you, I knew immediately that you are not ordinary. There is something special about you. While giving you *rotis* I observed the lines on your palms. It confirmed that you are a unique one. So I decided to do *seva* for you. Moreover I had a dream on the second day after meeting you. I saw in this dream an old woman telling me to take care of her child, pointing to you. Then I understood who you are, and what your birth is for. You have a special mission destined by your *Guru Parampara*. So I thought that by serving you, I will have the *ashirvaad* of the *Guru Parampara*. Bengali Baba was listening to all this. He asked me what I wanted to do next. I told him, "Baba, I have started *Tantra Sadhana* just out of curiosity. I need neither siddhis nor fame and wealth. I need only energy (*Shakti*) to do some service to the needy. My *Guruji* taught me to live for others always. I am trying to do that. And I know that at every moment, my *Guruji* is with me—guiding and protecting me!" Bengali Baba told me to do some more *mantra japa*. To my wonder, he gave me the mantra of '*Swayamvara Parvati*' (a *Yogini*) which I had already received from my father during my college days. He instructed me to do the japa for a few weeks, in a standing posture in the Ganga if possible. I was supposed to do *japa* standing in waist-high water, for at least 21 days. Bengali Baba was preparing to leave for his kutia at Tarapeeth in Bengal in a day or two. He told me, "In any case, you have completed the *japa* of *Tara*. Remember that now Tara is with you as a helping hand. Do not misuse this power. After completing your Yogini Mantra Japa for 21 days, you can leave Kashi. Come to Tarapeeth whenever you feel like it."

Bengali Baba left, and after some time Nakuli and myself talked about sadhana again. I told her of my wish to go to Narmada again. Nakuli said, "Narmada is a *Siddha Kshetra*. Now you possess certain siddhis too. All right so, go, you will definitely have good experiences there. But try to be solitary. Always move alone. As you are experiencing your *Guruji's* presence always with you, why do you need to worry?! She will take care of your life at every step."

The next day I began doing *Yogini Mantra Japa* standing in the Ganga. The water was unbearably cold. For a few minutes, I felt it difficult to stand in the water. I was losing my concentration due to the cold, but after ten minutes, I felt alright to stand and do my japa.

As usual daily Nakuli brought rotis for me. From early morning to noon I would do japa. After eating the rotis and taking rest for a few hours, I repeated the same japa from evening to midnight, standing in water. Almost two weeks passed this way. I was doing the japa standing in water when the night of my life that I shall remember always unfolded. It was almost midnight. I saw a beautiful woman emerge from the water in front of me, well dressed and decorated with ornaments and flower garland. She was young, in her teens. And the radiant glow on her face was wonderful and attractive. She looked at me and said, "Why are you doing this japa? And for what? If you are doing it for my *sakshatkara* (realization), look I am here. Tell me, what are you expecting from me?" With folded hands, I told her, "*Maa*,

I need nothing in particular. Only bless me, *Maa*! If I chant and do something for someone using this mantra, let the purpose be served successfully. Bless me *Maa* to be in bliss always and bless me to always do good for others!" She asked me to open my mouth wide. When I did so, she poured three handfuls of *Gangajal* with her hand into my mouth and merged with Ganga without saying anything. I went into trance. With much difficulty I returned to the ghat steps. Nakuli was sitting there. She had not slept, but was witnessing what had been going on. With a strange smile on her face, she said, "Son, you got it! You got it! Your coming to Kashi for *sadhana* has been successful. Now you have Tara and Yogini with you. You can do wonders! You can do miracles now!" I told her that I was not aiming for any miracles, though I would definitely make use of these powers for the betterment of ailing people. And not for any *kshamta* (capability or competence). Even now I use these two 'energies'—Tara and Yogini Mantra—for helping people come out of dangerous situations during illness, and get the expected results too.

I did the '*Yogini Mantra Japa*' for one more week and concluded the sadhana. I told Nakuli that I wanted to leave Kashi for Narmada (Omkareshwar) and if possible do Narmada Parikrama. She must have read the concern I had in my mind of how I was going to go there without money, for she opened her pottli and gave me a few *rupee* notes that she had received during *bhiksha* and said, "Son, this will be sufficient for your rail ticket. Go. Go now. But remember this old woman sometimes. Go son, go!"

I felt a deep ache in leaving her. With motherly affection she had taken care of my food for the past three months. With shaking hands and eyes in full of tears, I touched her feet and bid farewell to her. She pulled me up and embraced me once, murmured, "Go, son, Go. Go for the best."

Dom was looking at us. He also stepped down towards us and gave me a 100-rupee note, which he had got as *dakshina* for cremating a dead body. With a heavy mind and tears in my eyes, I left them both to go to the railway station to catch a train to Indore for my onward journey to Narmada.

Namami Devi Narmade

I was very happy to be back in Narmada. After two days of train and bus journey, I reached Omkareshwar and as usual, stayed at Markandeya Sanyas Ashram. Even though I was tired after my three-month sadhana, I took a staunch decision to go around the Narmada and let it not be a conventional pilgrimage. I decided to stay on the banks of Narmada for at least one year. For a few days I stayed at the ashram. Most of the old and known *swamis* were not there. A few new faces were there for their studies in Vedanta. I told my decision to Swami Ramanandaji that in a day or two I shall start my Narmada journey. If it was a conventional '*parikrama*', I would have to undergo certain rules and regulations. As I wanted it to be free from all these rituals and be without any bindings of *parikrama* rules I wanted to travel alone.

Swamiji asked me to be in the *ashram* until *Poornima* (full moon night) and then leave. So, I stayed there for a week more, waiting for *Poornima*. This time I did not visit Omkareshwar or Amalashwar (both being *Jyotir Lingas*) as I did not feel like going there. Even during my three months stay at Kashi I had not visited Vishwanatha Mandir or Vishalaskhi or Annapoorna Mandirs. Not because of any aversion, but I did not feel like visiting *mandirs*. My mind set had changed. I was wondering about the words of Nakuli when she had said that I was destined for a mission. I didn't know what that mission was? Only one thing I knew—I was like a football rolling in the court without reaching the goal! Of course, the Bengali Baba or Nakuli or others talked about the *siddhis*. There were no external, visible symptoms of *siddhis* in me. But these days I noticed one thing, whatever I thought or said it happened. I didn't know whether it was a siddhi nor not.

On Poornima day I left for my travel. I did not do any *sankalpa* (definite intention) for parikrama. Usually pilgrims on Narmada *parikrama* should take a *sankalp* and carry 'Narmada jal' in a bottle to do pooja daily. So, without any pre-conception I started my journey on the southern bank of the Narmada.

Daily after walking until noon, I would go to a nearby village for my bhiksha. I took food in my kappar, sat and ate on the banks of the Narmada, and then I rested till the next morning either on the banks of the river or at a nearby temple. And, again resumed walking the next morning. Except for taking food once a day, I never took any tea or snacks, even if someone offered it. Aimless, free of thoughts, without any calculations of the next moment, I simply walked. I saw so many people doing '*Parikrama Yatra*', but did not join any group, but walked alone reciting '*Devi Pranava*' at each and every step.

I stopped at a mandir one afternoon. There was a small crowd as villagers had brought a patient seeking blessing of the deity. It was a Shiv *mandir*. The patient was very restless and had symptoms of being 'possessed by a devil'. He had a well-built body, and was shouting, shivering and murmuring. Sitting on the *verandah* of the *mandir*, I was observing his actions. His wife and children were crying and a few villagers who had accompanied the patient were also very much worried. While they were offering some flowers and praying to the deity, the 'possessed' patient shouted and everybody was afraid. I thought I should do something to help him and held him with my left hand and pressed him in his '*Bhru Madhya*' (on the forehead in the middle of his eyebrows) and chanted *mantra* once. To my wonder he fell down at once and laid down calm. His eyes were closed. Now the shouting and shivering were not there. The villagers came near and saw that he was lying as if unconscious. They looked at me. When I took some water from my *kamandal* and sprinkled it on his face with the same *mantra*, he opened his eyes and sat up and did pranams to me.

The villagers were very happy as the man was normal now. They asked me about my whereabouts. I told them I was just a wandering monk, and will move after resting in this *mandir* tonight. All of them left in a happy mood.

Evening *arathi* was in progress. By this time another swamiji also reached there. He was also in Narmada *parikrama*. He said that he was from Bengal and belonged to *Bharat Seva Sangh*. The man, who was relieved from the 'possession', with his wife and children came with some food for me. I did not accept it for two reasons—one, I had already had my one-time *bhiksha* from the village at noon. Second, if I did accept this, it would be counted as a reward for relieving him from the possession. I told them that the swamiji sitting near had nothing to eat that day. So they better give the food to him. Happily they did so. I went to a corner of the *verandah*, and looking and praying to Narmada I lay down there.

Narmade Har ... Har ... Har

I heard the sound of '*Narmade har*' (salutations to holy river Narmada). The other swami was ready to move. The first rays of the sun were just shining. The customary greeting at Narmada by those who were doing parikrama was '*Narmade har*'. This phrase has a very deep meaning. *Nar + mad + har* (*nar* = man, *mad* = ego, *har* = wipe out). I felt that the meaning can be chanted as a prayer, 'wipe out the ego of man'. In another sense it is a prayer to Narmada and Shiva. The other swamiji left saying '*Narmade har*'. I woke and sat up. Now the *poojari* of that *mandir* (from the nearby village) also came. He was accompanied by a few villagers. Yesterday's 'possessed' man and his family came as well. He requested me to stay back at their village for a few days. The villagers from the banks of Narmada may be poor regarding worldly possessions, but they are rich in their hearts. If they liked a person or sadhu, they treated him as God! Once again they asked me to go with them to the village. I assured them that after my bath and pooja, I would definitely go to their village and will take '*Madukari Bhiksha*' (taking Bhiksha from five houses in *kappar*—the practice of wandering monks). They did their *pranams* to me and left. I too left to Narmada for bath, etc.

I never thought that such things will happen. After bath and after my japa I went to the village around noon for my bhiksha. I went to five houses, collected whatever they offered in my kappar and sat under a tree to eat. Three or four *rotis*, *dal*, little vegetables, rice and even butter milk and *chutney* was filled in my *kappar*. I was just washing my hand before offering my collected food to Narmada, and as I sat under the tree, a few villagers with their family (women, children and old people) came and sat around me.

I was wondering what was happening. I had just started eating food after mixing everything together. The villagers started telling me about their ailments, or some *bhoota baadha* (being possessed by a ghost), etc. Somehow these people came to know of the previous day's incident at the *mandir*.

They thought I was a *siddha*, and could solve any problem. I told them very humbly that I knew nothing to heal them from ailments or ghost possessions. By this time a few more villagers joined us. Each and every one had this or that problem. Even though I repeatedly told them that I knew nothing, they did not believe me as they had come to know of the previous day's episode. I wondered how I could get out of this situation. I told them to chant '*Narmade hara, Narmade hara*' and during their chanting, with a prayer in my mind, I started giving them a little bit food as '*prasadam*' from my kappar. Everybody was happy to receive it and one by one they left. I too completed my food immediately and left the village to the banks of the Narmada from the mandir. I thought, I must leave the place; if not there will be a bigger crowd next day. Immediately I resumed my journey.

Even though sunset time was near, I could not find a village or *mandir*. As I started immediately after food I was tired and felt my stomach very heavy. I decided to stay on the sands of the Narmada that night. This area was not in the forest so there was nothing to worry. From here and there, I collected some dry cow dung and some fire wood. At sunset I lit a fire. (Because of first yatra experience, this *yatra* I always kept one or two match boxes with me.) I had a bath and sat near the fire doing *japa*.

I slept on the sand and had a dream. I saw that I was in a fort in a dense forest. And I was locked in a room made of rocks. I could see through the window of the room a very big *homa kunda* (fire altar) in the courtyard of the fort, where fire in a homa kunda was burning. A teenage girl, who was fully naked, but wearing a flower garland and sword in her hand appeared in front of the homa kunda. She sat near it and lifted her hand with sword and started cutting off her hands, legs and other organs one by one and putting them in the homa *agni* (fire). Now as she was just cutting her head, a very big beam of light emerged from the *homa kunda* and for a moment everything vanished. I woke up from the dream. I was sweating. What a ferocious dream that was! What could be the meaning of this? I had to analyse the dream! At midnight on the banks of the Narmada, I sat near the fire, all alone. Again and again I tried to analyse the dream. I felt this dream was symbolic. Forest can be the symbol of materialism. The burning fire in the homa kunda could be desire. The naked girl—the *jeeva* (living being). So symbolically, when *jeeva* cut off her desires (different body parts) and when finally the ego (head) was cut, realization happened. When realization happened, a beam of light emerged! I thought that this could be the explanation for the dream. I did not know whether this was a message for me. Even now, I am unable to interpret the dream in detail.

I could not sleep after that. I simply sat near the fire and thought of several things. I could not concentrate and do japa either. I simply sat looking at the fire and thinking about the dream, until morning. I had my bath right away and resumed my walking.

Just a Journey—Neither Pilgrimage Nor Picnic!

I continued my journey. When I reached Hapeshwar, I remembered my last journey to Narmada how much I suffered because of diarrhoea and weakness. However, during the last few months' journey, my health had been quite good. I reached Soolpaneshwar mandir. The work at the dam site was yet to be completed. The old *poojari* who helped me reach Narpat Bhai during my last journey was not there. Here the Government was planning to shift the *mandir* from the original site to some higher place as this area would be submerged once the dam work was over. The *poojari* at Soolpaneshwar *mandir* had also been replaced. I slept at that *mandir* at night and resumed my journey next day early morning. Narpat Bhai and family were very happy to see me once again and they told me that they never thought I would be back again and meet them. Their children had grown up a little. They were still continuing their seva to the travellers doing Narmada *parikrama*. I stayed there for a few days.

On the other side was my old school Sri Rama Krishna English Medium school. Narpat Bhai said the *swamiji* was not there. Even then I sent a word to the people there that I was back. Some of the teachers came to meet me. That girl who 'loved' me and to whom I had initiated the '*Bala*' (child) *mantra* was also with the other teachers. She had married a person working in the government service and now had a child—boy. I was happy to hear that she had settled down and was happy with her family life. I resumed my journey next day via Garudeshwar, Nareshwar and after a few days journey reached at the confluence of Narmada.

I was told to cross this area by a boat in river to reach the other shore of Narmada. I waited for two days to get the country boat to cross the river. There were few more *parikrama vasis*, waiting for the boat. Because of high tide the boatman was not ready to row. On the morning of the third day, a few of us sat in the country boat and crossed that area of the sea. I was very much afraid to sit on the boat as it was jumping and dancing due to the waves of the sea. By evening we all reached safely to the other side of Narmada. This is the northern bank of Narmada. I stayed at the seashore itself on that day to avoid any company for my onward journey.

Next day I started the journey. Almost tired and bored, I wished to break my journey once again. On the other hand, my mind was arguing to continue the journey. Somehow, I continued my journey towards upper streams via Nareshwar and Garudeshwar. Nareshwar is the place where I visited the samadhi of the famous '*Ranga Avadhoota*'. Garudeshwar is a place known for Vasudevananda Saraswati (who is known as '*Datta Avatara*'). Once again I reached Kevadia where I had stayed in the school earlier. I stayed there for one day and resumed my journey for Hapeshwar next day.

I was told by the priest at Hapeshwar Shiva Mandir that the way through '*Lakad-kot-Jhadi*' will be very difficult as that area was infested with snakes. He instructed me not to go alone and be in the company of two or three to cover the day-long journey of that jhadi. As the priest instructed, I was accompanied by two-three *parikrama vasis* to cover the *jhadi*. This forest is inhabited by poisonous snakes. One has to cover the journey at a stretch. We tried to walk fast but I was tired in the middle of the journey. I sat under a tree for a few minutes to rest, while the others moved on. I was all alone. All of a sudden from the branch of the tree a snake fell down on my right shoulder. I was frightened and started running. For a few yards the snake also followed me. Somehow I reached the group with whom I started walking from Hapeshwar.

The journey was pleasant then onwards. I left those parikrama vasis on the north of Khedi ghat and again my journey was alone.

Without much hurry, I just walked towards the upper streams of the Narmada.

It took more than one month to reach Amarkantak after leaving the place known as '*Chaubis Avatar*' (the north bank, opposite to Omkareshwar). Amarkantak is the forest where Narmada originates. I stayed at '*Mayee Ki Bagia*' (a natural grove of trees, dedicated to Goddess Narmada—from where Narmada originates and flows from a *kund* [tank or small reservoir]) for three days. From there I had to travel about a quarter of the total distance to reach Omkareshwar. On the fourth day, I resumed journey towards Omkareshwar. Now I was again on the south bank of Narmada. Crossing dry and barren lands, hills, small forests and villages, I was moving towards Omkareshwar.

Near Mandala on the banks of Narmada, while I was taking rest one afternoon, I saw a young *sanyasini* in red clothes and kumkum tilak, holding a big *trishool* on her right hand sitting on the banks in *dhyana*.

After her *dhyana* she told me that she had always travelled on the banks of Narmada for past ten years. She never left Narmada and had never gone to any village to stay. Of course, daily she would go to some village to take *bhiksha* and rest on the sands of Narmada. She never took it as her parikrama but just being with Narmada always. She told her experiences of meeting several siddhas on the banks of Narmada. She had left her home at the age of 15 and for last ten years she had been living with Narmada. I was wondering about her life and sadhana.

Next day I resumed journey leaving her there. As usual taking daily *bhiksha* at a village and resting on the sand or rocks of Narmada, I travelled for over a month or so and finally reached my destination Omkareshwar. This was the nineteenth month after leaving Omkareshwar. I stayed at Swami Ramanandji's Ashram for a few days!

Life—A Dry Leaf

At Omkareshwar there is a Vigyansala Ashram near the Markandeya Sanyas Ashram. I used to see an old *swami* wearing only a loin-cloth sitting in front of Vigyansala, on the banks of Narmada. I had noticed that he was always busy, removing dry leaves lying scattered and gathered them at one place. With the flow of the wind the dry leaves would again spread here and there. Again he collected the dry leaves and kept them at one place. This was repeated the whole day. I was very curious about his action. He never talked to anybody and only concentrated on his work of collecting dry leaves the whole day. I was sure something mysterious was hidden in his actions. None of the *sadhus* ever went near him or talked to him or fed him. I think they thought that this old man could be mad. One day I decided to go to feed him something. I wrapped a few *rotis* and vegetable in one leaf from the *ashram* kitchen and went near him. Even though I was afraid of going near him, I prayed to my *Guruji* and went near and offered food to him. He looked at my face for a few minutes, with a calm and composed face but with a very serious look, and gestured me to keep it near him.

Now I felt he was not dangerous. I kept the *roti* near him and I sat down. I felt he did not like my sitting near him. Even his facial expression was like that; he said nothing for a long time and sat in silence looking at the food as if he was in a prayer. After some time I gained a little courage and told him, "*Baba*, please eat the *rotis*." He looked at me, then at the Narmada, then at his hands, and then started eating the rotis. I was happy and was relieved from tension. I brought Narmada jal in my *kamandal* and offered him for drinking.

As he was very old, and had no teeth, it took much time for him to chew the rotis. After he completed the food, drank water and washed hands, he again started to collect the dry leaves without caring about me.

I was simply sitting there and thinking what could be the meaning of this meaningless thing he was doing. All of a sudden he came near me and sat quietly. I took some courage and asked him, "*Baba*, the whole day you are collecting dry leaves and putting them at one place. But the wind takes them away. And again you collect the dry leaves; can you tell me what the purpose is for doing this?" He looked at my face; his face was like that of a small child. He said in a murmuring sound, "Son, this is the symbol of life. You earn wealth—material or spiritual—and just you are depositing it without proper use, the next moment the wind—death—comes and scatters whatever you collected. This is life. The earning—material or spiritual—must be utilized for the betterment of others. If not, then life of a person is irrelevant, meaningless, and immaterial!" I wondered, this old Baba in a loincloth talking about practical philosophy. So he is doing it and showing everyone, but nobody cares, everybody's eyes are covered with *Maya* (worldly illusions)—as they think whatever they accumulate, it will go with them even to *Para Loka* (world beyond death). He looked at me again and said, "Now again it is time for you to go to Himalayas. Go, go and have *darshan*[52] (an opportunity of seeing a holy person/ deity) at your Master's feet. Go to *Gyanganj*. *Gyanganj*! I was very astonished! This man knew about *Gyanganj*? The old *Baba* told me again, "I knew the day you came to Omkareshwar. I know your *Guru*, *Paramaguru*, even *Maha Tapa*—the head of *Gyanganj*— as I also belong to *Gyanganj*. Better that you go to Badrinath.[53] First spend one *chaturmas* (holy period of four months) there,

---

52 Auspicious sight of a holy person, which bestows merit on the person who is seen. 'Sight' here means seeing or beholding, and/or being seen or beheld.

53 A holy town in the state of Uttarakhand. It is the most important of the four sites in India's Char Dham pilgrimage.

then go to *Tapovan* (located above Gangotri). Someone will take you to *Gyanganj*." I was sweating after hearing all this. With an accumulated courage in mind I asked, "*Baba*, my *pranams* to you. You know everything, but I have one doubt, why are you hiding your identity. Instead of collecting dry leaves, you can go to the society and tell them how to live a practical life, materially or spiritually."

He laughed at me and said, "Son, this is *Kaliyuga*. No one will understand the real thing or real soul. Everybody is in their masks, and think they are wise and safe. So, instead of wasting my time with people, I am trying to show symbolically what is real. They think I am mad and never come to me. Now you go, let me do my job. Go!"

His face changed. I thought it was better to leave, before he got angry. I touched his feet with all reverence and was about to leave. He gave me a dry leaf as '*prasadam*' and asked me to keep it till I reach *Gyanganj*.

I returned to the ashram, sweating, and with a mind filled with thoughts about the old *Baba*, holding the 'dry leaf' in my hand.

Towards Badri
—Via Jammu, Haridwar

Next day, I went to Jammu *ashram* (which was under construction) and stayed there for a few days. *Guru Poornima* was nearing and I was planning to go to Haridwar enroute Badrinath for my stay during *chaturmas*. *Ashram* works were in progress. I told the devotees there that I would be moving to Haridwar to go to Badrinath for my *chaturmas*. Somehow my mind was not at all adjusting to stay at Jammu village. I stayed there for a week, only following the same routine I had.

The next week I reached Haridwar and stayed at Ram Kutir ashram for a week. I told Krishna Mataji about my plan to go to Badrinath before *Guru Poornima*, as the days of chaturmas began on the *Ekadasi* (the eleventh day in the lunar calendar as per the Hindi mythology) before *Guru Poornima*. There were only two weeks left for *Ekadasi*. So, I decided to start as early as possible. After a week's stay there, I left for Badrinath by bus. Krishna Mataji gave me Rs. 500 for my journey. I kept a pair of blankets and a plastic sheet, a set of clothes, my *kamandal* and *kappar* for journey.

Bus journey through the Himalayan hills was exciting. Second day I reached Badrinath. The priest (known as Raval) was from Kerala, and I knew him. After having *darshan* at the temple and meeting the priest, I went around in search of a room to stay for my *chaturmas*. But most of the rooms in the *ashrams* were meant for pilgrims and even at *Kalikambli kshetram*,[54] I failed to get a

---

54 Guest houses and inns started by Baba Kali Kambli Walla functioning in the Himalayas for poor and needy pilgrims, sadhus and ascetics.

room. I went to the hot water spring after a full day's search for a room. Tired and depressed, I just sat there during the whole night. It was very cold and it was drizzling. Early next morning, pilgrims, sadhus and others reached the hot water spring for their bath. A known old sanyasi was among them.

Seeing me, he came near and wished me. During our talk he said he was leaving for Rishikesh as he had already stayed in Badrinath for one or two months. He said he is vacating the cave where he stayed for the last two months and if I wished I could occupy it for my *chaturmas*. That cave belonged to one Udasi swami who stayed there for a few years. Dineshananda had left that cave and moved to Gangotri. Nobody had claimed authority of the cave, and I could stay there without any disturbance. I agreed and went with him to see the cave. It was behind the mandir, in the middle of the big snow-clad hill—known as Narayana *parvat*. It was a big cave, which could accommodate more than three people. I was happy to get an accommodation and was thanking the swami again and again. For *bhiksha*, I had to walk down to Kalikambli Annakshetra which was about 45-minute walk. So daily I had to walk about 1.5 hours, which I wanted to avoid. Before leaving, swamiji gave me an idea. He said it would be good to collect the leftover *rotis* and *puris* from the *annakshetra* and dry and store them in a covered cloth. Thus, daily I could take out a few rotis and eat. Swamiji left me in the evening.

Next day I contacted the *annakshetra* managers with a request to give me left over *rotis* and *puris*. I told them I was staying in the cave, and with their help I would be able to do my chaturmas at Badrinath. Before *Ekadasi* I collected *rotis/puris* from two or three annakshetras, and also purchased some salt and chilli powder. Water was not a problem as a small stream flowed near the cave. I spread the *rotis* and *puris* on the rock under the sun to dry them. It was an exercise for two–three days. I had to sit near the rotis and puris because if nobody was near them they might be eaten by grazing goats or animals. After drying I folded them in a piece of cloth and kept it in the cave.

On *Ekadasi* day I took the *sankalpa* for *chaturmas vrat*. After two days I felt simply sitting in the cave and looking at hills was not worthy. Anyhow I had to stay there for four months. Before *Deepavali* (the day of closing of the Badrinath temples for winter), I thought I could easily complete my japa purascharan on shodashi once again. So, on *Guru Poornima* day I took a *sankalpa* of my 11th *Srividya Purascharan*. There was no need for a daily bath as the weather was very good.

During my stay at that cave, I used to take bath very rarely. Daily after washing hands and face, before I started the *japa* chanting, I used to take two *rotis* or sometimes three *puris*. First l soaked it in water and then added some salt and chilli powder. I took this food daily. But it was not at all sufficient for my young body. But I was worried if I ate more, the *rotis/puris* will be over, and again I would have to go to collect it from the *annakshetra*. Daily I used to do *japa* for more than eighteen hours and slept only four hours at night. Here at this cave I developed the quality of not sleeping. Every evening before sunset, I went around for a walk for some 30 minutes. Except for the *Bhotia*[55] ladies who took their goats for grazing, there was no other visitor at the cave. They also never disturbed me, only just peeped in the cave to see whether I was there or not and just they did namaskars from outside and left silently.

My matted hair, thin body, dirty clothes, starved body, everything made me look very dull. I looked like a beggar or a mad man in those days.

---

55 An occupational community of shepherds, living as nomadic pastoralists.

Badrinath
—Chaturmas in a Cave

These were one of the best days during my *sadhana*. Cool wind from Himalayas, in serenity, without any disturbances, I continued my *japa*. Almost one month passed after my *japa* started and usually nobody visited me. I felt bored of eating the same thing daily. But there was no other way, as I did not want to disturb my *sadhana*, so the idea of going to any *annakshetra* and eating rice or *dal* was far from my mind.

Maya was not ready to leave me even at the Himalayan caves. One day the priest, Raval, who came to know that I was staying at the cave to do sadhana, sent a kerosene stove, a few small utensils, two packets of milk powder and a plastic container full of kerosene for my use. He also sent a tiffin carrier through his assistant with rice, vegetables and other eatables. Of course, I ate the rice and vegetable but returned the kerosene stove, etc., with a lot of thanks. Also I conveyed a message through his assistant not to send anything, even eatables, as I was happy with what I had.

One day I saw the *rotis* and *puris* covered with fungus because of cold. Moreover they were more than one month old. Now there was no way other than to go down to the *annakshetra* to collect food again and preserve it. Next day, I went to Kalikambili and Gujarathi *annakshetras* and collected maximum number of *rotis*. This time I could get only *rotis*. As before I dried and stored them. Now a new idea came to my mind. Next day onwards I collected few dry sticks and roots lying here and there. Daily I used to make little fire and warmed up 2–3 rotis before eating. I mixed a few drops of water with chilly and salt mix, and it looked like chutney now. In that cold, hot rotis with chilly *chutney* was a good relief.

But may be because of eating chilli powder, it was very difficult for me to urinate as it would burn. So I started drinking more water to neutralize the effect of the pepper.

One day one of the Bhotia ladies while going with her herd of sheep came to me with some *khichadi* made of *bajra*. Even though at first I denied needing it, but later I had it because of her affectionate cajoling. She told me that a *baba* stayed on the top of the hill in a cave. She used to take *khichadi* for him also often. Now the curiosity of meeting my neighbour developed in me. After a few days I went to the top of the hill to meet him. It took more than three hours to reach the front of his cave. Unlike my cave, his cave was big and had a wooden door too. Without a second thought, and not even exercising the courtesy of knocking the door, I pushed the door slowly and opened it. Nobody was there! To my wonder, I could see the *asan*, *jalpatra*, etc., intact and I heard the continuous chanting of '*Om*'. Of course, the *Baba* was there, but he was invisible! It was a shock to me. It may have been because of my ego that he was not visible, as I had entered the cave without permission. I felt bad for the mistake I had made. I did *namaskars* to the *asan* and told him to forgive my mistake. The '*Om*' sound was now very clear. I came out of the cave with a heavy heart. I was repenting the mistake I had committed.

Thinking that I missed meeting a *siddha* in the Himalayas, I came down to my cave. That day it was impossible for me to do the *japa* as I was thinking about the mistake I made. That night I simply lay down on my *asan* and did not do any *japa*. My mind was very much disturbed. I heard a sound calling, "*Baba, Maharaj*" from outside. I wondered who it could be this late at night. Even during the day time nobody came to me. I came out of the cave. With dim light from the sky I could see a *maharaj* with very long matted hair and beard standing there. I was very much afraid. He said, "Why be afraid? Come near me. I am the one staying at the in the cave above the hill. You came to meet me in the morning, but you were not able to. So, don't worry, I am here! I came to meet you *maharaj*."

I fell down at his feet and cried. I requested him not to curse me for the mistake I made by opening the door of his cave without his permission. He lifted me from his feet holding my both hands, embraced me and said, "To err is very common for man, don't worry about what happened. Now you forget what happened. Sit near me. I have something to tell you." I sat near him. Even now some fear was running in my mind. He said, "I know you are a good *sadhak*. Since the day you came here, I have been observing you. I am also doing *chaturmas* here. After *chaturmas* I am planning to go to Tapovan. If you are willing, you can come with me."

He told me in detail about Tapovan. We have to walk 3 or 4 days on the snowy hills to reach there. Usually nobody stayed there. But for past two years one Swamy Vijayanand was staying there alone. I told the *maharaj* that after completion of *chaturmas* and my *japa* I would happily join him to travel to Tapovan. He kept his hand on my head and murmured mantras for few seconds. He got up and walked away very fast to the higher hills. I sat there for a long time. I was unable to explain my feelings. I sat there till the morning as a stone idol. Even in the cold wind I was sweating.

Next morning, I started my japa. I was happy that the swamiji had forgiven my mistake and blessed me. He was even ready to take me with him to Tapovan. My *japa purashcharan* at the cave went on very well. Almost 75 days were over since I started staying at this cave, so once again I went to the annakshetra to collect my food. I got a large quantity of *puris* this time. This was the balance of previous days' *bhandara* (religious community feast) at the *kshetra*. As usual I dried it under the sun and kept it in a cloth bundle. l thought that this would be sufficient till my *chaturmas* ended.

End of Chaturmas

My body was getting weaker day by day as I was not taking proper food. Because of eating old *puris* my stomach got upset and daily I developed diarrhoea. I was thinking that I should stop eating the old *puris*. One day, one of the managers of the Gujarathi *annakshetra* came to meet me with a few visiting Gujarathi devotees. I discussed with him about my problem of eating old *puris*. He told me that from the following day onwards he would arrange to send daily rice and dal and also asked me to throw away the old *puris*. The devotees came with him offered some money to me but I did not accept it, as money was not needed during that time. What would I do with money in a cave? Next day onwards the manager of Gujarathi *annakshetra* sent me either rice and *dal* or *khichadi*. Now I was very happy. My *japa* was going on well.

There was a military camp near Mana village, a few hours walk from my cave. They brought some biscuits for me.

There was one Balan Nair from Kozhikode (Kerala) among the military jawans who visited me. They were wondering about my way of life there. They assured that they would send biscuit packets every week for me. But I told them not to send it as I was getting my bhiksha from Gujarathi *kshetram*.

I counted the number of days by keeping a pebble each day. This is the fourth month, and on Poornima, chaturmas would end. I thought in these three months I might have completed the *japa sankhya* of chanting 16 lakh times. Even then I decided to continue *japa* as usual until *Poornima*!

End of Chaturmas | 317

One day Raval, the priest from Badrinath, came to meet me with a few of his assistants. Raval was a native of Pazhayannur (Kerala). Ravalji asked me to come to the mandir and his residence after the completion of my *japa purascharan*. He also requested me to take *bhiksha* one day at his residence, near Badrinath *mandir*. He was happy that a sanyasi from Kerala was doing tapas at Badrinath. He also brought some old editions of *Mathrubhumi* (Malayalam newspaper) for me to read.

Daily I got *bhiksha* from Gujarathi *annakshetra*. One of the workers from the kitchen used to bring it. The bundle of puris was lying on one corner of cave. I asked the shepherd lady whether it was advisable to feed old *puris* to sheep/goats but she said she will take the *puris* to her house and prepare some dish out of those old puris. She took them, and next day she brought some dish made out of those old *puris*. She mixed it with onion, ginger, chilly, and boiled potato after powdering the dry *puris*. Of course it was a new thing to me but it was very tasty. I told her that I would leave for Tapovan after *Poornima*.

On *Poornima*, I concluded my 11th *purascharan* and the *sankalp* of *chaturmas*. I went up the hills next day to meet the *Baba* staying at the cave there. This time I was very conscious not to commit any mistakes. *Baba* was sitting on a rock outside the cave. Very happily he received me and took me to his cave. I told him about the conclusion of my *japa* and he was also ready to go to Tapovan in two or three days. He also offered me some *khichadi* made of *bajra*, which that *Bhotia* lady had brought for *baba*. Next day I visited Badrinath temple. Raval took me through another gate (the gate meant for priests) and I had a good darshan. I had a very nice *bhiksha* at his residence. They made food in Kerala style. With rice, *sambar*, curry, *papad*, pickles and even yogurt! The food took my memories back to Kerala. Near his residence I saw an Adi Shankaracharya Murthi. Here Shankara was not having a *dand* in his hands, and inside there is a Shankaracharya *gaddi* also. I did *namaskars* and left them for the Gujarathi annakshetra.

I conveyed my heartfelt thanks the manager and his assistants for sending me food during the last few days. I also informed them about my programme to go to Tapovan in a day or two. By evening I came back to my cave.

Next day morning the Baba who was staying up the hills came to me. He told me that he was ready to start the travel following day. I was also ready. There was nothing in particular to pack up. I was waiting for the Baba to come next day. He turned up in the morning and I kept my blankets on my shoulder, held the *kamandal* and *kappar* in hand, and said goodbye to the cave and Badrinath which accommodated me for four months.

Towards Tapovan

Just as I was coming out of the cave, the shepherd lady came running. She brought two packets of *khichadi* made of *bajra* one for me and the other for *baba*. She was very happy to reach in time before we left the place for our onward journey. We kept the packets of *khichadi* with us and slowly started walking.

This is life! To reach a goal one has to struggle like anything. Only then one reaches the goal either today or tomorrow.

It was more than five hours since we left Badrinath. I did not know the way or how to proceed on the snow-clad hills; I was just following that unknown *baba*, with one aim in my mind—Tapovan! After a few hours of journey, we sat near a stream and took the *bajra khichadi*. *Baba* told me that the shepherd lady used to bring food for him often. After eating again we resumed our journey. There was no sign of any village nor did we see anybody on those Himalayan hills.

All around there was a disturbing silence. I tried to concentrate on my *japa* of Devi Pranava. Baba was also walking in silence. By evening we reached a small forest. Here and there some snow was found. We decided to stay there at night. *Baba* said this area was haunted by Himalayan white bears, and they were dangerous. So, before sunset we collected some fire wood and built a camp fire. Fire would save us from wild animals.

Climbing up and down the hills, I was tired. My legs were aching and more over I felt hungry too. For both of us, there was nothing to eat. I put some ice in my *kamandal* and when it melted, I drank that water. On either sides of the fire we kept our *asan* and simply lay down.

In these unknown Himalayan hills, with an unknown *Baba*, I was alone. Of course by my *Guruji's Kripa*, nothing to fear, my mind was saying that again and again. Darkness covered the hills. My mind was wandering here and there even though I was tired of a day long walking; because thoughts were dominating my mind, I could not sleep. I got up and sat and started doing *japa*. *Baba* already slept on the other side of the fire.

After sometime I saw a very big man-like form appearing towards me. It came near. Now it was visible very clearly. Of course it was not a human being but a very big *bhalu* (white Himalayan bear). Slowly it came near—at a little distance. I was very afraid. I thought it might attack me any moment and I was shivering with fear; I tried to wake up *Baba* sleeping on the other side of the fire, but he was in deep sleep. Slowly time passed. The bear was sitting close by. Now *Baba* woke up and saw the bear. He told me that the Almighty had sent this bear as a guard, and by the first rays of sun the bear left us. After morning ablutions we both resumed our journey.

The second day of our journey was tougher than the previous day. There was no food for us. We were walking by just drinking ice water. By afternoon I felt that it would be very difficult for me to continue walking. My legs were aching badly and I felt I was very weak. But the encouraging words of Baba made me walk. The silence and serenity of the hills gave me more energy to walk.

Both of us were tired and we sat on rocks for some time. To the furthest distance, we could only see snow-bound hills. The cold wind was blowing. Baba told me to walk again as we had to reach some safe place before sunset. Constantly we were climbing up and down the hills. Even when it was almost sunset hour, we could not find a suitable place to take rest at night. So we decided to sit somewhere on the rocks, where there was no or little snow, for the whole night. It was a dangerous night. A disturbing and fearful night in total silence. *Baba* was lost in his thoughts. He talked very less. He said that if we walked at a good speed we would reach Tapovan by next evening. The whole night we sat on a big rock lost in our own thoughts. There was not much space for us to lie down. Suddenly it started drizzling. Even though we covered our bodies with a plastic sheet we were drenched and started shivering because of the cold. By morning the rain stopped and we resumed journey.

Today was the third day without food. The movements to the hilltop were very slow. Legs were aching and swollen due to frost bite. I did not have a pair of shoes. Baba was wearing a canvas shoe. The whole day we walked, walked and walked. By evening we had reached a small forest. Baba told me that we had reached Tapovan and Swami Vijayanand was staying here in a small *kutia*. We both went around in search of the *kutia*.

Tapovan

Tapovan is a small forest surrounded by snow-bound hills. The complete silence and non-polluted atmosphere was very pleasant. Usually nobody stayed there as there was no village or market nearby. Last few years Swami Vijayanand was staying there alone. Often he went to Joshimath to purchase essentials. A small kutia was built there by him for his stay. Swamiji was very happy to receive us. A pet, a big Himalayan white bear, was sitting near him. It seemed that the bear disliked our presence and made a '*gurrr...gurrr...*' sound; Swamiji introduced us to him and asked it to sit quietly. The bear went out; maybe our presence was disturbing it.

We did our ablutions and had *roti* and *dal* made by swamiji. It was almost dark. I was very tired and with permission of both *swamijis* I went to sleep in a corner of that room. Both of them sat near the *dhuni* and started talking. I had a very deep sleep and woke up late in the morning. When I woke up I saw that both *swamijis* were continuing their talks. On one corner the *bhalu* (pet of *swamiji*, the bear) was sleeping with loud snores which were a bit disturbing.

I had a detailed talk on *Gyanganj* with them. Of course, they had heard the name of *Gyanganj* or *Shambhala* or *Shangri-la*, but where the actual place existed was unknown to them. *Swamiji* told me that if I walked for a few days, l could reach Tibet. But he was in no mood to spare me as he was planning to go to Joshimath for his purchases. I was also tired. Vijayanand and the other *Baba* got ready to move next day. I was wondering why this *Baba* had travelled three days climbing hills and even without food - was it only to escort me up to Tapovan? I was in wonder, but was a little afraid of asking the *Baba* why he came to Tapovan and was leaving immediately. *Swamiji* showed his store (in a wooden box) of *atta*, *dal*, etc., also he instructed me to feed his pet and friend (the bear) three *rotis* two times a day. I was afraid. *Swamiji* called out for the bear and asked it to sit near me, and told that as *Swamiji* was going for purchases, I would have to take care of it. It seemed the bear fully understood. It was a lovely animal; even though it was stinking, I wanted to touch it.

Next day morning *Baba* and *Swamiji* left leaving me alone. Yes, of course the bear was there. I was afraid of staying alone. The bear used to sit at a corner or sleep on *Swamiji's asan* without any disturbance to me. I made *rotis* and some *dal*, and after feeding the bear, I also had my share. I felt it was like an offering of *naivedyam*. After food I sat near the *dhuni*. At such a high altitude, without fire nearby one cannot survive. Even though it looked dangerous, the bear was sitting very calmly near the fire, as if in deep meditation!

There was no need to sit and make efforts for meditation at Tapovan. The silence, serenity, surroundings, everything makes you meditate automatically, always! I was enjoying the deep silence in and around me. Hours and hours passed. I came back to normal mood after a long time. Now it was almost noon.

I came out of the *kutia* and walked a few steps. The bear followed me. I collected some fire wood lying here and there from that small forest. I felt that the bear was very clever. Swamiji might have trained it. Now there was no fear in me about that animal.

In the evening after feeding it, I took my food. It was severely cold. I slept early near the dhuni. At night I felt something spongy near me. I woke up and to my wonder I saw that the bear was sleeping next to me. Of course, I did not disturb its sleep, but my sleep was very much disturbed because of its smell as well as its snoring.

In the early hours, while it was near dawn, I heard a sound near me and woke up. To my wonder, Bhruguram Paramahamsa was standing near me. He was the same as I had seen him before. He said, "Oh! You are back in the Himalayas. I know that you have once again done *purascharana* at Badrinath. I am very happy with your *sadhana*. Be here till Swami Vijayananda comes. I will take you to *Gyanganj* this time. Remember one thing. You should be there for few days for your higher *sadhana* in *Srividya*."

I was happy to hear this. Now finally *Gyanganj* was being opened for me. There was no limit to my happiness. Bhruguramji said "I will come back to you after five days. Be ready to go with me. Also remember, life at *Gyanganj* is not so easy. You have to undergo very strict discipline. And you have to practice it. I am sure you are capable for it." He disappeared and I sat near the dhuni for a long time lost in my thoughts.

Towards Gyanganj - I

The bear was good company for me. But if I was late in making *roti* or feed it, it used to make '*grr...grr...*' sounds, in anger. I noticed that it never left the cottage for a long time. Three days passed very nicely in the company of the bear. I felt as if it was a near and dear one to me.

On the fourth day evening Vijayananda came back. One Bhotia coolie was also with him carrying some big bundles. The bear ran towards him, embraced him and started licking *Swamiji*. It was like a small child running towards his father, whom he meets after a long time. I told him that I was about to go to Tibet as I was expecting my *Paratpara Guru* any time now to take me to *Gyanganj*. He kept quiet for some time and told me it all can be an illusion as *Gyanganj* is a myth and not a reality. He said that people used to tell a lot of stories about their mysterious experiences of their Himalayan life, but most of them were myths or exaggerated stories of their intuitions. But I told him that what I experienced was true to me, and as he had not experienced it could be a myth for him. To me *Gyanganj* was a truth, from where my *Guru Parampara* originated. Next day while I was sitting near the fire, I heard somebody calling me from outside. *Swamiji* was sitting and reading some book. I went out and at last Bhruguram Paramahamsa was there. I told *Swamiji* that Bhruguramji had come and that I was leaving. I took my blankets, *kamandal*, *kappar* and came out ready to move. *Swamiji* also came out and said, "Nobody is here. Have you gone mad? Where are you going?" I did namaskars to Bhruguramji and started moving—but I heard the sound of Swamiji, "*Arre, Nadanand, pagalpan mat kar. Tum akele kahan ja rahe ho?*" (Hey Nadanand! Stop being crazy. Where are you going alone?) Now the bear also came near. I told him that I was going and touched the bear with affection and moved with Bhruguramji.

I was wondering why Bhruguramji was not visible to *Swamiji*. He was holding my hand and walking. It was a truth not a myth. Maybe by reading my mind, he said, "Son, everybody is not seen by everybody. Can you see the atoms near you? No! Like that I appeared as an atom and manifested only for your vision. Moreover, I have nothing to do with that Swamiji! I came for you only." This atom and manifestation—nothing could be digested by me. I asked him to make the theory clear. He said, "An atom of our existence (consciousness) can be sent anywhere with the thought waves. Once it reaches the destination with the *sankalpa*, it will take a form or manifest. I will teach you the technique of '*Doora Gamanam*'. It is pure science. If you fully concentrate, you can take the thought waves to another destination. This should be done with strong *sankalpa* and you can take out an atom and order it to go with your thought waves and manifest at the destination." Even now nothing was clear to me. I just walked with him. He was silent and was moving towards the hills very fast. After a long journey of six to seven hours, we reached the banks of a river. A small river, flowing down from the hills, with crystal-clear water, Bhruguramji opened a *pottli* from his shoulder bag and gave it to me. Few *rotis* and potato curry was there; he told me to eat and take rest there till he returns and he disappeared.

I ate those *rotis* and drank water from the small river. I felt sleepy and just laid down on the banks of that river waiting for his arrival. It was almost dark when I woke up from my sleep. Nobody was near me. Bhruguramji had not yet returned and it was almost dark. I was wondering what to do? A little fear was enveloping my mind. In this unknown Himalayan hill, near this river, in the cold wind—even without fire near me, I was alone! The whole night he had not returned, while I was sitting and doing my *japa*. Even though the *mantra* was on my lips, my mind was here and there, thinking what next! There was not even a single sound. Even the sound of wind was not there. I was shivering of cold and because of fear sleep also left me. After quite some time, finally, I saw a light appearing towards me. It came near; oh! It was Bhruguramji

Paramahamsa. With the dim light of sky I could easily recognize him. He came near to me and sat. He said, "It seems you are afraid to be alone here. Fear in the path of spiritual life is meaningless. Non-fear and non-attachment must be the first two qualities you have to develop in this spiritual life. You might have thought I left you alone here. Son, I went to your *Guru Tara* and told her about your journey to *Gyanganj*. Look, this is the *prasadam* from Mookambika." He opened his hands and gave me some *kumkum*, and it was of course the same as the Mookambika *kumkum*. Without doubting, I applied it on my forehead. I wanted to ask him about my *Guruji* and her health. Reading my mind he said, "Do not worry. Tara is fine in her health. She was happy to hear that you are with me." I felt at ease! My *Guruji* always remembered me. After a gap of several years', I got Mookambika *kumkum* again today. There was no limit to my happiness.

Towards Gyanganj—II

Early morning we both started climbing the snow-covered hills. Bhruguramji was in silence. I too was quiet, but I was thinking about myself! What is all this for? Endless journey and limit-less sufferings? Is it a must to reach the ultimate reality? Why sufferings to me only? I have seen so many *swamis* and *gurus* living high-profile lives, very happy. It seems in their life they have no sufferings. Very well-arranged rooms, good food, lot of assistants to take care of them, they are enjoying their lives royally. But for me it was constant travel, without food and sleep! Bhruguramji stopped for a while and looked at me pointedly. He might have read my thoughts, he said, "To make a necklace out of gold, the gold is first burnt in fire, and then hammered, finally the *mala* (necklace) is ready, and then only it is used to decorate a deity's idol. Your life is also like that. You have to be burnt in fire, hammered and filed, and now you are ready to be offered to the Almighty; you will be worn on the necks of the Almighty! Why are you bothering about your life? Often you forget, we - the *Guru Parampara* - are behind you to take care of you. Don't be childish and foolish. Face the present situation and get ready for a good future!" I kept quiet. Now I understood who was behind my sufferings. My *Guru Parampara* only! And that also for my purifications and to prepare me as a garland to be put in the neck of Almighty.

By afternoon I was tired from the non-stop walking. Climbing up and down the snow-covered hills was not easy. I was hungry and my legs were aching. Bhruguramji stopped walking near a stream. He opened his shoulder bag and gave me few *rotis* and vegetable. I was wondering why he was not eating, he was only feeding me. I collected my courage and asked, "*Maharaj*, are you not eating? Are you not hungry?" He smiled and said, "No son, I don't need food. I can gather my energy directly from the sun. For the last few years I do not eat or drink."

I heard that some Himalayan *yogis* never eat or drink. They are living on the energy of *pranayama*. More over *Gyanganj* is famous for *Soorya Vidya* (the science of sun) and *Chandra Vidya* (the science of moon). I told him, "*Maharaj*, a *sadhak* like me has to think about food and shelter every time. If I did not have that problem, I could have done my *sadhana* for more time!" He laughed and said, "Son, you have just started your spiritual journey. In due course you will get all these; don't be in a hurry. Let the destined things happen. Have patience. You have to eat away the *karma phalas* (fruits of your karma) of your previous births. Then only the total purification happens! Once you are totally purified, all doors will be opened for you. Wait for the time!"

I know this 'time' factor is very cruel. In the last few years I had suffered a lot. May be some balance was there. Bhruguramji may be pointing to this destiny. I completed eating the food. I was wondering where he was getting *rotis* for me in this Himalayan hill where there was not even a single village or human being! Once again Bhruguramji might have read my mind. He said, "Son, nothing is impossible in spiritual life. See this!" He took a magnifying glass from his bag and continued, "This glass will help me to manifest anything and everything in front of me. This is based on *Soorya Vidya*. Just having a strong *sankalp* looking into this magnifying glass, it will manifest whatever you need. Just like the *rotis* and vegetables for you, stare at this glass, and with a *sankalpa* ask anything in the world. It will be in front of you within moments." I was afraid to test it. I felt it was like the 'Aladdin's lamp'.

I did not do any *sankalp* nor did I look at the glass with a wish! I just told him to forgive me for my mistake of doubting him. He got up and started walking. I too followed. Before sunset we reached near a stream. He told me to take rest there at night. Except for the snow-covered hills, nothing was visible. Bhruguramji told me, "Son, in the morning itself start walking towards north. (He showed me the direction.) Walk for three days. Whenever you feel tired, take rest. I will meet you on the fourth day. Do not worry about your food. I assure you that you will not feel hungry or thirsty for three days. Do not be afraid you are alone. You are not alone. From the sky, the Mother Goddess *Lalitha*[56] in the form of *Soorya*[57] is looking at you always. So, don't worry and resume journey in the dawn itself." Saying this he disappeared.

Now I was all alone. I looked at the sun that was about to set and chanted *shodashi mantra* for some time with a prayer to take care of me. I laid out my blanket as bed near the stream and sat there. It was the snow-covered hills around and me, nothing else around. The sun had also set. Darkness covered the hills. I simply sat there, reciting *shodashi mantra*!

---

56 An incarnation of Lord Shiva's wife Parvati.

57 A form of Shiva, also known as 'Marthanda Bhairava', a well-known sadhak of Lalitha, who later took the form of Lalitha herself.

Towards Gyanganj—III

Of course, I knew I was not alone. The power of *guru mandala* was always with me. I started my journey towards the direction shown by Bhruguramji in the morning itself. I was constantly chanting *shodashi mantra* and walking. Climbing up and down the snow-covered hills was not so easy. After a long walk of five or six hours I reached the Tibetan Border and crossed it easily. There was nobody, neither a check post nor any military people around. Far away, at the next hill I saw many Buddhist flags. Now I was sure that there would definitely be some village or *gompa* or *vihara*. I tried to walk fast. By afternoon I had reached a small village of 15–20 houses and a Buddha *vihara*. I went there. A *lama* came out of the *vihara* and looked at me suspiciously. I told him that I was on my way to *Gyanganj*—moving towards north. He knew Hindi and invited me inside. I sat at the courtyard; four or five *lamas* were staying there. They offered me some food—a type of *khichadi* made of rice and leaves. I had it and sat there for some time. By this time the *lama* who invited me inside also came after finishing his food. He said if I desired I could stay there for the night and resume journey next day. As it was already afternoon, he said it would not be so easy to reach any village before sunset, as there were no villages nearby. I agreed to stay there as I was not in a hurry to move. Again at night the lama asked me to join for prayer and food with them. Of course, I joined them for prayer, but I did not feel like eating any food, as I had taken late lunch. I slept at the courtyard. I had a very strange dream at night. I dreamt that I was sitting near a dilapidated old *mandir*. Except for the idol there was nothing. It seemed as if there was no *pooja* or any *poojari*, yet all of a sudden a light appeared in front of me, which emerged from the *mandir*. It took the form of my *Guruji—Avadhoota Tara*

Mayee! She talked to me, "Son, the path of spiritualism is not so easy. Yet you have to proceed as you are destined for it. Proceed! Do not look back. Beware of the worldly people. They are there only for their selfish motives. They will come to you to spoil your accumulated energy for their selfishness. Do not entertain such people near you. With a mask of love and affection they will be around you. Do not encourage them. Be alone. One day, when you are 'full of energy' go back to them and serve them. Do not believe the mundane people. They are selfish!" She disappeared and I woke up. Till morning I could not sleep. I was contemplating on the words of my *Guruji* which I heard in the dream.

In Tibet, China, Japan, wherever it maybe, the Buddhists have a good system of analysing dreams. Early morning as I was ready to leave, I discussed my dream with the *lama*. He told me that it was a very positive dream and the instructions of my *Guruji* must be followed.

I resumed my journey; the *lama* gave me some food packed in a newspaper for my onward journey. He also asked me to move fast on the hills as I could reach a nearby village before sunset. After walking five or six hours on the hills I was tired, and saw a small hot water spring. I sat there. I had good bath in that hot water, had my food which the *lama* had given and resumed my journey. I was constantly walking. But even at long vicinity there was no sign of any village. I felt very tired. It was almost sunset time, but I failed to reach any village.

As I reached near a small stream, I decided to stay there that night. The stream was very small yet flowing in a speed downwards. After washing legs and hands I sat there chanting *mantra*. Darkness covered the hills in no time. I was all alone there. I could hear the sound of water flowing down on small rocks. I felt it is also doing some japa so started chanting "*Hara...Hara...Hara...*" I was thinking of my life. Why all this? For what? Where is the end to my sufferings? Slowly, I slept on the banks of the river, as I was driving to oblivion!

Towards Gyanganj—IV

In the morning I started moving towards north again. I felt there was no end to this hill. I walked at a very slow speed. One more day I had to walk alone. Then only I could meet Bhruguramji. It was the fourth day of leaving Tapovan. Even though I had very clear-cut instructions from Bhruguramji as well as my *Guruji* about the spiritual journey, somehow, sometimes my mind was very disturbed by the thoughts arising in me. I know I was destined for this life. But the question of what next was in my mind always. I knew very well that I had nothing at all left to lose as I had lost everything—my parents, friends, village, etc., so now whatever was left was only to be gained. I told myself I must be happy with what 'I am' in the present. But the problem with me was often I went back to my past, and felt bad about myself. At the same time I knew that the past had passed and I could not get it back. I never worried about the future! I knew from the core of my mind that whatever the future may be, will definitely be good for me.

Every step I was doing *japa*. By noon I reached a village. Comparatively this was a big village. While I was moving through the village, one of the villagers called me. I stopped and looked back. A few villagers came near and asked where I was going to (I thought it was so, as the language was Tibetan). I told them I was going towards north in search of *Gyanganj*. They took me to the *vihara*, just on the outskirts of the village. Two *lamas* welcomed me there. One of them knew little English. When I told him in English that I was in search of *Gyanganj*, he said, "Oh! *Shangri-La*. It is far from here. You have to walk three or four days to reach there." I was still in wonder whether *'Shangri-La'* and *'Gyanganj'* were the same or not?

They gave me some bread and black tea. After taking it I took rest there for a while and again resumed my walking. It was very cold in those snow-covered hills. Both my legs were swollen because of frost bite. My movements became very slow. I was very tired by the evening. At a distance I saw a hot water spring. I sat there and kept both my legs in hot water. After some time I felt a bit relieved. The salty hot water (usually hot water spring contains sulphur) gave relief to my pain as well as swelling. The sun was about to set. I thought I must stay there that night. Because of the cold wind it was very difficult for me to sleep at night. To my wonder I was not feeling lonely. I felt somebody was with me definitely, but was not visible. Once again I put my legs in the hot water and sat there simply. Not even doing *japa*. For hours together I sat there. My mind was in a void. Not even a single thought disturbed me. Slowly I lost my body consciousness. Only dim light of sky was there. I felt I had merged in that voidness of boundless sky. I was back to normalcy the next morning only. Now I felt my body, mind and intellect. I resumed my journey. The hot water treatment of the previous night had given me a new energy to walk. The leg ache had reduced. My mind was again wavering. I wanted to meet Bhruguramji. Where was he? He left me in this unknown land lonely! I was not aware when I would reach my destination.

By noon I had reached near a stream. From distance I could see someone sitting near the stream. Reaching there, there was no limit for my wonder. It was Bhruguramji! I went near him, did *namaskars*, and sat near him. He asked, "How was the journey? You might have enjoyed the lonely travel. Make this a habit. Always move alone. Do not try to be in any company. It will spoil you. Invisibly, of course, we the *Guru Mandali* are always with you. You have to believe this. Even now your mind doubts and you think you are alone. In the spiritual path, physically you may feel you are alone. But note always that *gurus* are with a true *sadhak*." As usual he opened his shoulder bag and took out a packet from it and gave it to me. It contained rice, *sambar*, etc. (The packet was done just like the food parcel packing in South Indian hotels. It was packed in Banana leaves and covered with a Tamil newspaper.)

I was wondering at the taste of South Indian food in the Himalayan hills. I ate the food with great happiness. Bhruguramji was looking at my face. Once I finished the food, he said, "Son, this feeling must go! When you get some food of South Indian taste you feel very happy and if the food is from other parts of the country you feel bit averse to, is it not? This has to go from your mind. Now you are a *sanyasi*—a universal being. Now you are not limited to any country, or state. Even you are not bound to *Chaturvarna*[58]—not a *Brahmin, Kshatriya, Vyasya* or *Shudra*. You have to experience that you are the ultimate being. The feelings of differentiation in language, country, caste and creed must go out from you." I felt ashamed. Even though after reaching a stage of 'Oneness' still that *Vibhageeya Chinta* (considering oneself different from others) was in me! Bhruguramji continued, "Never think that you are born! Born in a family, in a village, in a country of such and such language, of eating habits, etc. You are that 'energy' of whole existence. Now you have the five qualities of '*Paramatma*' (Almighty/Divine). Realize it and try to keep it up." He looked at me with a different smile and touched my forehead. I felt everything had vanished in front of me. No hills, no stream, nobody, no mind. I could see a beam of light around me and I merged in it. I went into a deep trance.

---

58 'Varna' is a Sanskrit word which means type, order, colour or class. 'Chatur' means four. Hindu literature classified the society in principle into four varnas: the Brahmins: priests, scholars and teachers; the Kshatriyas: rulers, warriors and administrators; the Vaishyas: cattle herders, agriculturists, artisans and merchants; the Shudras: laborers and service providers.

Towards Gyanganj—V

I was back to my normal stage by morning. I felt a new energy passing through me. Bhruguramji was sitting near the stream looking at the snow-covered hills. I got up and washed my face and hand and sat near him. I felt as if I was very intoxicated. Bhruguramji said, "Son, it is your real stage. You are neither body, mind nor intellect! You are that. The ultimate reality. Keeping this experience always with what you are. Do your work to uplift others to your stage. Do not merge with worldly things or people. Now you are out of *Maya*! Keep away from it; be in you always; and even when you work for the betterment, be non-attached! Now, let us go!" He started walking and I too followed him. There was no sun visible. The hills looked very dull without sunshine. Cloudy sky and cold wind was flowing. All of a sudden snowfall started. Bhruguramji was walking carelessly not even thinking of snowfall. My body was almost covered with snow. I looked like a white bear! After an hour of walking the snowfall stopped. Now the sun shone. Bhruguramji looked at me and told, "Son, this is the specialty of the nature. When it acts or reacts, nature only knows! Now you may be feeling cold of drenching under snowfall. But look at me. I am not shivering of cold. This is because of the fire burning within. You have to maintain this fire update. Today I will teach you the '*Doora Gaman Vidya*', which will be helpful for your future life: Remember we are siddha yogis. There is nothing impossible for guru mandali." We both sat on a big rock surrounded by snow. He taught me in detail about movements of *paramanu* (atom) and how to do sankalp to reach a particular destination, how to create strong *chinta tarang* (thought waves) and to send it to a known or even unknown place; he made me practice it. To understand the technical of '*Doora Gaman*' it took me more than three hours. In seconds he instructed me the 'rare technique' of *pranayam* (which you will not get in yoga books or even with ordinary yoga master) to help the fire (vital energy) in me to be kept intact always. He started walking again. I followed but I was a bit hungry. I asked him with an accumulated courage of mind (as I was hesitant with a reverence to him as he was one of the senior-most *Guru* of my *Parampara*) how to live without food and water (as he lived). He looked at my face and smiled and said, "Son, now you have to depend on food for a few more years. Of course, I will teach you all this; once you complete the higher studies on *Srividya* at *Gyanganj*." Maybe to change the subject, he said, "You know, today I will feed you with traditional Bengali *khichadi*." We both sat near a small waterfall. It looked very nice. I collected water in my kamandal and came near him. He spread a piece of an old English newspaper in front of me (he used to carry such things in his shoulder bag) then he took his 'magnifying glass' and looked through it, just keeping some distance from the newspaper he spread. I was wondering what magic was going to happen! His eyes were glowing like two red bulbs. To my wonder, as if someone had served it, the Bengali *khichadi* appeared on the newspaper which he had spread.

I was looking at the magic in front of me. Bhruguramji said, "Son, here is your food for the day. Eat it! My disciple Paramahamsa Visudhananda at Varanasi is having a magnifying glass like this. As you think, this is not magic. The sun's rays have the capacity to identify and produce everything in the world. Only you have to concentrate on the particular sun ray related to your need. For this also you have to practice strong *sankalpa*. One day I will give you a glass like this." For the first time, I negated Bhruguramji statement, "Master, I don't want it, as with it I will develop more ego in me. Moreover, I have the *kappar* of *Guru Parampara*, which my *Guruji* gave me while I started for my Himalayan journey. This *kappar* has all powers to give me what I need. I don't want your magnifying glass. Sorry!"

He was happy to hear that. He replied, "Son, I know better than you about the *kappar* which you have. During my stay at Haridwar/Kashi, I also used to take *bhiksha* in this. As you have said rightly, this *kappar* is enough. It is a living energy of our *Guru Parampara*." I ate that Bengali *khichadi*.

Of course it had the same taste of the khichadi made in Sri Ramakrishna Ashram in Calcutta. (Once I had a chance to get *khichadi* from Sri Ramakrishna Ashram at Dakshineshwar during my visit.) Bhruguramji suggested that we take rest there. We rested for a few hours and resumed walking again.

Towards Gyan Gunj—VI

Though my legs were aching, I still tried to walk with him at his speed. But it was barely possible. He was well accustomed to walking on snow-covered hills and I was not. I heard a thundering sound on my left side and saw a big rock coming down. "Run, Run," Bhruguramji said. When it was so difficult to just walk on these hills, how was it possible to run. I ran a few yards and by that time the rock just passed down with a thundering sound. On my right side, about a thousand feet down, the big rock had fallen at a very high speed. Bhruguramji looked at me and smiled. I was very frightened! If the rock had touched me, I would have been crushed underneath. We moved again towards the north. I was thinking to myself—in these hills anything can happen at any time, good or bad! After a few hours of walking we reached a village. He did not allow me to go through the village. He told me to avoid the village and go through another footpath leading towards another hill. If I were walking alone, I would definitely have gone to the village and rested there. He was not in a habit of staying at any village.

We climbed up and down several hills. It was nearing sunset. I was afraid of telling him that I was tired. But he read my mind again and said, "I see that you are tired. You can take rest on the next hill. There you will get good water too!" He pointed to a hill. It looked very near. But actually it was at quite a distance. When we reached there it was almost dark. Bhruguramji had me sit near a small waterfall, and disappeared without saying anything. Once again I was alone and wondering where he might have gone. Somehow I managed to wash my hands and legs in that ice-cold water. I sat near the waterfall, and in the dim light of the sky, I spread my blanket out for an asan.

I simply lay down for some time. I was tired, but could not sleep. The mind was very blank. Time passed by. I sat up, and slowly closing my eyes, slipped into deep meditation. Of course it was in deep, deep meditation that I saw myself with my *Guruji*, on the banks of the Sauparnika at Mookambika. I could hear Amma's voice. But nothing was clear. The vision disappeared. I felt I was in a forest, the same one where my Guruji stays. I heard the sound of her whistling (usually she makes that sound to call her pets to eat) once, twice.

Everything disappeared from my vision. I was sitting and sleeping!

Bhruguramji's voice was heard. He said, "Oh, you are sleeping in a sitting position! Get up, it is morning. Let us go." I opened my eyes. It was almost sunrise time and Bhruguramji was standing near me. I washed my face and got ready to move. On the way Bhruguramji said, "What you experienced at night was not fully true. One of your 'atoms' did definitely travel up to Mookambika. But it failed to manifest, because your *sankalp* was not strong enough. No problem, you will succeed next time."

We both walked slowly. By afternoon we reached near a small *kund* of hot water. While Bhruguramji sat there, I had a very good bath in that hot water spring. The fatigue had now vanished. I felt very fresh. As usual, he opened his pottli and gave me a few rotis and vegetable. After eating them, I slept there for some time. Once again the shouting sound of Bhruguramji reached my ears. "Get up! Let us move." I got up and moved with him. My mind was like that of a sheep, following its owner's orders. Just obeying the shouting! Just following! In one way my thinking was correct—*Guru* is the owner of *sishya*; and here, he was my great *Guru*. So I must obey this *Guru* every moment. And this would be for my own sake of course, only for my own betterment. I know that every action of a *Guru* is only for the betterment of the *sishya*. A *sishya* may have some selfishness, at least about his good *sadhana*. But *Gurus* are never selfish. Their lives are dedicated to all—everybody—equally. There will definitely be no partiality in the *Guru*'s mind.

Whether a *sishya* is doing well or not, is rich or poor, has no effect on the *Guru's bhava* (feelings) towards the *sishya*—the *bhava* will always be the same in the *Guru's* mind. It is the *bhava* of motherly affection, along with discipline like that of a father. All actions of *Gurus* are only for the improvement of *sishyas*. But *sishyas* may not be able to catch the mind of the *Guru* or experience his affection. That is due to the drawback of 'selfishness' present in the sishya, which forms an iron curtain between the two.

Bhruguramji looked at me and smiled. He had definitely understood what I had been thinking. He said, "Son, your thoughts are very right. If there is selfishness, a *Guru* is not a true *Guru*. If there is eagerness to earn wealth or fame, a *Guru* is not a true *Guru*. A *Guru* is a real *Guru* (*Sadguru*) only when he lives for his spiritual children, his *sishyas*."

We continued walking till he stopped for a while, and pointing to a distant, mist-covered hill, said, "Son, we have to reach there. That is our destination *Gyanganj*, but it is far. Tonight we will rest somewhere around here. Let us locate some water source and stay near it. If we start out early tomorrow morning, we will be able to reach there by afternoon for sure."

We walked a few hours more. I felt the mist-covered hills approaching near. I would be able to enter into *Gyanganj* the next day. My mind was dancing with joy. After walking for some time we found a small stream and sat there. With a mind full of joy, I slept early dreaming about the next day's entry into *Gyanganj*.

At Gyanganj

*E*arly in the morning, we started moving towards the neighbouring hills. Though it seemed to me like the mist-covered hills were very close, it was not as I had thought. Only by afternoon could we reach the valley of the mist-covered hill. My mind was filled with an unusual happiness. I recalled the last time when I had come up here, and returned in disappointment! Now by the Grace of the *Guru Mandali* I was being allowed to enter *Gyanganj*. I climbed the hill with a new energy. There was no mist anymore, it had vanished. I could easily see the hills. It took a lot of time to climb up to the top of the hill. Then we climbed down.

We were surrounded on all four sides by hills and in the middle was a big valley. No snow or mist was seen there. There were many caves visible in the hills around. I could easily see hundreds of caves. I saw a few swamis moving around in front of caves on the hills.

Bhruguramji asked me to sit outside a cave and he went inside. A swami came out and asked me to follow him. After walking for an hour or so, we reached another cave and the swami took me inside. There were three sadhus sitting there. It was a big cave (it seemed man-made) which could accommodate five or six people.

The *swami* asked me to be seated and went out. The other Swamis sitting there were busy reading. One of them, an old *sadhu*, stopped his reading and came near me and asked about my particulars. He talked to me in English. He looked Japanese, and his accent did not seem Indian. While I was narrating the story of my journey to *Gyanganj*, the other two *sadhus* also joined us.

One of them said, "This is *Gyanganj*! We also have a branch known as Sidhashram. You may not know, but this is more than a university. All spiritual subjects under the sun are preserved here, as well as the practices of all religions. Only a very few selected sadhaks are called in here for higher studies and sadhana. Which branch do you belong to?" I told them I was a Srividya sadhaka. Three of them were *Vedanta sadhakas*, based on the 'Trik' system of Kashmir Shaivism.

Of course, I had also read a few books on Kashmir Shaivism earlier; it was easy for me to talk to them. They told me that more than 150 sadhaks of different sections were staying there. Shri Mahatapa Babaji is the head of this institution. More than 300 years old, he had been sitting in trance for the last fifty years or more. My mind was in a happy space as I had finally reached the roots of my Guru tradition. Was it a myth? No, it was a reality. Now I was experiencing my presence here.

By this time Bhruguramji had come to me and asked me to follow him. He took me to another cave inside which on an asan was a swami with clean-shaven head and face, and with *vibhooti* and *kumkum* on his forehead. He looked Tamilian. Bhruguramji introduced me to him and told him about my *Srividya sadhana* and also about my 11 *purascharans*. That *swami* smiled and asked Bhruguramji what I needed next. Bhruguramji told me that swamiji would take care of my future *sadhana* and studies in *Srividya*, and that I should stay with him in that cave. And also to do seva to that *Swami*, by massaging his legs, washing clothes, cleaning cave and also cooking. And he left the cave.

Swamiji was sitting in silence. I placed my *kamandal* and *kappar* on one side of cave. When he noticed my *kappar*, he said, "Oh! This is with you. Now I understand. You are a disciple of *Tara*. I got acquainted with her when I was in the south."

In this remote corner of the earth in a cave, that an unknown swamiji knew my *Guruji*, this thought brought tears to my eyes. He asked in English again, "Are you also from South India? From Karnataka or Kerala?" When I told I was born and brought up in Kerala, to my wonder he started talking to me in Tamil! (Of course mixed with a few Malayalam words.) My intuition that this *swamiji* might be of Tamil origin was correct. *Swamiji* told me, "You are tired from continuous walking on snow-covered hills. Rest today. You can start your studies and *sadhana* tomorrow." He paused for a while and again said, "You can be here with me for three weeks. Are you prepared for strict discipline? If so, you will be able to complete your higher *sadhana*. Do not waste time. The days you stay here must be useful to you and your forthcoming disciples."

I agreed. I wanted to ask him whether I could meet the Great Mahatapa Guru. But I was a bit nervous, so I kept my mouth zipped. There were plenty of books in Sanskrit/English/Tamil/Hindi spread out in the cave. Perhaps they were all *Srividya*-related books. I went to the corner of cave and sat there on my *asan*. *Swamiji* was ready to cook something on his kerosene stove. I thought it would be awkward if I sat there idle without helping him in the cooking. But when I went near, *Swamiji* said again, "Take rest now. You can help me tomorrow. I will prepare some '*Pongal*' which both of us can eat."

I returned to my *asan*. Through the opening of the cave, the hill on the other side was very much visible. I could see a lot of caves. The valley was silent and full of vegetation. In its entirety, *Gyanganj* covers a very vast area. Even though the hill that was visible looked like it was near, it was not so. The caves on the other side were quite far away. One had to go down into the valley, walk through the forest, and then climb up the hills to reach the caves on the opposite side. I spotted some sadhus in front of those caves.

May be it was fatigue, or perhaps the calm and quiet atmosphere, or the cool breeze, but everything lulled me to sleep. I slept for a while leaning against the rock of the cave behind me. My mind was very calm!

Swamiji woke me up when food was ready. I wanted to wash my hands and face. He showed me a *jharna* near the cave. I went out, and washed my hands and face. There were big trees to be seen outside near all caves. It looked as if it were a big forest.

I had *pongal* with *swamiji*. It was a typical South Indian food and my mind immediately went to that thought, but I remembered Bhruguramji's advice about not going after *vibhageeya chinta*. I controlled my thoughts and ate the food.

Life at Gyanganj

The next morning *Swamiji* initiated me into to the practice of *'Hamsa Soham'*—the ultimate *mantra* in *Srividya*. This is to be done with *'Pranayama'*. He also taught me the practical worship of three aspects of *Pratyangira* (Hindu Goddess associated with 'Shakti' and the concept of eternal energy). I used to sit under a tree near the *jharna* and do *sadhana*.

In addition to my daily *sadhana*, I was supposed to do all types of *seva* there like washing *swamji's* clothes, cooking, cleaning, messaging his legs, etc. He was very generous to me and allowed me maximum time for *sadhana*. At night, he would teach me *'Soham Dhyan'*.[59] I sat in front of him, and with his directions was doing *sadhana* at night too.

One day *Swamiji* introduced me to a lama who was an *acharya* of *Srividya*, well versed in the Tibetan system. According to him, *Srividya* is known as *'Ugra Tara'*. The higher studies in *Srividya* were very difficult. Till then I had learned up to *'Para Vidya'* and *'Navavaran Pooja'* (stages of *Srividya sadhana*).

The difficult part now was that the present *sadhana* was not only *japa* or *pooja*, but was co-related with Tantra, Yoga, and Vedanta as well! Performing some *'mudras'* were very difficult for me. The lama with all patience, and supported me in my practice. He even taught me the secret of *'Antar yagya'* (internal worship) but though he did not allow me to take written notes of the practical

---

59 Soham Dhyana means 'Meditation on Soham mantra'—a central mantra practice of Yoga Meditation. Soham is a universal mantra as it relates to the breath, and everybody breaths.

aspect (*prayog vidhi*). I still memorized and somehow managed to write down a few important points on pieces of paper obtained from Swamiji. All my doubts were cleared during this higher study. During my stay and practice of *Srividya* in South India, I had heard of some of the techniques of this *sadhana*, but none of the *acharyas* there were fully competent about the practical part. Some of the Buddhist monks who migrated from the South took away all the knowledge of the practical aspects from Kerala or Karnataka.

Due to the intense cold weather, having food just one time a day, five or six hours of seva, and the rigor of continuous sadhana, I was very tired. But I liked and enjoyed my stay there. During the stay, I had opportunities to meet *sadhaks* of different practices like *Vedanta, Vaishanav, Tantra, Japa Yoga, Yoga*, etc. In fact I wanted to understand more about '*Soorya Vidya*' but the *Swamiji* told me to concentrate only on Srividya.

Ten days passed thus. Bhruguramji was not seen anywhere these days. When I asked *Swamiji*, he told me, "Mind your own business!" I was giving more and more importance to '*Soham Dhyan*'. *Pranayam* in '*Hamsa Soham*' was also of course going on. When *Swamiji* noticed that I was absorbed in deep meditation for more than 8–10 hours, he was very pleased. A new energy passed through me. The fatigue of long journey through Himalayan hills had now vanished.

One afternoon with *Swamiji's* permission, I went for a walk through the forest in the valley. At a distance under a tree, I saw Bhruguramji sitting deeply absorbed in '*Dhyan*'. Without making any sound of footsteps, I went near him and sat for hours till he opened his eyes and smiled. He asked me about my *sadhana*, and said he was happy with my progress in *Dhyan*. He said, "Son, you are lucky to be here. Make maximum use of your time for *Dhyan*. Do not waste time. After a week you have to leave *Gyanganj*. By that time clear all your doubts regarding *sadhana*. Once you are back with the *sansaris* (worldly people), you will not get as much time to do *sadhana* as you are getting here." He paused for a while. There was a deep silence between us for some time. He again said, "Once you return, start research works on '*Sri Chakra vibrations*'. Nobody has made attempts in that direction; you have to practice, experience, and write down everything. It will be useful to the coming generations!" Again there was silence! In fact I didn't want to leave that place. I would have liked to stay there all life long and do my sadhana. Reading my thoughts, Bhruguramji broke the silence, "No, son, even if you wished it a thousand times, you cannot be here for your entire long. You are destined for some other work. Remember, you have taken an oath, touching your *Guru Tara's* feet that you will live for others always. You have to do this life long. Even through suffering of body and mind, you will have to keep those words. You are destined for that."

I kept quiet. I was recollecting that moment of touching my *Guruji's* feet and taking the oath. Bhruguramji spoke again, "Son, living for others is not so easy. You have to detach yourself from worldly things first. Then with the accumulated energy of your *sadhana*, live in '*samsara*' like a lotus leaf in water! You may stay in your ashram or anywhere convenient to you, but keep the '*samsara*' out of your mind. Do not be tempted by worldly things. This life of yours is to prove that in this '*Kaliyuga*' yogis are for the sansaris, but samsara is not for yogis. The day you are supposed to leave *Gyanganj*, I will come and take you to '*Sidhashram*'. From there you can go through Arunachal to reach India. It would be better if on the way you can stay back at Kamakya for a few days." He stood up and moved away swiftly. I sat there for some more time and then returned to the cave where I was staying with *Swamiji*.

Last Days in Gyanganj

The last few days of *sadhana* at *Gyanganj* were very difficult. Swamiji taught me the '*secret sadhana of Srividya*'. I was supposed to meditate on *bhrumadhya* for hours together, standing on the right leg, keeping the left foot on the navel, with hands folded in the *anjali mudra*. I did this for three days, for hours together. The other *sadhana* being very secret, I am not supposed to write about them in detail.

One day I felt my back burning like fire. I was unable to stand or sit. *Swamiji* was happy, this being the symptom of an awakened *kundalini*. Sometimes I roared like a lion and at other times was deep in voidness. My body was full of heat. *Swamiji* told me that the '*kriya of Shat Chakra bhedan*' (the activation of the six chakras) was happening in me. He said, "Remember always your *guru Tara* who gave you '*Shakti paath*' *deeksha*; *Guru* is the reason and result of all this. Now you have reached a very good stage of *sadhana*. Even if you expend all your energy for some good purpose of healing others, etc., you will lose nothing. Whatever quantity of energy you spend, you will receive twice that by the grace of your Guru! Now I shall teach you *Anima, Laghima, Mahima*,[60] etc. Sit in *padmasan* (a yogic posture)."

I sat in '*padmasan*' and did '*pranayam*' as he instructed. After some time, I felt I was like a feather, weightless. And to my wonder, I was floating in air in the cave, about three feet up from

---

60 In Hinduism, eight siddhis or eight great perfections include Anima: reducing one's body even to the size of an atom; Mahima: expanding one's body to an infinitely large size; and Laghima: becoming almost weightless.

the ground. Slowly I descended back to the ground. *Swamiji* said, "Son, these are just mere *siddhis*—valueless! The real value of life lies in living for others, in doing good for others. Live in the way you have promised your *Guruji*. Live life for others, for every being at every moment, live, that is the only sadhana you have to do. Consider life itself as a *sadhana*, and live every moment for other beings, be they man, animal or plant!"

I learned a lot from *Gyanganj* about the theory and practice of *sadhana*. How to live for other beings! Even now at every moment, I am living for others. I forget to live for myself. *Swamiji* made sambar and rice that day. He did not allow me to help him. He said, "Take rest today, now that your studies are over. Tomorrow you have to leave this place. Now you are returning to '*samsara*'. Be careful. Do not get attached. Try to keep away from wealth and fame. Don't accumulate anything, money or any such worldly things! '*Aparigraha*' (the concept of non-possessiveness, non-grasping and non-greediness) must be the quality maintained in you."

In the evening Bhruguramji came by to tell me that I should leave the place next morning. They would come with me up to '*Siddhashram*'. Afterwards I had to continue my journey alone. I asked him whether I would be allowed to meet *Mahatapa Babaji*. He said, "No, Son, not now. As I told you, first complete your research work on *Srividya*. Then come back. Now *Gyanganj* is open to you." I was a bit disappointed. He introduced me to two or three *sadhaks* of *Srividya* staying there. They were in the stage of acharyas. All of them blessed me with good wishes for my future life. Bhruguramji said, "Son, to be here and be doing *sadhana* is in fact very easy. But to live among *samsaris* and live the life of a *yogi* is very difficult. Remember, you will meet with a lot of temptations on your journey, keep away from them. Your *Guru Tara's* eyes are on you always. So, do not worry at all. Whatever good or bad you are supposed to go through, it is destined, it is inevitable. Do not look back, whatever happens. Live and always live for the welfare of other beings!" He left the cave.

The next morning, a *sadhu* came by to say that Bhruguramji was waiting for me. It was time to depart! I felt very bad and sad.

I did *namaskars* to *Swamiji* who had helped me in higher studies and practice during the last three weeks. *Swamiji* gave me a handful of groundnuts fried in ghee, packed in paper, and said, "Son, I wish you all the best for your future life. Now you possess all types of *siddhis*. You are no more a *sadhaka*. Go forward, teach your disciples the proper way of *sadhana*. Bring them up to your level. This will be treated as your '*Guru dakshina*' to your '*Guru parampara*'."

I had tears when I left the cave. Bhruguramji was waiting for me. I went near him and both of us started walking. I could do only '*manasik pranams*' (paying my obeisance mentally) to the great *Mahatapa Babaji*. Slowly I began walking with *Swamiji*.

On the Way to India

To say farewell to *Gyanganj* was not so easy. *Swamiji* said, "If we walk fast, on the fourth day we can reach *Siddhashram*, which is near the Arunachal border, and from there you have to proceed alone." *Swamiji* told me that *Siddhashram* is the place which is the connecting link between *Gyanganj* and the other world. The needs of *Gyanganj* were being supplied through *Siddhashram*. The journey towards *Siddhashram* was quite normal. Without much difficulty, we travelled through snow-covered hills and reached there the third night.

I had previously thought that *Siddhashram* might be a conventional ashram. However, it was not. It was a replica of *Gyanganj*. There were a few caves here and there, where fifteen or twenty *sadhus* (of course great *siddhas*) stayed. Bhruguramji introduced me to the head of the *ashram* and asked me to stay there for a couple of days; he then left the place immediately.

My stay in *Siddhashram* was for a couple of days. It was a very calm and quiet place. Some of the *sadhus* asked me about the experiences during my stay there. The head of *Siddhashram* told me that if I walked for two days I could reach Arunachal, and from there I could take a bus to Guwahati. I told him that since I did not have money with me, I should walk all the way to Guwahati. He said, "Why do you worry unnecessarily? Bhruguramji told me to make arrangements for your onward journey." He gave me a thousand rupees for my journey. One of the *sadhus* was planning to go to Arunachal for some work the next day. I made a plan to go with him up to Zero, a place in Arunachal, from where I would get a bus to Itanagar and then to Guwahati.

We both set out for Zero by walk and on the third day we reached our destination. On the way, for two days we got food and shelter in villages. The *swamiji* with whom I walked to Zero was from Bengal. As we walked together, he narrated the experiences he had had during his *sadhana*.

We crossed the Brahmaputra River and reached India. Now Zero was near. This area has a very big military campus, and usually an inner-line permit was required to reach there. Vivekananda Kendra of Kanyakumari has more than 16 schools in Arunachal Pradesh. In the past, I had been a 'life worker' in the Kendra, and stayed for a long time in Kohima as well as the Dibrugarh branch for some time. Luckily, nobody asked me for a permit to enter at the border village.

I travelled to Itanagar, capital of Arunachal Pradesh, in a shared taxi jeep. By evening, I had reached Itanagar. I then booked a ticket to Guwahati by the evening bus, which would reach there next morning. I slept very well on the bus and reached Guwahati early morning.

Guwahati city and the surroundings were well known to me. My two brothers lived in Maligaon at that time, where they had jobs at the Northeast Frontier Railways (NFRLY) headquarters. I had visited Kamakhya several times before during my stay in Maligaon with them.

From the bus stop I took an auto-rickshaw to reach Kamakhya. Even though Kamakhya is near Maligaon (where my brothers stayed at the railway quarters), I neither informed them nor visited them. The auto-rickshaw dropped me off at the bottom of the hill from Kamakhya. I then started climbing the hills to reach the *mandir*.

At Kamakhya

I was once again at Kamakhya, after a long time. I just sat under a tree near the temple. I knew some *poojaris* there, as well as a great bhairavi known as '*Aghori bhairavi*' (an old woman staying there since a long time for her *sadhana*) at Kamakhya from my previous visits. I used to visit her to study and practice *tantra sadhana* during my stay at Tinsukia in upper Assam. After hours of search, I could locate her sitting under a tree near the Brahmaputra. This meeting was after a long gap. She recognized me and welcomed me with joy. She asked me about my *sadhana* and when I told her that I was on my way back from *Gyanganj* she was amazed. I told her in detail about my *sadhana* at Kashi also.

I was wondering why Bhruguramji told me to visit this place. I asked permission from that old *bhairavi mata* to allow me to stay with her for a few days. I did not know much about my future plans. She allowed me to stay at her *kutia*. She told me that I need not go here and there for food as she would feed me a part of whatever she cooked for herself.

I visited the mandir every day. Kamakhya is one of the famous Shakti peethams of India. It is also known as '*Yoni peetham*'. One day on my regular visit to the mandir in the evening, I met a swami from Kerala, known as Achyuthanand Giri, who was an acharya in yoga and tantra. He invited me to his room for *bhiksha*. I went there one day and during my *bhiksha* in my *kappar*, he said, "*Swamiji*, give this *kappar* to me. I need it." I told him of my inability to give it to him, as it was more precious to me than my own life since my *Guruji* had given it to me. He threatened me, saying that if I did not give it to him I would have to face huge difficulties as he would curse me! I was very afraid and ran away from his room without even finishing my food. The food remaining in my *kappar* I put into the Brahmaputra. I narrated this in detail to the *Bhairavi mata*. She got very angry and left to meet that swami who had threatened me. There was a quarrel between the both of them. My mind was disturbed, and I left Kamakhya next day.

Even at railway station, I had no idea where to go! I saw a train bound for Delhi on the platform. I bought a ticket to New Delhi and sat in the general compartment. My mind was still a little fearful that the swami who had asked me for the *kappar* would come here and snatch it from my hands.

However, thanks to God and to my *Guruji*, nothing adverse happened. As there was heavy rush in the general compartment, I could barely get a seat in a corner of the bench. On the third day morning, I reached Delhi. By that time I had decided to go to Panipat (Samalkha) for a few days and then on to Jammu where work at my *ashram* work was in progress.

And thus the river flows and the journey continues...

At that point in my life, I was eager to proceed with my intense *sadhana* and research on the Secrets of *Sri Chakra*. With my *Guruji* always beside me I was intensely keen on keeping my vow to Amma to lead my life in service to humanity.

There are so many incidents that I would like to share but it is not possible to record them all. I will continue to share some of them in my next volume. In the subsequent part of my autobiography I will share the experiences that I had during my childhood, and my long life as a *guru, sanyasi, Avadhoota* and a social worker. I will also share the experience of my completion of the voluminous *Sri Chakra* research study and the honor of once again visiting *Gyanganj* and presenting the work to Mahatapa Baba. And thereafter the life that I continued to live for the betterment of others.

I have been a lonely traveller all my life and continue to do so – moving alone in the crowd of my disciples, devotees and well-wishers. During this journey, some helped me; some harassed me; some criticized and scandalized me too; some just walked along side me as a witness to my pain and pleasures. But there is one person who walks behind me, in front of me, with me, in me, and that is my beloved *Guruji Avadhoota Tara Mayee*. It was *Amma's* ability of transforming mud into gold that she made a smooth and beautiful sculpture of the black and rough stone in her hand. A few kept that idol sculpted by *Amma*, in the altar of their heart and worshipped him as their Guru. That is me and my story.

Glossary

Arathi – worship ritual in which light, usually an oil lamp is offered to the deity, to the accompaniment of chants

Abhishekam – A devotional activity and/or religious rite or ritual involving pouring of a liquid as an offering to deity.

Adhyatma Ramayana – Medieval Sanskrit text extolling spiritualism in the story of Ramayana. It is embedded in the latter portion of Brahmānda Purana and philosophically attempts to reconcile Bhakti or devotion in Lord Rama and Shaktism, with Advaita Vedanta, spread over 65 chapters and 4,500 verses.

Adi Shankaracharya or Adi Shankara – Hindu philosopher of mid to late 8th century CE, widely accepted as incarnation of Lord Shiva. Author of over several hundred texts that are the foundation of Advaita Vedanta school of Hinduism. He cleansed the Vedic religious practices of ritualistic excesses, and ushered in the core teaching of Vedanta, which is Advaita or non-dualism

Advaita – Hindu philosophy of non dual nature of Reality

Advaita bodham – Understanding of non-dual reality or experiencing omnipresence of the Divine

Advaita siddhi – Oneness with the Almighty; non-dualism

Advaiti – follower of Advaita

Agarwal – A community found throughout North India. In this case, the last name of Avadhoota Nadananda's future disciples.

Agni – Fire. In this context, internal fire of purification lit through spiritual practice

Agni Lingam–(or Jyoti Lingam) A symbol of Shiva representing fire being one of the five elements, Temple in Arunachalam, Tamil Nadu

Ahmedabad – City in Gujarat, western part of India

Akash Vritti – a life without asking anything from anybody for day-to-day needs, and only accepting the minimum

Akhanda dhuni – 'eternal flame' or incessantly burning fire

Akshaya Tritiya – An auspicious festival in April

Alexandra David Neel – Belgian–French explorer and mystic who visited Lhasa in 1924, and wrote the book *Magic and Mystery in Tibet*

Alphy – A long shirt like dress made of country cotton fabric

Amaleshwar – in Madhya Pradesh renowned for Jyoti linga Shiva Temple

Amavasya – New moon

Amma – mother

Ananda – extreme happiness, one of the highest states of being

Anna(s) – Obsolete currency where 16 annas equals one rupee

Annadanam–an offering of food

Annakshetras – almonries, a place where free food is distributed to wandering monks

Annapurna – Hindu goddess of nourishment, and a form of Parvati, consort of Shiva

Antakarana suddhi – Internal purification

Antar yagya – Internal worship

Antaryami – omniscient, one who knows the hearts and minds of others

Anushtan – Firm conviction to do japa and mantra recitation a prescribed number of times

Aparigraha – The concept of non-possessiveness, non-grasping and non-greediness

Apavitrata – Impurity

Apmaan – Insult

Archana – Personal puja or prayers offered by a temple priest to the deity, on behalf of a devotee, to invoke blessings and guidance

Ardha nareeshwara – Lord Shiva and his consort Shakti in unity in the form of half man and half woman.

Arunachal/Arunachala/Arunachal Hill – A holy hill at Thiruvannamalai in Tamil Nadu, revered as the Kailash of South India

Asan – seat (used as a seat or bed in a cave)

Ashadha masam – fourth month according to Hindu calendar, between June-July, when the south-west monsoon hits India

Ashamayee – Mother Ashamayee is the spiritual sister as well as birth sister of Avadhoota Nadananda's Guru Maa Taramayee.

Ashirvaad – Blessings

Ashta siddhis – Eight Siddhis or yogic accomplishments

Atma Gyana – Knowledge of the Self

Atta – Wheat flour

Avadhoota – A mystic saint and a liberated ascetic who has gone beyond egoic-consciousness, duality and common worldly concerns and acts, and is often without standard social etiquette.

Avatar – a manifestation of a deity or released soul in bodily form on earth; an incarnate divine teacher

Baba – An ascetic/saint is addressed as Baba/Father

Badari – herbal leaf

Badha – obstacle

Badrinath – A holy town in the state of Uttarakhand. It is the most important of the four sites in India's Char Dham pilgrimage

Bajra – millet

Bajra roti – millet bread

Bala brahmachari – Young (bala) celibate on spiritual path. A brahmachari is a student of the Vedas, committed to celibacy and leading a virtuous and simple life of meditation and training for spiritual living.

Bala mantra – Chant or mantra of Balatripurasundari a form of Srividya

Balavat– Behavior as innocent as a child

Bali – Ritualistic sacrifice (slaughtering for sacrifice)

BAMS – Academic degree in traditional Indian system of medicine or Ayurveda

Beejam – Seed, or foundation

Bengali – Language spoken in the state of West Bengal

Beta – son

Bhagavat Gita – Literally, "song of the Spirit", it is the most famous of Hindu scriptures in Sanskrit, and is in the form of counselling by Lord Krishna to Arjuna. It is a section of the epic Mahabharata.

Bhagavan – Literally God, Sometimes one's Guru is referred to as Bhagavan

Bhagavan Govinda Pada – Guru of Adi Shankaracharya

Bhagavan Nityananda – A highly revered Siddha Guru who has an ashram in Ganeshpuri, Maharashtra.

Bhairavi – Devotee of Mother Goddess

Bhajan – Devotional song with religious or spiritual theme

Bhakti yoga – The yogic path of devotion to deity that leads to union with the Divine

Bhalu – White Himalayan bear

Bhandara – Food prepared on large scale, as a religious offering to the gods and eaten in a community setting

Bharat – Ancient name of India

Bhava – feelings

Bhikharin – Beggar woman

Bhiksha – Alms

Bhikshu – Monk, usually Buddhist

Bhoo Samadhi – Land burial (Dead body buried or cremated on land)

Bhooloka Vaikuntham – Literally 'Heaven on Earth', where the deity reveals Himself to His devotees

Bhoota (pronounced Bhutta) – Corn cobs

Bhoota badha – Being possessed by a ghost

Bhotia – An occupational community of shepherds, living as nomadic pastoralists

Bhrumadhya – The point in the centre of the forehead, commonly referred to as the third eye

Bhu Devi and Shri Devi – Consorts of Maha Vishnu – as depicted at the Tirupati temple, Andhra Pradesh, India

Bhumi Pooja – Prayers made at the time of laying foundation for building construction

Bidi – Indian hand-rolled cigarette

Bismillah mantra – A chant used by followers of Islam religion

Brahma sutra – Foundational texts in Sanskrit, of the Vedanta school of Hindu philosophy

Brahmanatwa – State of orthodox Brahminhood

Brahmaputra – A long river flowing through Eastern India

Glossary | 361

Brahmin – Commonly understood as a person belonging to the Hindu priestly class, but can also be viewed as one who has realized the Brahman or Self

Brahmins, Reddys, Vaishyas, Yadavas – Various castes prevalent in India

Buffalo – Referring to the Indian water-buffalo, which is domesticated

Bund – Embankment

Ceylon – Old name of the country Sri Lanka

Chaadar – Blanket

Chaar dham – Literally four abodes/seats, the names of four pilgrimage sites in the Himalayas—Badrinath, Kedarnath, Yamunotri & Gangotri—that are widely revered by Hindus

Chaitra Navaratri – The nine spiritual nights during spring or the Hindu month of Chaitra (March-April)

Chakrata – Town in Dehradun, North India

Chandan – Sandalwood paste

Chandi Paath – Religious text describing the victory of the Goddess Durga over the demon Mahishasura. It comprises 700 verses spread over 13 chapters. A ritualistic reading is often done during Navaratri celebrations and during Chandi Homam. Considered a powerful reservoir of mantras.

Chandra vidya – Science of Soma rites

Chaturdashi – Fourteenth day of waxing or waning moon phase

Chaturmas – holy period of four months (July to October)

Chaturvarna – Varna' is a Sanskrit word which means type, order, color or class. 'Chatur' means four. The society was classified in principle into four varnas: Brahmins as priests, scholars and teachers; Kshatriyas as rulers, warriors and administrators; Vaishyas as cattle herders, agriculturists, artisans and merchants; Shudras as laborers and service providers.

Chillum– Clay pipe for smoking

Chinmaya Mission– An organization dedicated to the spread of Advaita Vendanta across the world founded by Swami Chinmayananda

Chinta tarang – Thought waves

Chita bhasmam – Ashes from pyre

Chor – thief

Chottanikara, Cochin – Temple town in Cochin, Southern State of Kerala, India

Chowl – Town in the State of Maharashtra, Western India.

Coolies– Porters in stations

Dadar – A town in Mumbai, Maharashtra

Daksha yagya – The Hindu scriptures and mythology mention a huge sacrificial ritual conducted by King Daksha, father of Sati, Shiva's first wife.

Dakshin Bharatha Hindi Prachar Sabha – Organization promoting Hindi language in South India

Dakshina – Donation or payment for the services of a priest, spiritual guide or teacher, and ideally an offering of gratitude without expectation of personal gain

Dakshina Kailash – Kailash of the South

Dakshini – South Indian – a person belonging to Southern Indian states

Dal – Lentil (a warm gravy food made out of cooked lentils)

Damru – A small, hourglass-shaped hand-held drum

Dand – Long staff carried by some but not all sanyasis, depending on sampradaya

Darshan – Sighting of the idol of the deity

Dasamsh havan – Recitation of mantras, after completion of the main japa, for a number of times equal to one-tenth of total number of japa mantra recitations

Dasanami Sanyasi Parampara – Monastic order of sanyasis, established by Adi Sankara, the ten (dasa) name (nama) suffixes which these sanyasis adopt. These names are – Bharati, Sarasvati, Sagar, Tirtha, Puri, Aashrama, Giri, Parvata, Aranya and Vana.

Dashami – tenth day following the nine nights of Navaratri

Datta Bhagavan – referring to Lord Dattatreya, considered to be an avatar (incarnation) of the three Hindu gods Brahma, Vishnu, and Shiva, and as the exemplary type of the avadhoota. He can also be considered to be combining three figures in a paradigmatic way: the ascetic, the guru, and the avatara. He is often depicted with three heads and accompanied by a cow representing mother earth and four dogs representing the four Vedas.

Deepavali – Major religious festival, falling in October-November, and the day of closing of the Badrinath temples for winter

Devi Bhagavatham – Durga Saptasati or Chandi Paath/Devi Mahatmyam – religious text describing the Goddess as the supreme power and creator of the universe. It is also known as 'Chandi Paath'.

Devi Pranav Deeksha – Spiritual initiation with the mantra of the Goddess

Devi pranava – The seed mantra/chant to invoke Devi

Devprayag– A town in Uttarakhand, North India

Dhaba – Roadside eatery

Dharas – Distributaries, stream

Dharma – Duty

Dharmashala – Rest house for pilgrims

Dhokhla – A type of steamed dumpling made of chickpea flour—a Gujarati dish

Dhooly – Dust from beneath feet

Dhooni – Sacred fire, often kept lit perpetually. Symbolizes the purifying inner fire of Divine Love

Digh bandham – Contraction of the eight directions with chants

Deeksha – Spiritual initiation

Dom – Man responsible for burning corpses in a Crematorium

Doora Darshan – A siddhi or extrasensory ability to see things not in range of eyesight, without the use of instruments or equipment

Doora Gamanam – A siddhi or extrasensory ability to teleport

Doora Sravan – A siddhi or extrasensory ability to hear conversations far away, without the use of any instruments or equipment

Dr. S.Radhakrishnan – A highly distinguished scholar and philosophy professor, served as the second President of India, has written books on the Upanishads and Bhagvat Gita.

Durga – Principal form of the Mother Goddess, in her warrior manifestation

Bhagawatam– Religious text

Dvaita bhava – seeing others as different from oneself, duality in beliefs

Dwaraka – Sacred city in Gujarat, India

Easy chair – A folding chair for comfortable seating

Ekadasi – Eleventh day of waxing or waning moon phase

Ekakshari – Chant/mantra of one syllable

Etawah– A city in the banks of Yamuna River

Gaddi – Cushion

Ganeshpuri– City in Maharashtra, India – Ashram of Bhagavan Nityananda

Ganga jal – Water of River Ganga

Ganga, Ganges, Ganga Mata – The second largest riven in the Indian sub-continent, the river is revered and considered the heart of Hindu religion, tradition and living.

Gangotri – Hindu pilgrim town in the state of Uttarakand, Northern India

Ganja – Cannabis

Garbhagriha – Literally womb chamber, or innermost sanctum of a Hindu temple where resides the murti (idol or icon) of the primary deity of the temple

Garuda – A large mythical bird, sacred to Lord Vishnu

Gaya – An ancient city of historical and mythological significance, located in Bihar, India.

Giri Pradakshina – Circumambulation of the Arunachala Hill

Giri Pradakshina Veedhi – The path for the pradakshina or circumbulation

Gita or **Bhagavat Gita** – Hindu scripture in Sanskrit world renowned for its philosophical significance

Gompa – Tibetan monastery – a set of small Tibetan temple buildings and other places of worship or religious learning

Gomukh – The terminus of the Gangotri Glacier from where Bhagirathi River originates, Uttarkashi, North India

Gopuram – A pyramidical tower, usually ornate, at the entrance of any temple, especially in southern India.

Goshala – Cowshed

Govinda – One of the several names of Lord Krishna

Gufa – Cave

Gujjar – Community that keeps buffalos and sheep and moves around collecting grass for them

Gunny sack – Burlap

Guptavati Teeka – Commentary on the Durga Saptasati by Bhaskararaya

Guru mandal/mandala – The fraternity of sages, rishis and gurus who had themselves acquired a very high position in the hierarchy of spiritual evolution. All these sages were an 'Awakened' lot and formed a spiritual league to help humanity enjoy the divine bliss which they had themselves experienced.

Guru Mantra Deeksha – Initiation by the Guru who imparts a secret sacred chant of the Gurus.

Guru Parampara – The spiritual tradition or lineage of Gurus or Spiritual Masters

Guru tattva – The principle that the guru is the element that causes spiritual awakening within oneself, through a transmission process beyond the reach of the human intellect. The Guru is to be acknowledged as not a physical being but God Himself manifesting in a personal form to guide the aspirant

Gurubehan/behen –Fellow female student of the same spiritual master/lineage, considered as a sister

Gurubhais–Fellow male students of the same Guru, and so considered as brothers

Guruji – Spiritual Master – 'ji' is added as a mark of respect

Gurusthaan – literally, place of the Guru

Guruvayur– A famous and religious temple of Lord Krishna in Kerala, South India

Gyanganj – Legendary city-kingdom of mysterious immortal beings, from ancient Indian and Tibetan mythology. It is said to be inhabited by yogis and saints of high order, and is also a place of spiritual training. Situated in a valley somewhere deep in the Himalayas, and though hidden from the world, still influencing it in various subtle ways when necessary. It is said that Gyanganj is cunningly camouflaged or may even be existing in a completely different plane of reality.

Hamsa – literally swan, but also a mythical bird with knowledge and represents the individual soul or spirit.

Hamsa soham – Meditation on the Soham mantra, a central mantra practice of Yoga Meditation.

Haridwar – An ancient pilgrim city in Uttarakhand, Northern India

Har-ki-pauri – Revered ghat on banks of Ganga in Haridwar, where Lord Shiva and Vishnu are believed to have visited

Harsil – a village on the banks of Bhagirathi River

Haryana – A state in North India

Himavan – King of the snow-clad Himalayas and father of Parvathi

Hindi – India being a large country where several languages are spoken, Hindi is the national language and is spoken widely in the Northern part of India. However, Nadanandaji grew up in Kerala which is a state in South India where Hindi is not widely spoken.

Hindustan – India

Homa agni – The fire blazing in the homa pit

Homa kunda – Fire altar into which the homa offerings are made

Homam – Religious ceremony performed in temples and in homes that involves worship through the use of a sacred fire, and with recitations of mantras

Iccha – Desire

Idlis – Steamed rice cakes—a South Indian dish

Indore– A city in Madhya Pradesh, India

Ishta Devi – Literally 'cherished divinity' taken from the words iṣhṭa which means desired, liked, cherished or preferred and devi or devatā while godhead, divinity, tutelary deity is a term denoting a worshipper's favorite deity within Hinduism

Jaipur – Capital city of Rajasthan

Jal pathra – **Kamandal** – Water vessel carried by sadhu

Jal Samadhi – Internment in water – Dead bodies of saints are interned in flowing water

Jammu – State in the Northern part of India

Japa – Chanting of sacred mantras

Japa chakra – Prayer wheel

Japa mala – A string of prayer beads

Japa Samarpan – Offering of chants

Japa sankalp – Vow to recite mantra a prescribed number of times

Jaunsarbavar – A hilly region near Mussoorie in Dehradun, India

Jawan – Junior soldier or infantryman in the Indian Army

Jeeva – Living being (literally, that which has life)

Jharna – Waterfall

Jilebees – Sweet crullers

Jyotir Lingam – Please refer to Agni Lingam

Kaccha – Unpaved, not properly constructed

Kafni – A knee-length, loose robe-like garment

Kailash – Mountain peak in Tibet, legendary home of Lord Shiva and Parvati

Kala Kambaliwala/ Baba Kali Kamli Dharamshala – A resthouse for wandering monks/saints in Rishikesh, North India

Kali – Black one, or Goddess of Time, the destroyer of evil forces

Kalpavas – 14 days stay at Kumbha mela

Kamakhya – An important Hindu Tantric goddess of desire. The Kamakhya temple is a Hindu temple dedicated to the mother Goddess Kamakhya and is one of the oldest Shakti power centers.

Kamandal – Oblong water pot used by ascetics or yogis to store and carry water

Kambal – Blanket

Kamini and Kanchan – Lure of woman (kamini) and gold/wealth (kanchan)

Kanakadhara stotra – Sanskrit hymn composed by the sage Adi Sankara, believed to confer material benefits on the person reciting it. He is said to have composed it in compassionate response to a poor woman who was unable to offer him anything in alms except a gooseberry. The recitation of the hymn caused a shower of golden gooseberries.

Kancheepuram Ashram – Ashram located in Kancheepuram, city in Tamil Nadu, South India

Kanchi Sankara Mutt – The ashram in Kancheepuram established by Shankaracharya

Kankhal – A small colony in Haridwar, North India

Kappar – Vessel for receiving alms carried by a sadhu

Karma bhoomi – Land where the prevailing culture aids and supports a spiritual seeker in neutralizing his karmas through ritual and penance

Karma phala – Fruits of karma/destiny

Karma Yoga – Yoga of selfless action or service, whereby detaching oneself from the fruits of actions and offering them up to God, one learns to sublimate the ego

Karuna – Compassion

Karyalaya – Office

Kasba – Walled Township

Kashaya – Saffron, orange coloured robe

Kashaya dhvaja – Saffron flag

Kashaya vastra – Saffron-colored clothing typically worn by sanyasis

Kashi – Another name for the holy city of Varanasi

Kashmiri – From Kashmir, State in Northern India

Kayalu devata – Kala Bhairav or form of Lord Shiva

Keenaram Paramahamsa – The revered Guru of Avadhoota Nadananda's lineage, Keenaram Paramahamsa is Maa Tara Mayee's Guru, making him the Parameshti (great-grand) Guru of Avadhoota Nadananda

Keerthan – Bhajan singing by an individual

Kendriya Vidyalaya – Nation-wide schooling system administered by the Central Government of India

Kerala – State in the deep south of India, and the home state of Avadhoota Nadananda

Kevadia Colony – A colony at the foot of the Sardar Sarovar Dam, Narmada region, Gujarat

Khaddar – Handwoven cloth

Kheer – Pudding made with milk, sugar and broken grain

Kichadi/khichadi – Rice and lentil gruel

Kothari – Owners/caretakers of large granaries/storehouses

Krama deeksha – Step by step initiation process, moving into higher sadhanas

Krishna – Eighth incarnation/avatar of Lord Vishnu

Kriya of Shat Chakra bhedan – The activation of the six chakras

Krupa/Kripa – Grace

Kshamta – Capability or competence

Kula devi – Family deity, usually worshipped over generations. In Nadanadaji's case the goddess Sri Porkali Ma

Kumbha Mela – One of the largest human congregations of a faith, involving pilgrimage to one of four holy towns of Hindus and bathing in a sacred river

Kumkum – Vermillion, red powder worn as marking on forehead, made by combining turmeric with lime. It is offered to the goddess in puja/worship

Kund – tank or small reservoir

Kundalini – Dormant yogic life force that is believed to lie coiled at the base of the spine until awakened, when it is sent to the head triggering enlightenment

Kupathra – one ineligible for receiving a favor, unfit recipient

Kutia – A hut, dwelling place

Laddu– A sweet ball made out of powdered lentil

Lala – Common name for shopkeeper in North India

Lalitha Sahasranamam – Sacred and powerful hymn of thousand names of the Mother Goddess Lalitha

Lalitha Tripurasundari – Highest manifestation of Goddess Adi Shakti and the primary goddess associated with the Shiva-Shakti tradition.

Lamas – An honorific title applied to a spiritual leader in Tibetan Buddhism

Lashkar – City in Gwalior, North India

Leela – Divine play, or all reality, including the cosmos, as the outcome of creative play by the divine absolute

Lepanam – Application of sandalwood paste and vermillion

Lord Rama – Incarnation/avatar of Lord Vishnu and hero-king of the famous epic Ramayana

Lucknow – capital city of state of Uttar Pradesh

Lungi – A cotton cloth worn like a sarong by men around the waist, primarily in South India

Maa – Mother

Maan – Respect

Maayee/Mayee – Mother

Madhya Pradesh – A state around the middle part of India

Madrasi – South Indian (from Madras)

Madukari Bhiksha – literally collecting like a honeybee, taking bhiksha a little from each house

Maha Tapa – The Head of Gyanganj, Mahavatar Babaji

Maha Kali – Goddess of time and death

Maha Lakshmi – Goddess of abundance and prosperity

Maharaj – Sadhus in North India are respectfully addressed by this title

Maharashtra – State in the western part of India

Maharshi Aurobindo – Indian nationalist, guru, and spiritual reformer

Maha Saraswathi – Goddess of the arts, knowledge, and wisdom

Mahatma – Literally great soul, or person of advanced spiritual stature

Mahatma Gandhi – Prominent leader of the Indian Independence movement, relentless practitioner of karma yoga, world renowned.

Mahavatar Babaji or Babaji – Indian saint and yogi, believed to have revived the ancient science of Kriya Yoga, Head of Gyanganj

Makara Sankranti – A Hindu harvest festival that marks the transition of the sun into the zodiacal sign of Makara (Capricorn) on its celestial path. The day is also believed to mark the arrival of spring in India.

Mala – necklace

Malayalam – Language spoken in south India, predominantly in the state of Kerala

Mama – Mother's brother; uncle

Manasarovar – Freshwater lake in Tibet near Mt.Kailash, bathing in and drinking its water is believed by Hindus to cleanse all sins.

Manasik pranams – Paying obeisance mentally

Manava – Human being

Mandali – Group of sanyasis

Mandir – Temple

Mangalore – Port City in the state of Karnataka in Southern India

Manikarnika Ghat – One of the ghats in Varanasi and is most known for being a place of Hindu cremation

Mann – 240 kilograms

Glossary | 373

Mantra – A sacred utterance, sound, syllable, word or phonemes, or group of words in Sanskrit believed to have psychological and spiritual powers. The sounds may, or may not have literal meaning.

Marwari – A native or inhabitant of Rajasthan in India

Masala – A powdered blend of spices

Mauna – Vow of silence

Maya – Name, fame, wealth – created by the obscuring power that conceals the true character of spiritual reality. The manifested world of creation is constantly changing and thus considered unreal.

Mellaril and Dizepam – Names of medicines

Mohi – A devotee of Avadhoota Nadananda

Moksha – Salvation or freedom from rebirth

Mookambika – The Kollur Mookambika Temple located at Kollur, Udupi district in the state of Karnataka, India, is a Hindu temple dedicated to Mookambika Devi.

Mookambika, Chottanikara Bhagavati, Kodungalur Bhagavati, Vaishno Devi, or Nayana Devi – Different names of Goddess Parvati or Shakti

Moorthy – Idol of God

Moorti sthapana – Installation of the idol with rites and rituals

Mudra – Symbolic hand gestures used in Hindu and Buddhist ceremonies, movement or pose in yoga

Mukhiya – Village chief

Nada – energy of music

Naga sadhu – Shaivite saints, who live in the Himalayas and occasionally come down to the plains

Naivedyam – Food offered to a Hindu deity/guru as part of a worship ritual, before eating it

Namami Devi Narmade – Salutations to Devi Narmada (River Narmada respected as a Devi or Mother)

Namaskar – A traditional Indian greeting or gesture of respect, made by bringing the palms together before the face or chest and bowing

Nambudiri – The Malayalam speaking Brahmins of Kerala

Narmada – A River that flows through Central/Western India

Narmade har – Salutations to holy river Narmada

Nashta – Breakfast

Navami – Ninth day of the fortnight in the Hindu Lunar Calendar

Navaratri – Literally 'nine nights' in Sanskrit, *nava* meaning nine and *ratri* meaning nights. The Goddess Shakti is worshipped in her different manifestations for nine nights and ten days. This is a major Indian festival occurring in autumn (September-October) and spring (March-April)

Navavaran Pooja – The highest Pooja ritual of the Goddess, aimed at removing the nine concealments or obstructions to self-realization that are within one's mind and ego

Nirakara – Formless

Nishkaam karma – Selfless action without expectation or agenda, non-attached action without obligation

Nishkalankata – Quality of purity and innocence, and being selfless

Nitya karma – Daily ablutions

Niyogam – Plan or destined arrangement

Omkareshwar – Hindu temple dedicated to Lord Shiva, situated on an island called Mandhata or Shivapuri in the Narmada River

Oottupura – Temple dining hall

Pada – As in padyatra, pilgrimage on foot

Padmanabha sahodari – Sister of Padmanabha or Vishnu

Padmasan – The Lotus Pose, a yogic posture of Hatha Yoga

Padmavathi – Consort of Venkateshvara, enshrined in the temple at Tirumala

Paisa – One hundred paisa equals one rupee

Palash stick – Stick made from wood of the tree Butea monosperma. The wood is used in fire ceremonies and nearly as common as the holy Tulsi in homes of Namboodiri Brahmins in Kerala.

Panchadasi – Devi mantra of fifteen letters

Panchajanyam – Periodical, popular in Kerala, South India

Panchang – A Hindu calendar and almanac which follows traditional units of Hindu timekeeping, and presents important dates and their calculations in a tabulated form.

Panchayat – Village governing body, assembly of village elders

Panditji – Priest

Papad – Fried lentil wafers

Para Loka – World beyond death

Para Vidya – Higher or spiritual knowledge of the inner world, as opposed to knowledge of the material world

Param guru/ Paramaguru/Parmeshti Guru – Guruji's Guruji (Master's Master – Grand Master)

Parama virakt – Person with absolute indifference to worldly pleasures. Renouncer of all material things.

Paramanu – Atom

Paramatma – The Supreme Divine Soul

Parampara – A succession of teachers and disciples in traditional Vedic culture; guru–sishya tradition.

Paratpara Guru – Guruji's Guruji's Guruji (Great Grand Master)

Parigraha/m – intention to accumulate material possessions for future use

Parikrama – Circumambulation

Parivrajaka – Wandering monk

Parnasala – Hut made of leaves

Parvat – Mountain

Pathankot – City in the Indian State of Punjab

Pathra/Patra – Vessel, utensil

Pathrata – Eligibility

Payasam – Pudding sweetened with sugar or jaggery, and made with dairy or coconut milk and broken grain

Peepal – Ficus religiosa or sacred fig tree

Peetham – University or academic institution

Pishachavat – Sudden fits of anger etc. Literally means like a ghost. A realized one who is a loner and exhibits strange behavior and hence feared by people because they do not understand such a one

Pitthu – Large backpacks

Pongal – Dish of rice, moong lentils cooked together with spices and clarified butter

Pooja pathra –Utensils used for worship in the Temple

Pooja samagri – Materials used for worship

Poojya – Respected, honorable

Poori – Deep fried wheat bread

Poornima – Full moon

Poorva janma karma phalam – The result of the deeds of one's previous birth

Poorvashrama – Previous stage of life, before Sanyasa/renunciation

Pottli – Small cloth bag

Pradakshina – A ritual of circumambulation around the inner sanctum in a temple

Prakruthi – Nature

Pralobhan – Temptation

Prana Shakti – Prana (vital energy), Shakti (Awareness), in this context, the awareness of the vital energy

Pranava – 'Om' mantra considered the symbol or representation of the individual soul which sanyasis must always chant

Pranayama – Science and practice of control of breath as part of yoga

Pranta Karyavah – Official of civil organization

Prasadam – Food that is a religious offering, consumed after worship or religious ceremony

Prashtana Trayee – (i.e., *Gita, Upanishads* and *BrahmaSutra*)

Pratyangira – An extremely powerful and fierce form of the Goddess, worshipped with very specialized rites or sadhana

Prayag – Ancient name for the city of Allahabad, site of the sangam or confluence of the Rivers Ganga, Yamuna and Saraswati

Prayoga vidhi –– Method of usage

Presh mantra – Standing in water, this mantra is chanted as a vow of renunciation of the world, worldly relations and material wealth.

Preta yoni/atma – Ghost state after death

Pujari – Priest who performs puja

Pukka – In this context, solidly constructed

Pulyodhara prasadam – Spiced tamarind rice offering to deity

Punya karma – Meritorious deeds

Purascharan – A vow to repeat a mantra a fixed number of times, usually a very large number, with complete concentration and rigid discipline, with the aim of spiritual progress

Pushkar – town in Rajasthan, known for its lake and the temple of God Brahma

Ragam – The six basic musical modes which express different moods in certain characteristic progressions, with more emphasis placed on some notes than others, *of Indian classical music. A scientific, precise, and aesthetic melodic form with its own distinct ascending and descending movement, consisting of combinations of notes of the octave. One raga is demarcated from another in the way the notes are combined. The music created by a raga is known to color the mind in a particular way, creating distinct moods or feelings.*

Rahasya– Sacred Secret

Rajasthan – State in Northwestern India

Rajasthan Patrika–A periodical

Rajkot – A large city in the state of Gujarat

Rakta chandan – Red sandalwood

Ramana Maharishi–A renowned and revered Indian sage who lived in the Arunachala hills of Thiruvannamalai, Tamil Nadu

Ravi – (River 'Iravati' of *Puranas*) River Ravi

Rishi – A seer who realizes eternal knowledge beyond the mundane world and gives expression to those truths in the form of hymns, many such hymns are found in the scriptures, the Vedas

Rishikesh –Ancient pilgrim city, Dehradun, Uttarakhand, North India.

Romaharsha – Bristling of the hair in rapture, feeling of ecstasy

Roti – Unleavened wheat flatbread

Sabji – Cooked vegetable dish

Sadguru – An honorific title given to an enlightened Master

Sadhana – Daily spiritual practice

Sadhu – Hindu monk; an ascetic, holy man

Sadhvi – Female ascetic

Sahasrara – Crown chakra is generally considered the seventh primary chakra, according to most tantric yoga traditions and is the one which integrates all the chakras with their respective qualities. It is the last milestone of the evolution of human awareness.

Sakamata – The desire to gain something materialistic

Sakshatkara – Realization

Saligram – spiraled ammonite stone, worshipped as iconic symbol of Vishnu

Samadhi – Stage of union with the Divine, the highest bliss

Samadhi mandir – When an enlightened being leaves his mortal body, a temple is built over when the mortal remains are buried.

Samatva bhavana – Viewing all beings impartially, without attachment or bindings

Sambar – a lentil-based vegetable stew made with tamarind and spices

Samhar – Annihilation and reabsorption

Sampraday bheda – Differential treatment pertaining to spiritual tradition

Sampradaya name – Traditional religious title

Samsara – Terrestrial

Samyak nyasa – To renounce worldly and material aspects of living and lead a life of intellectual contemplation

Sandhya Arathi – (Refer to Arathi) Arathi performed during evening time

Sandhyavandan – Oldest extant liturgy in world religion, consisting of verbal chants from the Vedas, done three times a day, at dawn, noon and dusk

Sangeet – Music

Sangh pracharak – Volunteer of a civil organization

Sankalp – Solemn vow or determination

Sankalpa Siddhi – The power to fulfill desires or wishes effortlessly

Sankalpam – a prayer of offering made with some desire

Sansaris – Worldly people

Sanskrit – Primary sacred language of Hinduism

Sanyasa – State of renunciation, asceticism

Sanyasa Sanskara – Rituals related to initiation to sanyasa

Sanyasi – Renunciate

Sapta sarovar – Seven streams – a picturesque place near Haridwar

Saraswathi Mandapam – The name of a hall at the Sri Ramakrishna Yogashram

Sardarji – Sikh gentleman

Sari/Saree – A female garment traditionally worn in India

Sarva Sanga Parityaga Sanyasi – One in complete freedom from all attachments, unruffled and immune to all temptations, because of seeing the Self in all

Sashtanga namaskara – A form of salutation where the eight limbs of the body, namely, two hands, two legs, two arms, chest and forehead, touch the ground. It symbolizes the nullification of one's ego before Guru or God.

Sat-chit-ananda – Truth, consciousness, bliss

Satram – A resting place for pilgrims where rooms and food are provided by a charitable institution for nominal rates or for free

Satsang – A gathering of people for spiritual discourse

Sauparnika – River flowing near the Mookambika Temple, Kollur

Seva – Service

Shakha – Branch

Shakta – Worshipper of Shakti

Shakteya – A sub-sect of Hinduism in which the followers worship Mother Goddess in Her various avatars and incarnations.

Shakti – The female principle of divine energy, especially when personified as the supreme deity.

Shakti peetham – A shakti peeth is a place of recognized harnessed power or Shakti that has the ability to plug us into the Greater Source. The Indian subcontinent has several such sacred sites where there are temples dedicated to the Goddess. From Hindu mythology, each of these places has a correspondence to a body part of Goddess Sati that fell to earth.

Shakti tatva – The principle of Shakti tradition

Shaktipath deeksha – Initiation through spiritual transfer of energy from the touch of a Guru

Shangri-La – A mystic place hidden in the Himalayas covered with snow and mist

Shankhdhwani – Sound from blowing of conch

Shastras – Scripture

Shava – Corpse

Shava sadhana – A ritual done in the presence of a corpse

Shava Suddhi – Purification of the corpse

Shavasana – Supine corpse pose in Hatha Yoga

Shetty – Merchant

Shiva Mahimna stotra– A Sanskrit composition in devotion of Lord Shiva

Shivalingam / lingam– Abstract or an iconic representation of Lord Shiva

Shivananda ashram – An ashram and spiritual center in Rishikesh, founded by Swami Sivananda

Shivaratri– A festival celebrated annual in honor of Lord Shiva

Shodasi mantra – Sixteen-lettered mantra of the Goddess, recitation of which leads to liberation. This is considered secretive in nature, and only to be imparted by a Guru on initiation.

Shri Shivanand Paramahamsa of Vatakara, Kerala – A revered sage and founder of Siddha Samaj of Kerala

Shuddhi – Purity; righteousness

Siddha – masters who have acquired siddhis and achieved some degree of spiritual perfection or enlightenment.

Siddha Parampara – Traditional lineage of adepts, and ascetics who have achieved enlightenment

Smashaan – Cremation ground

Soham Dhyan – Meditation on the Soham mantra, a central mantra practice of Yoga Meditation. Soham is a universal mantra as it relates to the breath, and everybody breathes

Soolpaneeshwar Mandir – Temple dedicated to Lord Shiva, Narmada area

Soorya – A form of Shiva, also known as 'Marthanda Bhairava', a well-known sadhak of Lalitha, who later took the form of Lalitha herself.

Soorya/Surya vidya – Science of the solar system, especially the sun

Sparsan – Touch

Sramadan – Donation of time and effort, excluding money, for a good cause

Sri Chakra – a sacred geometrical construction of nine levels representing the Cosmos within which the Mother Goddess is considered to manifest herself along with Her parivara (family) yoginis. The Shiva and Shakti aspects of Consciousness and Awareness reside on the peak at the Navama (ninth) Avarana (level) called Bindu. Visualization and internal contemplation of the manifestation of this Sri Chakra within the physical body in a subtle form is the secret of Sri Vidya.

Sri Raja Rajeswari – Presiding deity of Sri Chakra, the Divine Mother

Sri Ramakrishna Mission – A monastic organization brought into existence by Sri Ramakrishna Paramahamsa, the great 19th century saint of Bengal

Sri Ramakrishna Yogashram – Name of the Ashram

Sri Vidya Sadhana – Sri Vidya is an ancient and influential school of Goddess-centered Shakta Tantrism. The goddess is worshipped in three manifestations, as the beneficent deity Lalita Tripurasundari/ Raja Rajeswari, through her mantra and through her yantra known as Sri Chakra.

Srisailam – In Tamil Nadu

Srishti – Creation, emanation, projection

Srividya – Tantric or Shakta theology where the Goddess is worshipped as the Supreme, transcending the cosmos that is her manifestation.

Stithi – Continuation and maintenance

Stotras – Sacred hymns

Svan bhiksha – Food intake similar to that of a stray dog, which eats wherever it finds food

Swabhava – Nature or habit

Swami – An ascetic/saint is addressed as Swami

Swami Vivekananda – Hindu monk and direct disciple of Ramakrishna Paramahamsa and a major force in the modern revival of Hinduism. Founder of the Ramakrishna Mission

Swamy Ayyappa – A Hindu deity worshipped as Manikandan or Sasta. The famous temple of Swamy Ayyappa is located in Sabarimala in Kerala

Swapna – Dream

Swayamvara Parvati mantra – special yogini mantra

Syana – Chief

Tamil – Language of Indian state of Tamil Nadu

Tantra/Tantric – An ancient Indian tradition of beliefs and ritual practices that seeks to channel the divine energy of macrocosm of God into the human microcosm.

Tapara – Cottage

Tapas – Connotes certain spiritual practices in India related to asceticism, including meditation, austerities, body mortification and penance

Tapovan – Forest of austerities or spiritual practice. In this context, the area above Gangotri

Tara Mayee – The Guru of Avadhoota Nadananda

Tarpan/a – Offering/ritualistic worship made to departed entities (ancestors)

Teertham – Holy water associated with a temple or deity, or from a reservoir/river near such sacred sites

Tehsil – An administrative division of a city or town

Thalam – A traditional rhythmic pattern in classical Indian music, usually expressed with percussion instruments

Thava – griddle

Thoriyali – Region in Gujarat

Tibet – Region in the Tibetan plateau in Asia

Tilakam – marking on forehead, usually with a fragrant paste, such as of sandalwood or kumkum

Tirumala/Tirupathi – One of the most famous temples in the Indian state of Andhra Pradesh, where the presiding deity is Lord Venkateshvara or Vishnu, and also known as Balaji. It lies in the midst of seven peaks or group of hills in the Eastern Ghats Range

Tiruvannamalai – Please refer to Arunachala

Trayodashi – Thirteenth day of waxing or waning moon phase

Trichur (Thrissur) – City in the southern state of Kerala

Tripura – Northeastern state in India

Trishool/Trishul – Trident, a symbol of Lord Shiva and Shakti

Triyuginarayan – A village in Rudraprayag, Uttarakhand, North India

Trtva bhava

Tryakshari mantra – Mantra of three letters

Tulsi – holy basil

Turiyateeta – One who has attained Turiya or Avadhoota state, the state beyond waking, dream, and deep sleep states. In such a one's eyes, nothing is pure or impure anymore because, transcending duality, he has realized the Supreme Unity.

Udasi Sampradaya – Udasi is a religious sect of ascetic sadhus centred in northern India. It is based on the teachings of Sri Chand (1494-1643), the son of Guru Nanak, the founder and the first Guru of Sikhism.

Ugra Tara – Literally Fierce Tara, an emanation of the Divine Mother

Unmadavat – Literally means madness, a state of such complete absorption in Divine Love and oblivion to the material world, that conventional people view it as madness

Upadesa – Advice

Upanishads – Collection of texts containing central philosophical concepts of Hinduism, concerning the nature of ultimate reality and describing the path to human salvation

Upavas – Timed fasting as part of religious observance

Uttarakhand – formerly known as Uttaranchal, it is a state in the northern part of India. It is often referred to as the Devbhumi (literally: "Land of the Gods") due to the many Hindu temples and pilgrimage centres found throughout the state.

Uttarkashi – Hindu pilgrim town in the state of Uttarakand, Northern India

Vairagya – Dispassion or detachment

Vaishnav – Worshipper of Vishnu

Vaishno devi – A manifestation of Hindu Mother Goddess Mahalakshmi, the temple of Vaishno Devi is located in Katra, Jammu and Kashmir

Vaishya – Person from business/merchant community

Vamachar Tantra – Branch of Tantra, where a particular mode of worship uses the kind of elements of deity worship which are not used in the orthodox religion. This is known as panchamakara (five 'M's) five species of pleasure, namely: meat (mamsa), cereal (mudra), fish (matsya or machli), wine (madya or madira) and ritual sexual intercourse (maythuna).

Vanaprasthi – forest-dwelling ascetic in the 3rd of four *ashrama* (stages) of human life, the other three being Brahmacharya (bachelor student, 1st stage), Grihastha (married householder, 2nd stage) and Sanyasa (renunciate ascetic, 4th stage).

Vanavasi Kalyan Ashram – an Indian social welfare organization based in Jashpur, in the Chhattisgarh state of India

Vandevata – Forest angel

Varanasi – Also known as Kashi or Benaras is a city on the banks of the Ganges in Uttar Pradesh, North India. An ancient city and the spiritual capital of India, it draws millions of pilgrims throughout the year

Vastram – Clothing

Vayu Bhagavan – Wind God

Veda vakya – Great saying or pronouncements, words of wisdom accepted without question as coming from great sages

Vedanta – A Hindu philosophy based on the doctrine of the Upanishads, especially in its monistic form

Vedi – Altar

Veena – Traditional Indian stringed musical instrument

Venkateshvara – A form of Lord Vishnu, presiding deity of the Tirumala temple

Vibhageeya Chinta – Considering oneself different from others

Vibhuthi/Vibhoothi – sacred ash

Vidya – knowledge

Vidyaranya Muni– An accomplished philosopher and chief proponent of the Dvaita school of Vedanta, popularly known as Madhavacharya. He was the Supreme Master of the Sringeri Sharada Peetam

Vihara – Buddhist monastery

Vijaya Dashami – see Dashami

Viraja Homam – An oblation to fire (homam), for the purpose of self-purification from ego. This is a part of the Hindu ceremonies, whereby a monk enters into sanyasa or renunciation

Vishwanath – Lord Shiva, presiding deity of the Kashi Vishwanath Temple, Varanasi

Vrata – Religious vow

Vrithy – Physical cleanliness; virtue

Vyas ghat – Along the banks of Ganges, Uttarakhand, North India

Yagnopavita sanskar – A traditional rite (sanskar) of passage that marks the acceptance of a student by a guru. The sacred thread (yajnopavita) is received by the boy during this ceremony, that he continues wearing across his chest forever thereafter.

Yagya – elaborate ceremony around a fire, with oblations offered as worship to the accompaniment of sacred chants/ mantras

Yama – A Hindu unit of time; one-fourth of a day + night is a yama

Yamuna – The longest and second largest tributary of the Ganges in northern India

Yatri – Traveler

Yogini – A woman proficient in yoga; a female yogi

Zilla pracharka – District in-charge